Springer Proceedings in Business and Economics

Springer Proceedings in Business and Economics brings the most current research presented at conferences and workshops to a global readership. The series features volumes (in electronic and print formats) of selected contributions from conferences in all areas of economics, business, management, and finance. In addition to an overall evaluation by the publisher of the topical interest, scientific quality, and timeliness of each volume, each contribution is refereed to standards comparable to those of leading journals, resulting in authoritative contributions to the respective fields. Springer's production and distribution infrastructure ensures rapid publication and wide circulation of the latest developments in the most compelling and promising areas of research today.

The editorial development of volumes may be managed using Springer's innovative Online Conference Service (OCS), a proven online manuscript management and review system. This system is designed to ensure an efficient timeline for your publication, making Springer Proceedings in Business and Economics the premier series to publish your workshop or conference volume.

More information about this series at https://link.springer.com/bookseries/11960

Alina Mihaela Dima · Ion Anghel ·
Razvan Catalin Dobrea
Editors

Economic Recovery After COVID-19

3rd International Conference on Economics and Social Sciences, ICESS 2020, Bucharest, Romania

Springer

Editors
Alina Mihaela Dima
Bucharest University of Economic Studies
Bucharest, Romania

Ion Anghel
Bucharest University of Economic Studies
Bucharest, Romania

Razvan Catalin Dobrea
Bucharest University of Economic Studies
Bucharest, Romania

ISSN 2198-7246 ISSN 2198-7254 (electronic)
Springer Proceedings in Business and Economics
ISBN 978-3-030-86640-2 ISBN 978-3-030-86641-9 (eBook)
https://doi.org/10.1007/978-3-030-86641-9

This Springer imprint is published by the registered company Springer Nature Switzerland AG
The registered company address is: Gewerbestrasse 11, 6330 Cham, Switzerland

Preface

This proceedings constitutes a selection of papers presented to the 3rd International Conference on Economics and Social Sciences, Innovative Models to Revive the Global Economy, ICESS 2020 Bucharest, Romania.

The COVID-19 crisis has practically imposed a new way of life and work globally, which offers research opportunities in terms of inquiring benefits and disadvantages, as well as finding solutions for individual safety and maintaining the efficiency of the economic, social and environmental systems. COVID-19's global spreading and the consequent drastic public response have quickly brought new economic policy challenges to the fore. Many researchers have responded by reviewing recent data and publishing brief articles in order to better comprehend the size of the issues confronting challenging regions and the best policy responses. It is critical that the scientific community provides a mechanism for this research to be published as soon as practicable. Our objective is that this collection of articles will contribute to a better understanding of the issues and policies surrounding the crisis, as well as serve as a constructive example of how the set of techniques for top-level research publications in economics should be expanded.

This volume is a collection of research findings and perspectives related to recent economic challenges determined by the global crisis due to COVID-19, resulted from a research project "Restart Economia" implemented by The Bucharest University of Economic Studies in the period April—August 2020 with the support of the Ministry of Education and Research from Romania. The project's main goal was to find solutions for the Romanian SMEs in order to help them survive the actual COVID situation and to support them through recommendations in order to avoid a real economic crisis. The data and the information collected derived from the main sectors of activity as follows: water distribution, sanitation, waste management, decontamination activities, building industry and real estate transactions, wholesale and retail trade, hotels and restaurants, fiscal environment, higher education, healthcare system, macroeconomic policies, public administration and regional development, consumers' behavior, banking sector, international trade in goods, international trade in services, transportation and storage sector and agricultural sector. The presented data include the evolution, impact, main effects and challenges of the COVID-19 pandemic on each of these sectors.

The performance of the companies will be increased by delivering them researched recommendations after an integrated analysis is performed by economic experts. Moreover, economic recommendations were sent to the institutional and decision-making factors to develop enhanced policies destined for improving the economic situation. The economic and social effects of the pandemic phenomena have imposed the necessity in many countries of government interventions in order to maintain the stability of the system or innovative solutions.

Bucharest, Romania

Alina Mihaela Dima
Ion Anghel
Razvan Catalin Dobrea

Contents

Challenges in the Romanian Healthcare System in the Context of the COVID-19 Pandemic

Anghel Ion, Drăgoi Mihaela Cristina, Anica-Popa Adrian, Ştefan Simona Cătălina, and Ciocodeică David-Florin

1 Analysis of the Healthcare Field

The public healthcare system in Romania rests on a centralized health insurance model, which is based on a two-fold command: the Ministry of Health (tasked with the general governance) and the National Health Insurance House (CNAS), a body that manages and administers the funds in public health care. The two entities, the Ministry of Health and CNAS, are represented at local level by public health county authorities and, respectively, by the county health insurance houses. The medical services are provided in the 41 counties and Bucharest based on the centrally agreed rules.

1.1 Number of Employees in the Healthcare Sector

In 2016, the medical sector accounted for almost 261,000 employees versus 215,000 employees in 2009, most of them healthcare professionals with secondary education and ancillary staff—support staff (56%), followed by medical doctors (24%), pharmacists and dentists (7% each). From the ownership point of view, it is noteworthy a reduction of the staff working in the public healthcare system, both in absolute terms,

A. Ion (✉) · D. M. Cristina · A.-P. Adrian · Ş. S. Cătălina · C. David-Florin
Bucharest University of Economic Studies, Bucharest, Romania
e-mail: ion.anghel@cig.ase.ro

D. M. Cristina
e-mail: cristina.dragoi@rei.ase.ro

A.-P. Adrian
e-mail: adrian.anica@cig.ase.ro

Ş. S. Cătălina
e-mail: simona.stefan@man.ase.ro

A. M. Dima et al. (eds.), *Economic Recovery After COVID-19*, Springer Proceedings in Business and Economics, https://doi.org/10.1007/978-3-030-86641-9_1

Table 1 Developments in staffing the public medical sector

Indicators	2009	2011	2012	2014	2015	2016	2017	2018
Total staff per 1,000 inhabitants	**10.41**	**10.75**	**10.93**	**11.54**	**12.03**	**12.48**	**12.94**	**13.40**
Doctors per 1,000 inhabitants	2.44	2.58	2.65	2.74	2.82	2.89	2.98	3.11
Pharmacists per 1,000 inhabitants	0.61	0.66	0.68	0.74	0.78	0.83	0.80	0.84
Medical nurses per 1,000 inhabitants	0.21	0.34	0.47	0.59	0.65	0.70	0.74	0.79
Number of nurses/1 doctor	**2.57**	**2.40**	**2.33**	**2.35**	**2.37**	**2.40**	**2.43**	**2.40**

Source adaptation after the National Institute of Statistics 2009–2016, 2017, 2018 and 2019
Note The WHO guidelines provide for a ratio of 2.5 per 1 medical doctor

from 169,080 people in 2009 to 152,942 people in 2018 and in terms of share, from 78.7% in 2009 to 58.5% in 2018. In 2009–2018, the number of staff in the private sector increased 2.3 times, i.e., it came to account for 108.441 persons (National Institute of Statistics 2009–2016, 2017, 2018, 2019) (Table 1).

In comparison with 2009, we can notice a significant improvement in the number of doctors and nurses per 1,000 inhabitants as well as the constant compliance with the adequate nurses-to-doctors ratio, in public sector.

1.2 Financing Scheme in the Healthcare System

The healthcare system in Romania is about 80% funded from public sources, out of which around 63% from the National Health Insurance Fund (FNUASS) and 14% allocated by the Ministry of Health, in 2019. It is worthwhile that these public sources are also complemented by an estimated 20% out-of-pocket payments as well as by local budget allocations and funds of the different public bodies that own a medical network. The main financing drawback in the public system stems from the small number of individual contributors to the health insurance system and although the scheme is supposed to provide coverage for the health needs of a large number of citizens, the developments in the last few years are rather alarming. In 2019, only 25% of the total resident population accounted for insurance payers, 56% were non-paying and 19% non-insured.

Although healthcare expenditure has lately increased, spending per capita in Romania amounts to less than half of the EU average. In 2017, Romania's healthcare spending per capita was about EUR 1,029 (adjusted by purchasing power), whereas the EU average was EUR 2,884, in other words, 5% of the Romanian GDP (in comparison with the average GDP share in the EU of 9.8%). More than 75% of the healthcare expenditure comes from public funds (79.5% in 2017), which is similar to 79.3% EU average.

The funding sources of the Romanian healthcare system are the following: FNUASS, government health expenditure, direct payments and the clawback tax. The main funding source is FNUASS, a fund that totaled approximately EUR 8.8 billion in 2019, out of which 73% employee contributions (cash), 14% public subsidies, 9% clawback tax and 4% contributions for sickness leave. The fund almost doubled in 2008–2019, from EUR 4.3 billion to EUR 8.8 billion.

The healthcare system in Romania points to an unsustainable situation, under the circumstances where contributions only amount to 49% and the spread is covered from the state budget (23%), out-of-pocket payments (20%), the clawback tax (6%), local budgets and other sources (2%).

If we consider that the share of the insurance payers is extremely low (approximately 25% out of the total resident population in 2019), the contribution amounts to 10% of the salary, one of the lowest shares in Europe and salaries in Romania are among the lowest in Europe; then, the financing of the system is unsustainable, since there cannot be significant differences between Romania and other EU member states with respect to cost (medication, medical materials, salaries).

Under these circumstances, the system is forced to keep alive an unsustainable cost pyramid in which 42% of the total health expenditure is still channeled to in-hospital care (versus 29% EU average). It is noteworthy that the total amount per capita is still lower in absolute figure, i.e., it overall represents about half of the health spending per capita in the EU.

Primary and out-of-hospital care account for 22% of the EU average spending (EUR 188/capita versus EUR 858/capita), whereas preventative care amounts to 20% of the EU average (EUR 18/capita versus EUR 89/capita), under the circumstances where the GDP per capita in Romania is only 63% of the EU average (EUR 18,000/capita versus EUR 30,000/capita) (Eurostat 2017) (Table 2).

Table 2 Expenditure on public health care in Romania versus the EU average (EUR/capita 2017)

Indicator	Ro	EU avg	Ro (%)	EU avg (%)	EUR/cap. expenditure (RO/EU avg.) (%)
In-hospital care	432	835	42	29	52
Pharmaceuticals	280	522	27	18	54
Primary and out-of-hospital care	188	858	18	30	**22**
Long-term care	65	471	6	16	**14**
Prevention	18	89	2	3	**20**
Other costs	46	109	4	4	42
Total	**1029**	**2884**	**100**	**100**	**36**

Source adaptation after Eurostat database, 2017

1.3 Operational Capacities of the Romanian Healthcare System

Romania used to have over 150,000 hospital beds in 368 hospitals. In the last few years, we can see that the number of beds has become relatively stable, of about 133,000 in 2018, slightly under the 2009 level, of 137,000. One also has to take into account that no significant and consistent investment has been made in the last few years.

The total number of hospital admitted patients dropped from 5.35 million in 2009 to about 4.2 million in 2018, on the one hand because the population dropped by more than 5.5% in the ten years under review and, on the other hand, due to the improvement of the healthcare system and the fact that the Romanian population may access the medical services provided in other member states of the European Union, a possibility that developed in time.

One of the major indicators in the calibration of the necessary healthcare expenditure is the average hospital stay, which went slightly down, from 7.4 days in 2009 to 7.2 days in 2018.

1.4 Performance Results in the Healthcare System

The public healthcare system does not yet rely on a consistent set of performance indicators, a situation that adds to underfunding the risk of spending the healthcare resources in an inefficient way.

Healthy life years, one of the relevant economic and social indicators, shows a widening gap from the EU average measure, although public health expenditure has markedly gone up and the private healthcare system has significantly developed (Table 3).

Table 3 Healthy life years developments in 2010–2018

Indicator	Ro	EU avg	Spread Ro versus EU avg	Gap Ro versus EU avg (%)
Healthy life years at 65 years old (2010)	5.5	8.4	−2.9	65
Healthy life years at 65 years old (2018)	6.1	9.9	**−3.8**	62
Healthy life years at birth (2010)	57.4	61.8	−4.4	93
Healthy life years at birth (2018)	59.4	64.0	**−4.6**	93

Source Eurostat database, 2020

Table 4 ECHI score—Romania versus the EU average

Indicator	Romania	EU average	Romania versus EU average (%)
Patient rights and information	96	101.26	94.81
Service accessibility/waiting time	175	157.06	111.42
Outcome	133	212.09	62.71
Range of medical services	52	84.46	61.57
Prevention	54	108.03	49.99
Pharmaceuticals	39	64.11	60.83
Overall EHCI score	549	696.83	78.79

Source adapted after Björnberg and Phang (2019, p. 20)

Other such analysis-relevant indicators are avoidable mortality (preventable and amenable) and unsatisfied medical care needs.

In this context, the overall performance of the Romanian healthcare system can also be pictured in terms of satisfaction of the patients' core needs—split into major areas of interest (Table 4): (1) service accessibility/waiting time, (2) patient rights and information, (3) range of provided medical services, (4) preventive actions, (5) pharmaceuticals and (6) outcome. All these different dimensions are addressed in questionnaires that are filled out by patients from 34 countries, based on which the national healthcare systems are given a total score—Euro Health Consumer Index (EHCI). The following table shows the results for each of these areas, as well as the overall EHCI score (Björnberg and Phang 2019).

It emerges that, except for the accessibility of the medical services, health care in Romania scores under the EU average, with the widest gap in prevention actions. This situation is also reflected in the overall EHCI score, where Romania ranks last out of the 34 countries under review.

1.5 Medium- and Long-Term Dynamics

In the long term, we expect to see a higher demand for healthcare workers as well as an increase in expenditure. The higher demand for medical doctors stems from the savings of the upper middle class (featuring higher income and a fast-paced increase of the population over 65).

The major challenges are: pandemic risk, population aging, the increase in the number of disabling conditions, changes in disease profile, higher income of the general population and higher expectations.

Additional challenges for Romania are: securing the adequate funding of the system in the next period, demographic developments, the aging of the healthcare staff, feminization of the profession and increased pressure at the workplace (notably in the public hospitals).

2 Impact of the COVID-19 Pandemic on the Healthcare System

2.1 Materials and Methods

The analysis of the current situation of the Romanian healthcare system was aimed at conducting a research that would yield topical and relevant data about the impact of the COVID-19 pandemic, both from the perspective of those directly engaged, i.e., the medical staff and medical unit managers and that of different other stakeholders. The research pursued several objectives:

1. To establish the direct and indirect effects of the COVID-19 crisis on the overall healthcare system, on the organizations within the system as well as on their different functional components;
2. To identify the main challenges that the medical staff and the managers of the medical units were faced with in their effort to manage the COVID-19 crisis;
3. To identify whether the different features of the health organizations yield any significant differences with regard to the manifestation of the elements mentioned before, which would allow to capture a more nuanced representation as well as to design measures that would address specific root causes of the particulars of each organization;
4. To identify short-, medium- and long-term actions aimed not only at managing the current situation and at mitigating the effects of the COVID-19 crisis, but also at increasing the responsiveness of the Romanian healthcare system in front of similar potential challenges in the future.

The first stage in achieving these objectives consisted of the collection and analysis of the secondary-source data, which helped us build an overall image on the social and economic effects of the sanitary crisis as well as on their repercussions healthcare-wise.

The second stage focused on a deeper analysis of the healthcare system, by means of an online survey that we conducted on August 5–15, 2020. The survey targeted healthcare personnel who played an active role in managing the COVID-19 crisis, i.e., the medical staff and the managers of different healthcare organizations.

Considering that healthcare organizations were supposed to have suffered a different impact based on their different features and that the suggested measures must be tailored to concrete situations, the surveyed population included respondents from all the Romanian development regions as well as from hospitals, outpatient units, pharmacies, individual medical practices, etc., both from the public and the private systems. In order to ensure the representativeness of the sample, both with regard to its size and structure, we designed a sampling framework that included accredited suppliers for the entire range of medical services that work with county health insurance houses—the contact data of the medical services suppliers is public, on the webpage of the county health insurance houses.

The 11 questions included in the questionnaire—predefined or open answers—were structured so as to facilitate the collection of the data needed to achieve the research objectives. In this paper, only those reflecting the impact of the current situation on the core activity of the medical units and main difficulties encountered in the medical practice were analyzed.

The questionnaire was sent in electronic format (Google Forms) to the email addresses of the providers of medical services in a 10-day time slot. We collected 373 responses, out of which 5 respondents declined; therefore, we processed 368 questionnaires altogether.

Considering the size of the research sample (368 respondents) as well as the territorial breakdown, since the respondents represent healthcare units in different development regions (National Institute of Statistics 2020), we may conclude that the sample is representative at national level, with results yielding a margin of error of ±5,1%.

2.2 *Analysis of the Healthcare Impact of COVID-19 Based on Secondary-Source Data*

The emergence of COVID-19 as a global pandemic disrupted the operation of all companies across the world. The virus has significantly hindered the economy and social life and generated, alongside the pandemic, a world economic crisis.

Aware that numerous countries were faced with difficulties and that the cases would skyrocket, the World Health Organization declared the state of global pandemic on March 11, 2020 and urged all national governments to "fully mobilize the healthcare systems, the medical equipment and the workers in the national medical system." The WHO also advised to distribute antiviral protection equipment as well as other medical materials in accordance with the national plans (Cadis 2020).

At the beginning, the crisis caused by the number of infections put pressure on the sanitary systems across the world, as the need for ICU ventilators was very high.

At that time, the Romanian public system had about 2500 ICU beds, which could be made available to treat the severe cases. Also, the big private players claimed that they were in close contact with the authorities and offered to make their equipment available, if necessary.

On March 23, 2020, the Private Medical Service Suppliers Association (PALMED), an organization that includes the large private healthcare networks, required an analysis of the situations provided under Order 74,527 of March 23, 2020, which suspended for 14 days any hospital admission for surgery procedures, in-hospital therapy or interventions for all cases, excepting life-threatening conditions that could not be rescheduled. According to the president of PALMED Cristian Hotoboc: "We need an urgent analysis of the situations where we can actually apply this order, we cannot do it overnight. There are many different types of situations and such restrictions can cause the loss of human lives. Someone who suffers from a chronic condition or a patient under palliative care do not count as medical emergencies, but releasing them from hospital may end up in complications or, even worse, in death. The Romanian health care system is already insufficient, so we cannot afford to restrict access to medical services even more" (Ziarul Financiar 2020a).

The pandemic touched the sore spot of understaffing in the Romanian medical system—a 17.4% deficit, according to the Sanitary Solidarity Federation, i.e., public hospitals are short of about 40,000 employees, doctors and nurses, in comparison with the standard ratio. At country level, the most severe understaffing is felt in Mehedinți, Giurgiu, Galați and Olt, whereas the best staffed are the hospitals in Bistrița and Harghita. The former category was not only the least prepared to fight the COVID-19 pandemic, but also the hardest hit (Ziarul Financiar 2020b).

On March 26, 2020, Ziarul financiar (2020a) already singled out the serious difficulties emerging at national level, more precisely:

- There were already 153 people infected with the new coronavirus among the medical workers and ancillary medical staff, i.e., 15% of the total number of infections;
- The outbreaks of Bucharest and Suceava marked a high infection rate for doctors, with 36 and 90 medical workers infected, respectively;
- The Romanian College of Physicians asked the authorities to test patients and doctors, even if they did not match the established criteria;
- In a context where the need for medical equipment and pharmaceuticals is critical at global level, Romanian authorities should urgently restart local production.

In the same period, the number of patients admitted in private clinics plummeted to less than half, which reduced the income of the doctors from the private system. Some private clinics even suspended their activity altogether (Bădescu 2020).

A particular case is the impact of COVID-19 on dentistry services. Since dentistry is a medical profession that supposes direct and close contact with the patient, the measures taken at national level in order to curb the spread of the new coronavirus specifically targeted the activity in this field. Thus, during the lockdown initiated by the president of Romania, according to the Military Ordinance no. 1, Article 1, the activity of dentistry practices was suspended and only a limited number of practices, which were authorized by the Public Health Directorates, were allowed to provide emergency dental care in that period. Consequently, dentistry, a medical field that mainly operates as a private practice, was strongly affected by the COVID-19 pandemic. Dentistry practices practically recorded no revenue, although fixed operating cost stayed largely unchanged. The effect was equally felt by the patients who saw themselves forced to postpone or discontinue dental treatment. Even if dental practices reopened after May 15, 2020, the additional measures (natural under the circumstances of a pandemic), such as cleaning and disinfecting, the increase of time between patients, the need for additional individual protection equipment etc., added new cost elements, which were felt by the dentists, but finally incurrent to the paying patients.

The economic impact of COVID-19 is highlighted in the next table, which shows a 15% drop in the FNUASS collected contributions in March 2020 versus March

2019 and especially an increase of the subsidies, i.e., RON 826 billion in March 2020 versus RON 40 billion in March 2019 (2023% more year-on-year). It is also noteworthy that the collected insurance contributions in May 2020 are 85% of the amounts collected in May 2019 (Table 5).

2.3 *Analysis of the Healthcare Impact of COVID-19 Based on Primary-Source Data*

In order to deepen the direct analysis of the healthcare system, on August 5–15, we conducted an online survey that targeted the persons who played an active role in managing the COVID-19 crisis, i.e., the medical staff and the managers in the healthcare organizations. From the point of view of territorial distribution, the shares of the respondents representing the medical organizations headquartered in different development regions and the shares of the respondents in the sample are not very different from the shares of the medical units in Romania in 2018 (National Institute of Statistics 2020). As expected, the largest share of the respondents originates from București-Ilfov Region (17.12%), whereas at the bottom of the representation are the southwest (10.05%) and central regions (8.42% of the total number of respondents).

The first cluster of questions was aimed at the impact of the COVID-19 crisis on the healthcare organizations (on the whole) as well as on their various functional components. The analysis of the answers yielded the following:

- In most of the cases, there was an adjustment of activities so as to prevent the spread of COVID-19, with adjustment averaging 35.33% for management activities and 52.88% for the core medical activities of the units.
- Telework can also be seen as another type of adjustment, although it is more frequent in management activities (17.39%) and less frequent in the provision of medical services (8.97%).
- Unfortunately, in some situations the activity was altogether suspended (not an unexpected outcome, though), although it was less noteworthy when it came to the management activities.
- The distribution analysis based on the type of delivered medical services mainly yielded the following (Table 6):
- Except for dental care practices, most of the medical units reported an adjustment of their core activities, i.e., they had to take preventative measures in order to curb the spread on COVID-19.
- Dental practices make a particular situation, since more than half (58.33%) reported that they had to temporarily suspend their activity, whereas 33.33% related that they had to adjust and take preventative measures in order to curb the spread on COVID-19.
- Regarding to the stay of the activity, we note that the measure was not really necessary except for 0.91% of the general practice offices and none of the pharmacies.

Table 5 Monthly dynamics of FNUASS revenues in 2020 (RON thousands)

Indicator	Program for 2020	Collected in Jan. 2020	Collected in Feb. 2020	Collected in March 2020	Collected in April 2020	Collected in May 2020
Total revenues	42,293,540	2,843,582	3,694,101	3,246,524	2,660,271	3,343,357
Currend revenues	36,817,782	2,918,700	3,642,993	2,427,908	2,628,881	3,291,783
Insurance contributions	33,502,223	2,909,804	2,714,740	2,267,681	2,534,144	2,392,303
Out of which payments due by insured employees	30,957,644	2,743,022	2,501,846	2,103,004	2,389,330	2,236,276
Subsidies	5,364,254	25,968	24,940	826,133	25,486	26,453
Year-on-year situation	Progr. 2020/progr. 2019	01.2020/01.2019	02.2020/02.2019	03.2020/03.2019	04.2020/04.2019	05.2020/05.2019
Total revenues	101%	102%	109%	120%	100%	94%
Currend revenues	102%	102%	110%	90%	103%	92%
Insurance contributions	103%	102%	107%	85%	100%	85%
Subsidies	94%	165%	152%	2032%	98%	105%

Source http://www.cnas.ro/

Table 6 Impact of the current situation on the core activity of the medical units based on type of medical care

Impact	Type of medical care						
	GP (%)	SA (%)	H (%)	PH (%)	MR (%)	P (%)	DM (%)
Temporarily suspended	0.91	8.70	11.76	0.00	33.33	7.14	58.33
Adjusted to telework	13.24	10.87	2.94	20.00	11.11	10.71	8.33
Adjusted to the preventative measures taken to limit the spread of COVID-19	56.16	71.74	73.53	70.00	55.56	64.29	33.33
Not affected	9.59	6.52	2.94	0.00	0.00	3.57	0.00
Work is more intense than before	18.26	2.17	8.82	0.00	0.00	10.71	0.00
Not applicable/I do not know	1.83	0.00	0.00	10.00	0.00	3.57	0.00

Note GP = Primary medical care/general practitioners, SA = Specialized medical assistance, H = Hospital, PH = Pharmacy, MR = Medical rehabilitation, P = Paraclinical investigations, DM = dentistry medical services
Source own elaborations based on the survey results

Throughout this period, the medical and non-medical staff had to cope with countless difficulties in their professional activity. The survey results emphasized that the biggest difficulties were the lack/shortage of protective equipment and adjustment to the new working conditions, both mentioned by about half of the respondents (50.82% and 47.01%, respectively). In descending frequency order, the other major difficulties refer to the following: poor cooperation from some patients (31.25%), lack of/failure to implement procedures (22.01%), extended working hours (12.23%), lack of/failure to create medical circuits (10.60%), poor engagement from some colleagues (8.70%) and defective organizational management (3.80%).

Besides choosing an answer from a predefined list of difficulties that they encountered in their professional activity, 5.89% of the respondents also mentioned other difficulties, such as: ambiguity with regard to information, deficiencies in the organization of the healthcare system, poor coordination between different organizations and ministries with respect to the adopted decisions, deficiencies with respect to coordination and engagement of bodies such as the Directorate for Public Health, Bucharest Health Insurance House or city halls, increased operating expenditure for a shrinking number of patients, difficulties and delays in the reimbursement of the medical services by the health insurance houses, as well as negative repercussions on the staff.

It is also noteworthy that 6.25% of the respondents stated that they encountered difficulties in the performance of their professional activity.

Based on the type of healthcare services provided by each medical unit, the respondents highlighted the following major difficulties (Table 7):

Table 7 Main difficulties encountered in the performance of professional activity based on the type of medical care provided

Difficulties	Type of medical care						
	GP (%)	SA (%)	H (%)	PH (%)	MR (%)	P (%)	DM (%)
Lack/shortage of protective equipment	60.73	42.39	32.35	10.00	27.78	42.86	27.78
Lack of/failure to implement procedures	27.85	20.65	14.71	0.00	11.11	17.86	11.11
Lack of/failure to create medical circuits	12.79	11.96	11.76	0.00	11.11	17.86	2.78
Adjustment to the new working conditions	45.21	46.74	55.88	50.00	38.89	46.43	55.56
Extended working hours	15.07	6.52	11.76	0.00	5.56	3.57	13.89
Defective organizational management	5.02	4.35	5.88	0.00	5.56	3.57	2.78
Poor engagement from some colleagues	10.50	6.52	17.65	0.00	16.67	14.29	5.56
Poor cooperation from some patients	32.88	32.61	29.41	30.00	27.78	50.00	27.78
No difficulties	5.94	6.52	0.00	10.00	16.67	0.00	0.00

Source own elaborations based on the survey results

- Irrespective of the type of medical assistance provided, the difficulties that the healthcare workers most often encountered were the following: lack/shortage of protective equipment, adjustment to the new working conditions and poor cooperation from some patients.
- Lack/shortage of protective equipment and lack of/failure to implement procedures are most often singled out by GPs.
- Adjustment to the new working conditions and poor engagement from some colleagues were most often noted by the respondents from the hospital environment, whereas lack of/failure to create medical circuits and poor cooperation from some patients were most often singled out by respondents from medical units that provide paraclinical investigations.
- The largest share of the medical units where respondents singled out that they encountered difficulties in performing their activity corresponded to the medical rehabilitation facilities and to pharmacies.

Besides the analyses of the answers collected from the entire sample, which helped shaping an overall image of the problematics addressed in the survey, the research also highlighted numerous particular aspects which are rather specific to each development region, to the type of ownership and to the kind of medical care provided by the medical units, all of them useful to project short-, medium- and long-term actions. Equally useful were the opinions and suggestions that the respondents expressed when they answered the open questions and we are grateful for their engagement.

3 Suggested Measures Aimed at Mitigating the Effects of COVID-19 and at the Recovery of the Field on the Short, Medium and Long Terms

The suggested measures in the field of health care equally address punctual aspects and more general orientations, which are meant to generate better responsiveness, should to those generated by the COVID-19 pandemic occur again. They represent the synthesis of the quantitative and qualitative research that we performed in this study, some of them relying on the answers we received at the open questions that we included in the previously described questionnaire.

The new circumstances generated by the COVID-19 pandemic turned everyone engaged in the different healthcare specialties into "first-line" workers, irrespective of whether they conduct their activity as medical workers in hospitals, as GPs, dentists or pharmacists. Consequently, some measures and actions are of general nature, transgress medical specialties and can be beneficial for all medical fields. We only list a few:

- Efficient management of the available financial and medical resources—rearranging financing scheme priorities according to the needs and eliminating useless or discretionary investment and expenses. Such goals can be achieved through:
  - Lower political involvement in the healthcare system or cooperation with experts in the field of economics in order to make resource-use more efficient;
  - Better matching the number of positions in the healthcare system with the real local and regional needs and filling positions through transparent and methodologically correct selection procedures;
- Consistency in the adoption of decisions—preliminary debates and discussions with all the social and professional categories concerned by the decisions;
- Creation of equitable and fairly remunerated jobs—based on the work done, an approach that would ensure human resource retention in the healthcare system;
- Closer focus on prevention programs—Prevention is undoubtedly less costly than medium- and long-term interventions and results in a better general health status.
- Parallel investment in the education system—A population that has access to information and good-quality education services can have a clearer understanding of things and embraces a more responsible response to the measures enforced by the authorities in order to protect the common good.
- Specific financial support for the SMEs that operate in the medical field;
- An overarching approach to the concept of quality of life—besides ensuring access to good-quality medical and education services, it also takes an adequate infrastructure that would limit the number of road injuries and reduce transit as well

as commuting time, etc., a reduction in air, ground and water pollution, an end to massive deforestation, in other words the protection of the environment; practically speaking, the general population health status is directly affected by all these factors, not only by the deficiencies in the healthcare system;
- Eradication or reduction of corruption to the largest possible extent at all levels of the administration and support for professional pathways based on ethics.
- Furthermore, in order to counter the spread of COVID-19 and support the efforts made by all the categories of medical staff, there are other measures to be considered, such as:
- More substantial checks and sanctions for those who do not comply with social distancing, disinfection and the mandatory mask-wearing in crowded and closed spaces;
- Wide-scale testing of the population and compensation (at least partial) of the cost of testing;
- Subsidizing the cost of masks and of disinfectant solutions for the vulnerable social categories/categories found at and under the threshold of poverty;
- Regulation of staggered export in order to replenish national stocks;
- Repeated population information (without inducing any panic) about the medical and social effects of COVID-19 infection—to that end, it is also useful to inform the population about the economic and social cost of the disease (both at individual and local/national level);
- Attracting volunteers for all the activities associated with the fight against COVID-19.

4 Conclusions

The data and the information presented in this study reflect without any doubt the countless challenges in the healthcare system, all of them having repercussions first of all on the citizens' state of health and then on economic productivity. It is a well-known fact that a population that enjoys a good health status is, on the one hand, more productive and, on the other hand, puts less pressure on the budgetary health expenditure.

The context of the COVID-19 pandemic requires a set of immediate actions in order to curb the unfortunate sanitary and socioeconomic effects that we have already explained. Nevertheless, we ought to warn on the need of equally adopting an overall approach that should include medium and long-term measures, since the healthcare system cannot improve through short-term actions, but requires a long-term vision that relies on the strategic input of all the direct and indirect stakeholders engaged in or affected by the healthcare system.

Moreover, integrated investment targeting the education system, as well as the economic capacity of the country will make it easier to manage the effects of any economic or sanitary crisis like those that we have experienced in the past 15 years while also spending less of the government funds.

Comparative figures between the past decade and 2019 indicate that we have made progress and partly reformed and strengthened the system, but the indicators regarding the general state of health and healthcare financing are very disturbing. Thus, although in comparison with the previous decade, the developments are encouraging, we must note that only by implementing articulated reform actions throughout the system and by investing more in health care can we build a solid foundation for the medical staff and patients alike, which would help attain a better general state of health and counter the emergency situations or cases through avoidable morbidity and mortality. Last but not least, an economy based on sustainable growth, on a well-educated human capital, on accessible and good-quality public services, on large investment projects in all the key areas is much more resilient to any type of macro-instability.

References

Bădescu, A.: Ziarul Financiar. [online] Available at: https://www.zf.ro/opinii/spune-adrian-badescu-directorul-clinicilor-medici-s-timisoara-imi-19081329. Accessed May 3, 2020 (2020)

Björnberg, A., Phang, A.N.: Euro Health Consumer Index 2018 Report. [online] Available at: https://healthpowerhouse.com/media/EHCI-2018/EHCI-2018-report.pdf. Accessed on May , 03, 2020 (2019)

Cadis, A.: Ziarul Financiar. [online] Available at: https://www.zf.ro/eveniment/ce-se-intampla-dupa-ce-oms-a-declarat-pandemie-de-coronavirus-18969826. Accessed on 7 May 2020 (2020)

Eurostat: Eurostat. [online] Available at: https://www.oecd.org/health/health-at-a-glance-europe-23056088.htm. Accessed on May 7, 2020 (2017)

Eurostat: Eurostat, Data, database, Health care expenditure by function. [online] Available at: https://appsso.eurostat.ec.europa.eu/nui/show.do?dataset=hlth_sha11_hchp&lang=en. Accessed on May 8, 2020 (2020)

Mihalache, G.: Ziarul Financiar. [online] Available at: https://www.zfcorporate.ro/zf-print/prima-pagina/masurile-care-trebuie-luate-urgent-in-sanatate-testarea-tuturor-pacientilor-care-intra-in-spitale-si-preluarea-spitalelor-mari-de-catre-ministerul-sanatatii-19023361. Accessed on May 5, 2020 (2020)

National Institute of Statistics: Alte publicații, arhiva Activitatea unităților sanitare 2009–2016. [online] Available at: https://insse.ro/cms/ro/content/alte-publica%C8%9Bii. Accessed on May 8, 2020 (2009–2016)

National Institute of Statistics: Activitatea unităților sanitare anul 2016. [online] Available at: https://insse.ro/cms/ro/content/activitatea-unit%C4%83%C5%A3ilor-sanitare-%E2%80%93-anul-2016. Accessed on May 8, 2020 (2017)

National Institute of Statistics: Activitatea unităților sanitare anul 2017. [online] Available at: https://insse.ro/cms/files/publicatii/publicatii%20statistice%20operative/activitatea_unitatilor_sanitare_anul_2017.pdf. Accessed on May 8, 2020 (2018)

National Institute of Statistics: Activitatea unităților sanitare anul 2018. [online] Available at: https://insse.ro/cms/ro/content/activitatea-unit%C4%83%C5%A3ilor-sanitare-%E2%80%93-anul-2018. Accessed on May 8, 2020 (2019)

National Institute of Statistics: TEMPO online. [Interactiv]. Accessed on August 13, 2020 (2020)

National Institute of Statistics: SAN101A—Unitati sanitare pe categorii de unitati, forme de proprietate, macroregiuni, regiuni de dezvoltare și judete. [online] Available at: http://statistici.insse.ro:8077/tempo-online/#/pages/tables/insse-table. Accessed on August 14, 2020 (2020)

Ziarul Financiar, 2020a. Ziarul Finaciar. [online] Available at: https://www.zfcorporate.ro/pharma/patronatul-furnizorilor-servicii-medicale-private-suspendarea-internarilor-spitalele-private-nevoie-analiza-urgenta-situatiilor-aplica-adevarat-acest-ordin-19012551. Accessed on May 5, 2020 (2020)

Ziarul Financiar: Ziarul Financiar. [online] Available at: https://www.zfcorporate.ro/pharma/federatia-solidaritatea-sanitara-spitalele-au-intrat-in-lupta-impotriva-coronavirus-cu-un-deficit-de-40-000-de-angajati-la-spitalele-de-boli-infectioase-lipsesc-698-de-angajati-19015551. Accessed on May 3, 2020 (2020b)

The Impact of COVID-19 Crisis on the Romanian Agricultural Sector

Istudor Nicolae, Popescu Gabriel, Begalli Diego, Ignat Raluca, Petrescu Irina-Elena, and Petre Ionuț-Laurențiu

1 Introduction

Agriculture operates in two systems, with different speeds. The first, and the closest to the level of current technical–scientific progress, is the industrial, intensive type. It is the system in which the results register sustained rhythms, the behavior in the market is more and more competitive, and it is positioned, especially, in the lowland areas, where the suitability is highly favorable for cereals and oleaginous.

The second is the traditional slow-moving system away from the market. It is the dominant system in over 3.2 million small and very small entities and is based on family, property, and self-consumption.

Integration into the European Union has been beneficial in terms of economic growth, especially for the industrial system. Dynamism and competitiveness in the market are recognized and appreciated forces.

I. Nicolae · P. Gabriel · I. Raluca · P. Irina-Elena (✉) · P. Ionuț-Laurențiu
Bucharest University of Economic Studies, Bucharest, Romania
e-mail: irina.petrescu@eam.ase.ro

I. Nicolae
e-mail: nicolae.istudor@ase.ro

P. Gabriel
e-mail: gabriel.popescu@eam.ase.ro

I. Raluca
e-mail: raluca.ignat@eam.ase.ro

P. Ionuț-Laurențiu
e-mail: laurentiu.petre@eam.ase.ro

B. Diego
Universita Di Verona, Verona, Italy
e-mail: diego.begalli@univr.it

A. M. Dima et al. (eds.), *Economic Recovery After COVID-19*, Springer Proceedings in Business and Economics, https://doi.org/10.1007/978-3-030-86641-9_2

For traditional entities, integration, which has allowed the influx of cheaper foreign products and increased state aid, has meant in significant proportions, the removal and, what is really worrying, the abandonment of agricultural activities.

Currently, on the rural, but especially on the agriculture act two important natural risk factors, respectively, prolonged drought and coronavirus pandemic, factors that can induce a strong and deep crisis, with multiple effects in Romanian society. The drought, which began in August and September 2019, has already compromised much of the autumn crops (wheat, barley, oats), and in the crops sown in spring, the plants do not have the necessary water resources for germination and growth. The coronavirus pandemic, although it started in the first part of March 2020; however, its effects can be as harmful as drought, even more so because:

- It overlaps and amplifies the effects of the swine fever that brought down the herd of pigs with millions of heads;
- It restricts the movement of the population and, implicitly, of the labor force, fact that will compress the economy through all its components;
- It can generate a strong food crisis, with much more acute manifestations than in 1945–1946, recognized as the worst in recent history. Now, unlike then, peasant families, even if they have a much-improved standard of living; however, their vulnerability to risk factors is arguably much higher due to:
  - High dependence on public aid;
  - Volatility of ties with agriculture;
  - Decrease, until the disappearance of the interest for the establishment of stocks of agricultural products in households, and, equally, for the breeding of animals.

Also, the impact of COVID-19 on the agricultural systems is an important aspect that was considered by all the stakeholders, not only from Romania. Haqiqi and Horeh (2021) reached the conclusion that in the USA the impact of COVID-19 was higher on the small-scale farmers and that the innovations and technical progress may exclude pandemics effects. Obviously, the impact of the COVID-19 was quite high on agricultural exports (Lin and Zhang 2020), and on the system itself in several countries around the world (Middendorf et al. 2021; Gu Wang 2021).

The issue is much more important as the organic food market will develop more (Stoian and Caprita 2019), the sustainable development of agriculture represents the new trend (Pargaru et al. 2019; Drăcea et al. 2020) and any shocks may even crash the agri-food system. Moreover, the circular economy will be introduced in the agriculture system also (Busu and Trica 2019), as the innovation may be the development key of the field business. Obviously, the strategic success factors need to be modeled (Mazurencu-Marinescu and Pele 2012) in order to implement innovation into the agriculture and, nevertheless, the European funds for agriculture are one of the key factors (Dinu 2020).

Therefore, there is no other possibility for Romanian agriculture to be developed then to consider the pandemic context, to draw conclusions, and to implement the necessary measures in order to eliminate as much as possible the effects and minimize the negative impact.

Thud, the COVID-19 impact is huge on the economy and the agri-food sector just takes its part.

2 Evolution of the Sector

2.1 *Number of Employees*

In agriculture, the employed population decreased from 2.4 million people to 1.76 million people, respectively, by 27%. Of these, on average 112 thousand people (5.3%) were employees, their share during the period increased to 7.3% and 129.3 thousand people, respectively. Out of the total number of people employed in agriculture, 0.3% (6.7 thousand people) were employers, which increased significantly, to 12.4 thousand people in the last year (Fig. 1).

Even if the first two categories increase, the general downward trend is given by the other two categories in which more than 90% of people employed in agriculture are found: self-employed and unpaid family workers. On average, self-employed workers have a share of 47.3% (1.033 million people), but they register a decrease of 29%. Of those who deal with agriculture, 47% are unpaid family workers, so we can emphasize through this indicator the traditional part of agriculture, they are on a downward slope, decreasing in the analyzed period by 30%, reaching 766 thousand people.

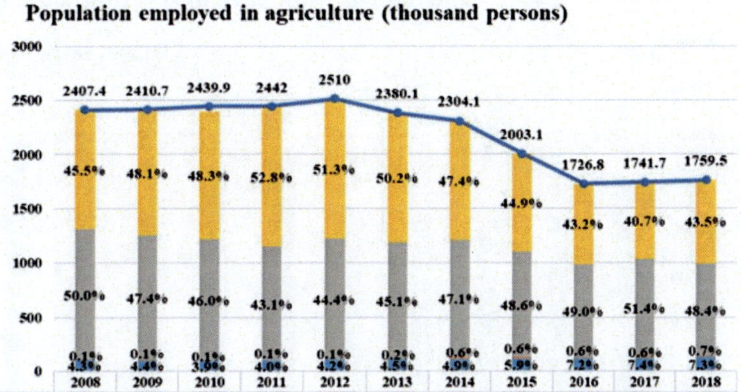

	2008	2009	2010	2011	2012	2013	2014	2015	2016	2017	2018
Unpaid family workers	1095.5	1160.1	1178.7	1290.5	1287.9	1193.9	1091.4	899.4	745.6	708.8	766.1
Self-employed	1204.9	1142	1122.7	1051.9	1115	1072.6	1085.8	972.9	846.2	894.6	851.7
Owners	3.4	2.4	1.3	1.6	1.9	5.4	13.1	11.7	10.6	9.7	12.4
Employee	103.6	106.2	95	98	105.2	108.2	113.8	119.1	124.4	128.6	129.3
Total	2407.4	2410.7	2439.9	2442	2510	2380.1	2304.1	2003.1	1726.8	1741.7	1759.5

Fig. 1 Dynamics of the number of employees. *Source* own processing based on NIS data, 2020 (National Institute of Statistics 2020)

From the point of view of evolution, those employed in agriculture registered an average annual growth rate of 2.24%, from 103 thousand people to 129 thousand people, the average number being 112 thousand people, from this value there is an average deviation of 12 thousand people which determines a coefficient of variation of 10.7%.

2.2 *Gross Value Added*

The gross value added, in agriculture, registered an increasing evolution in the analyzed period, registering a total increase, in 2019 compared to 2008 by 38%. If in 2008, there was a gross value added of about 30.8 billion lei, in 2019 it increased to 42.6 billion lei (Fig. 2).

The lowest gross value added was recorded in 2009, being 27.1 billion lei, immediately with the outbreak of the economic crisis of that period, and the second-lowest value was recorded in 2012 when the value of production was low given small productions in the vegetal sector due to the climatic conditions.

On average, the gross value added was 32.3 billion, with a deviation of 4.8 billion, which determined a coefficient of variation of about 15%.

The increase in GVA was due to the increase in the value of production and less to the reduction in intermediate consumption, so it can be said that this increase is due to either the increase in production or the increase in the capitalization price.

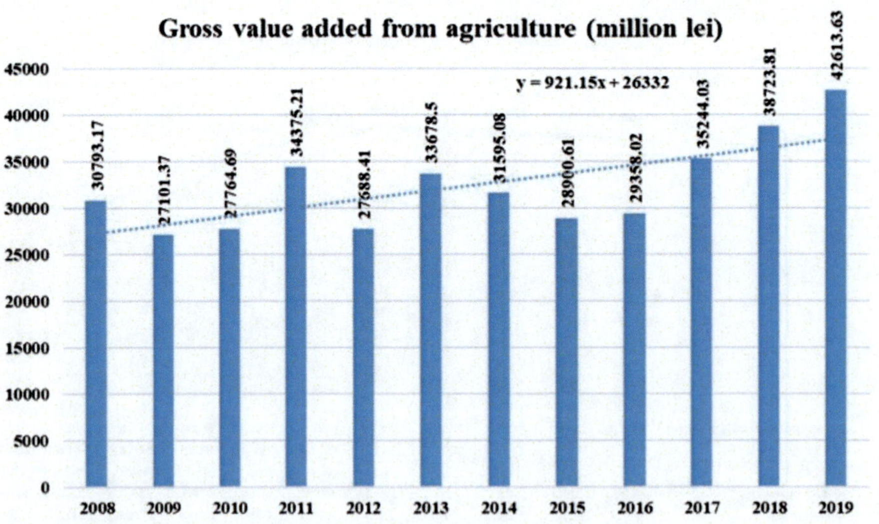

Fig. 2 Dynamics of added value. *Source* own processing based on NIS data, 2020 (National Institute of Statistics 2020)

The average annual growth rate was 4.63%, and if we analyze the equation of the trend line established in the graph, we can see that the value of the coefficient of x is 921.15, which may lead to the hypothesis that, annually, GVA increases, in the middle, with 921 million lei.

2.3 *Investments*

Investments in the agricultural sector (agriculture, forestry, and fishing) are increasing during the analyzed period, registering a minimum level of them (2.66 billion lei) in 2010, when the most intense economic crisis was felt, at new in the country, and the maximum value was registered in 2017, the investment level being 5.88 billion lei (Fig. 3).

Overall, the average investment in this sector of the economy was 4.125 billion lei, with a rather high deviation of 1.1 billion lei, which determined a coefficient of variation of 26, 6%.

In the last year, the value of investments in agriculture increased by 67% compared to the first year, but in this period, there were also decreases; thus, calculating the pace, there is an average annual increase of 4.97%.

In addition to the agricultural sector, industry is also registered in the branches of the economy, and it includes several sub-branches, including the manufacturing industry, which includes the categories of food industry and beverage industry. Adding the level of investments in these two categories to the agricultural sector, the investment level of the agri-food sector was determined.

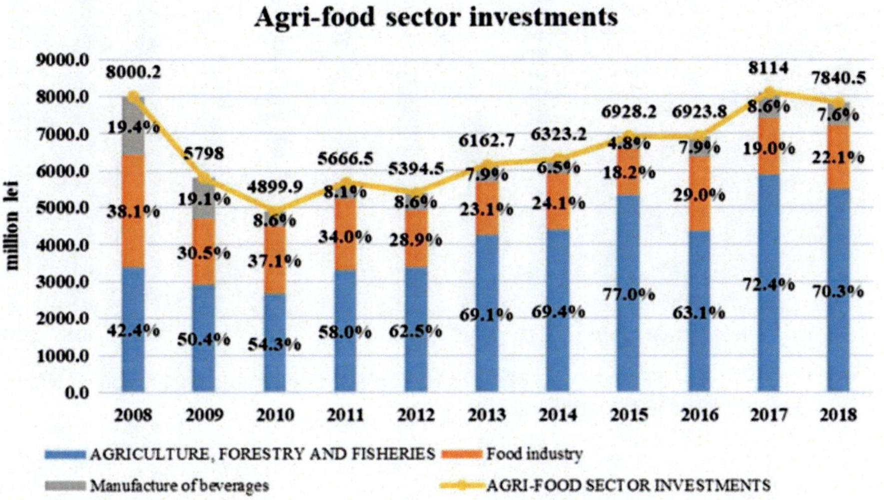

Fig. 3 Investment dynamics. *Source* own processing based on NIS data, 2020 (National Institute of Statistics 2020)

From the graph, it can be seen that out of the total investments in the agri-food sector, investments in agriculture have a share between 42–73%, which increases over time, on average the share being 62.6%.

In the food industry, there is a level of investments between 1.26 billion lei and 3.05 billion lei, the average for the entire period being 1.78 billion lei, which represented a share of total investments of 27.6%, investments in this category are declining, on average by 5.5% annually.

In the beverage industry, there is a level of investments between 334 million lei and 1.55 billion lei, the average for the entire period being 643 million lei, which represented a total share of investments of 9.7%, investments in this category being decreasing, on average by 9.1% annually.

Analyzing as a whole it can be seen that investments in the processing area have decreased, and their place has been taken by investments in the agricultural sector, given that the level of investment between the two ends of the analyzed time interval is very similar, around of 8 billion lei. This can be seen from the annual rate of −0.2% per year, so it can be said that the level of agri-food investments was constant, on average, because compared to the average of 6.55 billion lei, it is registering a rather large deviation of 1.1 billion yards, respectively, a variation of 16.8%. Thus, even if the level of investment fluctuated during this period, on average it remained unchanged over the 11 years (Fig. 4).

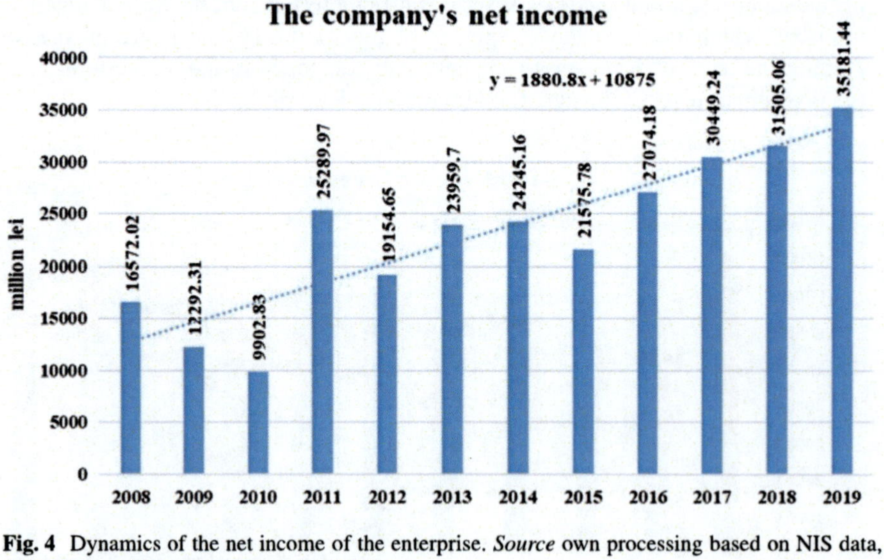

Fig. 4 Dynamics of the net income of the enterprise. *Source* own processing based on NIS data, 2020 (National Institute of Statistics 2020)

2.4 Agricultural Income

According to the Economic Accounts in Agriculture, the net income represents the gain of the entire sector following the taxation and deduction of any kind of taxes. As can be seen, the company's net income recorded a significant increase in the period under review, from 16.57 billion in 2008 to 35.2 billion in 2019, an increase of 112%. The lowest net income of agricultural enterprises was registered in the period of economic recession, respectively, in 2010, when this indicator registered a value of 9.9 billion lei.

On average, the net income of agricultural enterprises was 23.1 billion lei, with a rather large deviation from it, of 7.66 billion, representing a variation of 33%. This variation characterizes this data series as inhomogeneous, given that it has grown very steeply. The average annual growth rate is 11.1%, and looking at the equation of the trend line we see an average annual growth of 1.88 billion.

This doubling of the net income of the agricultural enterprises in the analyzed period is attributed to the increase of the production value, respectively, to the increase of the yield per hectare, or per animal head, but also to the increase of the capitalization price. At the same time, it should be mentioned that a very important role on this indicator has the volume of subsidies, these being included in this income, representing about 30% of it.

2.5 Cultivation of Plants

Romania owns about 3.4 million agricultural holdings, of which about 3.3 million represent agricultural holdings without legal personality, respectively, individual agricultural holdings or individual or family enterprises. About 26,000 agricultural holdings have legal personality and are constituted in: autonomous companies, agricultural associations, commercial companies, cooperative units, and other types. There is an increase of 55.6% in the number of companies whose object of activity is cultivation of plants, in the period 2008–2018, simultaneously with a decrease in the number of agricultural holdings without legal personality. This is due to the infusion of non-reimbursable European funds, available after Romania's accession to the European Union. Thus, in the first programming period, 2007–2013, the Romanian agri-food sector benefited from about 8.2 billion euros in non-reimbursable European funds, and in the period 2014–2020, it benefited from another 9.4 billion euros (Fig. 5).

Of the 8765 companies, in 2018, those that deal with the cultivation of cereals represent 85.5%. The interest of agricultural producers for these types of crops is also reflected by the high share of areas cultivated with cereals in the used agricultural area of Romania. In the same year, out of the over 8.4 million hectares cultivated, the area cultivated with cereals was over 5.2 million hectares, representing 62.2%.

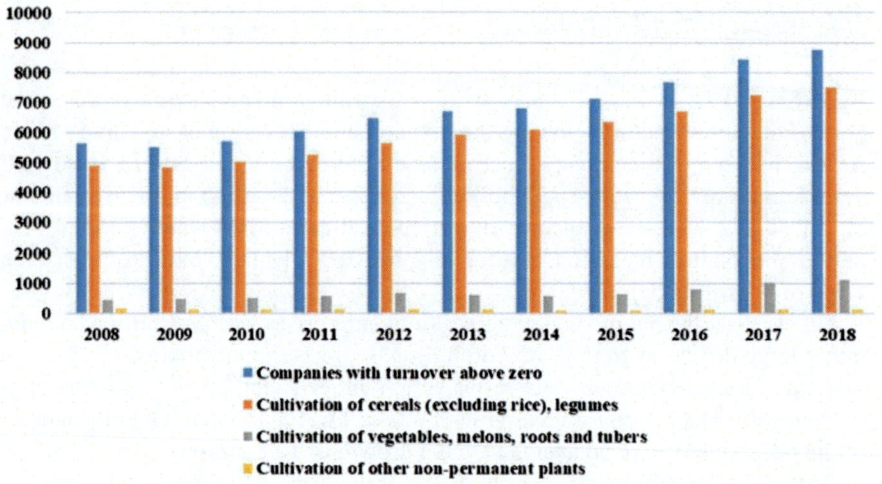

Fig. 5 Evolution of the number of companies with the object of activity Plant cultivation, in the period 2008–2018. *Source* Trade Register data processing (Trade Register Office 2020) and (National Agency for Fiscal Administration 2020)

The increase in the total number of companies whose object of activity is the cultivation of plants is due, for the most part, to the increase in the number of companies growing cereals, but also companies growing vegetables, melons, roots, and tubers.

2.6 Livestock

Regarding the number of companies whose turnover is positive, in the livestock sector, a slightly increasing evolution can be observed, from 1648 to 2029 companies, respectively, an increase of 23.1%. The average number of companies for the entire period was 1833, with a deviation of 133, respectively, a variation of 7.2%. Out of the total number of companies, on average, 500 are dairy farms, respectively, a share of 27.3%. However, these companies are decreasing, on average by 0.38% annually, from 2008 to 2018, decreasing by 3.8% (Fig. 6).

Out of the total number of companies, on average, 433 are poultry farms, respectively, a share of 23.6%. These companies are growing slightly, on average by 1.9% annually, from 2008 to 2018, increasing by 20.7% (Fig. 7).

Out of the total number of companies, on average, 355 are pig farms, respectively, a share of 19.3%. These companies are growing, on average by 3.34% annually, from 2008 to 2018, increasing by 39%. Out of the total number of companies, on average, 149 are sheep and goat farms, respectively, a share of 8.2%. These companies are growing, on average by 6.3% annually, from 2008 to 2018, increasing by 83%.

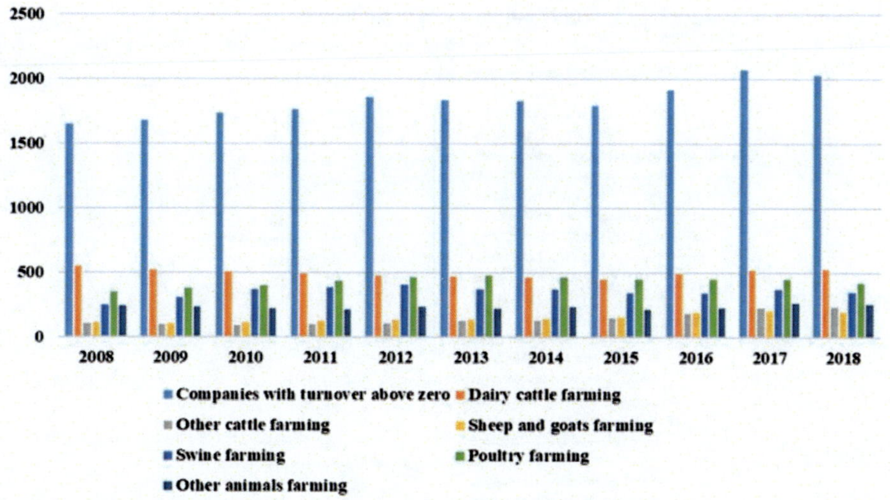

Fig. 6 Evolution of the number of companies with the object of activity Animal breeding, in the period 2008–2018. *Source* Trade Register data processing (Trade Register Office 2020) and (National Agency for Fiscal Administration 2020)

2.7 *Trade Balance*

Analyzing in the sections of the nomenclature, those that record a surplus on the trade balance is that of vegetable products (due to the very high level of exported cereals), the surplus of the entire section being 1.37 billion euros, the section of animal or vegetable fats and oils, registers a surplus, amounting to 50.7 million euros, and on the other hand, there is a surplus in the wood products section. Respectively in the category of raw wood, timber, the ex-assignor being 855 million euros.

Within the chapters, there is a surplus for: live animals (253.1 million euro, here contributing a lot to the export of sheep), cereals (2.2 billion euro); oil seeds and oleaginous fruits (686.5 million euro), tobacco and substitutes (583.5 million euro).

Analyzing the deficit in foreign trade of the agricultural sector by far the largest deficit is recorded in the food section, beverages being 1.6 billion euros. The second section with a significant deficit is that of live animals and animal products, of 1.04 billion euros, here contributing a lot to the chapter that brings us with a deficit of 701 million euros.

Although the largest deficit for a section was recorded for food products (processed) in this section is included a category with the largest deficit of 2019, namely that of meat and fish preparations, registering—there is a deficit of 3.58 billion euros, this situation can be explained by the fact that this year there was a crisis regarding swine fever and the actual bankruptcy of certain farms whose object of activity was raising pigs.

Another chapter that registers a significant deficit for one is the one referring to edible fruits, the trade balance being negative by 593 million euros.

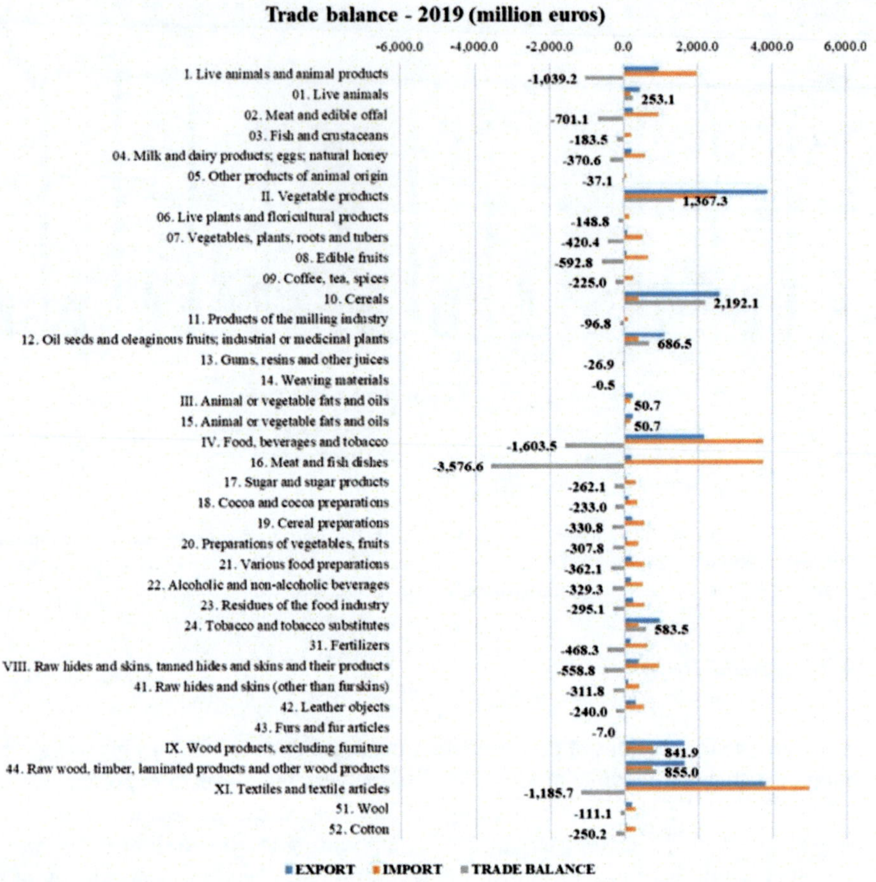

Fig. 7 Trade balance analysis. *Source* own processing based on NIS data (National Institute of Statistics 2020)

3 The Impact of COVID-19 Crisis and Drought on the Sector

3.1 Social Impact

The social impact of COVID-19 has been lower on agriculture, as the demand for food is inelastic, especially in the short term, and agricultural and food products have been consumed a lot during this time. The largest share of the population infected with COVID-19 is not from the rural environment.

In addition, field crops are carried out in the open air, with day laborers, in particular, and virus has not posed a major risk to these businesses.

One problem would have been in livestock farms, but no outbreaks of COVID-19 have been reported in such businesses. Farmers have requested that the competent authorities, in such a situation of illness with COVID, be isolated inside the farm, unless the medical situation requires other measures.

3.2 Economic Impact

The economic impact of COVID-19 is insignificant to be quantified at this time (National Bank of Romania 2020). Agricultural farms did not close, they continued to produce and sell, the demand for agricultural and food products even increasing in the first part of the emergency period, amid emotional consumption.

Agricultural production has its specificity, the production cycle in the plant sector being an annual one. Under these conditions, production cycles have not been affected either by the infection of the population, the activities taking place in the open air, or by the decrease in demand, as the products obtained are at the base of the pyramid of needs and will therefore continue to be consumed.

However, agriculture has been affected differently by this pandemic, a qualitative research being extensively carried out in the next chapter.

Large-scale farms faced other risk factors, drought, and early frost. On the other hand, they harvested for the first time in June, so in the period March–June 2020 they have not registered problems with sales, and their distribution channels are already contracted. However, low agricultural production meant increased per capita income for the agricultural producer, as there was no competition on the national cereals market.

Small vegetable farms have had to look for new distribution channels and, for the most part, have succeeded. The promotion of local products through social networks has facilitated the retail trade of small farms and farms. Costs increased with the value of transport/delivery costs, but no significant losses were recorded.

Large livestock farms continued to deliver to processing companies, milk, meat, etc., with no changes in either the structure of demand or its volume, as there has been no decrease in final consumption in the supply chain.

Small- and medium-sized livestock and vegetable farms that worked with HoReCa sector and those that sold through traditional fairs, street-food events, vineyards and wineries, fruits, flowers, suffered heavy losses, because the HoReCa sector did not work at all between March and June 2020 (Agricultural exploitations 2020). These farms did not even have the possibility of concluding distribution contracts through retail networks, because in order to be able to accept their products on the shelf, they would have to meet the conditions very firm: high volume of production to ensure a certain flow of supply and to be able to recover all the taxes imposed by these retail chains, special packaging conditions, ensuring traceability, etc. These were, in most cases, impossible to adapt to the conditions imposed by the COVID-19 pandemic and suffered heavy losses.

3.3 Qualitative Research in Romanian Agriculture

The beginning of 2020 brought to Romanian agriculture several stressors, including the deepening effects of the drought, the delay in the collection of some of the subsidies granted, the decrease of the value of the national currency (RON) against the euro, the COVID-19 pandemic. All this has led to individual decisions at the level of agricultural producers in order to raise the chances of survival of farms and individual businesses. For a clearer perspective of the impact of stressors on farmers, we conducted a qualitative research based on in-depth interview, applied in April–May 2020.

The motivation for choosing the method is given by the fact that the team decided to conduct a qualitative research because the main objective of the approach is an exploratory one, as a starting point for identifying the effects of economic–eco–social and environmental phenomena in which we are, in accordance with the criteria described by Taris (2010), Creswell (2000). The objective of the research was to identify the nature of the problems currently facing agricultural producers in Romania.

The secondary objectives were:

- Establishing the most important stressors faced by agricultural producers;
- Identifying the main negative effects that these stressors have on business, business behavior;
- Creating the premises for quantifying the impact that some of the identified stressors have on national agricultural production;
- Generating proposals for relevant measures and consolidation of activity, as well as to be taken at the level of local, central, European administration for the next period.

The sample consisted of 17 agricultural producers (2 from Botoșani County, 9 from Teteleorman County and 6 from Călărași, Giurgiu, Ialomița, and Tulcea counties), representatives from all fields of activity: vegetable production—large crop, vegetable growing, and zootechnical production: farms large, individual producers, beekeepers, etc., from all over Romania and with businesses of different sizes: from small farms to large farms, thousands of hectares and heads of animals.

Sampling targeted a wide range of respondents in order to be able to explore as clearly as possible the nature of the stressors of this period and the effects of the COVID-19 panic attack on all. The main objective being the context, the subjects in the sample did not need a unique profile, but rather a deeper heterogeneity (Popa 2015).

The most important stressors faced by agricultural producers, unlike the main object of activity are:

- Drought: all interviewed farmers identified this factor as the most important;
- Late frosts: some of the farmers in the southeast have identified this factor;
- COVID-19: the factor on the second position;
- African swine fever: for pig farms and farms;

- Use of pesticides non-compliant with the Carpathian bee: identified on the third position by beekeepers;
- Use of sunflower hybrids: identified by a single beekeeper;
- Unidentified diseases in bees: identified by a single beekeeper;
- Delay in payment of subsidies in 2019, identified by a single farmer;
- Absence of slaughterhouses in the vicinity of animal husbandry businesses: identified by a single animal husbandry.

The most important negative effects that stressors have on business activity and behavior are:

- Drought: production per hectare has decreased by up to 30% at the moment, costs for additional treatments have increased, additional treatments have been applied to combat the effects of drought, but have led to the death of bee families and rising feed prices, in-capacity to meet the payments of annual installments on loans, some of which are 200,000 euros for the purchase of equipment;
  - The application of new treatments to combat drought, but the very absence of rain prevented the absorption of these substances;
  - There is a mistrust in accessing non-refundable funds, given past experiences with accessed funds;
- Late frosts: the cost of additional treatments;
- COVID-19: generated an increase of approximately 30% in the costs of transport and delivery of products to the poultry farmer who had to deliver them at home, in compliance with the specific equipment conditions, finding new transport routes;
  - The poultry farmer has discovered new transport routes, a primary customer management system to which he has delivered live birds to the yard;
  - Vegetable farmers delivered to wholesale markets for vegetables and fruits and sold at prices imposed by intermediaries;
- African swine fever: for pig farms and farms, through high costs for control and low effects;
- The use of pesticides that do not comply with the Carpathian bee: leads to the death of hundreds of bee families annually;
- The use of sunflower hybrids: determines the inability of bees to produce honey, because these new hybrids self-pollinate;
- Delay in payments of subsidies in 2019, for example, for alfalfa, which determines negative effects on cash flow;
- Absence of slaughterhouses in the vicinity of animal husbandry businesses.

The creation of the premises for quantifying the impact that some of the identified stressors have on national agricultural production led to the following conclusions:

- A decrease of about 30% in yields per hectare for large crops has led to an increase of about 30% in the costs of applying treatments that could combat this drought, which will lead to increased production costs and increased selling prices, the effect being perpetuated up to the level of the citizen;

- The application of protection measures during the COVID-19 pandemic generated an increase in operating costs of up to 20%, which will be reflected in the selling price.

The coronavirus pandemic produces little noticeable effects, and not in the actual processes inside agriculture, but in the upstream and downstream areas, effects determined by the movement of prices, usually upwards, both at inputs and outputs.

4 Proposed Measures for Increasing the Competitiveness of Agriculture

The current situation requires a multi-perspective approach. The combined effort of all factors is desirable, in the context in which each participant in the economy obviously generates chain effects (Government of Romania 2020). The measures are taken in this sector of activity target three major levels: measures to be taken by the government, measures to be taken by large companies, and measures to be taken by small economic actors.

4.1 Government Actions

I. Upstream of Agriculture

Emergency relaunch of domestic production of tractors and agricultural machinery, adapted to the activity of small and medium farms (20–45HP tractors), with the appropriate machine system.

Increasing the degree of coverage in domestic production, the own need for chemical substances—fertilizers, herbicides, fungicides, insecticides, medicines, etc.

II. Downstream of Agriculture

The increase, in emergency regime, of the surfaces arranged for irrigation, as well as of those actually irrigated, within modern systems in which the gravitational force for the transport and administration of water to plants predominates.

Setting up a system of incentive levers and networks of internal and external markets capable of mobilizing the interest of agricultural producers, in order to capitalize on the production obtained with high efficiency.

Increasing the degree of stimulation and involvement of national agricultural research in an active and mutually beneficial partnership with the productive sector, downstream of agriculture.

Relaunching the activities of processing agricultural production, especially sugar beet, technical plants, oilseeds, vegetables, fruits, livestock products, etc.

Development of capacities for storage, transport, and marketing of agricultural products.

Computerization of all structures subordinated to the Ministry of Agriculture and Rural Development.

4.2 *Fertilizers*

The objectives are to cover the needs of agriculture from domestic production and, in addition, to create availability for export, which were definitively abandoned. Now, most of the domestic demand comes from the industrial agriculture segment, which covers less than half of the cultivated area, and the main suppliers of chemicals are from abroad.

This new change in the chemicals market requires a double-entry judgment. First of all, there are the positive aspects, resulting from the reduction and even elimination of the sources of environmental pollution. Secondly, however, the social risks resulting from the dismissal of the employed personnel increased and even worsened, who, in the areas where the respective plants were active, had significant shares in the total employed population. To the social risks are added the economic ones, caused by the bad action of the scissors of the prices of industrial products to the detriment of the farmers.

The future for all industries related to agriculture, implicitly also for the chemical ones, can unfold on two distinct variants:

(a) Either by maintaining the current structure, which in time, can only deepen the dependence of domestic consumption on the external market, which leads to the even deeper vulnerability of the national economy, to which social pressure is added objectively and in depth, with consequences that are difficult to anticipate;
(b) Either on the basis of a superior and long-term strategic vision, the industries concerned would be relaunched, in technical, technological, and high-efficiency conditions, a variant which is obviously much more expensive from an investment point of view and which, in addition, should be to avoid the mistakes of the regime in the command economy.

4.3 *Irrigation*

Irrigation has always been a problem with many unknowns. The vast majority of disputes on this topic start from the fundamental question with Hamletian references: whether or not irrigation is efficient. The communists, who paid a lot of attention to them, but starting only with the “era” after ‘65, sought to motivate their huge investments, in the approximately 3.2 million ha arranged in the value of 13–14 billion dollars, with the possible increase in production.

However, toward the final years of the regime, it focused more on the power of production to cover the costs of both investments and the operation of the system, i.e., efficiency, which, in real terms, was demonstrated by the inability of the system to operate at full capacity All the inefficiency in the last resort, brought the system in the current dramatic situation, when, actually exploited, in 2015, there were around 300 thousand ha, i.e., less than 10% of the entire developed area from the '90s. As such, any strategic vision for the relaunch of irrigation in agriculture must meet the following challenges or targets:

- the extent to which the projected production increase takes place in the current global market conditions;
- the extent to which the stability in production obtained through irrigation proves to be appropriate for strengthening food security alongside the agri-food reserve fund, which is currently very low;
- what is the irrigated area that can operate in conditions of real efficiency. Against the background of these three major challenges, two defining strategic lines are outlined, namely
- the first, but not the most important for the present conditions, has as targets the increase and the stability of the production. It is the variant in which the efficiency lies in the plan, which, of course, requires non-reimbursable public or private financing. Natural risk factors, especially as a result of prolonged droughts, as well as social and political imbalances, the coverage of which can extend beyond national borders, can contribute to the adoption of this option. It was the option adopted by the communists because it satisfied their unwillingness to produce and created some stability in the market supply. But when production entered free market competition, the system of large farms and, with it, the entire scaffolding in the irrigation network collapsed irreparably.
- the second variant, which considers the principles of efficiency, can be manifested in the following directions:

  - by perpetuating the current situation, when less than 15% of the total arrangements from the 90s remained in operation, and with clear decreasing tendencies;
  - by adding to the surfaces of the old facilities, but possible to operate efficiently, approx. 1,500 thousand ha of another 700 thousand ha of the Siret–Bărăgan system, which remained unfinished after the collapse of communism, but in which the water supply would be made by gravitational force, which would substantially reduce energy consumption;
  - by adopting new technical and technological solutions, which would reduce operating costs such as water supply from deep sources, distribution of water to plants through the drip system, replacement of sprinklers with mobile watering systems and others.

4.4 Actions of Large Companies

Large agricultural companies need to increase their resilience to risk factors, as well as permanent factors that affect their activity.

In order to do this, it needs to formulate a number of objectives and define very clearly the measures it should take. These could be:

- Increasing the irrigated areas and increasing the share of investments for the realization of irrigation systems in total investments;
- Identifying strategic partnerships with private and public partners to increase the areas covered by systems specific to smart agriculture;
- Increasing the degree of digitalization of the business/activity;
- Increasing the storage capacity of production by making investments in the construction of silos and storage centers, both for cereal females and for vegetable farms;
- Involvement in the creation of consolidated channels for the sale of animal husbandry products;
- Implementation of measures to diversify the customer portfolio and thus reduce the degree of dependence on customers of HoReCa, which is vulnerable during financial crisis, economic, health, or food processing industry, which imposes the price purchase of traded products;
- Increasing the added value of the products obtained by implementing projects aimed at integrating agricultural production in the processing industry, businesses that can be developed by agriculture or within strategic partnerships;
- Strengthening the entrepreneurial skills of those working in large farms, to facilitate the identification of market opportunities and their transformation into successful businesses.

4.5 Actions of SMEs, Households, and Other Small Actors

Romanian agriculture is characterized by this very large number of peasant households, small farms, and other actors with limited economic power and limited production. Their impact on agriculture is very high, as they integrate most of the labor force employed in agriculture. In order to increase the competitiveness of Romanian agricultural products and to facilitate the overcoming of crisis situations, they could adopt some of the following measures:

- Integration of the production activity in sales cooperatives, collection centers, channels created by large retailers;
- Increasing the share of investments in irrigation systems;
- Integration of the production storage activity in specific storage centers that could be built/realized by associations/cooperatives of producers;
- Increasing the entrepreneurial skills of farmworkers, in order to strengthen the connection of production to market demand and to facilitate the sale of production;

- Accessing agricultural marketing cooperatives to increase the competitiveness of the products obtained;
- Acquiring correct fiscal behaviors and compliance with the rules for the application of pesticides that would lead to the elimination of fraud in the sector and the consolidation of public confidence in these products;
- Accessing crop insurance policies.

5 Conclusions

The main effect of these measures is to increase the resilience of Romanian agriculture to crisis factors, as well as to ensure the food security of the Romanian population, to increase the competitiveness of Romanian agricultural products. The expected effects are mainly (Project "Restart Economia" 2020):

- Increasing irrigated areas and, respectively, ensuring increased yields per hectare;
- Ensuring the necessary fodder for the livestock sector;
- Increasing the added value of the products obtained by Romanian agriculture by making processed food products;
- Increasing the adaptability of agricultural farms to crisis conditions and strengthening their survival capacity;
- Development and consolidation of agri-food chains;
- Creating a taxed market, perfectly functional, modern, and articulated to the new models of food consumption.

References

Busu, M., Trica, C.L.: Sustainability of circular economy indicators and their impact on economic growth of the European Union. Sustainability **11**(19), 5481 (2019)

Creswell, J.W., Miller, D.L.: Determining validity in qualitative inquiry. Theory Pract. **39**(3), 124–131 (2000)

Data from The National Institute of Statistics. Accessed April 2020

Data from the Trade Register Office. Accessed April 2020

Data from the National Agency for Fiscal Administration. Accessed April 2020

Data from agricultural exploitations. Accessed June 2020

Dinu, M., Pătărlăgeanu, S.R., Chiripuci, B., Constantin, M.: Accessing the European funds for agriculture and rural development in Romania for the 2014–2020 period. In Proceedings of the International Conference on Business Excellence **14**(1), 717–727 (2020)

Drăcea, R.M., Ciobanu, L., Buziernescu, A.A.: The impact of environmental protection expenditure on environmental protection in Romania. Empirical analysis. Strategica, 10 (2020)

Government of Romania: "National investment plan and economic recovery" (July 2020)

Gu, H.-Y., Wang, C.-W.: Impacts of the COVID-19 pandemic on vegetable production and countermeasures from an agricultural insurance perspective. J. Integrat. Agric. **19**(12), 2866–2876, ISSN 2095–3119, https://doi.org/10.1016/S2095-3119(20)63429-3, https://www.sciencedirect.com/science/article/pii/S2095311920634293 (2020)

Haqiqi, I., Horeh, M.B.: Assessment of COVID-19 impacts on U.S. counties using the immediate impact model of local agricultural production (IMLAP), Agricultural Systems, Volume 190, 2021, 103132, ISSN 0308–521X, https://doi.org/10.1016/j.agsy.2021.103132, https://www.sciencedirect.com/science/article/pii/S0308521X21000858 (2021)

Lin, B., Zhang, Y.Y.: Impact of the COVID-19 pandemic on agricultural exports. J. Integra. Agric. **19**(12), 2937–2945 2020. ISSN 2095–3119, https://doi.org/10.1016/S2095-3119(20)63430-X, https://www.sciencedirect.com/science/article/pii/S209531192063430X (2020)

Mazurencu-Marinescu, M., Pele, T.D.: Modelling the strategic success factors of the Romanian ICT based Companies. Procedia Soc. Behav. Sci. **58**, 1111–1120 (2012)

Middendorf, B.J., Faye, A., Middendorf, G., Stewart, Z.P., Jha, P.K., Prasad, P.V.V.: Smallholder farmer perceptions about the impact of COVID-19 on agriculture and livelihoods in Senegal. Agric. Syst. **190**, 103108, ISSN 0308–521X, https://doi.org/10.1016/j.agsy.2021.103108, https://www.sciencedirect.com/science/article/pii/S0308521X21000615 (2021)

National Bank of Romania: "Report on financial stability", Year V (XV), no. 9 (19), New Series, June 2020

Pargaru, I., Stancioiu, F., Ladaru, R G., Teodor, C.: Sustainable development in agriculture at the level of Romania and the European Union: Acces la success. Calitatea, 20, pp. 446–450. Retrieved from https://www.proquest.com/scholarly-journals/sustainable-development-agriculture-at-level/docview/2198414152/se-2?accountid=50247 (2019)

Popa, M.: "APIO- Metodologia cercetării" (note de curs): 11_Noțiuni de cercetare calitativă (2015)

Project "ReStart Economia. Măsuri de combatere a efectului economic și social al COVID 19 în România", implemented by The Bucharest University of Economic Studies in the period april–august 2020, financed by Ministry of Education and Research from Romania (2020)

Stoian, M., Caprita, D.: Organic agriculture: opportunities and trends. In: Agrifood Economics and Sustainable Development in Contemporary Society, pp. 275–293, IGI Global (2019)

Taris, T.W., de Lange, A.H., Kompier, M.A.J.: Research methods in occupational health psychology. In: Leka, S., Houdmont, J. (Eds.), Occupational Health Psychology, pp. 269–297. Blackwell Publishing Ltd. (2010)

The Challenges of the Higher Education Sector. The Impact of COVID-19 Crisis on the Educational Process—Case of Romania

Dima Mihaela Alina, Fonseca Luis Miguel, Nastase Marian, Busu Mihail, and Vargas Madalina Vanesa

1 Introduction

The COVID-19 virus generated a general crisis that encompassed the entire society. According to Bratianu (2020), this pandemic has all the characteristics of a Black Swan phenomenon having the power to change daily lives (Baicu et al. 2020) and causing consequences for social, economic, education, political and human security (Abodunrin 2020). The education system has also been strongly shaken by this threat, because by its nature could contribute to a very rapid transmission of the virus and the gain of the associated problems in the community. The research trend after COVID-19 pandemic will be changing and more challenging. More research in health science will be preferred (Maulana 2020), but education could be considered a source of new studies in the field.

Due to the expected economic downturn, a considerable number of students might defer entering the university. The travel restrictions could mean a drop in international students' applications (that in some institutions represent up to 30% of total tuition fees). In an investigation addressing the impact of COVID-19 pandemic on international higher education and student mobility, Mok et al. (2021) conclude

D. M. Alina (✉) · N. Marian · B. Mihail · V. M. Vanesa
Bucharest University of Economic Studies, Bucharest, Romania
e-mail: alina.dima@ase.ro

N. Marian
e-mail: marian.nastase@man.ase.ro

B. Mihail
e-mail: mihail.busu@fabiz.ase.ro

V. M. Vanesa
e-mail: vanesa.vargas@fabiz.ase.ro

F. L. Miguel
School of Engineering of Porto (ISEP), Polytechnic of Porto, Porto, Portugal
e-mail: lmf@isep.ipp.pt

A. M. Dima et al. (eds.), *Economic Recovery After COVID-19*, Springer Proceedings in Business and Economics, https://doi.org/10.1007/978-3-030-86641-9_3

that the COVID-19 pandemic significantly decreased international student mobility and also shifted the mobility flow of international students. Online learning is not able to provide the same social interaction or access to laboratory work as face-to-face learning. The social dimension of higher education is valuable to students. The prospects of weaker student demand and pressure to decrease tuition fees could represent a significant challenge to higher education institutions. Without proper action and support, significant cost reductions could harm employment and research and the subsequent loss of vital capabilities.

Depending on the exposure to the new coronavirus and the recommendations of the Ministry of Health or other decision-making bodies, established to manage the situation, Ministry of Education and Research from various countries decided to lock down the education for all levels, for different periods of time, depending on the general and particular evolution of the pandemic. In this way, almost 1.7 billion young people worldwide were affected by the closure of schools in March 2020.

These decisions taken by the governments of most countries represented a brutal change in the pace of life of children, young people, but also of families as a whole, representing a shock to the entire society.

This shock was also determined by the characteristics of this crisis generated by the COVID-19 pandemic, respectively:

- Virus spread rate;
- Geographic coverage rate;
- The complexity of the crisis;
- Unpredictability;
- Difficulties in predicting the evolution of the pandemic;
- Direct and propagated impact throughout society;
- Direct and propagated impact in the educational system.

At the same time, praiseworthy, the educational activity has not been definitively stopped, but it has adapted and taken on new forms, passing mostly in the online environment. It is gratifying that beyond the real threats to public health, governments and local governments have found the right ways to ensure a fundamental right for citizens of a state, namely the right to education. During this pandemic period, many companies, schools, and public organizations all around the world asked their employees to work from home, i.e., to adopt what are called "smart working" modalities (Bolisani et al. 2020).

2 Specific Elements to Higher Education in the Context of the Pandemic

Higher education is essential for human development (Schofer and Meyer 2005) and the role of higher education institutions in educating decision-makers and leaders, and therefore contributing to progress and the public good, has been widely acknowledged (Waas et al. 2010). Moreover, the access to quality education (to ensure inclusive and equitable quality education and promote lifelong learning opportunities for all) has been recognized as a United Nations Sustainable Development Goal that positively correlates with other goals, such as no poverty, zero hunger, good health and well-being, and decent work and economic growth (Fonseca et al. 2020). Higher education was a component of the national education system that reacted quickly and found those options that allowed the continuation of the educational process in fairly good conditions, at different stages of study.

The new conditions created a high pressure on all educational units, generating major barriers that could affect the access to education of a large number of students. Among the main obstacles encountered by students as a result of the new online learning system, we mention:

- Low access to computers or other means of online communication;
- Poor online communication infrastructure (Internet);
- Lack of knowledge of operating online learning platforms;
- Improper study conditions (large family, insufficient space, several family users for the same equipment, etc.);
- Difficulties in interacting with the teacher;
- Difficulties in understanding the materials displayed online;
- Stress due to isolation;
- Stress due to the possibility of illness.

The pandemic has affected all the major functions of a university, whether we are talking about the educational, research or social, which involves a strong anchor in the problems of the community in which they operate. Leaders of educational institutions must take into consideration the capacity to adapt to the new circumstances paying attention to the fact that there are generational differences for the stages and typology of education programs (Abrudan 2021).

Although the impact of the pandemic was quire severe, the response capacity of higher education institutions can be considered as appropriate one, in terms of adaptation and the development of educational processes for time crisis. However, a better collaboration among higher education institutions is needed to strengthen the practices in the curriculum and make it more responsive to the learning needs of the students even beyond the conventional classrooms (Toquero 2020).

Some of the factors that contributed to this favorable situation are based on university autonomy, academic management and leadership, adaptability of students to online forms of study, professionalism of teachers; degree of technological endowment with computer equipment, study platforms; availability of educational materials already in electronic formats, etc.

Higher education institutions have proven from the beginning that they have real opportunities for retreat and through proper management they have managed to maintain a high commitment to the educational community. This involved a focus on students, on their needs to continue training activities for further studies, but also to develop the skills expected of them in the future labor market.

High attention was also paid to the teaching staff, its training, the establishment of working procedures to clarify and facilitate the development of the activity in a period of uncertainty. It was especially important to communicate during all these months, with all university stakeholders, so that through a correct information about the existing problems, the available resources, the vision of the institutions, the best educational strategies can be developed and applied.

It is important to notice that each country tried to find out specific approaches that have been considered to reflect in the best ways the education realities caused by pandemic, but also paying attention to the resources, tradition and culture of that system, with a particular impact from the managerial style practiced in education organizations (Raducanu et al. 2020). In research encompassing the biggest US higher education institutions in the USA, Freeman et al. (2021) found variability in COVID-19 prevention and testing strategies among the institutions. This emphasizes the need for national recommendations and equitable distribution of sufficient pandemic response resources to those institutions. Higher education institutions from almost all European countries decided in the spring of 2020 to move to online courses, and only a few of them started in a hybrid form in the autumn. The University of Twente in Netherlands took this approach of teaching both online and in class. However, De Bour affirmed that this type of blended learning is time-consuming and it led to even more work pressure, uncertainty and frustration, both among students and teachers. On the other hand, Tsinghua University (China) had a positive experience with the hybrid education. According to Yang and Huang (2021), it can be achieved richer education goals such as capability improvement, community building, and value shaping, in addition to knowledge transfer.

Roman and Plopeanun (2021) investigated the effectiveness of the emergency eLearning during the COVID-19 pandemic in higher education economics in Romania. The research results indicate that psychological distress and increased concerns about the COVID-19 pandemic harm learning effectiveness. They also found that Internet access, working space at home and the university infrastructure for online activities are critical for eLearning success.

The efforts within the educational units will be enhanced as a result by collaborating with the stakeholders of the educational community. In this regard, we point out the efforts to ensure access to online education for students, given that some families are facing increasing pressure on parents to provide the necessary means to participate in the educational process of children. According to Wahab (2020), the society needs flexible and resilient education systems as we face unpredictable futures.

A timely and quality educational process leads to the avoidance of internal conflicts due to the burden of parents' time budget and support activities for children's education, as well as the need for parents to assist children in some cases in teaching activities. Decreased parental productivity due to increased family involvement, especially through children's attention and support for educational activities, can be avoided by asserting teachers' willingness to counsel students, depending on their educational needs, in a student-centered approach.

The impact of the transition to online education and the lack of student mobility generates direct and indirect influences in society, in the local community. It is easy to perceive this impact if we see, for example, unused accommodation in large cities, university centers, due to lack of vacancy by students, who stayed at home or problems raised for some buildings due to lack of rent, payment of utilities for spaces that were intended for rent to students in the province.

A major challenge for higher education institutions was represented by graduation of the senior students (third-year bachelor students and second-year master students), and for this it is worth mentioning that the students received tutoring in that period of time. At the same time, it is particularly important the preparation of universities for admission and to integrate new students into the university education system, according to all the existing norms and legal procedures in force.

It is also important that, in addition to the characteristics of this period of pandemics, with multiple direct effects and propagated in the educational system, that we also pay attention to lessons that recent human history has offered us. Thus, the financial crisis of 2008, although it did not have the same impact on society as a whole as the COVID-19 pandemic, showed us that the education system, although it is considered a strategic area of any country, is very exposed to the economy shocks.

We could recall that, in several countries, during the financial crisis of 2008, for example, teachers' incomes were reduced or frozen, at best, even by significant percentages, which led to difficulties in providing teaching materials, of the possibilities to pay bank rates and even in their daily existence.

Teachers' motivation also suffered, given that the investment regime in the educational field was severely affected. The effects were not only short term, since the impact of the 2008 financial crisis was felt later in terms of lower funding for the education system, given that GDP was significantly lower than in the previous period.

The economic deadlock and the struggle for survival of most companies mean that the financial resources available to the education sector are shrinking a lot, amplifying competition and leading to a massive reduction in institutional investment.

3 Specific Elements of the Romanian Higher Education Institutions Compared to the European Union

In the European Union in 2018, more than 19 million students were registered in the tertiary education sector, universities and colleges included. Although the total number of students decreased at EU level in the period 2014–2017, it can be seen that Romania did not follow this trend, but the total number increased during the analyzed period.

Romania's average allowance per student is one of the lowest in the European Union, the average value being, in 2014, about 12,655 EUR in OECD countries and about 12,680 EUR in EU, and in 2015, about 14,670 EUR in OECD countries and approximately EUR 15,000 in the EU. As shown in the Table 1, Romania allocated only 1,238 euro in 2014 and 1,310 in 2015.

The status quo of financing higher education in Romania can be better characterized when placing it in a European context, especially that defined by the European

Table 1 Average allowance per student Romania (2008–2018)

	2008	2009	2010	2011	2012	2013	2014	2015	2016	2017	2018
Average allowance/student (lei)	6.004	5.930	5.828	5.090	5.107	5.461	5.503	5.823	7.149	8.272	10.187
Exchange rate lei-Euro	3,6827	4,2373	4,2099	4,2379	4,4560	4,419	4,4446	4,445	4,4908	4,5681	4,6535
Average allowance/student (euro)	1.630	1.400	1.384	1.201	1.146	1.236	1.238	1.310	1.592	1.811	2.189

Source CNFIS, 2020, National Council for Financing Higher Education, Romania, 2020

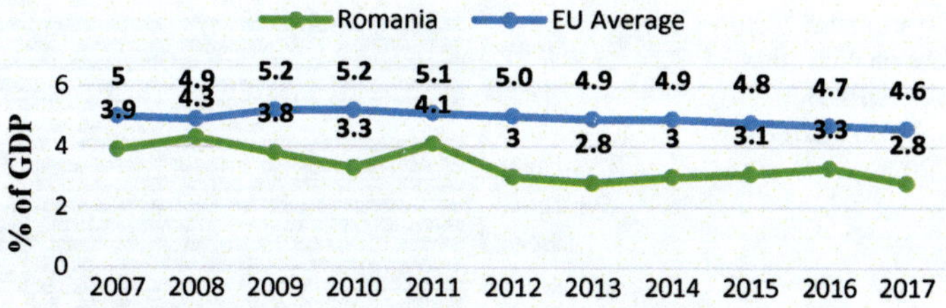

Fig. 1 Share of government expenditures on education in GDP, Romania versus EU-28 average, in the period 2007–2017. *Source* Eurostat, 2020

Union. For this, however, the indicators used in the analysis must be comparable in terms of content and measurement methods. Although data is collected at the level of the European Union accordingly to a system of indicators developed to characterize this field, statistics in Romania only partially cover the issue of financing higher education.

A relevant issue in the analysis of the Romanian education system is the comparison of government expenditures for education in 2017 for each European country. As can be seen in the Fig. 1, Romania has so far invested little and continues to invest little in education compared to other countries in the European Union, placing it at the end of the EU ranking of education expenditure, being far from the goal of 6% of GDP, established by the National Education Law.

It could be stated that the data in the figure above is just a matter of time, unfavorable to Romania, but, as can be seen, the situation was not so different in previous years, and no changes are foreseen based on the expenses of the current year. According to Eurostat, the highest funding received in Romania was in 2008, with a share of 4.3% government expenditures on education in GDP. It should be noticed not only the non-compliance with the commitment to prioritize education by bringing it to a higher level of funding, but also the difference between government spending on education at national level compared to the European average. As can be seen in Fig. 2, Romania maintains a significant distance from the European average, a distance that has constantly placed our country at the bottom of the rankings.

4 Analysis of the Students' Perceptions on the Educational Process Implications During Pandemic Period

4.1 Methodology

The purpose of this research is to study the impact of the COVID-19 on the educational process, from the students' perspective. The role of the learners in educational process and the analysis of their perception to improve the educational policies was

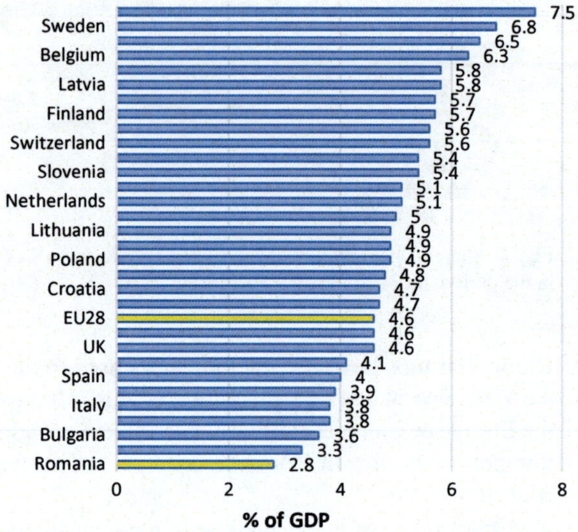

Fig. 2 Government expenditure on education, total (% of GDP). EU countries, 2017. *Source* Eurostat, 2020

studied by Aristnovik et al. (2020) with a sample of 30,383 students from 62 countries, and it revealed that teaching staff and universities' public relations offered students the most important support at the university during the pandemic. However, they were unable to perceive a higher level of success when adjusting to the "new standard," namely, distance education, due to a lack of computing skills and the perception of a higher workload. During the lockdown, students were often anxious and expressed worries about their potential professional careers and study issues. Another experiment conducted by Gonzales et al. among 450 students from Universidad Autónoma de Madrid, Spain, reveals that there is a significant positive effect of COVID-19 confinement on students' performance and that students get better grades in activities that did not change their format after the COVID-19 confinement.

The statistical survey aims to collect and analyze data on the impact of the pandemic caused by COVID-19 on students at the Bucharest University of Economic Studies (BUES), as part of the university community, to obtain relevant information to the challenges they faced during this period. Information obtained may be the basis of recommendations on educational policies and practices for the development of the education system as a whole.

The sample was selected using the "snowball sampling" method. This method consists of initially contacting a small number of subjects in a population, which then attracts other people belonging to the same category studied.

Snowball sampling uses a small initial pool of respondents, selected via email or social media, or other participants who meet the eligibility criteria and could contribute to the specific study. However, the degree of success of this technique depends largely on the initial contacts made, but also on the connections made by each respondent. Thus, it is important that, in order to conduct a good survey, we have a credible and reliable reputation, so that the respondents' answers are qualitative but also quantitative.

Thus, applying this method, we started from a group of 50 students from BUES, who were sent by email the invitation to complete this statistical survey and to pass on this request to other students and so on.

The statistical survey was conducted between June and August 2020. The questionnaire contains 30 questions and was created on the website: http://www.isondaje.ro/sondaj/814189698/. The survey was answered by 369 of the students to whom the questionnaire was sent, but the success rate cannot be determined, as the number of requests to answer sent is not known.

There are several opinions regarding the making of a sample. If Bell and Bryman (2007) state that the absolute size of the sample is more important and not its relative size, relative to the entire research population, Afifi and Clark (1990) consider that the number of questionnaires should be between 5 and 10 times higher than the number of questions, thus reducing the errors of answer. In the case of our analysis, this ratio is 12.3 times (369/30), a result that exceeds the upper limit of the range indicated by the two statisticians.

4.2 Description of Statistical Research

The tool used to obtain the data was the questionnaire, the purpose of the research being to know the opinion of BUES students on the implications generated by the COVID-19 pandemic on the educational process.

The construction of the questionnaire was complex, including questions of identification, opinion, factual behavior, related to the future intentions of respondents. The questionnaire includes both closed questions (dichotomous, multidichotomic with single and multiple answers—for which the 7-point Likert scale was used), as well as open, unstructured questions. It was decided to use asymmetric bi-directional scales, as the possibility was taken into account that the interviewee may have a neutral position or not know how to answer those questions.

We also followed the "funnel technique" on the dynamics of questions, as the questionnaire begins with simple questions, and along the way we approached progressively, more and more precise and difficult questions. Questions identifying demographic characteristics were placed at the end of the questionnaire.

4.3 Characteristics of Respondents

Next, the structure of the sample will be presented, in terms of both demographics and studies (age, gender, education, professional status, etc.). The demographic data of the respondents to this questionnaire can be seen in the Appendix.

The grouping of respondents by age categories (Table 2) reveals the fact that most are aged between 18–22 years (86.2%), followed by those in the category 23–27 years (11.7%). However, this is a distribution as expected, being a questionnaire applied to students from the Bucharest Academy of Economic Studies, as part of the university community, in order to obtain information relevant to the challenges they faced during the pandemic caused by COVID-19.

Regarding the gender of the respondents (Table 3), out of the 369 interviewees, 78.3% are female and 21.7% male. Depending on the level of education (Table 4), most respondents pursue undergraduate studies (78.6%), 21.1% of respondents and doctoral studies (0.3%). The grouping of respondents according to their domicile indicates that the 369 respondents come mainly from Bucharest (40.8%), followed by those domiciled in urban areas, but a different city than Bucharest (39 0.1%), and 20.1% are domiciled in rural areas.

In terms of the professional status of the respondents (Table 5), most of them do not work (65.2%), followed by those employed in the private sector (26.4%) and those employed in the public sector (4.9%). The least represented are the category of entrepreneurs (2.7%) or another category (0.8%).

In the statistical survey, the interviewees were asked about their residence during the teaching activities in the context of the restrictions imposed by the COVID-19 pandemic. Thus, as can be seen in the figure below, most respondents lived at home, with their parents (78%), followed at a great distance by the category of those who lived alone, in the specially rented home (8.1%) or at home alone (7.9%). There are very few who lived in the rented house, with colleagues (2.4%) in the other category (2.7) or in the student dormitory (0.8%).

4.4 *Interpretation of the Results from the Questionnaire*

The results obtained from the analysis of the answers of the students included in the statistical research reveal the implications of the restrictions generated by the COVID-19 pandemic on the challenges that the students faced in the development of the teaching process.

Thus, being asked to appreciate the accessibility of services within the university during the pandemic in terms of services: administration, library, accommodation and medical care, the answers were as follows (Fig. 3).

When asked to what extent during the pandemic the possibility of attending the planned university courses was affected, the average of the answers was 3.06/7.

Very small

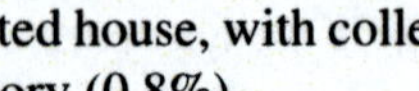

Very high

3.06 / 7

This indicates that the possibility of taking classes during the pandemic was rather small.

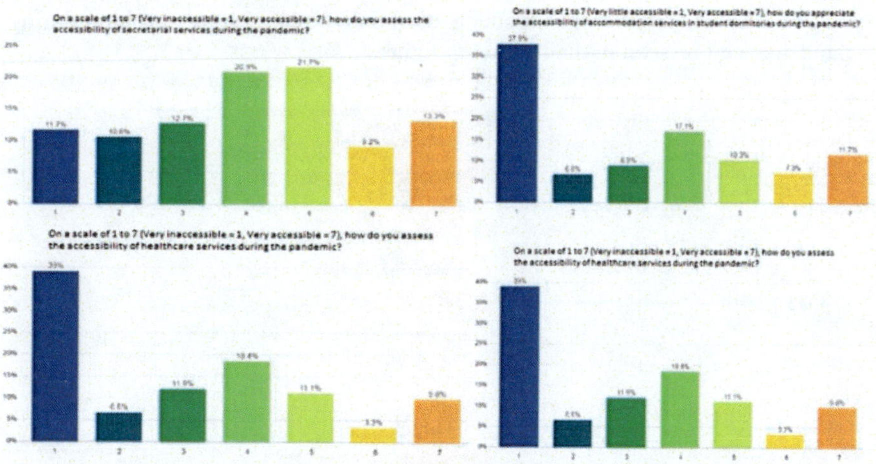

Fig. 3 Accessibility of services within the university during the pandemic in terms of services. *Source* Authors' processing based on statistical data, National Council for Financing Higher Education, Romania, 2020

Regarding the alternative communication channels that students carried out their teaching activities, from the chart below it can be seen that the majority (66.4%) used the university platform, while WhatsApp was used in a smaller measure (8.7%). Other platforms were used by 10.8% of the surveyed students, and other options were chosen by 11.1% of the respondents (Fig. 4).

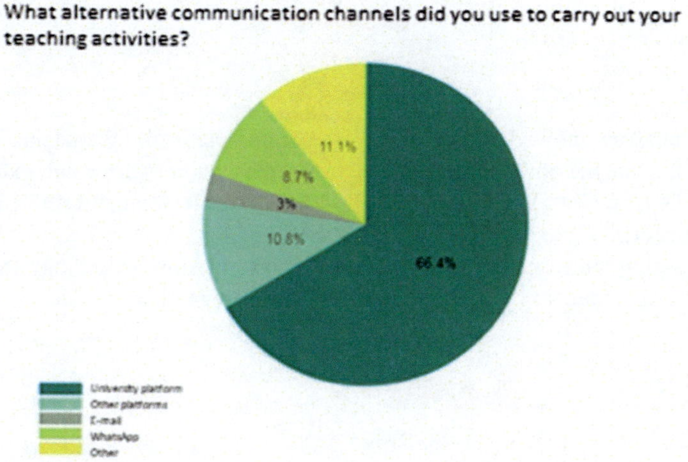

Fig. 4 Alternative communication channels for educational activities used during pandemic. *Source* Authors' processing based on statistical data, National Council for Financing Higher Education, Romania, 2020

The frequency with which students used online platforms in teaching during the pandemic can be seen in the following figures.

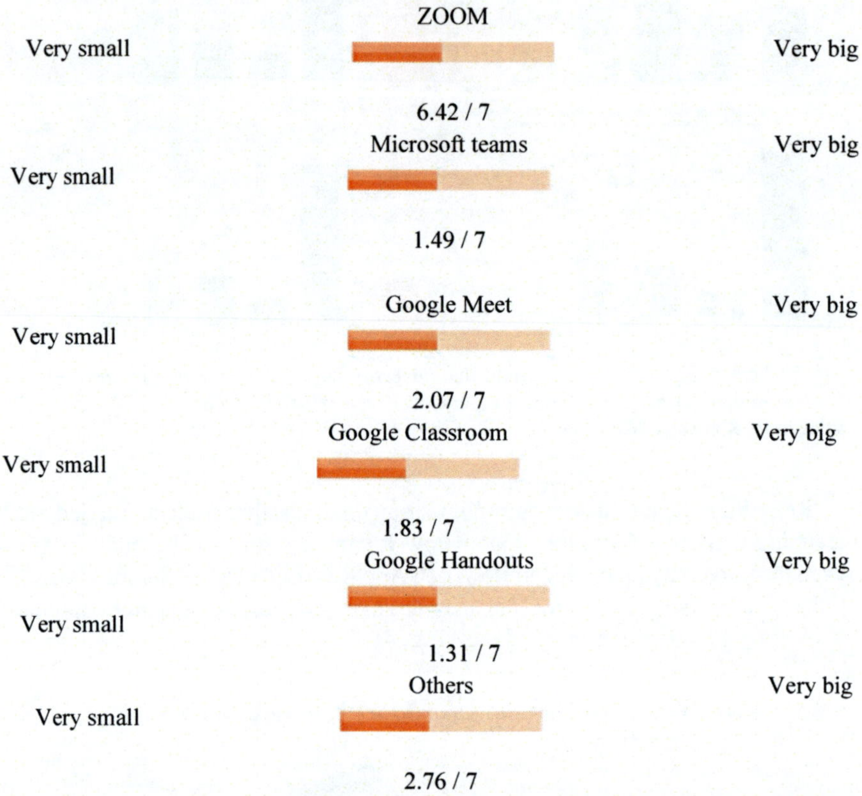

The analysis showed that the most used online platform by students was ZOOM (6.42/7), while the other platforms were used to a small or very small extent: Google Meet (2.07/7), Google Classroom (1.83/7), Microsoft Teams (1.49/7) and Google Hangouts (1.31/7).

Regarding the extent to which the use of information technology increased the presence of students in teaching activities, the average of the results was 4.22 /7.

This highlights the fact that the use of information technology has increased the presence of students in teaching activities to a small extent.

The quality of students' interaction with teachers, colleagues and administrative staff can be seen in the following Fig. 5.

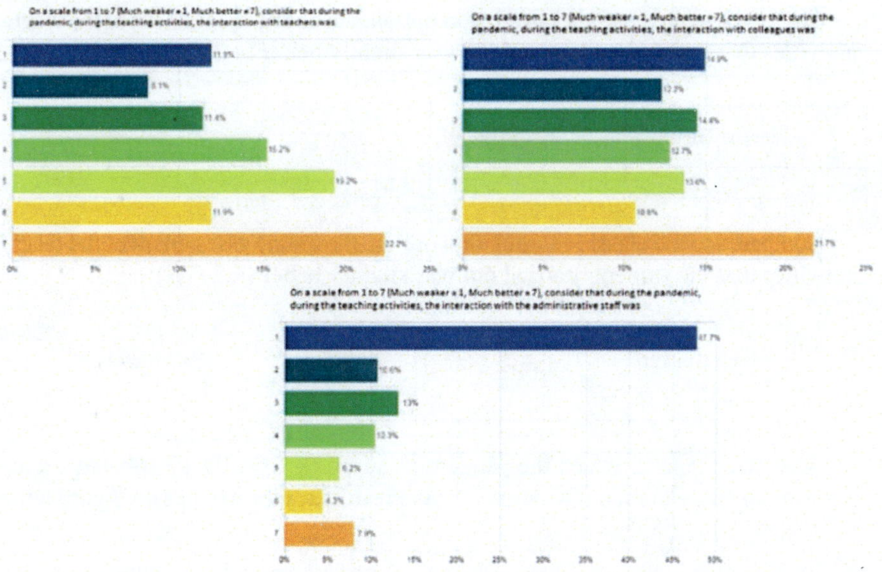

Fig. 5 Quality of interaction of students with teachers, colleagues and administrative staff. *Source* Authors' processing based on statistical data, National Council for Financing Higher Education, Romania, 2020

From these figures, during the pandemic, students had a very good interaction with teachers (22%) and colleagues (21%), but less good with administrative staff (7.9%).

Also, when asked whether the use of information technology stimulated their involvement during online activities, the average student responses were average to good (4.45/7).

To a very small extent  To a very large extent

4.45 / 7

Regarding the degree of load with didactic activities, compared to the previous period, on a scale from 1 to 7, the average of the answers was: to a large extent (5.15 /7).

Very little  Very much

5.15 / 7

When asked what the specialized practice was during the pandemic, the average of the answers was close to the average (3.84 /7).

Compared to the classic examination option, the online assessment of the teaching activities that the students carried out was slightly better (4.3 /7).

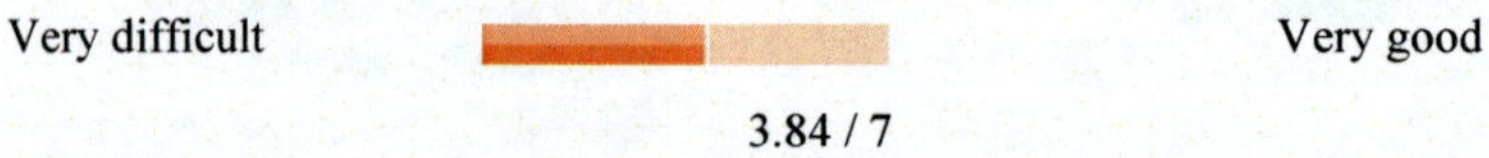

Compared to the classic examination option, the online assessment of the teaching activities that the students carried out was slightly better (4.3 /7).

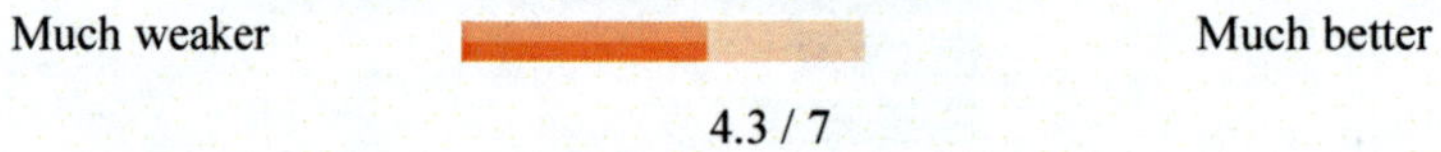

Also, the extent to which the pandemic caused by COVID-19 affected students' decision to study abroad (Question 12); the results can be seen in the figure below.

Thus, on a scale from 1 to 7, the average response was 3.35, which shows that the decision of students to study abroad was affected to a small extent to the average pandemic.

Regarding the desire to study abroad, as can be seen in the following figure, it was slightly affected by the pandemic.

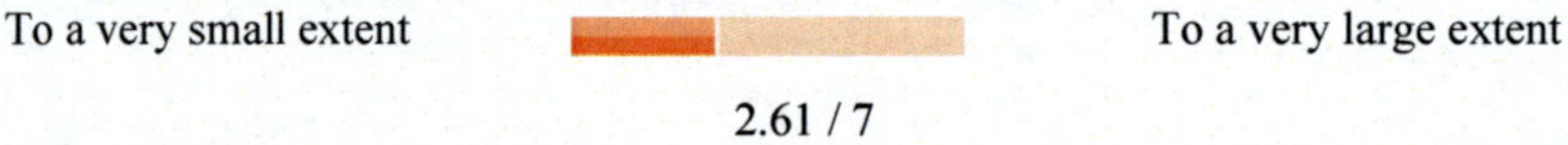

The students also listed the main difficulties encountered in the educational process during the pandemic. As can be seen in the chart below, the main difficulties were: the level of stress felt (27.6%), collaboration with colleagues (17.2%), communication with teachers (17.2%), collaboration with employers or potential employers (13.6%), lack of documentary materials (12.5%) and access to infrastructure (9.6%) (Fig. 6).

Regarding the level of discomfort/anxiety that students experienced during the pandemic, the average response was 4.77/7, which means that this discomfort was felt to a medium to high extent.

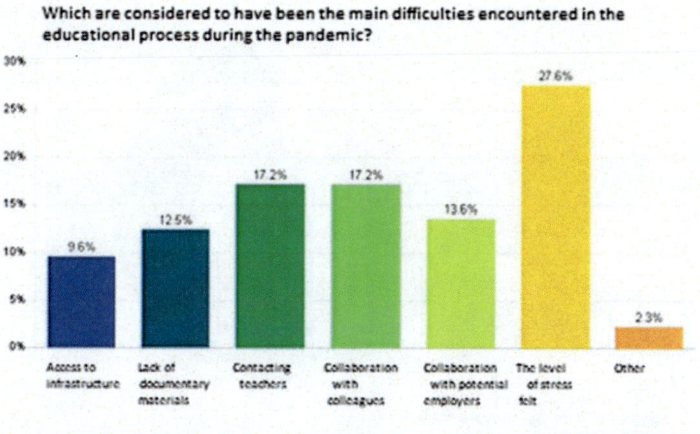

Fig. 6 Main difficulties encountered in the educational process during the pandemic. *Source Authors' processing based on statistical data,* National Council for Financing Higher Education, Romania, 2020

The biggest opportunities that students benefited from during this period were: saving time (26.4%), flexibility to attend courses and seminars (23.6%), developing digital skills (20.1%), diversification of online documentation sources (17.4%). At the same time, opportunities of lesser importance were: high interaction with the teaching staff (6.3%) and interaction with colleagues (5.1%).

Compared to the classic version, the educational experience in the online system was appreciated by the respondents as being approximately equal, the average of the answers being 3.94/7.

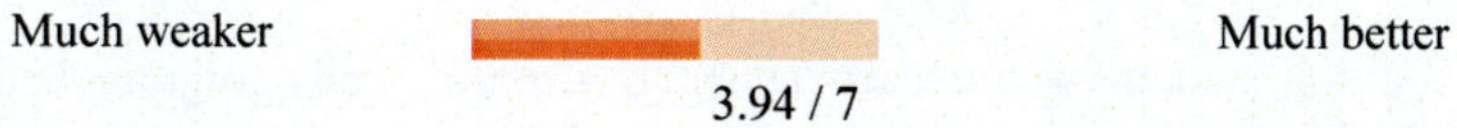

Also, the expenditures with the educational process during the pandemic were appreciated by the respondents as being lower than the previous period, the average of the respondents' answers being 2.41 on a scale from 1 to 7.

As for revenues, they were slightly lower during the pandemic than in the previous period, as can be seen from the Fig. 7.

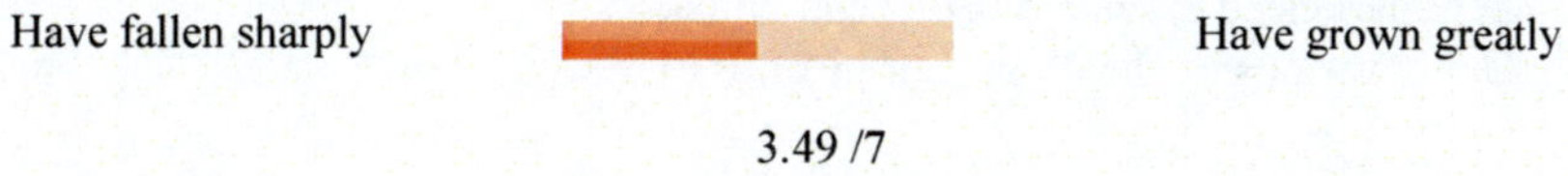

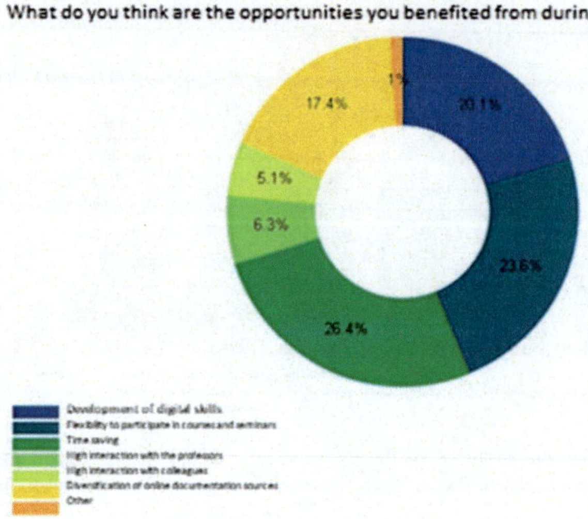

Fig. 7 Opportunities that students benefited from during the pandemic. *Source* Authors' processing based on statistical data, National Council for Financing Higher Education, Romania, 2020

When asked to what extent the pandemic could negatively affect graduation, the mean of the answers was very close to neutral (3.45/7). Thus, we can say that the pandemic caused to a very small extent the graduation of studies.

In addition, students would like to benefit from online study programs in the future, with 4.54/7 being the average of the answers of the respondents to this question.

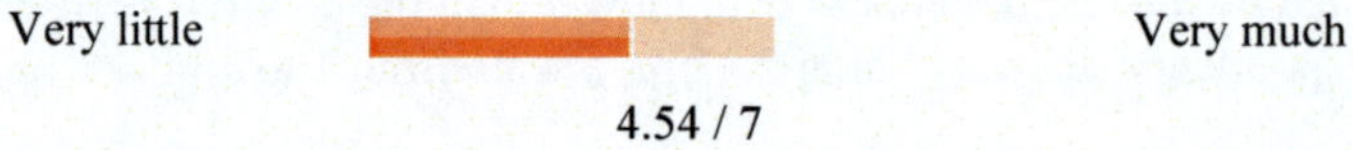

Except for the demographic questions, the last three questions in the questionnaire were open-ended questions.

Thus, the question: What are your suggestions for improving online courses have been given interesting and substantial answers that can help to better develop the way online teaching of teachers. The most common answers were:

- "To involve absolutely all teachers and give us understanding, because we have not experienced ex-ante this difficult situation";
- "Using various applications, not just the BUES platform";

- "It should become mandatory for classes to be taught on Zoom or such platforms, as it is not effective for a subject to be explained on the university platform chat";
- "For those subjects where it is traditionally written on the board, teachers need equipment, tablets on which to write with a digital pencil but not with the mouse, because it is very difficult to write";
- "I would not like to improve anything; my opinion is that all teachers have been very involved. Some maybe more than was needed"
- The question related to the suggestion for improving online seminar hours, was also given many interesting answers, including:
- "Let's do all the seminars on online interaction platforms (Zoom, Discord, etc.). I consider this method more advantageous, because we need explanations, debates with teachers to understand and assimilate information effectively";
- "Recording and sending them so that working students can see them when time allows. There are students who really want to learn, but at the same time they have to work and they can't participate in all the classes";
- "To be much more interactive, to take place on platforms where you can communicate verbally";
- "If all students have access to any seminar in the same subject and the classes are diversified. This also gives access to working students";
- "The preparation of the materials should be adapted to remote operation, i.e., slightly more detailed than in the case of face-to-face hours";

In conclusion, making a brief analysis of the students' answers to the questionnaire, we can see that they have adapted very easily to the online learning environment, appreciating to a large extent this way of teaching. The main advantages of this type of education are according to the respondents: the diversity of teaching and assessment methods, the elimination of lost time with transport, direct and indirect interaction with teachers, the use of online and offline platforms for courses and seminars.

At the same time, however, there are multiple disadvantages, the main disadvantages being: the reduced possibility of socializing online, lack of interaction with colleagues, reduced possibility to create connections with the business environment and reduced possibility to have group discussions online.

There are also many good things that need to be improved in the future, such as: better adaptation of online teaching methods, more diverse assessment methods, pre-session exam preparation sessions and better communication, and interaction with the administrative environment.

5 Conclusions and Recommendations

The complete analysis performed on available data from educational sector, as well as all the effects generated by the state of emergency, involves the developing of a plan of potential actions, to be applied in the central and local organizations.

Obviously, the action plan reflects the vision of the drafting team, at the time of the analysis, based on the data and information available from the various public sources of information. Given the major involvement of a significant number of institutions in the development of solutions dedicated to the "Education" sector, there is a possibility that some of them may be similar to the vision of others, or even in a different approach. Also, during the implementation of this project, local and central public authorities initiated and implemented various actions and interventions. Some of them were aimed at solving problems of a strictly temporal nature, and others with the role of creating the framework for the redesign a system and component of the organization and functioning level.

When drawing up the proposed plan of measures, a series of major long-term challenges were underlined, some of a structural nature (i.e., chronic underfunding of education, inequalities between regions, localities and socioeconomic areas, insufficient resources available through local budgets) and others of a conjunctural type or specific only to certain communities or organizations. Their classification on the two categories reflects the opinion of the team of experts involved, being influenced by the ongoing developments, in relation to the external environment.

The proposed actions have a potential character in terms of convergence of objectives of the institutions involved, the existing legislative framework and possible proposals for change that can be argued, but also from the perspective of existing resources, both in the central and local public system. The option of applying them may be subject to further debate and deepening, highlighting other categories of positive and negative impacts on the overall system, but also on the entities involved.

The approach of the proposed plan of measures must also be interpreted from a temporal perspective, respectively of the time horizon necessary for their application. Obviously, the options for resolving, as a matter of urgency, unpredictable, cyclical situations reflect the level of knowledge, the available information but also the existing constraints. Moreover, the effects of the state of COVID-19 were also manifested in the obligation to solve some general problems of the system, such as those determined by the use of information systems in specific processes such as teaching, knowledge assessment, admission, etc. Basically, the six months have shown that certain obstacles, apparently insurmountable (i.e., transmission and recognition documents online system) were resolved quickly to pressure all parties that have recognized the effects immediately.

The educational sector, as a component part of the public system, has undergone multiple transformations over the last thirty years in the context of challenges and opportunities, both nationally and especially internationally. The opinion of the experts involved in the elaboration of the present analysis takes into account the multiple interdependencies between the evolutions of the educational system and those of other fields such as health, social, financial and informational. The options of the states analyzed in this report, regarding the functioning of the educational system starting with September 1, 2020, integrate a common set of intentions / interventions (i.e., the clear option to start study programs, face to face or at least mixed) but also independent, individual actions, as a reaction to the different evolution of the number of diseases. Also, the operational approach of the process benefits from a high degree of decentralization of decisions, from central to regional and even local. Such a situation may be favorable to those entities that are prepared in terms of human and financial resources, but also unfavorable to those organizations that are inexperienced or do not want to take various risks.

The educational system is over regulated: There is already a critical mass of direct regulation related to the educational services, as well as indirect regulations, related to particular aspects of quality such as health, welfare, hygiene, transport, energy and infrastructure. The synthesis and systematization of these regulations, from the perspective of quality management and decentralization, may represent an opportunity for future approach.

The perspectives of decentralization of the educational sector, as they are proposed and applied, could represent opportunities, but also vulnerabilities. We refer here to those opportunities generated by the implementation of flexible solutions, able to provide a quick response to some problems, but with a limited degree of extension or multiplication over time.

Certainly, other opportunities for decentralization have also generated different evolutions of the institutions in the educational system in the university area. Thus, some component parts of the educational system, and here we refer to schools and universities, reacted differently, with different performances and immediate results. An additional condition for the firm and positive reaction to various challenges is related to the strategic alignment of local and central policy-makers with experts in the field of educational, financial and information management. A major advantage generated by the consequences of the state of emergency/ COVID-19 alert, in the six months of the event was related to the opportunity to develop a common dialogue between the parties involved, which went beyond the institutional or political framework and generated effects on the convergence of objectives in the fields of health, education, social, economy.

For university education, the plan of measures is structured on two directions of intervention, respectively of the central authority (Ministry of Education and Research) and that of the management of universities, mainly public ones. We appreciate that the size of the private university system is more difficult to approach in terms of independence in educational and financial management but also the potential conditions. However, this fact does not exclude that some proposed measures should be adopted by the private education system, in order to increase the level of performance and alignment with common standards, promoted by specialized institutions, namely ARACIS and ARACIP.

In defining those measures, the following dimensions were considered: the observance of the principle of university autonomy, public responsibility, the efficiency and effectiveness of the educational act, the orientation toward quality, transparency and ethics.

Appendix: Demographic Distribution of Respondents

See the Tables 2, 3, 4 and 5.

Table 2 Sample structure according to respondents' gender

Answer	Number of respondents	Percentage of respondents (%)
Female	288	78.3
Male	81	21.7

Source Proceedings of their authors based on statistical data obtained

Table 3 Level of education

Answer	Number of respondents	Percentage of respondents (%)
License	290	78.6
Master	78	21.1
Doctorate	1	0.3

Source Authors' processing based on statistical data obtained

Table 4 Distribution of respondents by domicile u

Answer	Number of respondents	Percentage of respondents (%)
Bucharest	150	40.8
Urban (another city)	144	39.1
Rural	74	20.1

Source Authors' processing based on statistical data obtained

Table 5 Distribution of respondents according to residence during the teaching activities in the context of the restrictions imposed by the pandemic

Answer	Number of respondents	Percentage of respondents (%)
In the student dormitory	3	0.8
At home with my parents	287	78.0
Home alone	29	7.9
Alone, in the specially rented house	30	8.2
In the rented house, with colleagues	9	2.4
Other	10	2.7

Source Authors' processing based on statistical data obtained

References

Abodunrin, O., Oloye, G., Adesola, B.: Coronavirus pandemic and its implication on global economy. Int. J. Arts Lang. Bus. Stud. (IJALBS) **4**, 13–23 (2020)

Abrudan, D.: The impact of multigenerational leadership on organizational performances. Ecoforum J. North America (2021)

Afifi, A.A., Clark, V.: Computer-Aided multivariate analysis, edn. Available online: https://www.jstor.org/stable/2533984?origin=crossref&seq=1. Accessed 23 July 2020 (1990)

Aristovnik, A., Keržič, D., Ravšelj, D., Tomaževič, N., Umek, L.: Impacts of the COVID-19 Pandemic on life of higher education students: a global perspective. Sustainability. **12**(20), 8438 (2020). https://doi.org/10.3390/su12208438

Baicu, C.G., Gârdan, I.P., Gârdan, D.A., Epuran, G.: The impact of COVID-19 on consumer behavior in retail banking. Evidence from Romania. Management Marketing. Challenges Knowl. Soc. **15**(Special Issue), 534–556. https://doi.org/10.2478/mmcks-2020-0031 (2020)

Bell, E., Bryman, A.: The ethics of management research: an exploratory content analysis. Br. J. Manag. **18**(1), 63–77 (2007)

Bolisani, E., Scarso, E., Ipsen, C., Kirchner, K., Hansen, J.P.: Working from home during COVID-19 pandemic: lessons learned and issues. Management & Marketing. Challenges Knowl. Soc. **15**(Special Issue) 458–476. https://doi.org/10.2478/mmcks-2020-0027 (2020)

Bratianu, C.: Toward understanding the complexity of the COVID-19 crisis: a grounded theory approach. Manag. Mark. Challenges Knowl. Soc. **15**(Special Issue), 410–423. https://doi.org/10.2478/mmcks-2020-0024 (2020)

De Boer, H.: COVID-19 in Dutch higher education. Studies in Higher Edu. **46**(1), 96–106. https://doi.org/10.1080/03075079.2020.1859684 (2021)

Europe Direct: Available online: https://europa.eu/european-union/contact/europe-direct-answering-your-questions-about-eu_ro (2019)

European Commission. Education and Training Monitor 2019. Available online: https://ec.europa.eu/education/sites/education/files/document-library-docs/et-monitor-report-2019-romania_en.pdf (2019)

Eurostat: Tertiary education graduates. Available online: https://ec.europa.eu/eurostat/web/products-datasets/product?code=educ_itertc (2019)

Eurostat: Europe 2020 indicators—education. Available online: https://ec.europa.eu/eurostat/statistics-explained/index.php/Europe_2020_indicators_-_education#Increasing_attainment_at_tertiary_level (2020)

Fonseca, L.M., Domingues, J.P., Dima, A.M.: Mapping the sustainable development goals relationships. Sustainability **12**, 3359. https://doi.org/10.3390/su12083359 (2020)

Freeman, S. et al.: COVID-19 response strategies at large institutes of higher education the united states: a landscape analysis, Fall 2020. J. Adolescent Health **68**, 683–685. https://doi.org/10.1016/j.jadohealth.2021.01.016 (2021)

Gonzalez, T., de la Rubia, M.A., Hincz, K.P., Comas-Lopez, M., Subirats, L. et al.: Influence of COVID-19 confinement on students' performance in higher education. PLOS ONE **15**(10), e0239490. https://doi.org/10.1371/journal.pone.0239490 (2020)

Maulana, N.: Research trends in marketing science before COVID-19 outbreak: a literature review. Management Marketing. Challenges Know. Soc. **15**(Special Issue), 514–533. https://doi.org/10.2478/mmcks-2020-0030 (2020)

Mok, K.A., Xiong, W., Ke, G., Cheung, J.O.W.: Impact of COVID-19 pandemic on international higher education and student mobility: student perspectives from mainland China and Hong Kong. Int. J. Educ. Res. **105**, 101718. https://doi.org/10.1016/j.ijer.2020.101718

National Committee for Special Emergency Situations (Comitetul Național pentru Situații Speciale de Urgență): Decision no. 7/11.03.2020 on measures to prevent the spread of COVID-19 (2020)

National Committee for Special Emergency Situations (Comitetul Național pentru Situații Speciale de Urgență): Decision no. 10/14.03.2020 on the proposal to establish a state of emergency in Romania and to approve additional measures to manage the SARS-CoV-2 Coronavirus pandemic (2020)

National Committee for Special Emergency Situations (Comitetul Național pentru Situații Speciale de Urgență): Decision for the application of the provisions of Law no. 19/2020 regarding the granting of some days off to parents for the supervision of children, in case of temporary closure of educational units (2020)

Raducan, M., Vrabie, T., Colan, A., Colan, G., Cristache, N., Cristia, V.: The influence of management style and socio-cultural factors on the education system in the European Union Countries. Ann. Univ. Dunarea De Jos of Galati: Fascicle: I, Econo. Appl. Inform. **26**(1), 115–120 (2020)

Roman, M., Plopeanu, A.-P.: The effectiveness of the emergency eLearning during the COVID-19 pandemic. The case of higher education in economics in Romania. Int. Rev. Econ. Educ. **37**, 100218. https://doi.org/10.1016/j.iree.2021.100218 (2021)

Schofer, E., Meyer, J.W.: The worldwide expansion of higher education in the twentieth century. Am. Sociol. Rev. **70**(6), 898–920 (2005). https://doi.org/10.1177/000312240507000602

Toquero, C.M.: Challenges and opportunities for higher education amid the COVID-19 Pandemic: the Philippine context. Pedagog. Res. **5**(4), em0063, https://doi.org/10.29333/pr/7947 (2020)

Waas, T., Verbruggen, A., Wright, T.: University research for sustainable development: definition and characteristics explored. J. Clean. Prod. **18**, 629–636 (2010). https://doi.org/10.1016/j.jclepro.2009.09.017

Wahab, A.: Online and remote learning in higher education institutes: a necessity in light of COVID-19 Pandemic. Higher Educ. Stud. **10**(3), 16–25. https://doi.org/10.5539/hes.v10n3p16 (2020)

Yang, B., Huang, C.: Turn crisis into opportunity in response to COVID-19: experience from a Chinese University and future prospects. Stud. High. Educ. **46**(1), 121–132 (2021). https://doi.org/10.1080/03075079.2020.1859687

Public Administration and Regional Development

Profiroiu Constantin Marius, Constantin Daniela Luminiţa, Goschin Zizi, Iorga Tudose Elena, and Nastacă Corina-Cristiana

1 Introduction

Public administration is a key area for the well-functioning as well as for the economic and social development, with a direct impact on the governance system and on improving the quality of citizens' lives. The evolution of the main macroeconomic indicators, such as the growth of the national, regional, or per capita Gross Domestic Product, the decrease in the unemployment rate, or the increase in productivity are closely related to public administration and public services' efficiency, performance and resilience.

When any type of shock occurs (such as economic crises, epidemics, the current COVID-19 pandemic or natural disasters), public administration institutions are the first to respond and implement policies developed to manage and overcome the new situations caused by these unforeseen events, in an efficient manner. The COVID-19 pandemic and its management showed public administration's need to modernize. Although the administrative reform has been a priority objective for all governments, a significant progress has not been achieved yet (European Commission 2019). The situations caused by the coronavirus pandemic revealed that public institutions need to develop their own and also human resources' resilience. They need well-trained specialists and civil servants who can adapt to crises and adjust their behaviour as to respond rapidly and efficiently to citizens' new needs. The emergence of the COVID-19 pandemic shows that public administration needs to become more adaptable, flexible and transparent. This area requires to implement changes as to improve public services' quality and to professionalize public positions by attracting specialists in various fields, such as public health or information and communication technology. Moreover, this health crisis entails economic imbalances resulting in the economic crisis. For these reasons, the public administration must be prepared to minimize

P. C. Marius · C. D. Luminiţa · G. Zizi · I. T. Elena · N. Corina-Cristiana (✉)
Bucharest University of Economic Studies, Bucharest, Romania
e-mail: corina.nastaca@amp.ase.ro

A. M. Dima et al. (eds.), *Economic Recovery After COVID-19*, Springer Proceedings in Business and Economics, https://doi.org/10.1007/978-3-030-86641-9_4

as much as possible, the impact of the economic crisis on citizens' well-being and business environment.

In addition, the public administration and the governance process are basic factors for the cohesion policy-related investments to be translated into sustainable economic growth. Public investments' impact depends, to a large extent, on how they are managed. From this perspective, increasing administrative capacity for funds absorption implies coordination between the administrative levels and the applied policies, promoting coordination and exchange of good practices between administrative levels. The administrative capacity is closely related to the investment capacity, being influenced by the poor coordination, lack of staff stability, lack of required skills and frequent institutional changes. Maximizing the European Funds' results involves competent civil servants, appropriate tools for managing complex projects as well as multi-level governance to support public investments. Public procurement also plays a key role, which must be guided by precise, binding rules to follow in all cases where public authorities use public resources.

The present study has a worthwhile contribution to the literature because it presents a comprehensive picture of the Romanian public administration by approaching the field through various perspectives such as human resources who play a major role in developing an efficient and resilient public sector, digitalization which is a necessity for the efficiency of the public institutions and the public utility sector, an area with major impact on the society's development and well-being. More than that, the research also explores a subject of great interest—the impact of COVID-19 pandemic on Romanian regional economy. Both subjects are related to each other because public administration has impact on the development of regional economy, through its institutions, public services, human resources and level of digitalization, all influencing the socio-economic dynamic and quality of life.

The study comprises three sections. The first section is dedicated to the literature review concerning Romanian public administration and COVID-19 pandemic impact on regional development. The second section presents the analysis of the public administration in the 2009–2019 period from the human resources, digitalization and public utility sector perspectives. The third section approaches the COVID-19 pandemic impact on regional economies development, investigating the degree of local vulnerability to the negative economic effects caused by this medical crisis and proposing policy measures for reducing the negative effects of the COVID-19 pandemic and reviving the regional economies. The study ends with conclusions and recommendations for improving the weaknesses of the public administration.

2 Considerations Regarding Public Administration and Regional Development in Romania. Insights from the Literature Review

In Romania, public administration is still facing problems such as the public service low level of professionalization, excessive politicization, a low degree of responsibility, public services' low quality and a low level of digitalization. The low administrative capacity is caused by a series of factors mentioned in most strategies and reports regarding Romanian public administration and its functioning. It can be observed that in the analyses conducted on this subject for long periods of time, public administration's problems have not changed, being solved only to a small extent (Radu 2015; Dragomir 2019; Petrescu and Mihalache 2020; Stan et al. 2020).

The latest data from the Country Report (European Commission 2019) showed that Romania is still struggling with the low administrative capacity with negative impact on economic and social development. This situation influences negatively not only the efficient functioning of the public services and institutions but also investments' level, Romania remaining quite unattractive to foreign investors. The excessive bureaucracy, as well as the administrative system's inefficiencies, reduced Romania's attractiveness for foreign investors, which may also have a negative impact on overcoming the economic crisis (European Commission 2019). In addition, the partnership agreement between Romania and the European Union for the 2014–2020 period (Ministry of European Funds 2014) revealed a series of causes underlying the low level of the administrative capacity. This includes human resources management, where there is no integrated long-term policy that leads to unitary and stable management. The identified problems regarding human resources management in public administration are: the inflexible methods used for civil servants' recruitment, selection, evaluation and promotion, the instability of the execution and management positions, bureaucracy, the measurement of performance based on procedures and not on the achievement of the established objectives and the lack of an integrated approach to ethical values and professional integrity. In 2019, the new Administrative Code (Romanian Government 2019) was adopted, which should put the premises of a series of long-term changes, including regarding the public service.

Concerning other measures which should be considered in the administrative reform, the European Commission (2019) noted that in terms of decentralization, consolidation of the local authorities' capacity, the public consultation process as well as the development of the e-Government process, there are still major shortcomings and the solving process is lagging behind. Moreover, the recommendations from the European institutions are implemented at a slow pace, and the economic crisis caused by the COVID-19 pandemic could also negatively influence all the progress made in terms of public administration and public services.

The COVID-19 pandemic had negative impact on the well-functioning of all types of public institutions and the provision of public services. Moreover, this has led to the need of implementing a series of rapid changes in areas such as health, education or public order. The activity of public institutions has been disrupted, and public sector employees have had to adapt in a very short period of time to situations that have never been encountered before. In a world of global interdependencies, risks are also global and no country can prevent them alone. Concerning the COVID-19 pandemic, each country is interested in finding adequate answers to its challenges, considering that the global risks manifest themselves nationally, regionally and locally and no country alone can prevent these events or reduce their impact (WEF 2020).

In the context generated by this crisis, not only the public administration, but also the regions and local communities are interested in strengthening their resilience, defined as "the ability of a region to anticipate, prepare for, respond to and recover from a disturbance" (Foster 2006, p. 14), in other words, "the capacity of a regional economy to withstand change or to retain its core functions despite external upheaval" (Davies 2011, p. 370). It is closely connected with regions' resources and their inherent vulnerabilities. Vulnerability is a concept associated with resilience and is understood as "propensity or predisposition to be adversely affected" (Gitz and Meybeck 2012, p. 19), being dependent upon economic, social, environmental, institutional, etc., factors. The local authorities are at the forefront of crisis management, with important responsibilities for containment measures, the application of a wide range of health measures, the provision of social services of general interest, a viable economic environment and an investment environment (OECD 2020). More than that, human resources in the public sector and their competencies, the degree of public services digitalization, and their well-functioning represent key aspects for managing the pandemic's effects with impact on the regional economies development. Resilient and well-prepared authorities both at the central and local level help at managing efficiently the management of the European funds as well as the other factors influencing the regional development.

3 The Analysis of the Public Administration Field in the 2009–2019 Period

The present chapter aims to investigate Romanian public administration in terms of public employment, civil servants' recruitment and management, the provision of the essential public services as well as the digitalization process in order to propose recommendations that might improve the problematic issues encountered in the analysis in order to achieve a proper administrative reform and improve public services' quality. In order to analyse the mentioned aspects, an exploratory study using secondary data analysis has been conducted, for the 2009–2019 period, regarding the human resources in the Romanian public administration, focusing on aspects as recruitment, selection, management and continuous professionalization, the public services' development and the process of digitalization in the public sector. All the analysed aspects have a direct impact on public services' quality and the development of a modern, efficient and resilient public administration.

3.1 *The Human Resources from the Romanian Public Administration*

Human resources are an important component of the administrative capacity, and the adopted measures regarding public service management should materialize in increasing performance and efficiency, as well as in the development of a body of professional civil servants who can successfully implement and manage administrative reforms and stressors or shocks that might appear at the national, regional or local level. Moreover, human resources and their level of resilience might influence the management of crises and the implementation process of the measures adopted by the central government in order to surpass such shocks (as the COVID-19 pandemic) and return to a new state of economic and social equilibrium.

Different studies and reports mentioned certain aspects related to human resources management as causes of the Romanian low administrative capacity. In various studies developed in the context of the negotiation process between the Romanian Government and the European Commission for drafting the Partnership Agreement for the 2014–2020 period (Ministry of European Funds 2014) and in the context of the Strategy for strengthening the Romanian public administration 2014–2020 development (Romanian Government 2014), a series of factors that led to the decrease of the administrative capacity have been presented, such as

- The large number of approvals issued by the National Agency of Civil Servants in order to modify the structure of the public positions and to reorganize different activities. This situation has been encountered every time the government changed revealing public administration's high level of politicization. Also, the public administration is facing far too many administrative reorganizations and a high degree of instability in terms of administrative activities and public positions' structure.
- The increased instability in the management levels due to the high number of approvals issued for the temporary exercise of management and senior civil servants' positions.
- A large number of amendments to Law no. 188/1999, republished (Romanian Parliament 2007), and additions that caused disturbances in the public institutions' activities.
- The recruitment system is a hybrid one, situated between the career system and the position-oriented system. World Bank experts have noted inconsistencies between the national legislation which aimed for the depoliticization process in public administration and existing practices, which led to the development of a politically motivated position-oriented system. Because the legislation stipulates that senior civil servants, as well as management positions, can be held temporarily, a significant number of positions are often occupied without passing through a competitive recruitment system (World Bank 2017).
- The recruitment and selection processes are problematic, targeting rules and procedures instead of skills and competencies correlated with the public positions' specificities (World Bank 2011, 2017, 2018).

- There is no strategy to promote public sector as an employer (OECD 2016), although more online promotion, together with a high level of transparency in the recruitment process, would increase the number of candidates and attract more young people into the system.
- The evaluation of the public service is purely formal, being just another task related to the bureaucracy of human resources management. Also, the evaluation process lacks the free discussions and feedback phase between the evaluator and the evaluated civil servant. Basically, the evaluation process is exclusively on paper (Deloitte Report 2013, pp. 18–19).
- The promotion system does not consider civil servants' developed competencies, acquired skills, or the results from various forms of vocational training (World Bank 2017). This manner of promotion, based on the transformation of the public position, does not contribute positively to public administration's performance or to the public service professionalization.

Moreover, the public administration is facing a shortage of specialists and staff with specific qualifications, such as specialists in information and technology, education or health (World Bank 2017).

Public administration's age structure reveals another problem, namely the ageing phenomenon of the civil servants' body. Consequently, it can be considered that the public administration's degree of attractiveness for graduates is low, although there are several bachelor and master programmes in this field. Moreover, the low proportion of young people in the civil service will continue to have a negative impact on the capacity to adapt and transform the administrative system (National Agency of Civil Servants 2019).

As regards civil servants' training opportunities, the National Agency of Civil Servants manages the specialized training programme for the public positions corresponding to the category of senior civil servants. The existing data indicate a decrease in the number of participants to these courses between 2011 and 2018 (National Agency of Civil Servants 2013, 2018, 2019). Another problem is that the civil servants' evaluation process does not take into account the results achieved on these trainings (The National Agency of Civil Servants 2019). An important step towards the development and civil service professionalization was the implementation of the Young Professionals Scheme programme and the initiation of a new training programme for future public managers (The National Agency of Civil Servants 2015).

3.2 The Analysis of the Public Services' Development in the 2009–2019 Period

The new Administrative Code (Law no. 57/2019) defines public administration as *all the activities of organizing the execution and execution of the law conducted under public power and the provision of public services in order to satisfy the public interest.*

In Romania, the public utility sector comprises eight services: *water supply, sewage, and sewage treatment, collection, sewerage, and discharge of rainwater, heat supply in a centralized system, sanitation of localities, public lighting, natural gas supply and local public transport of passengers*. These services should be available for all citizens, regardless of the area of residence (urban or rural), respecting the following principles: quality, safety, accessibility, equal treatment, promotion of universal access and user rights, permanent character and continuous operating regime. However, the reality shows major differences in terms of ensuring that all Romanian citizens have access to a minimum package of public utility services, especially in rural areas. Also, *the public services' quality* concept is still far from being clearly defined as to measure the local administrations' performance in fulfilling the obligation to provide public services, as stipulated by the law, using performance indicators.

As regards the management of these services, there is a large variation in the models used in practice—from direct management to partial or total concession to private operators, and the degree of liberalization of public service markets differs from one type of utility to another, being also directly dependent on the local authorities' decisions.

In terms of regulations, the legislation on public utilities was adopted in 2006, with the emergence of the first unitary law—the *Law on Community Public Utilities Services No. 51/2006,* which has undergone several amendments so far (Romanian Parliament 2013). The majority of subsequent laws applicable to each public service appeared in 2006.

In 2011, following the transposition of the Directive 2008/98/EC (Eur-Lex 2020), Law No. 211/2011 was adopted (Romanian Parliament 2014). The law made significant changes in the provision of the sanitation service by introducing the *selective collection mechanism,* the *pay-as-you-throw* principle, the contribution to the *circular economy* (authorities pay for the quantities of waste deposited above the performance indicators set out in the contracts). Moreover, Law No. 211 is the first legislative act governing a public service and specifically referring to the *performance indicators* to be provided in the contracts for the delegation of service to private operators, having as a reference basis the recycling targets that should have been achieved in each category of waste until 2020. In 2013, the government introduced the notion of *essential public services* and nominated the community utility services on the list of essential public services without which the administrative–territorial units in financial crisis or insolvency cannot operate. In 2012, the Law on Electricity and Natural Gas (Law no. 123) (Romanian Parliament 2012) defined the activity of electricity distribution and the distribution of natural gas as *public services of general interest,* and the transmission of electricity and gas as *public services of national interest.* However, the gas supply was included on the list of community utility services only in 2018. Neither the law nor the specialized literature (pretty sporadic) identified at that time the differences between *community utility services* and *those of general/national interest*.

In 2015, new conditionalities arose in the provision of the sanitation services, also as a result of the transposition of the European Directive on the packaging—introducing new obligations for the sanitation services operators concerning the separate collection of packaging waste from the population by Law No 249/2015 (Romanian Parliament 2015). In 2016, the *management of the public and private domains of administrative–territorial units, as well as others,* were removed from the list comprising community public utilities services—activities that covered a multitude of fields (building/modernization/repairs, roads, planning, and maintenance of green areas, parks, sports grounds, lakes, construction, modernization and exploitation of markets, urban movement, dispensing, parking planning and management).

Since 2004, the public utility sector was set as regulatory priority, in line with the European Commission' requests, through the updated strategy of the Romanian Government on accelerating the public administration's reform 2004–2006, which identified the *decentralization and decentralization of public services* as one of the three areas in which Romania had to make significant progress. In 2020, we still do not have a database in Romania with information on how many localities have/do not have electricity, drinking water, district heating, sanitation, public transport, etc.

The Strategy for Strengthening Public Administration 2014–2020 (Romanian Government 2014) the first integrated strategy for administrative reform since 2006, introduced for the first time, explicit references regarding the measurement of performance in public administration—including in the provision of public services—by *setting up benchmarking, bench doing and bench-learning mechanisms.* This strategic approach required both the development and implementation of mechanisms to compare and prioritize the performance achieved by public authorities and institutions inclusively in the provision of certain public services, as well as encouraging public authorities and institutions to establish partnerships to identify common solutions to the existing problems. Moreover, the only explicit reference in this document to community public utility services is in the context of the proposed measure *of developing a minimum package of public services, necessary and mandatory to be provided at each administrative level,* complying with minimum quality and efficiency requirements. In addition to the minimum package of services, the strategy also mentioned *the optional package of public services,* for which quality and cost standards would be established, as more developed administrative and territorial units to provide additional services.

The same strategy mentions the *establishment of modern management in institutions and authorities providing public services* from several perspectives: linking strategic planning to budget and human resources; spending public funds efficiently; tracking quality assurance; openness, promptness, and anticipation in relation to customers; accountability for both actions and inactions.

Although there are formal commitments to introduce unified mechanisms to measure the performance of local public authorities in providing public services to citizens throughout the country, in reality, all the steps taken by the Ministry of Administration since before 2009 have not been completed.

3.3 *The Digitalization Process in the Romanian Public Administration*

The pandemic triggered by the COVID-19 virus put enormous pressure on individuals, organizations and governments regarding *digitalization* and the widespread use of digital platforms to counter the major bottlenecks this crisis caused to our lives, society and the environment in which we live. With the increasing number of cases and the need to preserve indefinitely a new social code that involves less direct interaction in all aspects of social and economic life, the scientific community has already begun to investigate how COVID-19 will irreversibly impact *digital transformation.*

Although it was the pandemic that revealed the acute need for digital transformation in the public sector, specialists in the field affirm that the design of viable strategies for public administration digitalization should *not* be done in times of crisis, when unpredictable circumstances arise and the opportunity costs are disproportionately high.

One of the most advanced analyses and support initiatives for the development of *digital administrations* is the World Bank's GovTech project, initiated in 2019—a macro-approach to the modernization of the public sector that promotes the principle of simple, accessible and efficient governance. This principle translates into the use of technology to transform the public sector, improve the quality of the provided services for citizens and businesses, and increase transparency, efficiency and accountability.

The main objectives of this global project are:

- *The citizen comes first*—the development of affordable, cost-reasonable and inclusive services.
- *Civic involvement*—increasing participation, transparency and accountability, with the ultimate aim of building public trust in governments.
- *Bringing governance standards to the level of the twenty-first century*—information technology and artificial intelligence have the potential to transform the efficiency of key government functions, including *public finance management and tax systems, public procurement, human resources management, mobilization and monitoring of the use of national resources.*

At the European level, concerns for the digitalization of the governments' services have started systematically since 2009, firstly in the health field (eHealth), continuing with the analyses of the government e-services' maturity and constantly evolving through annual monitoring of the development level of digital service infrastructure in the Member States (e.g. series of DESI reports—Digital Economy and Society Index).

3.3.1 The Current Stage of Digitalization in the Romanian Public Administration—Statistics Compared at European Level

The latest report released in this regard, the *Digital Economy and Society Index (DESI), Digital public services 2020* (European Commission 2020b) shows that Romania is almost without exception on the last place for all the indicators measuring the degree of services digitalization at the EU level:

1. *Users of e-Gov services-* calculated as the percentage of all internet users in the Member States that should submit online forms reported to those who actually used these services. The EU average for 2019 was 72.2%, with Romania registering the lowest indicator (below 60%) (Fig. 1).
2. *Pre-completed electronic forms-* the indicator evaluated the extent to which the already known data by the public administration is automatically completed in online forms, with a maximum score of 100 points. Romania is situated in the last place, with less than 30 points (Fig. 2).
3. *Online services-* the indicator assesses the extent to which certain steps that are needed in interaction with the public administration can be solved completely online. The average score at the EU level is 90, Romania being in the last place, with a score well below 80 (Fig. 3).
4. *Digital services for the private sector* represent the extent to which public services for private companies are interoperable, including at the international level (including start-ups, regular business operations, etc.). Services that are provided through portals receive a higher score, while services that provide information online but require offline operations receive a lower score. For the fourth consecutive indicator, Romania is also the last in terms of digital services for the private sector (Fig. 4).

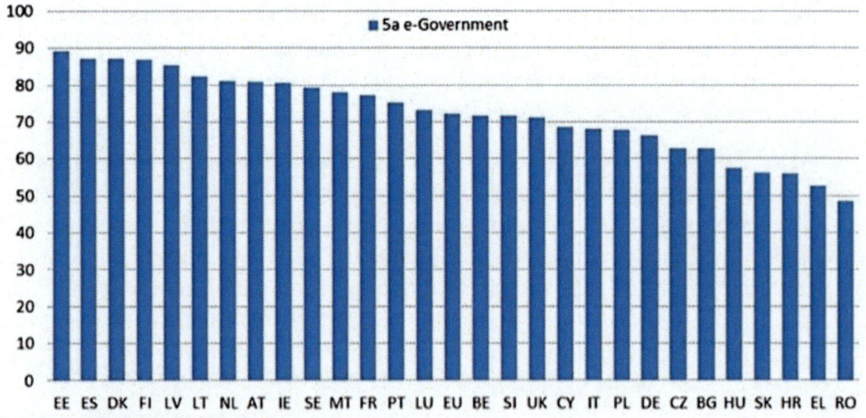

Source: DESI 2020, European Commission.

Fig. 1 Users of e-Gov services at European level

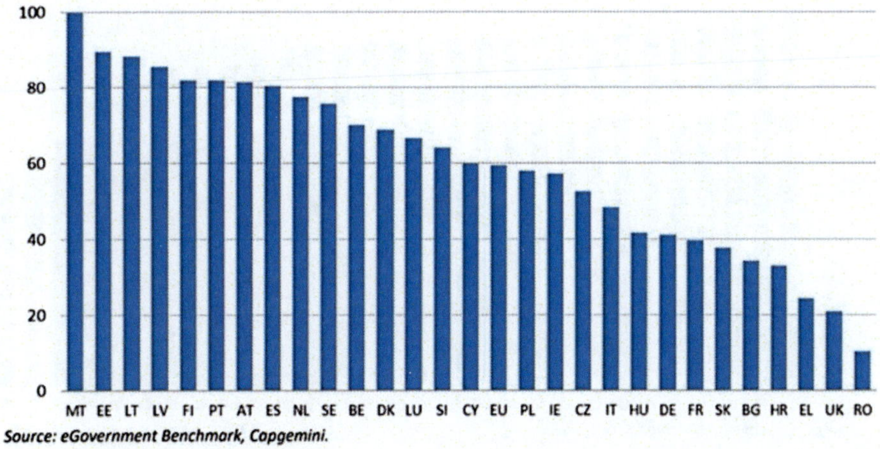

Fig. 2 Pre-completed electronic forms

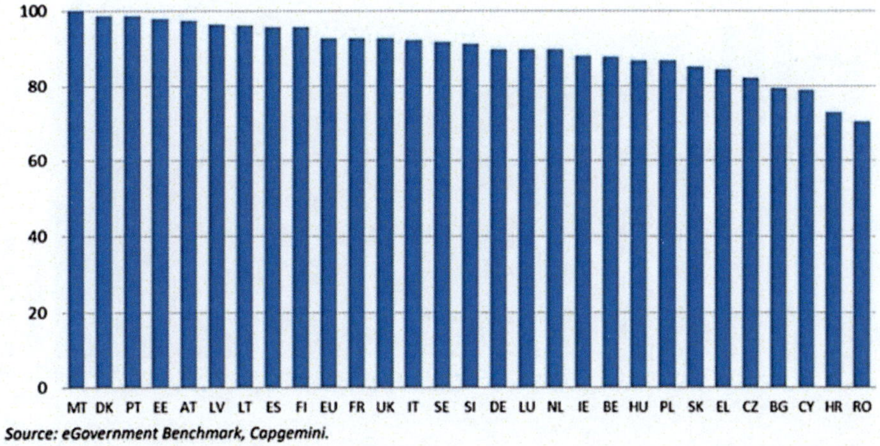

Fig. 3 Online services

5. *Open Data—the indicator measures* the governments' readiness and commitments to provide open data, measured since 2018 by *national open data policies, open data portals, the impact of open data and the quality of open data.* Romania is still in the last sequence of the ranking, but ahead of countries such as Hungary, Slovakia, Malta or Portugal (Fig. 5).
6. *User focus*—measured based on three dimensions: *available public services, online support in use* (e.g. online chats) *and versions of mobile-friendly services.* The European average score for this indicator is almost 90, Romania being situated in the last position, with a score of less than 75 points (Fig. 6).

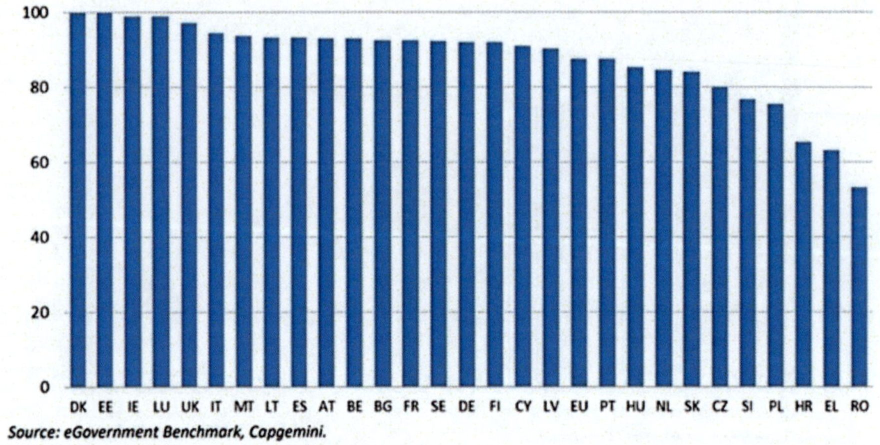

Fig. 4 Digital services for the private sector

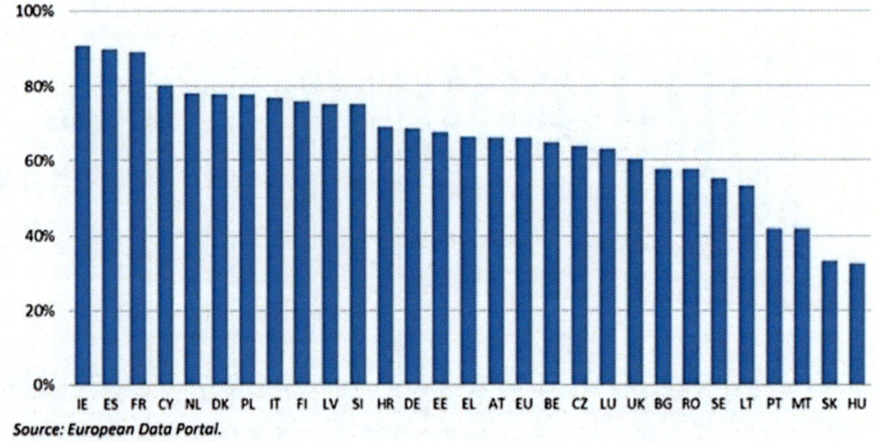

Fig. 5 Open data

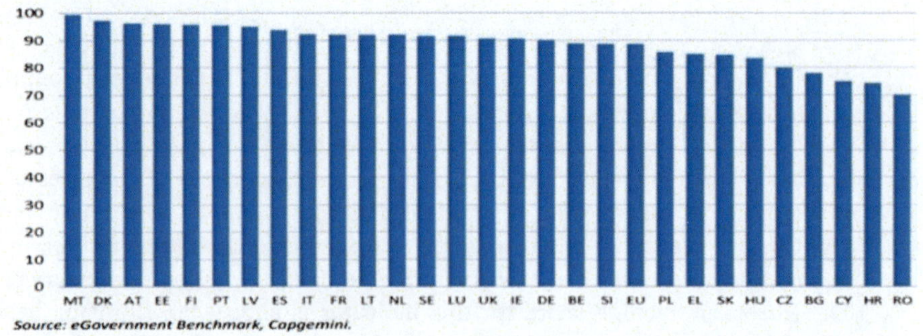

Fig. 6 User focus

7. *Key factors in digitalization*—this category includes *electronic identification* (a document issued by a public authority for identification and authentication), *e-documents* (documents authenticated by the issuing authority, electronic signature certificate), *authentic source documents* (electronic registers used by public authorities for automatic validation of data), *digital mails* (only digital communication between citizens and administration). Malta, Estonia, Lithuania, Denmark and Latvia lead the rankings, with scores of more than 90 points, while Romania situates at the bottom of the ranking, far behind Greece, scoring approximately 20 points (Fig. 7).
8. *Cross-border mobility of online services* indicates the extent to which the users of public services from another Member State can use the online services of the evaluated State. Romania's score is below 30 points (Fig. 8).

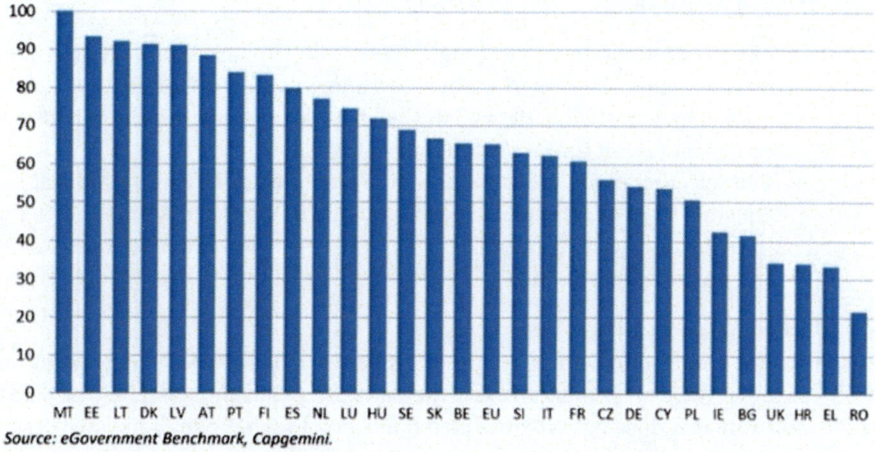

Fig. 7 Key factors in digitalization

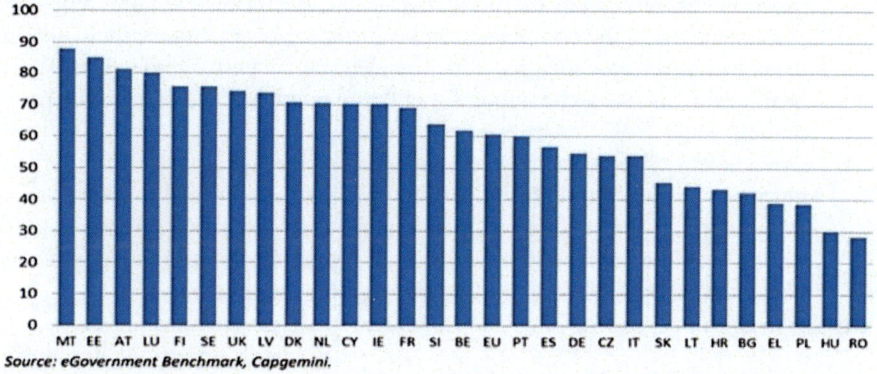

Fig. 8 Cross-border mobility of online services

Although at the formal level, Romania adopted in 2015, the *National Strategy on the Digital Agenda for Romania 2020,* having institutions responsible for the digitalization process such as the *Romanian Digitalization Authority,* the situation outlined above, in which Romania formally ranks last at almost all indicators measuring public services digitalization (and on the last place globally in the DESI report), indicates that the country has systemic difficulties that make the digital transformation process, a difficult one.

3.4 Recommendations for the Digital Transformation of the Romanian Public Administration

1. Digital transformation of public institutions

   - The transformation of the Single Electronic Contact Point (PCUE) into a real communication interface between citizens and the Romanian state. Any document deposited in the PCUE shall have legal value and enter in the legal document circuit for all institutions.
   - The selection of key institutions/areas (identified as having significant risks affecting large-scale social or economic functioning) and developing digitalization strategies in these areas as a priority—as *tax administration* (ANAF) and *public procurement.*

2. Interoperability of services

   The construction of digital highways between database-holding institutions, in order for them to communicate efficiently. No public money should be paid for software that does not provide interconnection to the digital highway network.
3. Electronic identity

   The electronic ID card-The law on electronic identity cards was adopted by the Romanian Parliament on 14 July 2020 (Romanian Parliament 2020). The main benefits brought by this normative act are that the beneficiaries will be able to authenticate in the computer systems of the state's institutions and not only, using their electronic identity card. The electronic identity card will replace the health card, and it can be issued for children under the age of 14 if the parents request it.
4. Government Cloud—the full responsibility of the government to provide the necessary infrastructure for all institutions that are obliged to take over and store information to public services' beneficiaries and to protect their data. The project was launched in 2018 with a budget of EUR 45 million but is far from being complete.

4 The Regional Effects of the COVID-19 Crisis

The section focuses on COVID-19 impact on regional economies development, trying to estimate the degree of local vulnerability to the negative economic effects of the COVID-19 crisis. The research method used combines own calculations on each region's dependence on the most severely affected activities with the information provided by the National Strategy and Forecast Commission on the foreseeable short-term contraction of these activities. The working hypothesis on which the chapter is based is that the regional distribution of COVID-19 infection cases in Romania, but especially the economic implications of the social distancing measures taken in the context of emergency ordinances, has an unequal regional distribution. Even areas with a low incidence of disease are severely affected by the reduction of economic activity, especially if sectors such as hotels and restaurants, transport and construction. They have a high share in the local economy. As in the case of "classic" crises, the economic shock caused by the pandemic seems to be closely linked to the sectoral structure of local economies, the main cause of vulnerability being high dependence on sectors of activity directly affected by strict health crisis management policies.

4.1 The Vulnerability Index by Development Region

4.1.1 Method and Data

As mentioned before, to estimate the degree of local vulnerability to the negative economic effects of the COVID-19 crisis a new method that combines own calculations on each region's dependence on the most severely affected activities with the information provided by the National Strategy and Forecast Commission on the foreseeable short-term contraction of these activities have been used. The sectoral structure of the regional economies has been investigated with the localization coefficient (Florence 1939), also known as the Hoover–Balassa coefficient. It is a simple indicator, able to express the position of each economic activity in the economy of a region, providing a realistic estimate on region's dependence, hence on region's vulnerability to the decline of that activity. The localization coefficient of activity j in region i can be calculated starting either from the concentration rate g_{ij}^{C} or the specialization rate g_{ij}^{S}, as follows:

$$LQ_{ij} = \frac{E_{ij}/E_j}{E_i/E} = \frac{E_{ij}/E_i}{E_j/E} \Leftrightarrow LQ_{ij} = \frac{g_{ij}^{C}}{E_i/E} = \frac{g_{ij}^{S}}{E_j/E} g_{ij}^{S} = \frac{E_{ij}}{\sum_{j=1}^{m} E_{ij}} = \frac{E_{ij}}{E_i} \quad (1)$$

g_{ij}^{C}—the concentration rate, computed as the share of region *i* in the economic activity *j*;

g_{ij}^{S}—specialization rate, representing the share of the economic activity *j* in the total employed population of region *i*;

E_{ij}—the population employed in activity *j* relative to total employment in region *i*;

E_j—total employment in the economic activity *j* for the whole national economy;

E_i—total employed population or gross value added in region *i*;

E—total employed population at national level;

i—region;

j—economic activity.

The magnitude of the localization coefficient is interpreted as follows:

- LQij > 1 shows that economic activity *j* holds an important position in the economy of region *i*, having a higher than average share (at national level);
- LQij < 1 indicates that economic activity *j* is underrepresented in the economy of region *i*, having a lower share than the national average of activity *j*.

For the computation of the localization coefficients, we have used the official statistics on the civilian employment by activity at the NACE-2 level, by development region and county (National Institute of Statistics 2020). The time span was from 2008 to 2018 (the latest statistics available at territorial level).

The variations in the coefficients level are also influenced by the degree of data disaggregation by economic activity. The simplicity of the localization coefficients makes them useful tools in the initial research stages. Based on the results regarding the localization coefficients by county and by economic activity, the next step has been the calculation of the index of economic vulnerability to the current crisis caused by the measures aimed at mitigating the epidemic impact. This vulnerability index is built by combining the answers to the following two questions:

1. What is the contraction forecasted for the activities most affected by the crisis?
2. What is the importance of each of these activities in the region's economy?

To answer the first question, we have employed the forecast provided by the National Commission for Strategy and Forecasting (NCSF) via "The current context of the Romanian economy and the impact of coronavirus on the main macroeconomic indicators" Report (NCSF 2020), while for the second aspect we have calculated the localization coefficients according to Formula (1), for each economic activity, each county (NUTS3) and each development region (NUTS2).

Finally, we have combined the two criteria into a synthetic indicator of economic vulnerability to the COVID-19 crisis by calculating a weighted arithmetic mean according to the following formula:

$$V_i = \frac{\sum_j \sum_{j=1}^{k} LQ_{ij} \cdot \left(D_j \big/ \sum_j D_j\right)}{100} \tag{2}$$

where

V_i—the vulnerability index;
LQ_{ij}—the localization coefficient of activity *j* in region *i*;
Dj—the decline forecast for activity *j* at national level;
k—number of activities affected by the crisis.

The level of the vulnerability index is interpreted as follows: supra-unit values indicate the regions likely to be severely affected by the crisis, with a higher degree of risk than the national average; on the contrary, sub-unit values correspond to regional economies with below-average risk. The higher the value of the indicator, the more exposed the region is to the economic risks posed by the COVID-19 crisis.

4.1.2 Results

The contraction of the activities hardest hit by the COVID-19 crisis in the period envisaged by our research (March–May 2020) was estimated by the National Forecast Commission as follows (in descending order of damage):

- Hotels and restaurants: −45,8%;
- Transportation: −32,3%;
- Manufacturing industry: −17,7%;
- Performing, cultural and recreational activities: −11,2%;
- Real estate transactions: −9%;
- Construction: −7%;
- Retail: −7,7%.

The localization coefficients by these activity sectors, counties (NUTS3) and development regions (NUTS2) for the latest year available in the period in which the research was conducted—2018—are presented in Tables 1 and 2. The significant spatial polarization illustrated in these data is an indication of the differences in the level of specialization of counties, as well as of the inequalities in the territorial distribution of economic activities. The differences are larger at county level than at regional level, the aggregate values partially hiding the inequalities of the component parts.

Next, in order to determine the vulnerability index (see the same tables as above) we combined the level of dependence of a territorial unit's economy on the activities most affected by the crisis, as measured by localization coefficients, with information provided by the National Commission for Strategy and Forecast (NCSF) in connection with estimates of short-term contraction of these activities. Basically, we calculated a weighted average of the localization coefficients for the activities severely affected by the crisis (hotels and restaurants, transport, manufacturing and retail), using as weights the NCSF estimates on their short-term decline. The weights used to express the gravity of the evolution of the respective activities in the short term, and the average of the localization coefficients thus weighted is an estimate of the degree of vulnerability of the territorial units to the current crisis. Although the calculations on location coefficients are limited in time by the available official statistics, the most recent data being for 2018, the results obtained are little

Table 1 Economic vulnerability to the COVID-19 crisis on the short term for the Romanian counties

County	Localization coefficient							Vulnerability index
	Manufacturing industry	Construction	Retail trade	Transportation	Hotels and restaurants	Real estate transactions	Performing, cultural and recreational activities	
Brașov	1.299	1.288	1.085	1.063	1.775	1.460	1.085	**1.395**
Constanța	0.676	1.488	1.176	1.645	1.564	1.320	0.981	**1.374**
Bucharest Municipality	0.464	1.470	1.271	1.003	1.317	1.877	2.386	**1.261**
Ilfov	1.065	0.720	1.475	1.438	1.053	2.377	1.085	**1.247**
Sibiu	1.657	0.875	0.875	1.140	1.195	0.909	1.286	**1.196**
Cluj	0.972	1.025	1.059	1.181	1.101	0.970	1.172	**1.094**
Covasna	1.423	0.643	0.965	0.890	1.327	0.608	0.878	**1.091**
Prahova	1.274	1.186	1.007	1.139	0.944	1.316	0.869	**1.070**
Bihor	1.253	0.772	0.948	1.154	1.089	0.766	0.869	**1.061**
Vâlcea	1.012	0.995	1.041	0.878	1.161	1.619	0.534	**1.035**
Arad	1.609	0.798	1.013	1.200	0.812	0.829	0.733	**1.017**
Caraș-Severin	1.010	0.858	0.789	1.089	1.095	0.727	0.700	**0.994**
Bistrița-Năsăud	1.295	1.162	0.879	1.100	0.999	0.200	0.744	**0.989**
Timiș	1.392	0.610	1.000	1.054	0.850	1.147	0.858	**0.988**
Mureș	1.147	0.809	1.026	0.994	0.974	0.877	0.950	**0.988**
Galați	0.803	1.126	0.969	0.932	1.007	1.123	1.043	**0.977**
Harghita	1.236	0.782	1.012	0.844	1.210	0.388	0.480	**0.974**

(continued)

Table 1 (continued)

County	Localization coefficient							Vulnerability index
	Manufacturing industry	Construction	Retail trade	Transportation	Hotels and restaurants	Real estate transactions	Performing, cultural and recreational activities	
Alba	1.532	0.674	0.910	1.121	0.912	0.462	0.508	**0.968**
Argeș	1.549	0.980	0.756	0.995	0.714	0.897	0.946	**0.941**
Brăila	1.058	1.428	0.912	0.741	0.958	0.847	0.875	**0.926**
Hunedoara	1.138	0.924	1.212	0.826	1.008	0.451	0.559	**0.913**
Dâmbovița	1.272	0.434	1.006	1.290	0.742	0.544	0.505	**0.911**
Satu Mare	1.204	1.061	0.877	0.889	0.766	1.053	0.797	**0.898**
Iași	0.755	1.101	0.878	0.765	0.991	0.958	0.935	**0.897**
Tulcea	0.871	0.871	0.865	0.858	1.134	0.316	0.522	**0.896**
Maramureș	1.349	0.773	0.828	0.901	0.843	0.644	0.585	**0.885**
Neamț	0.932	0.690	1.038	0.867	0.992	0.723	0.537	**0.884**
Suceava	0.820	0.672	0.968	0.935	0.994	0.456	0.611	**0.870**
Sălaj	1.296	0.742	0.882	1.076	0.797	0.256	0.422	**0.865**
Gorj	0.629	1.554	0.856	0.852	0.931	0.578	0.716	**0.858**
Dolj	0.749	0.844	1.001	0.790	0.808	1.117	0.880	**0.836**
Mehedinți	0.828	1.234	0.700	0.840	0.856	0.261	0.540	**0.793**
Buzău	1.051	0.549	0.937	0.853	0.760	0.629	0.454	**0.785**
Bacău	0.925	1.623	0.998	0.690	0.646	0.878	0.622	**0.779**

(continued)

Table 1 (continued)

County	Localization coefficient							Vulnerability index
	Manufacturing industry	Construction	Retail trade	Transportation	Hotels and restaurants	Real estate transactions	Performing, cultural and recreational activities	
Ialomița	0.692	0.907	0.948	0.830	0.796	0.567	0.468	**0.762**
Vrancea	0.981	0.925	0.784	0.808	0.718	0.576	0.475	**0.759**
Botoșani	0.830	0.531	0.815	0.702	0.767	0.379	0.547	**0.705**
Giurgiu	0.397	1.286	0.635	1.282	0.344	0.630	0.650	**0.689**
Călărași	0.763	0.721	0.730	0.821	0.538	0.575	0.712	**0.674**
Olt	1.077	0.795	0.638	0.695	0.411	0.165	0.545	**0.596**
Vaslui	0.843	0.540	0.724	0.798	0.380	0.407	0.503	**0.583**
Teleorman	0.739	0.390	0.798	0.715	0.413	0.378	0.312	**0.539**

Source Authors' calculations

Table 2 Level of economic vulnerability to the COVID-19 crisis in the short term for the Romanian development regions

Region	Localization coefficient							Vulnerability index
	Manufacturing	Constructions	Retail trade	Transportation	Hotels and restaurants	Real estate transactions	Performing cultural and recreational activities	
București—Ilfov	0.551	1.360	1.300	1.066	1.279	1.950	2.196	1.259
Centru	1.369	0.901	0.988	1.031	1.257	0.880	0.913	1.129
Sud-Est	0.868	1.126	0.984	1.085	1.097	0.922	0.783	1.021
Nord-Vest	1.185	0.923	0.941	1.077	0.980	0.741	0.856	0.999
Vest	1.349	0.752	1.020	1.050	0.903	0.874	0.747	0.981
Sud-Muntenia	1.123	0.868	0.872	1.042	0.708	0.813	0.699	0.868
Sud-Vest Oltenia	0.855	1.031	0.877	0.805	0.827	0.836	0.677	0.827
Nord-Est	0.843	0.920	0.917	0.796	0.839	0.684	0.664	0.813

Source Authors' calculations

affected by the impossibility of updating the data, given that there were no significant changes in the territorial distribution of economic activities, as suggested by the variation of localization coefficients in the period 2008–2017 also studied in the research undertaken.

The values of the crisis vulnerability index (Table 1, last column) show that the counties of Brasov and Constanta are the most affected, primarily due to the high share of tourism in the economy of each county. In the context of this crisis, additional risk factors are, in descending order of severity: transport, construction and real estate transactions for Constanța County and real estate transactions, manufacturing and construction in the case of Brașov County. A high level of vulnerability is also displayed by the Municipality of Bucharest (entertainment, cultural and recreational activities, real estate transactions, hotels and restaurants, construction, trade), as well as the counties of Ilfov (real estate transactions, trade and transport) and Sibiu (manufacturing industry, activities of shows, cultural and recreational, real estate transactions, hotels and restaurants). The counties of Cluj, Covasna, Prahova, Bihor, Vâlcea and Arad have a comparatively lower degree of vulnerability, slightly above the national average. At the opposite pole, with a level of vulnerability of approx. 30% below average, are the counties of Botoșani, Giurgiu, Călărași, Olt and Vaslui, in whose economies the activities strongly affected by the crisis have lower shares than in the other counties.

In the case of the development regions (Table 2), the most vulnerable is the Bucharest–Ilfov region, which brings together the weaknesses of Bucharest Municipality and Ilfov county in terms of the large share of activities affected by the crisis: performance, cultural and recreational activities, real estate transactions, hotels and restaurants, construction, trade and transport. The centre region is particularly weakened by the scale of the manufacturing industry and the activities of hotels and restaurants, and the south-east region is affected by the location of construction activities, hotels and restaurants and transport. Vulnerability ratios slightly below 1 have the north-west (manufacturing and transport) and west (manufacturing industry is the strongest risk factor) regions. The north-east region is the least vulnerable.

Our investigation and findings bring about an original perspective for the analysis of the COVID-19 economic effects at regional level, opening the door for relevant comparisons with other studies in the same field (e.g. Niembro and Calá 2020; Bachtrögler et al. 2020; Kitsos 2020).

However, these results represent only a first estimate of the crisis impact at regional level, revealing the degree of vulnerability to the crisis for regions and counties. The official information available later on the level of unemployment by counties is to provide a first real quantitative assessment of the impact of the crisis at the local level.

4.2 *Policy Measures for Reducing the Effects of the COVID-19 Crisis and for Relaunching the Regions' Economies in the Short and Medium Terms*

Given the global nature of the COVID-19 epidemic and the multiple interdependencies that exist between the economies of the world's countries, the first message from the experience acquired so far in managing the effects of the crisis aims to treat each country as a system composed of horizontally and vertically integrated subsystems and, at the same time, as part of a much more comprehensive, global system that affects its resilience. Global risks may have profound effects on the functioning of the governance system, government–business relationship, efficiency of government spending and implementation of reforms, public confidence, anti-corruption measures and the provision of services designed to improve business performance (WEF 2020).

The second message—essential for the topic of our research—highlights the strong territorial dimension of the global crisis COVID-19. As demonstrated in Romania, in each country the regional and local impact of the crisis is asymmetric, with some regions affected more than others, at least in the early stages of the pandemic. In economic terms, the impact of the crisis differs from one region to another depending on its economic specialization, exposure to foreign trade, the degree of connection to global value chains.

At regional and local levels, reducing the effects of the COVID-19 crisis and reviving the economy implies concerted measures in the short, medium and long terms. International studies suggest that short-term measures should focus on managing the emergency and crisis of the public health system, while medium-term policy measures should focus on managing the economic, social and public finance crisis (OECD 2020).

More than that, an essential aspect for ensuring an adequate response to the challenges of the crisis is, in this context, coordination between the actors involved in crisis management at national and local levels, accompanied by combining the opportunities arising from economic, financial, social decisions at national scale and the European support with those able to strengthen regional and local economies, taking into account their structure and the vulnerabilities manifested during the crisis.

Regarding the development models, the variation of the economic impact of the COVID-19 crisis from one economic sector to another, from one region to another and even from one company to another determines the need to rethink, find answers to the actions of factors such as "exposure to of China as a source of intermediate inputs, the possibility of resorting to alternative suppliers, the existence of stocks or dependence on 'just in time' production processes" (European Commission 2020a). Thus, the current that supports the reconsideration of current development models based on Global Production Networks (GPN) in favour of "classic" models such as local production systems (LPS), with a high degree integration at national level and, at the next level, at European level. This will lead to "economic restructuring" measures in combination with "spatial restructuring" measures, leading to rationally designed economic systems in terms of reducing the vulnerability to global shocks.

5 Conclusions

The study revealed a series of important facts regarding the development of the Romanian public administration and the negative effects of the COVID-19 pandemic on regional economy. Nevertheless, some research limitations have been generated by the lack of data for 2020 and 2021 and by the fact that the local vulnerability was calculated using only data from the beginning of the pandemic. Regarding the future trends of research, the present study will be continued as soon as new data will be available as to create a clearer picture regarding COVID-19 impact on regional economy and to observe if during this pandemic, the digitalization process in the public administration, has been improved and if the public utility sector suffered any kind of changes. Also, other studies regarding the human resources from public administration will be conducted as to observe the changes made in this field after the adoption of the new Administrative Code in 2019.

The analysis of the Romanian public administration from the human resources perspective reveals that this area is facing with an ageing body of civil servants, with instability caused by the frequent changes in legislation, the need to train civil servants and a difficulty in attracting and retaining personnel specialized in areas with deficit (IT, education, health). These problems affect public administrations' efficiency and performance and the successful implementation of reforms and strategies.

Government policies must meet the turbulent environment and design optimal policies, tactics and strategies. All these aspects require a new vision, alternatives and methods to ensure the continued improvement of the use of scarce resources in order to achieve maximum impact and benefits. Public administration must ***continuously strengthen its capacity to improve results, incorporate permanent change and improve its vision and manner of work.***

At strategic public policy level, the reform in the field of community utility services needs to be considered in a broader perspective: (a) identify the current state of development of public service networks throughout Romania, with a view to targeted investments from national and external funds and (b) connecting with tax decentralization reform in order to increase the financial capacity of localities and reduce their dependence on the state's budget—that will also have a positive impact on the community utilities sector.

From a managerial perspective, the public services sector requires an urgent transformation on the basis of efficiency and economic efficiency, while respecting the minimum principles of ensuring fair access for all residents to a minimum package of services. But further investments, without prior analysis of the best manners to implement them as to maximize the benefits of some projects, must stop. The most common example in this register is the projects meant to extend water supply and sewage networks in rural areas: although significant investments have been made, the costs for these services are sometimes prohibitive for citizens, who prefer not to connect to the water network and continue to use the fountain in the yard—one of the reasons why statistics indicate that two out of three Romanians in rural areas do not have access to running water.

As far as the public service market is concerned, it is still far from being transparent and competitive: the duration of public service concession contracts is still very high in some cases (25 years), which basically makes a private operator, once the service has been leased, no longer motivated to improve his service if there is no real prospect of competition. Similar to public procurement, the concession of public services should be made using a national platform where information is available in real time to all potentially operators interested in taking over the management of a public service in a locality.

Last but not least, one requirement that extends itself to all strategies is to ***digitalize the entire utility supply chain: the relationship between the public authority and the operator (if the service is delegated), as to allow real-time monitoring of the performance indicators established by contract and the customer—citizen relationship***, who must have unrestricted access to information about the cost and quality parameters of the service he pays. The aim of the administrative reform can simply be defined as providing better services to citizens. In the government's institutions, the significance of this goal must be carefully examined, understood, developed and effectively implemented.

In addition, the economic crisis generated by the COVID-19 pandemic brings to Romania a series of new challenges related to the European funds' absorption, especially since we are at the beginning of a new financial cycle, 2021–2027. A particular emphasis must be placed on the administrative absorption capacity, which is considered essential for the effective and efficient implementation of investment programmes and on maximizing the potential of the European Structural and Investment Funds to contribute to regional, national and EU development as a whole (OECD 2020). This requirement has a special significance in Romania's case, which has committed itself to continue at a steady pace the improvement of its administrative capacity after joining the EU.

Also, Romania should take advantage of opportunities for creating a more resilient society, focusing on revising and strengthening multi-level governance, providing basic quality services accessible for all areas of the country and for all citizens, developing digital services and tools, adopting new models of regional and local development, increasing the importance of participatory mechanisms, involving civil society, citizens and the business environment in public governance, supporting the transition to a low carbon economy.

References

Bachtrögler, J., Firgo, M., Fritz, O., Klien, M., Mayerhofer, P., Piribauer, P., Streicher, G.: Regional differences in the economic vulnerability to the current COVID-19 crisis. WIFO Working Paper. Online, available at: https://www.wifo.ac.at/jart/prj3/wifo/resources/person_dokument/person_dokument.jart?publikationsid=65871&mime_type=application/pdf. Accessed 15 September 2020 (2020)

Capgemini: EGovernment Benchmark 2019: governments are empowering more Europeans through trusted digital public services, Online, available at: https://www.capgemini.com/news/egovernment-benchmark-2019/. Accessed 15 August 2020 (2020)

Davies, S.: Regional resilience in the 2008–2010 downturn: comparative evidence from European countries. Camb. J. Reg. Econ. Soc. **4**, 369–382 (2011)

Deloitte: Raport privind transparența, Online, available at: https://www2.deloitte.com/content/dam/Deloitte/ro/Documents/about-deloitte/ro-md-raport-privind-transparenta-032913.pdf. Accessed 15 August 2020 (2013)

Dragomir, C.: Quality of public services and promotion of quality management in public institutions in EU member states. Rev. Gener. Manag. **30**(2), 43–54 (2019)

European Commission: Country Report Romania 2019. Including an In-Depth Review on the prevention and correction of macroeconomic imbalances, Online, available at: https://ec.europa.eu/info/sites/info/files/file_import/2019-european-semester-country-report-romania_en.pdf. Accessed 15 August 2020 (2019)

European Commission: The Digital Economy and Society Index (DESI), Online, available at: https://digital-strategy.ec.europa.eu/en/policies/desi. Accessed 15 September 2020 (2020a)

European Commission: European Structural and Investment Funds—Data, European Commission, Online, available at: https://cohesiondata.ec.europa.eu/overview. Accessed 15 September 2020 (2020b)

Eur-Lex: Directive 2008/98/EC of the European Parliament and of the Council of 19 November 2008 on waste and repealing certain Directives, Online, available at: https://eur-lex.europa.eu/eli/dir/2008/98/oj. Accessed 15 September 2020 (2020)

Florence, P.: Report of the Location of Industry. Political and Economic Planning, London (1939)

Foster, K.: A Case Study Approach to Understanding Regional Resilience, Working Paper 2007–08, Institute of Urban and Regional Development, Berkley University (2006)

Gitz, V., Meybeck, A.: Risks, vulnerabilities and resilience in a context of climate change, Agriculture and Consumer Protection Department, FAO, Rome, Online, available at: http://www.fao.org/fileadmin/templates/agphome/documents/faooecd/gitz.pdf. Accessed 15 September 2020 (2012)

Kitsos, A.: The uneven spatial footprint of the COVID-19 shutdown. ERSA. Online, available at: https://ersa.org/wp-content/uploads/2020/04/Blog_Resilience.pdf. Accessed 25 July 2020 (2020)

Ministry of European Funds: Partnership Agreement between Romania and the European Union 2014–2020, Online, available at: http://www.fonduri-ue.ro/files/documente-relevante/acord/Acord_de_Parteneriat_2014-2020_RO.pdf. Accessed 15 September 2020 (2014)

National Agency of Civil Servants: Report on the management of public service and civil servants for 2012, Online, available at: http://www.anfp.gov.ro/R/Doc/2014/Materiale%20utile/Rapoarte/ANFP%20RaportManagementFunctiePublica2013.pdf. Accessed 18 September 2020 (2013)

National Agency of Civil Servants: Analiză privind evaluarea implementării programelor YPS (Proiectul Tinerilor Profesioniști) și *BSGR (Bursa Specială "Guvernul României") și bune practici identificate*, Online, last accessed on: http://www.anfp.gov.ro/R/Doc/2015/Studii%20si%20prezentari/3_NEW%20final%20analiza%20yps%20si%20bsgr%202015.pdf. Accessed 18 September 2020 (2015)

National Agency of Civil Servants: Report on the management of public service and civil servants for 2017, Online, available at: http://www.anfp.gov.ro/R/Doc/Ionut/Raport%20Management%20FP%20%202017.pdf. Accessed 18 September 2020 (2018)

National Agency of Civil Servants: Report on the management of public service and civil servants for 2018, Online, available at: http://www.anfp.gov.ro/R/Doc/2019/rapoarte%202019/Raport%20privind%20managementul%20func%C5%A3iei%20publice%20%C5%9Fi%20al%20func%C5%A3ionarilor%20publici%20pentru%20anul%202018.pdf. Accessed 18 September 2020 (2019)

National Institute of Statistics: Populația ocupată civilă pe activități ale economiei naționale la nivel de secțiune CAEN Rev.2, pe regiuni de dezvoltare si județe, Baza de date TEMPO, Online, available at: http://statistici.insse.ro:8077/tempo-online/#/pages/tables/insse-table. Accessed 18 August 2020 (2020)

Niembro, A., Calá, C.D.: A first exploratory analysis of the regional economic impact of COVID-19 in Argentina. ERSA. Online, available at: https://ersa.org/wp-content/uploads/2020/08/Niembro-Cala_Regional-Impact-of-COVID19-in-Argentina.pdf. Accessed 25 September 2020 (2020)

OECD: OECD Public Governance Reviews: Romania, Online, available at; https://www.oecd.org/gov/public-governance-review-scan-romania.pdf. Accessed 18 August 2020 (2016)

OECD: The territorial impact of COVID-19: managing the crisis across levels of government, OCDE, Online, available at: https://read.oecd-ilibrary.org/view/?ref=128_128287-5agkkojaaa&title=The-territorial-impact-of-covid-19-managing-the-crisis-across-levels-of-government. Accessed 18 August 2020 (2020)

Petrescu, C., Mihalache, F.: Perceptions towards the quality of public services in Romania. Poor outcomes  of public administration reforms?. Calitatea vieţii, XXXI(2), pp. 263–285 (2020)

Radu, L.: How to develop sustainable public administration reforms, Transylvanian Review of Administrative Sciences, No. 44 E/2015, pp. 180–195 (2015)

Romanian Government: The Strategy for Strengthening the Romanian public administration 2014–2020 development, Online, available at: http://scap.gov.ro/welcome/page/scap. Accessed 18 August 2020 (2014)

Romanian Government: Ordinance of Emergency no. 57 from 3 July 2019 regarding the Administrative Code, published in the Official Monitor no. 555 from 5 July 2019 (2019)

Romanian Parliament: LEGE nr. 188 din 8 decembrie 1999 (**republicată**) privind Statutul funcționarilor publici, published in the Official Monitor no. 365 from 29 May 2007 (2007)

Romanian Parliament: LEGE nr. 123 din 10 iulie 2012 energiei electrice și a gazelor naturale, published in the Official Monitor no. 485 from 16 July 2012 (2012)

Romanian Parliament: Law no. 51 from 8 March 2006 (republished) on Community Public Utilities Services, published in the Official Monitor, no. 121 from 5 March 2013 (2013)

Romanian Parliament: *LEGE nr. 211 din 15 noiembrie 2011 (*republicată*) privind regimul deșeurilor*, published in the Official Monitor no. 220 from 28 March 2014 (2014).

Romanian Parliament: LEGE nr. 249 din 28 octombrie 2015 privind modalitatea de gestionare a ambalajelor și a deșeurilor de ambalaje, published in the Official Monitor no. 809 from 30 October 2015 (2015)

Romanian Parliament: LEGE nr. 162 din 3 august 2020 pentru modificarea și completarea unor acte normative care cuprind dispoziții privind evidența persoanelor și actele de identitate ale cetățenilor români, published in the Official Monitor no. 698 from 4 August 2020 (2020)

Stan, S.E., Stan-Oprean, C., Țîțu, A.M. (2020). Digitalization—sustainable development convergence: metrics and effects in Romania. Manag. Sustain. Develop. **12**(1)

WEF: How to boost global resilience to COVID-19?, Online, available at: https://www.weforum.org/agenda/2020/04/how-to-boost-global-resilience-to-covid-19. Accessed 18 August 2020 (2020)

World Bank: Public Administration Reform: a general picture of cross-cutting issues, Washington (2011)

World Bank: Regulatory Impact Assessment Report: A better employment system at the level of central public administration, Online, available at: https://sgg.gov.ro/new/wp-content/uploads/2016/04/RIA-Report-NACS_RO.pdf. Accessed 18 August 2020 (2017)

World Bank: GovTech: Putting people first, Online, available at: https://www.worldbank.org/en/topic/governance/brief/govtech-putting-people-first. Accessed 18 August 2020 (2019)

World Bank: From Uneven Growth to Inclusive Development Romania's Path to Shared Prosperity Online, available at: https://openknowledge.worldbank.org/bitstream/handle/10986/29864/9781464813177.pdf?sequence=2&isAllowed=y. Accessed 18 August 2020 (2018)

Restart the Hotel, Restaurant, and Travel Industry in Romania After the COVID-19 Pandemic

Tigu Gabriela, Ciora Costin, Petcu Monica Aureliana, Boboc Dan, Crismariu Oana Diana, and Curteanu Adrian Bogdan

1 Introduction

Tourism, an important economic, social, and cultural phenomenon, has significantly developed on a worldwide scale in the past years. In this context, tourism, including the hospitality industry, is an essential part of many national and regional economies. It is a critical factor in the development process when it is managed accordingly. Tourism generates, both directly and indirectly, a variety of workplaces. It contributes to the social and economic development of poor regions when managed durably.

The tourism activity worldwide has severely decreased due to the sanitary, economic, and social crisis that occurred after spreading the new COVID-19 virus. In Romania, despite the potential value of our country for tourism development, the industry is not a significant source of contribution to the Gross Domestic Product (only 2.8%). But tourism is not a neglected sector as it could be evaluated in a larger sense by focusing on its multiplicative effect.

The objectives of this paper are: gradual analysis of the evolution of hotels, restaurants, and the tourism industry during the pandemic, correlating the situation of the sector with the activity of other sectors of the national economy (given the multiplier effect of tourism), but also finding solutions for safe resumption activity of this sector.

T. Gabriela (✉) · C. Costin · P. M. Aureliana · B. Dan · C. O. Diana · C. A. Bogdan
Bucharest University of Economic Studies, Bucharest, Romania
e-mail: gabriela.tigu@ase.ro

C. Costin
e-mail: costin.ciora@cig.ase.ro

P. M. Aureliana
e-mail: monica.petcu@cig.ase.ro

B. Dan
e-mail: dan.boboc@ase.ro

A. M. Dima et al. (eds.), *Economic Recovery After COVID-19*, Springer Proceedings in Business and Economics, https://doi.org/10.1007/978-3-030-86641-9_5

The originality of the approach is, in our opinion, the main advantage of this research. Also, until now, we have not identified a similar, comprehensive study on the impact of the pandemic on tourism and the hospitality industry in Romania. Thus, our study starts from the identification of similar studies in the international literature, from the analysis of the sector until 2020, following to evaluate the effects of the pandemic on the activity and to highlight some measures that can be taken for business recovery.

2 Related Work

In the literature, the vulnerability of tourism has been presented in correlation with climate change, terrorist attacks, natural disasters, or economic shocks. We are currently facing vulnerability related to the SARS COV-19 pandemic (Duro et al. 2021).

Tourism vulnerability is the extent to which a destination is prone to damage due to accidental risk exposure, which is influenced by two characteristics: the degree of risk exposure and the ability to cope (resilience-overcoming impacts and continue activity and resilience-recovering from a crisis situation). However, measuring the vulnerability of tourism is complicated by its multidimensional nature (Duro et al. 2021).

Quarantine is the most critical decision adopted during the pandemic, significantly affecting the hospitality industry. Decisions on quarantined regions also directly affect national economies. They can affect all areas, especially the tourism industry and the supply chain. In order to mitigate the negative consequences of the pandemic situation, prioritizing causal relations between regions is essential. Therefore, a systematic approach in making the decision to quarantine a certain area is preferable (Altuntas and Gok 2021).

The crisis caused by the SARS COV-19 pandemic is different from the crisis situations previously encountered in the tourism industry. First of all, it marked a decline in travel, the global hospitality industry, not just in small areas. Second, the economic downturn is more dramatic. Third, the crisis caused by SARS COV-19 has the potential to delineate fundamental changes in the functionality of several segments of tourism. Last but not least, it creates long-term uncertainty due to the fact that the end of the pandemic cannot be predicted (Collins-Kreiner and Ram 2020).

The effects of the COVID-19 pandemic cannot be still predicted because mankind has never experienced such an event globally. Governments are enforcing travel bans and closing borders. The present findings are based on previous pandemics, but their power to predict the effects of the current pandemic on tourism is limited. Studies can analyze the long-term or short-term effects of the pandemic on tourist arrivals using quarterly/annual data from one or more countries (Karabuluta et al. 2020).

According to a World Travel and Tourism Council (WTTC) report, the travel and tourism sector is facing new challenges caused by the situation created by the emergence of the COVID-19 virus. The sector can be mentioned as one of the most affected, and according to WTTC estimates, by the end of 2020—almost 197 million jobs and 5.5 trillion dollars will be the losses recorded globally (World Travel & Tourism Council (WTTC) and G20 2020 Saudi Arabia 2020).

According to another report realized by the G20 and the WTTC, international coordination needs to be improved to remove barriers and strengthen travelers' confidence, which is vital for the sector's recovery. Also in this regard, it is necessary for tourists to be informed about passenger safety, travel restrictions, and domestic or international travel policies. This situation must also be seen as an opportunity for collaboration between the public and private sectors, the aim being both—the economic recovery of the tourism industry, while respecting the necessary measures to prevent the spread of COVID-19 and creating jobs (World Travel & Tourism Council (WTTC) and G20 2020 Saudi Arabia 2020).

3 Research Methodology

The analysis of the hotel, restaurant, and travel industry sector is based on a secondary research, using the statistical information provided by the National Institute of Statistics of Romania, by the Ministry of Labor or by the Ministry of Finance. The data were collected from the respective sources, analyzed, and interpreted by the authors, using statistical tools. In order to highlight the effect of tourism on other sectors of activity, the Leontief quantitative input–output model was used, helping us to identify the values of the backward and forward multipliers.

3.1 The Industry Evolution Between 2014–2019

Hotel Sector

During this time, the number of active companies reported in the Ministry of Finance database showed an increase of 26%, with a growth of the average number of employees by approx. 14%, turnover by 56%, and total assets by 23%. The higher growth rate of the turnover compared with the number of employees determined an increase of the turnover per employee by 37%.

The average occupancy rate of the accommodation units was relatively modest, with values between 25 and 35%, which means an insufficient capacity of use and, at the same time, suggests a strong seasonality (usually with a peak season in summer and with greater intensity on weekends) (Fig. 1).

Restaurant sector

The number of active companies reported in the Ministry of Public Finance database has increased by 2% compared to 2014, with superior use of human resources, which

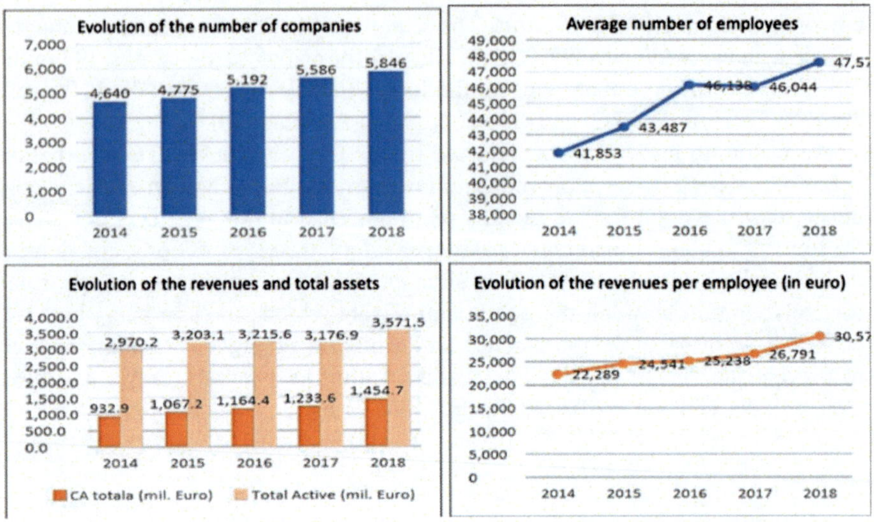

Fig. 1 Evolution of main economic indicators in hotel sector. *Source* https://mfinante.gov.ro/

increases 14%. The turnover registered a rise by 86.74%, resulting in an increase of the turnover per employee by 64%. The value of total assets reached about 2 billion euros, up 43% from 2014. The gross profit margin is about 10%, while expenses with suppliers are estimated at 30–50% (Fig. 2).

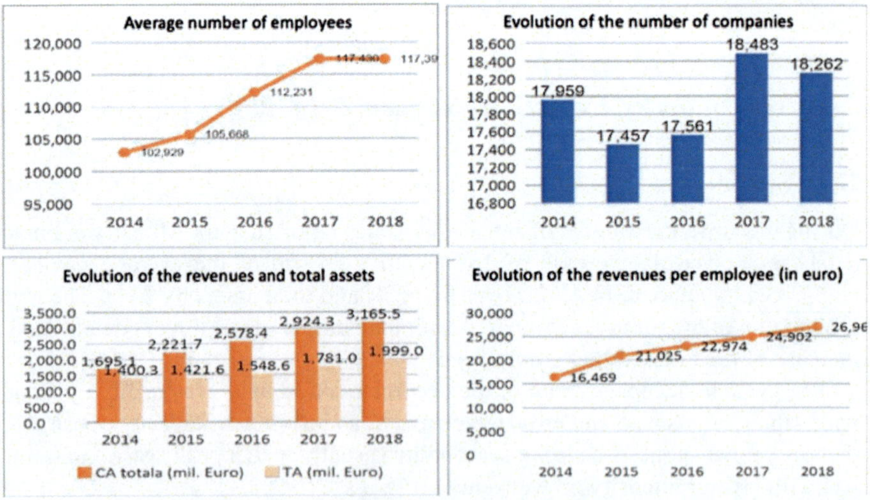

Fig. 2 Evolution of main economic indicators in restaurant sector. *Source* https://mfinante.gov.ro/

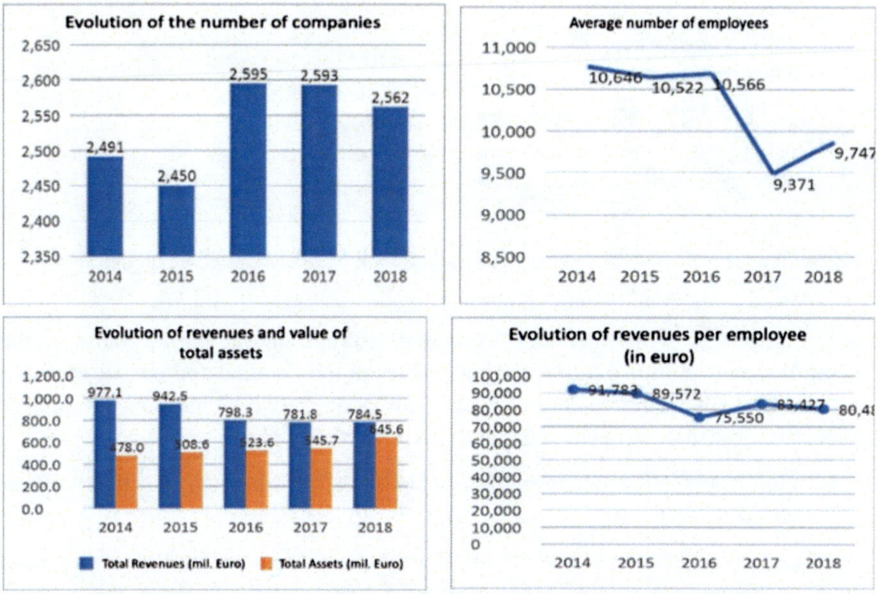

Fig. 3 Evolution of main economic indicators in travel sector. *Source* https://mfinante.gov.ro/

Travel sector

The number of companies that operate in this sector has fluctuated in this time with maintenance in the conditions of an average annual index of 100.71%. The average number of employees showed a different dynamic, with a decrease of 9% compared to 2014 (Fig. 3).

Between 2014 and 2017, the fiscal value in the sector decreased by every year until the value of 781.8 million euros (followed by an increase in 2018 to 784.5 million euros), while the value of total assets increased to 645.6 million euros (for the last analyzed year the increase was 18.3%).

3.2 *Analysis of the Correlation of the Sector with the Other Sectors of the National Economy—Leontief Model*

The quantitative input–output model proposed by Leontief highlights the interdependencies between different sectors within an economy, based on the premise of the balance between resources and consumption. In this model, the transactions in an economy are grouped by sectors in a matrix whose rows reveal how the output of each sector is distributed among the other, and the columns highlight for each sector the inputs of goods and services provided by the other sectors of the economy. If the matrix I—A is invertible, it is thus determined simultaneous equations with a unique

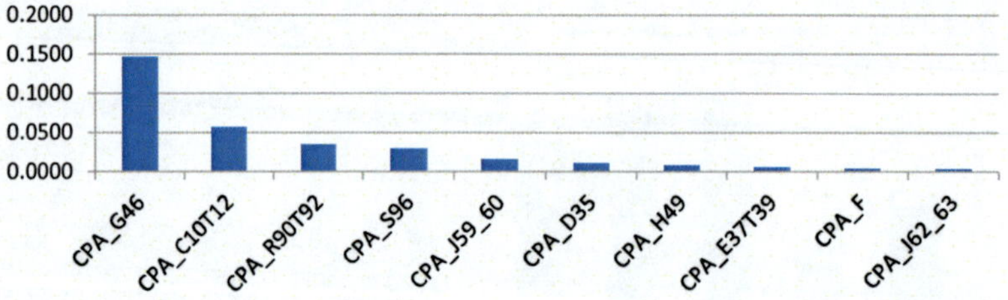

Fig. 4 Ten main areas of the industry's providers. *Source* calculations based on INSSE data

solution, and for a final demand vector, the required output can be found. Considering Hawkins–Simon condition, if all entries of the demand and output vectors are nonnegative, the required output vector x is nonnegative. Regarding the analyzed industries, the main aspects and results are described below.

(a) ***Hotels and other accommodation facilities, restaurants, and other foodservice activities***

The hospitality industry's activity implies intermediary consumption with a certain level of dependency on the inputs offered by other sectors. In the graph below, we can find the top ten areas of the industry's providers (Fig. 4).

The analysis of the technical coefficient suggests that the highest values of inputs for this sector are generated by the following areas: trade with the exception of auto vehicles and motorcycles—CPA_G46 (0.1471 RON); the food industry, beverage manufacturing, tobacco manufacturing—CPA_C10T12 (0.0571 RON); activities of creation and artistic interpretation, activities of libraries, archives, museums, and other cultural activities, gambling activities—CPA_R90T92 (0.0354 RON); other activities of services—CPA_S96 (0.0300 RON); activities of cinematography production, video, and television; audio recordings and music editing recordings; broadcast activities and transmission of programs—CPA_J59_60 (0.0160 RON); production and providing of electric and thermal energy, gas, hot water, and air conditioning—CPA_D35 (0.0116 RON); terrestrial and underground transportation—CPA_H49(0.0093 RON); collection and purification of wastewater, collection, treatment and purification of waste; collection of recyclable materials; activities and services of decontamination—CPA_E37T39 (0.0062 RON); construction CPA_F (0.0046 RON); services within technological information, computer services—CPA_J62_63 (0.0039 RON). 1 LEU of generated output at the level of this sector implies an input of 0.3212 RON to these ten areas and 0.369 RON at the economic level.

On the other side, the outputs of the sector are the inputs of other sectors, the most significant ten influences being presented in the following graph: (Fig. 5)

The main contributions of the hospitality industry (or HoReCa—hotels, restaurants, catering) are evaluated through technical coefficients, and they are found at the level of the following areas: activities of tourism agencies and tour operators; other services of reservations and touristic support—CPA_N79 (0.0502 RON); air transport—CPA_H51 (0.0342 RON); public safety administration; social insurance of

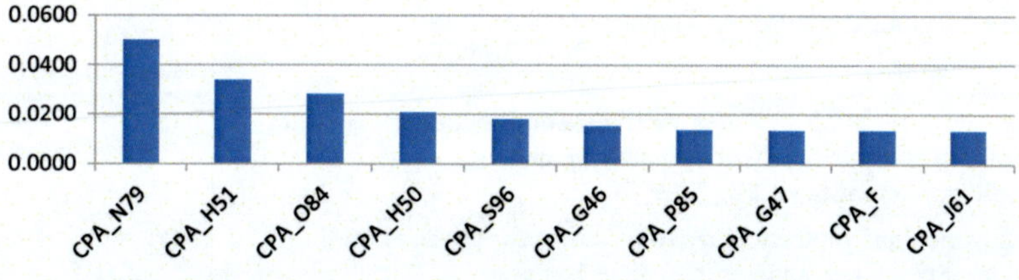

Fig. 5 Ten main sectors-output. *Source* calculations based on INSSE data

the public system—CPA_O84 (0.0284 RON); water transport—CPA_H50 (0.0207 RON); other service activities CPA_S96 (0.0182 RON); trade with exception to car and motorcycle trade CPA_G46 (0.0154 RON); educational system CPA_P85 (0.0139 RON) retail, with exception to cars and motorcycles—CPA_G47 (0.0138 RON), construction—CPA_F (0.0137 RON), RON telecommunications CPA_J61 (0.0134 RON).

(b) ***Activities of tourism agencies and tour operators; other reservation and tourism support services***

The ten main areas which provide inputs in the tourism industry are presented in the following graph: (Fig. 6) (Table 1)

1 RON of output generated at the level of industry implies an input of 0.4115 RON from ten areas and 0.607 RON at the economic level.

The tourism agencies, other services of reservations, and touristic support are materialized in inputs of different areas, the ten main influences being presented in the following graph: (Fig. 7) (Table 2)

To analyze the interconnection of the considered sectors, two multipliers are determined: ***Backward multipliers*** (from the perspective of demand) and ***Forward multipliers*** (from the perspective of supply) (Table 3).

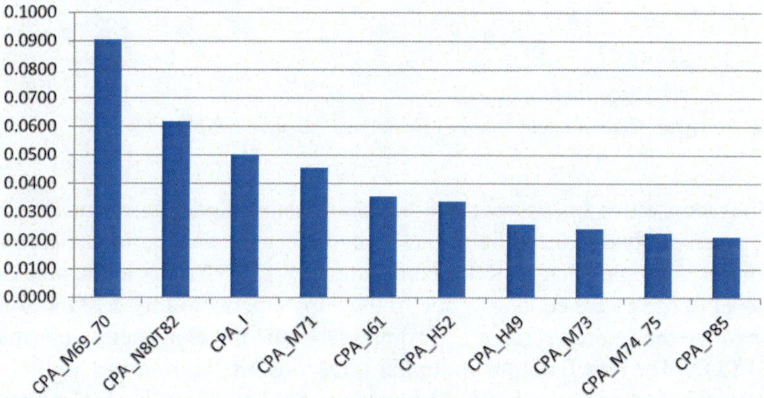

Fig. 6 Ten main areas of the industry's providers. *Source* calculations based on INSSE data

Table 1 Technical coefficient—input

Sector—input	Technical coefficient
Legal and accounting activities, Activities of directorates (central), centralized administrative offices; management and management consultancy activities—CPA_M69_70	0.0905
Investigation and protection activities, Landscaping and building services, Secretarial, support, and other business activities—CPA_N80T82	0.0618
Hotels and other accommodation, restaurants, and other foodservice activities—CPA_I	0.0502
Architectural and engineering activities; testing and technical analysis activities—CPA_M71	0.0456
Telecommunications—CPA_J61	0.0356
Storage and ancillary transport activities—CPA_H52	0.0338
Land and pipeline transport—CPA_H49	0.0257
Advertising and market research—CPA_M73	0.0241
Other professional, scientific, and technical activities; Veterinary activities—CPA_M74_75	0.0227
Educational system—CPA_P85	0.0214

Source calculations based on INSSE data

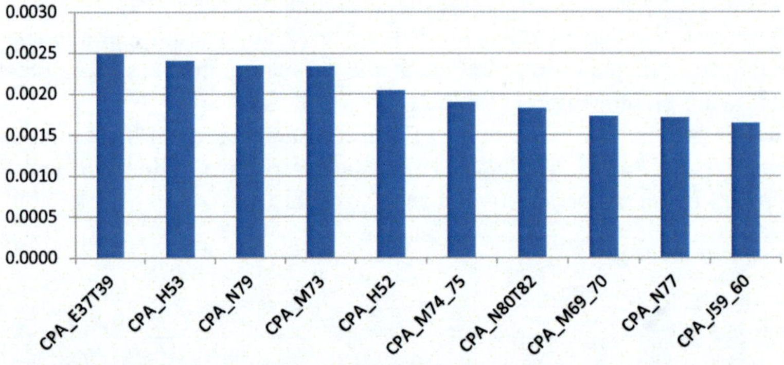

Fig. 7 Ten main sectors-output. *Source* calculations based on INSSE data

The comparative analysis of the indicators reveals a higher impact on the pandemic sector than the one induced before it. Thus, before the pandemic, the type I output multiplier highlights that HoReCa contributes with 1.672 RON to the total output at the level of the entire economy, due to the supplementation by 1 RON of the final demand for the offered services. In comparison, the travel agencies contribute with 2.031 RON. The type II output multiplier is responsible for the direct, indirect effects and those induced due to the supplementation by 1 RON of the final demand from a specific branch on the total output at the level of the entire economy. In the case

Table 2 Technical coefficient—output

Sector—output	Technical coefficient
Wastewater collection and treatment, waste collection, treatment, and disposal; recyclable materials recovery activities; Decontamination activities and services—CPA_E37T39	0.00249
Postal and courier activities—CPA_H53	0.00241
Activities of travel agencies and tour operators; other reservation services and tourist assistance—CPA_N79	0.00235
Advertising and market research activities—CPA_M73	0.00234
Storage and ancillary transport activities—CPA_H52	0.00204
Other professional, scientific, and technical activities, Veterinary activities—CPA_M74_75	0.00190
Investigation and protection activities, Landscaping and building services, Secretarial, support, and other business activities—CPA_N80T82	0.00183
Legal and accounting activities, Activities of directorates (central), centralized administrative offices; management and management consultancy activities—CPA_M69_70	0.00173
Rental and leasing activities—CPA_N77	0.00172
Film, video, and television production activities; audio recordings and music editing activities, broadcasting and broadcasting activities—CPA_J59_60	0.00165

Source calculations based on INSSE data

Table 3 Backward multipliers impact analysis

CAEN CODE	Before COVID-19			During COVID-19		
	Type I output multiplier	Type II output multiplier	Induced effects	Type I output multiplier	Type II output multiplier	Induced effects
*55 + 56**	1.672	2.188	0.516	1.7657932	2.3092995	0.5435063
*79**	2.031	2.608	0.577	2.0987994	2.7197788	0.6209794

* 55 + 56 —Hotels and other accommodation, Restaurants, and other foodservice activities
*79—Activities of travel agencies and tour operators; other reservation services and tourist assistance
Source calculations based on INSSE data

of HoReCa, the type II output multiplier is 2.188 RON, of which the value of 1.672 RON is related to the direct and indirect effects of the services provided and 0.516 RON to the induced effects. For travel agencies, the type II output multiplier is 2.608 RON, of which the value of 2.031 RON is generated by direct and indirect impacts and 0.577 RON by the induced effects. During the pandemic, the changes registered in the demand for tourism services determine values of the type I output multiplier of 1.7657932 RON—HoReCa, respectively, of 2.0987994 RON—travel agencies. The

Table 4 Income multiplier

CAEN CODE	Before COVID-19				During COVID-19			
	Direct effects	Indirect effects	Induced effects	Type II multiplier	Direct effects	Indirect effects	Induced effects	Type II multiplier
55 + 56	0.1663	0.1027	0.0616	0.3305	0.1443	0.1192	0.0768	0.3404
79	0.1090	0.1917	0.0688	0.3696	0.0954	0.2057	0.0878	0.3889

Source calculations based on INSSE data

type II output multiplier is 2.3093 RON for HoReCa, of which the value of 1.7658 RON is related to the direct and indirect effects of the services provided and 0.5435 RON to the induced effects. The travel agencies register a value of 2.7198 RON of the type II output multiplier, of which 2.0988 RON is generated by the direct and indirect impact and 0.6210 RON by the induced effects.

The output multiplier can be calculated in terms of income, gross value-added, and employment, highlighting the impact of changing demand by 1 RON for a particular sector on each variable considered (Table 4).

Deepening the analysis also highlights the increase in the impact of the change in demand for services in the sectors considered in the pandemic, compared to the period before it. Before the pandemic, the value of the income multiplier for HoReCa reveals that at an additional 1 RON of the final demand for such services, the incomes of all employees in the economy will increase by 0.3305 RON, of which: 0.269 RON represents the increase of workers' incomes both from hotels and restaurants (direct effect of 0.1663 RON), and from the industries with which this sector of activity interconnects (indirect effect of 0.1027 RON), and 0.0616 RON represents an induced effect. For travel agencies, an additional 1 RON of demand generates an increase of 0.3696 RON in the income of all employees in the economy, of which: 0.3007 RON represents the increase in income of workers in the sector (direct effect of 0.1090 RON), as well as from the industries with which this activity sector is interconnected (indirect effect of 0.1917 RON), and 0.0688 RON represents an induced effect. As a result of the pandemic, the income multiplier values reveal that all employees' incomes will change by 0.3404 RON to a change by 1 RON of the final demand for services for HoReCa and by 0.3889 RON in the case of travel agencies. There is a change in structure, increasing the impact-induced in other branches of the economy. Thus, although the sectors have a low share in GDP, the impacts they generate multiply in the economy (Table 5).

Before the pandemic, at an additional 1 RON of the final demand for HoReCa services, the gross value-added multiplier is 0.96 RON, generated directly by this sector (0.47 RON), indirectly by the sectors with which the HoReCa industry is interconnected (0.28 RON), as well as the induced effect of all sectors of the economy that can determine the additional increase of consumption in this sector of activity (0.20 RON). The effect induced during the pandemic remains relatively constant, with a structural change, by increasing the impact in other branches of the economy.

Table 5 Gross value-added multiplier

CAEN CODE	Before COVID-19				During COVID-19			
	Direct effects	Indirect effects	Induced effects	Type II multiplier	Direct effects	Indirect effects	Induced effects	Type II multiplier
55 + 56	0.47	0.28	0.20	0.96	0.4116	0.3261	0.2316	0.9692
79	0.34	0.45	0.23	1.02	0.2999	0.4923	0.2645	1.0568

Source calculations based on INSSE data

For travel agencies, the value of the multiplier, before the pandemic, is 1.02 RON, of which 0.34 RON corresponds to the direct effects in this sector, the value of 0.45 RON is generated indirectly by the industries with which the sector is interconnected, and 0.23 RON represents the induced effect of all sectors of the economy that may lead to further growth in consumption in this sector of activity. The incidence is amplified during the pandemic, with the same exacerbation of the other economic branches' multiplier effect.

Forward Multipliers Impact Analysis

The analysis of the impact of the total production's increase from the considered sectors on the whole supply for all the other economy's sectors, which use the products from HoReCa and the travel agencies as inputs in their production processes, supposes the calculation of the forward multipliers (Table 6).

During the pandemic, the output multiplier highlights that a change in supply by 1 RON in the HoReCa sector generates an output of the entire economy of 2.378 RON, of which 1.570 RON is the type I multiplier and 0.808 RON is the induced effect. Overall, the effect is more significant than the period before the pandemic, increasing incidences in other branches of the economy. In travel agencies, the value of the output multiplier is 1.251 RON, of which the value of 1.061 RON is related to the type I multiplier and 0.191 RON to the induced effect. The impact in the crisis is smaller (Table 7).

The value of the employee income multiplier registered by HoReCa during the pandemic highlights the fact that when the supply changes by 1 RON, the income of employees in the economy changes by 0.456 RON, of which: 0.144 RON at the

Table 6 Forward multipliers

CAEN CODE	Before COVID-19			During COVID-19		
	Type I output multiplier	Type II output multiplier	Induced effects	Type I output multiplier	Type II output multiplier	Induced effects
55 + 56	1.766	2.309	0.544	1.570	2.378	0.808
79	2.099	2.720	0.621	1.061	1.251	0.191

Source calculations based on INSSE data

Table 7 Income multiplier

COD CAEN	Before COVID-19				During COVID-19			
	Direct effects	Indirect effects	Induced effects	Type II multiplier	Direct effects	Indirect effects	Induced effects	Type II multiplier
55 + 56	0.144	0.119	0.077	0.340	0.144	0.113	0.199	0.456
79	0.095	0.206	0.088	0.389	0.095	0.011	0.047	0.153

Source calculations based on INSSE data

Table 8 Gross value-added multiplier

COD CAEN	Before COVID-19				During COVID-19			
	Direct effects	Indirect effects	Induced effects	Type II multiplier	Direct effects	Indirect effects	Induced effects	Type II multiplier
55 + 56	0.4742	0.321	0.381	1.176	0.4118	0.249	0.385	1.046
79	0.3427	0.032	0.090	0.464	0.2991	0.027	0.091	0.417

Source calculations based on INSSE data

level of income within the sector, 0.113 RON income of sectors using as inputs the services in the sector, and 0.199 RON the induced effect for the other sectors of the economy. The effect is more significant compared to that generated in the period before the pandemic. If the direct effect is kept constant (usually, the labor force is remunerated with an income close to the minimum wage in the economy), the induced effect increases.

For travel agencies, the total effect on the economy is 0.153 RON, lower than previously recorded (Table 8).

Before the pandemic, the supplement with 1 RON of the HoReCa offer determines an increase of the gross value added at the level of the entire economy of 1.176 RON, of which: the amount of 0.4742 RON represents the value generated directly in this industry, 0.321 RON represents the value registered in the sectors the industry is interconnected, and 0.381 RON represents the induced effect. The impact is much lower in the case of travel agencies (0.464 RON). During the pandemic, the change in the supply of services on gross value-added decreases at the analyzed sectors' level.

4 Results and Discussions: The Impact of the COVID-19 Pandemic on the Industry

The tourism industry in 2020 has been strongly affected by restrictions on the activity and movement of people, as response to the pandemic, and the consumer's new behavior, generated by awareness of the risk of contamination.

To evaluate the impact of COVID-19 on the analyzed sectors, we propose the following impact matrix, developed on two main axes (Fig. 8).

Based on this matrix, we will place the sector's activity according to the impact and the related operation on four areas: Green, Yellow, Orange, and Red, with the substantiation of some measures accordingly.

4.1 Social Impact

Measures to restrict HoReCa activities have led to a massive suspension of the employment contracts. Firstly, on 30.03.2020, they represented 18.1% of the total of individual suspended employment contracts, the sector being one of the first affected. On May 5, 2020, their share decreased to 12.3%, in the context of a continuous increase but at a lower rate of individual employment contracts suspended in the field than the entire economy. On June 16, 2020, their share increased to 23.1%, in the context of a continuous increase but at a higher rate of individual employment contracts suspended in the field than the entire economy. In the same time, another

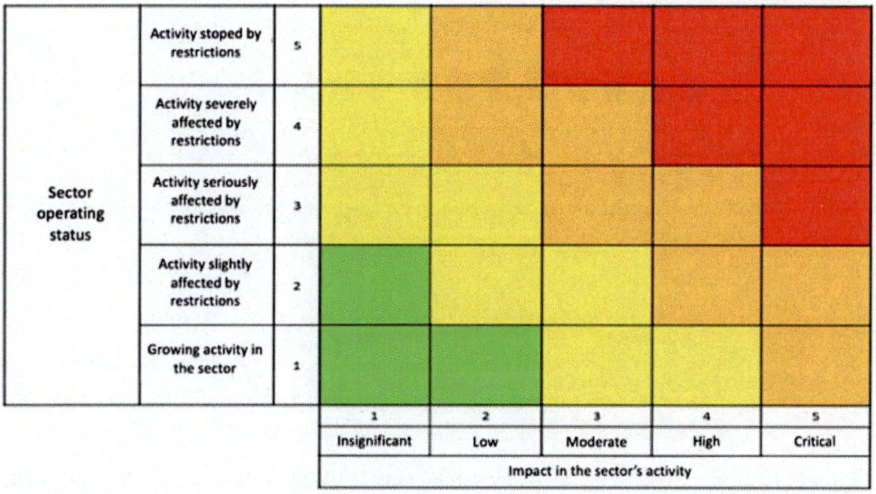

Fig. 8 Impact Matrix. *Source* Realized by the authors

measure was the closure of some individual employment contracts. Correlating with the share of the sector in GDP, we can mention a significant discrepancy.

Specific to the tertiary sector, the activity in hotels and restaurants involves a large workforce, with a differentiated level of qualification depending on the type of unit, classification, and quality of services provided. The average gross monthly earnings in hotels and restaurants are lower than the average in the economy, registering a ratio of 0.56 in February 2020.

These measures' social impact is amplified by the high seasonality of the activity, which involves a large number of individual employment contracts signed for a short period. As a result, at the beginning of the lockdown period, a significant number of workers were already unemployed.

The socio-human dimension of these activities must also be included in the social impact assessment of COVID-19. Tourism, by its nature, has an impact on the quality of life of both tourists and the local population. Tourism satisfies people's need for relaxation, recreation, affecting his productive capacity.

4.2 Economic Impact

The impact of the crisis generated by COVID-19 on this sector can be highlighted by the evolution of arrivals and employment over the last 16 months (Figs. 9, 10).

Analyzing the monthly situations (March to June) in terms of the number of arrivals in accommodation units—total, of which Romanians and foreigners—in the last three years, we can also see the drastic decrease in tourist traffic in this period compared to the same period of previous two years (Fig. 11).

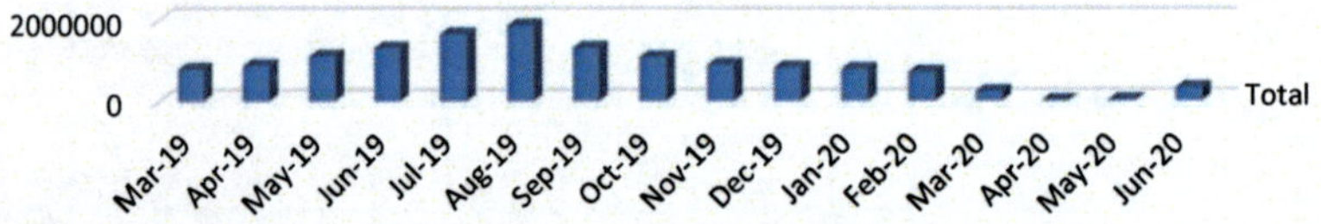

Fig. 9 Monthly evolution of tourist arrivals in the accommodation units 2019–2020. *Source* INS, data series 2019–2020

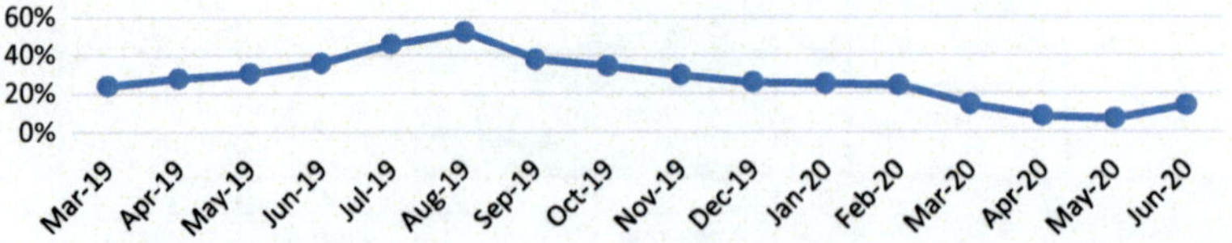

Fig. 10 Occupancy rate of the accommodation units 2019–2020. *Source* INS, data series 2019–2020

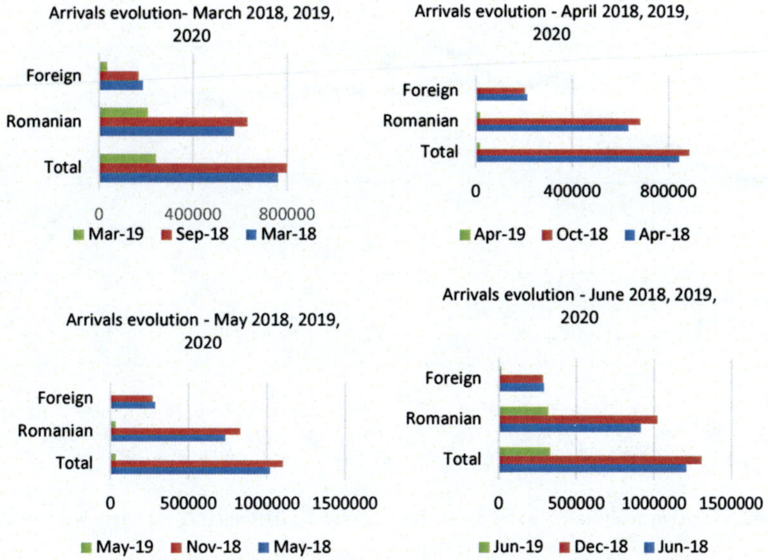

Fig. 11 Monthly arrivals evolution between 2018 and 2020. *Source* INS, data series 2018–2020

In the restaurant sector, the activity was stopped for several months in the first part of 2020, and even if they turn to specific home delivery or drive-in activities, the economic impact was major.

The impact on travel agencies can be seen in the value of turnover, the number of employees and companies in the sector, in the volume of activity, and in the number of customers affected. At the same time, the impact is also given by the need for customers to reimburse the amounts paid (used by tour operators to book packages and early booking offers, amounts that have been already used by airlines, hotels, or other suppliers). Thus, the sums' reimbursement puts the travel agencies between the clients who want the sums back and the hotels and airlines that propose instead providing some tourist services in the future.

The hotel and restaurant sectors can also be analyzed in terms of supply chain partnerships. HoReCa sector is supplied through several channels: suppliers, distributors, large retailers, retailers, and online orders. Taking into account the last one and a half year, we can make considerations using the chart below, which represents the percentage evolution of sales (August 2019 represents 100%) (Fig. 12).

In the context in which the activity in HoReCa was restricted only to home delivery orders and to online commerce, corroborated with the mutations in the family supply basket, a decrease of up to 90% can be considered for beverages, but an increase for water, vegetables, and staple foods, which led to an average reduction of sales to HoReCa by only about 65% in the case of large distribution.

Based on the proposed analysis methodology, we consider that the three sectors are in the RED impact area within the impact matrix, with a major risk of bankruptcy.

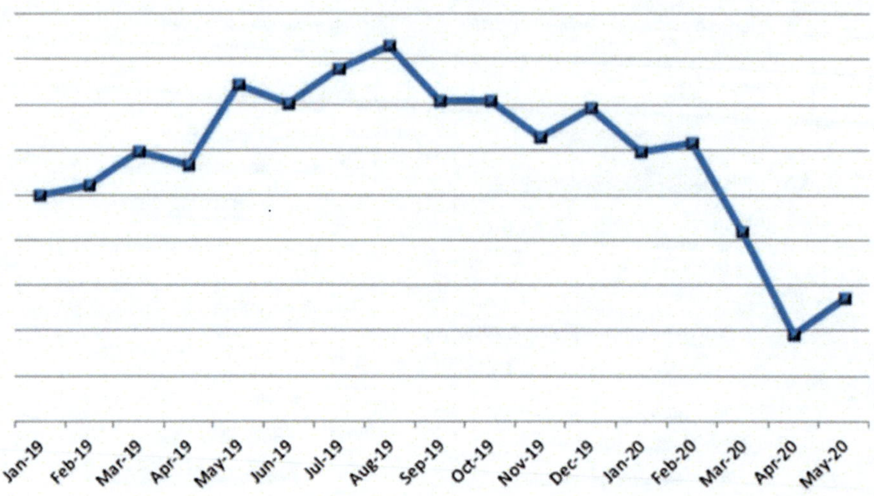

Fig. 12 Relative evolution of sales for HoReCa (August 2019 = 100%). *Source* Nielsen Consumer LLC

- *Hotels.* The impact on hotels is felt both by banning the activities of their restaurants and by organizing events. Also, the movement of spa tourism was suspended. We believe that although the actions of hotels were not banned, the impact was significant.
- *Restaurants.* The activity of serving and consuming food and alcoholic and non-alcoholic beverages, organized by restaurants, cafes, or other public places, in the spaces intended for this purpose inside or outside the location was prohibited through the first administrative decisions in March 2020. Moreover, the closure of the shopping centers' activity implicitly affects the restaurants' delivery activities.
- *Travel agencies.* The impact on travel agencies has been critical due to pressure from tourists to reimburse the value of travel packages already booked. Moreover, a series of traffic restrictions and the fear of the pandemic supported the crisis in this sector.

Consequently, the state was affected by decreasing the VAT and other taxes collection, and increasing budget expenditures. For providers, late payments or non-payments, as well as other bottlenecks, have been strong negative effects. And last but not least, the customers have suffered by the travel restrictions, difficult health rules, financial constraints, but also illness risks (Figs. 1, 2, 3, 4, 5 and 6).

Some urgent measures have been taken with a short-term impact. The government decided to support SMEs with a specific financial program (INVEST ROMANIA), helping also all companies and employees with some financial facilities. The companies from HoReCa and travel sectors tried to adapt the business models to this specific crisis, reducing activities, the operational costs, rents, or even close some units, negotiations with financial-banking institutions to ensure the necessary liquidity, new strategic partnerships (e.g., between hotels or restaurants and hospitals), etc.

5 Proposed Measures to Reduce the Effects of COVID-19 and to Restart the Sector in the Short and Medium Terms

Following the impact matrix mentioned earlier, we can develop a scenario matrix, which includes two coordinates (Figs. 7, 8, 9, 10, 11, 12 and 13):

- positioning the sector within the impact matrix;
- estimating the level and speed of support measures: authorities, funding, or own resources (Fig. 13).

Thus, 12 scenarios are starting from 0.1—the most critical impact level (Red zone) and low level of support measures, to 3.3—the lowest impact level (Green area) and high level of support measures (Tables 1, 2, 3, 4, 5, 6, 7 and 8):

Further, considering the effects of the economic and social pandemic on the analyzed sectors, briefly highlighted above, and considering the degree of urgency with which recovery measures should be taken, we can place: the *hotel sector in Scenario 0.2*, *restaurant sector in Scenario 0.1*, and *travel sector also in Scenario 0.1*.

Measures proposed at the Government level

A. Measures for the employees:

- modification of the contribution period of at least 12 months in the last 24 months before the date of registration of the application to benefit from unemployment benefit for 2020–2021 (Implementation: EMERGENCY ORDINANCE No. 70 of 14 May 2020. Limit: persons unemployed at the decree of these emergency states—especially those employed in the hotels on the coast—cannot benefit from this provision);
- granting insertion incentives to HoReCa companies to maintain jobs after returning from technological unemployment for the period 2020–2021 (Implementation: Emergency Ordinance No. 92 of May 28, 2020. Limit: disadvantage of companies whose activities are still restricted to 1.06.2020,

	Impact				
	Impact zones	0	1	2	3
Level and speed of support measures: authorities, funding, or own resources	Low Level	0.1	1.1	2.1	3.1
	Medium Level	0.2	1.2	2.2	3.2
	High Level	0.3	1.3	2.3	3.3

Fig. 13 Scenario matrix for hotel, restaurant, and travel sectors. *Source* Realized by the authors

in that the ordinance stipulates that companies that have portfolios of activities, of which at least one is subject to restrictions established by the competent authorities, will choose either to apply the active measure of a settlement of part of the salary or to pay technical unemployment from June 1, 2020; the treatment activity was restricted until June 14, 2020);
- introduction of a mixed employer-state remuneration system (salary and compensation for income reduction) in case of reduction of work schedule (Implementation: Emergency Ordinance no. 132/2020).

B. Measures about support activities:

- holiday vouchers for 2020; investments in general infrastructure; investments in specific infrastructure; elaboration of a plan for promotion for a minimum of five years of the destination Romania; promoting domestic tourism, as well as incoming, through sustained campaigns but also through fiscal facilities; promoting the forms of ecotourism, rural tourism, health tourism (spa, medical), cultural tourism, cycling, mountain tourism; grants for resilience projects, but also for investments in digitization; supporting the financing, through European funds, of investment projects in sustainable development at the level of tourism economic agents and local administrations; supporting the implementation of ecological certification systems for accommodation units and destinations; continuing to provide holiday vouchers, encouraging travel in the off-season; encouraging the process of setting up the DMOs; supporting dual education; supporting food waste reduction campaigns/projects.

C. Measures regarding taxes, duties, and other fiscal obligations:

- extension of the term of application of the provisions regarding the postponement of the payment of the specific tax in case of issuing measures restricting the activity of HoReCa after leaving the state of emergency (Implementation: Emergency Ordinance no. 99/25.06.2020. Limits: lack of coherence of the legislative act, there is a period for which the facility is not granted (15.05.2020–24.06.2020), granting bonuses for the advance payment of tax obligations, for 2020 (Implementation: Emergency Ordinance no. 33/2020, Emergency Ordinance no. 99/2020), compensation of allowances for sick leave to be recovered with the due contributions, but also with other fiscal obligations exemption from social insurance contributions in case of compensatory incomes insured by the state.

D. Various measures

- granting allowances to persons who do not benefit from unemployment benefits or other compensatory income (individuals who obtain income from the transfer of the use of goods, respectively, from renting rooms located in personal property, having a capacity for tourist accommodation between one and 5 rooms including those that derive income from independent activities, respectively, from the rental for tourist purposes of the rooms located in privately owned dwellings, with an accommodation capacity of more than 5 rooms for rent, as well as travel agencies—guides).

Measures proposed for the large companies

- *Objectives*: diversifying the offer to increase the attractiveness, preventing the spread of COVID-19, maintaining employees, streamlining supply management and reducing costs, maintaining customers, reducing cash flow deficits, presenting the entity and tourist products offered, stimulating demand, differentiating the tourist product, influencing consumer behavior.
- *Measures*: adaptation of the tourist offer—intern tours and destinations; reconfiguration of tourist service packages; investments in high-performance cleaning and hygiene systems; digitization (for check-in, room access, reservation, check-out, payment, etc.); reconfiguration of spa activities, treatment that involves collective procedures; implementation of ecological and food hygiene certification systems (HACCP, for example); reconfiguration of serving spaces; reconfiguration (redesign) of the meal service (probably the elimination of the Swedish buffet), development of the roomservice; flexibility of personnel policy; adoption of "resilience" measures after the period of technical unemployment; shortening the supply chain and using local suppliers; continuity in communication with customers; issuing vouchers to customers who have purchased service packages during the period for which the state of emergency was declared or in the immediately following period, provided that there are no provisions regarding the date of resumption of activity; investments in the development of the tourist offer; promotion; public–private partnerships.

Measures proposed for SMEs and households

- *Objectives*: diversification of the offer to increase the degree of attractiveness; capital infusion to support the investment processes and to finance the current activity; capital infusion to develop the tourist offer; preventing the spread of COVID-19, making the reservation system more flexible, maintaining employees, maintaining customers, reducing cash flow deficits; presentation of the entity and tourist products offered, stimulation of demand, differentiation of the tourist product, influencing consumer behavior, neutralization of negative information; integrated destination development; promotion.
- *Measures*: diversification of activity; recourse to loans for investments and working capital, guaranteed by the state—SME INVEST ROMANIA Program; EU funding; promoting tourist activities in nature; programs for small groups of tourists; integrated reservation systems (in the pension network, for example); implementation of ecological certification and food hygiene systems (HACCP, for example); reconfiguration of serving spaces; reconfiguration (redesign) of the meal service (probably the elimination of the Swedish buffet), development of the roomservice; reconfiguration of spa activities, treatment that involves collective procedures; flexibility of personnel policy; adoption of "resilience" measures after the period of technical unemployment; emphasis on cleanliness and hygiene; continuity in communication with customers; issuing vouchers to customers

who have purchased service packages during the period for which the state of emergency was declared or in the immediately following period, provided that there are no provisions regarding the date of resumption of activity; promotion; public–private partnerships.

6 Conclusions

The tourism industry has experienced significant growth in recent years, which is based on many reasons. Thus, tourism is an activity that has facilitated global economic growth; many governments have considered tourism a growing sector, providing jobs; tourist flows were directly proportional to the quality of life in each state; gradually, global tourism has become accessible to all social classes (by diversifying low-cost travel, price reductions, etc.).

In the current context, the emergence of the new COVID-19 coronavirus has led to the rapid and brutal decline of tourism, making it the most affected industry in the world. The reduction of the tourist activity in Romania, as it was demonstrated in our study, was in line with the trends registered worldwide, respectively, a decrease of about 70%, on average, in the analyzed sectors. More, a noticeable effect of this situation will be the change in tourists' behavioral habits, as soon as the restrictions are reduced and travel will be resumed.

As a consequence of the multiplier effect of tourism, many companies have reached or will go bankrupt, encouraging an increase in the sector's concentration around international players who have liquidity and can resort to market repositioning.

Therefore, to limit this pandemic's negative effects, synchronizing the efforts of the state and the private environment is the best option. These measures must refer to employment, support for business, and, last but not least, the adoption of temporary decisions on taxes, duties, or other fiscal obligations.

The limits of this study are related to the period in which we did the research, respectively, April–July 2020, with the data available at that time. The effects of the pandemic can be analyzed in more depth on the basis of complete statistical information recorded at the end of 2020 and perhaps even at the end of 2021, as the effects of the pandemic on tourism and the economy in general are far from over at this time, just like the pandemic itself. Our study can be continued in another year or maybe two, in order to better see the immediate effects of the pandemic, but also of the measures taken quickly in this field.

References

Altuntas, F., Gok, M.S.: The effect of COVID-19 pandemic on domestic tourism: A DEMATEL. Int. J. Hosp. Manag. (2021)

Collins-Kreiner, N., Ram, Y.: National tourism strategies during the covid-19 pandemic. Ann. Tour. Res. (2020)
Duro, J.A., Perez-Laborda, A., Turrion-Prats, J., Fernandez, M.: Covid-19 and tourism vulnerability. Tour. Manag. Perspect. (2021)
Karabuluta, G., Huseyin, B.M., Demirc, E., Dokerd, A.C.: How pandemics affect tourism: international evidence. Ann. Tour. Res. (2020)
World Travel and Tourism Council (WTTC) and G20 2020 Saudi Arabia: 100 Million Jobs Recovery Plan Final Proposal. Saudi Arabia (2020)

Romania's International Trade in Goods After the COVID-19 Crisis: Where to? An Empirical Investigation Based on Granger Causality Analysis

Paraschiv Dorel Mihai, Davidescu Adriana AnaMaria, Popovici Oana Cristina, and Gerard Cazabat

1 Introduction

Seen as a minor threat at the end of 2019, the Covid-19 virus soon engulfed the whole world and only three months after China has officially reported the several cases of pneumonia caused by a novel coronavirus, it generated measures hard to imagine before, which restricted free movement and led to the closure of manufacturing and of a large part of the economic activity. The pandemic has severely affected the global economy and daily life (Baicu et al. 2020). Globalization at its highest was hardly hit, vulnerabilities being exposed, while the largest economic drop in the last 40 years (IMF 2020), altogether with the most difficult health crisis were experienced. The crisis had asymmetrical impact on industries (Staszkiewicz et al. 2020) and, like any other crisis, will generate lasting consequences for a vast number of sectors. Among them, international trade was one of the most affected and it is also envisaged to be shaped by important alterations.

P. D. Mihai (✉) · D. A. AnaMaria · P. O. Cristina
Bucharest University of Economic Studies, Bucharest, Romania
e-mail: dorel.paraschiv@ase.ro

D. A. AnaMaria
e-mail: adriana.alexandru@csie.ase.ro

P. O. Cristina
e-mail: oana.popovici@rei.ase.ro

D. A. AnaMaria
National Research Institute for Labor & Social Protection, Bucharest, Romania

P. O. Cristina
Institute for Economic Forecasting, Romanian Academy, Bucharest, Romania

G. Cazabat
EDC Paris Business School, Courbevoie, France
e-mail: gerard.cazabat@edcparis.edu

A. M. Dima et al. (eds.), *Economic Recovery After COVID-19*, Springer Proceedings in Business and Economics, https://doi.org/10.1007/978-3-030-86641-9_6

International trade was affected by the containment measures which included the closure of the borders, the reduction of the transport activity or restrictions on trade. In addition, the development of international trade based on global production networks or global supply chains had a supplementary effect in quantifying the impact of the pandemic (Fonseca and Azevedo 2020). Literature evidence that the actual crisis was different than the one in 2008–2009 because it generated not only a shock in demand, where uncertainty affected the economic agents' behavior, but also a shock in supply, exacerbated by the lockdown policies and after that by the contagion which spread all over the supply chains (IFC 2020) due to spill-over effect (Brinca et al. 2020). Saif et al. (2021, p. 6) describes the actual crisis as a "hybrid supply–demand shock generating domino effect", while Baldwin and Tomiura (2020), Friedt and Zhang (2020) and Kejžar et al. (2021) point towards the "triple pandemic effect" related to trade, as a consequence of the reverberations on supply, demand and value chains shocks. In order for Romanian micro and small businesses to better cope with the disruption created by the Covid-19 pandemic, they must, first and foremost, demonstrate openness to production innovation and adaptability to new demand, as well as provide strong support for customers and communities (Păunescu and Mátyus 2020).

This paper analyzes the evolution of Romania's exports and imports during the development of Covid-19 crisis, in an analysis of monthly data since the beginning of 2020. Romania is integrated in global value chains, the automotive industry being one of the most important sector for the economy. The paper begins with a brief literature review related to the consequences of the measures taken at domestic and international level on international trade. This provide the opportunity to further place the evolutions in Romania in the global context and to identify the medium and long term expected transformations. We then assess the evolution in the trade of goods in Romania and make comparison with the evolution of international trade during the actual crisis and the one in 2008–2009. Back then, Romania had the opportunity of a quick recovery in exports, which also influenced the restoration of the whole economic activity. Based on that, we can draw a picture of actual evolutions and risks.

In the context of Romania's integration in the global value chains, high trade dependence with the EU market, and increasing importance of China's as a supplier for the Central and Eastern European countries, we are interested in investigating the relationship between Romanian exports and EU imports and exports of goods and services using the Granger causality analysis. In this aim, we perform a VECM analysis using quarterly data from 2000 until 2019.

2 Measures and Consequences Affecting International Trade as a Result of the Covid-19 Pandemic

Starting with March 2020 and even earlier in China, countries in the European Union (EU) resorted to lockdown and social distancing measures, which affected both supply and demand in each economy and which subsequently influenced the performance in international trade. Demand was affected by a more cautious behavior of both consumers, which oriented towards savings, and companies, which delayed their investments, due to uncertainty, while public spending patterns were affected (Gruszczynski 2020; Saif et al. 2021). Supply was hit by the closure of factories following containment measures, which further affected manufacturing in the other countries integrated in global value chains. Estimates at the beginning of the pandemic showed that almost one fifth of global trade in intermediate goods originated in China (Milea 2020). Therefore, the reduction of China's supply of intermediate goods also had a major impact on the global economy, given its importance in world trade (Vidya and Prabheesh 2020). This have led to the closure of factories in North America, Europe and the rest of Asia, due to shortage of supplies (ECLAC 2020). Moreover, EU is one of the most affected economies, according to UNCTAD (2020). A drop in the production of intermediate goods in China highly impact the sectors of construction, equipment, cars and chemicals.

Shutdown and lockdown measures led, in a first instance, to a shortage of resources and inputs. Secondly, commodities were confronted with an increase in prices (Saif et al. 2021). These factors affected the domestic capacity of production which further resulted in lower capacity to export. Vidya and Prabheesh (2020) describe a global production network that characterized international trade, which include trade diversification, production fragmentation and a multitude of intermediaries intervening in the production of the final good. In fact, global value chains are responsible for the reduction of the average real GDP downturn by a quarter, according to Bonadio et al. (2020), while IFC (2020) goes further and describe a "contagion" of such networks. In a gravity model including final goods trade in the EU countries, Kejžar et al. (2021) establish that the transmission channels for the shocks generated by the pandemic were mostly caused by the position of a certain country in the supply chain. Therefore, increase of Covid-19 incidence affected the exports toward countries which were positioned downstream in the global supply chain, which further determined a decrease in imports. The role of the Central and Eastern European countries in the global value chains (GVC), among which Romania, is to provide mostly advanced manufacturing and business services exports (World Bank 2020). Therefore, they were caught in the middle, strongly depending on both the demand of older EU Member States specialized in innovative and sophisticated GVC, and on the supply of inputs from factories located in countries such as China. At the same time, they were also confronted with social distance measure. This vicious circle strongly affected their performance in trade.

Soon after the first set of containment measures, several countries turned to export prohibitions and restrictions, given the need to secure medical and food supplies

(Gruszczynski 2020; Saif et al. 2021). The closure of free trade agreement fell into the background, prioritizing the resources towards supporting the epidemiological situation, even in the EU (Milea 2020).

Reorientation and readjustment of the supply chains may follow (OECD 2020), as the need of having production facilities closer to the sale market and more regionally diversified was highlighted during this crisis. Not only US (Gruszczynski 2020), but also European countries (Baldwin and Tomiura 2020) envisage such a solution in the near future, which could be helpful in eliminating supply shortages. Given the strong international trade in intermediate goods, a change in the pattern of global imports and exports might appear. Vidya and Prabheesh (2020) show that we assist at changes in the structure of the trade network, characterized by an important reduction of trade interconnectedness as a result of COVID-19 outbreak. IFC (2020) envisages the emergence of smaller trade hubs, which will reduce the previous long global supply chains. Positive repercussions might appear, as a result, for countries harnessing their competitive advantages, with influence on the reorientation of trade all over the world.

3 The Evolution of International Trade in Romania During the Covid-19 Pandemic

3.1 The Situation in Romania's International Trade Before the Covid-19 Crisis

After the fall of the communism, Romania's trade in goods was enhanced by the opening of the economy and the perspectives of the EU adhesion. A positive and sustained growth rate in both exports and imports could be noticed since the beginning of 2000s (Fig. 1). Before the pandemic, in 2019, the value of exported goods amounted to EUR 63.1 billion, while imports hit EUR 80.1million. The financial crisis in 2008–2009 generated a shock which was reabsorbed in 2010 and, for a

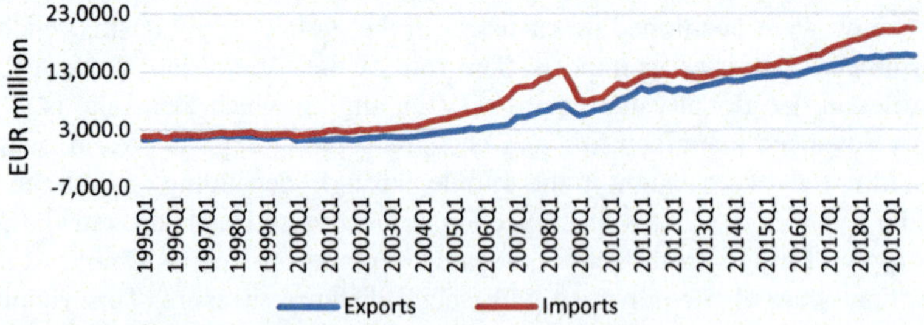

Fig. 1 Romania trade in goods, quarterly data, 1995–2019. *Source* Authors' own elaborations based on Eurostat data

period of five-six years, the trade deficit was under control. In the last two years before the pandemic, the trade deficit burst on the background of a rapid increase in the purchasing power generated by increases in pensions and public wages. The deficit of consumer goods is mainly generated by food goods (National Bank of Romania 2018), although the agricultural potential of the country is one of the most important in the EU. The roots of this situation resides in the lack of investment made in time and a severe fragmentation of agricultural areas.

3.2 Romania's Trade in Goods During the Covid-19 Pandemic

Figure 2 presents the evolution of the exports in goods, in a comparative framework based on the value in 2019 and 2020. The latest available data for 2021, covering the period January-March, are also added. Goods exports started the year of 2020 with higher values than in the previous year, on an ascending trajectory. Exports in January 2020 were 3.2% higher than in the same month of 2019, even better than the debut they had in 2019. However, in the month of February, the global tensions started to be felt in Romania, and the level of exports was only 0.7% higher than in February 2019, a much more reduced increase than in 2019 (when the growth was 8% higher than in February 2018). Lockdown measures in China and in Italy started to be already implemented (Minodo 2021). Since March, there is an acute drop in exports, following the quarantine measure and the emergency state which was adopted in Romania and in all the EU countries, which are Romania's most important trade partners. As a consequence, exports were 11.4% lower in March 2020 than on the same month of the previous year, the negative evolution sharpening until a 47% drop in April. The comeback in May, once with the end of the emergency state, was lower than expected. The gap as compared to the previous year reduced only to 40%. We notice a similar evolution of exports in Romania with the one noted by Minodo (2021) for Spain: the relaxation of the measures taken by the governments reduced the difference as compared to 2019 until 12.9% in June and 5.1% in July. However, in August it increased again to 8%, potentially as a result of new restriction measures taken in some European countries, among which Germany, which is Romania's

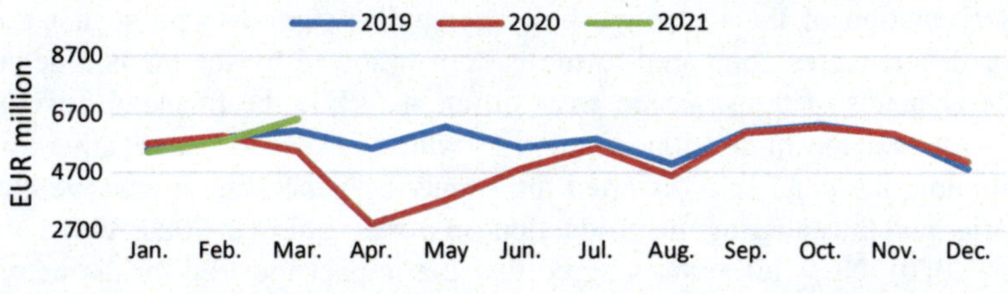

Fig. 2 Romania's monthly exports, 2019-March 2021. *Source* Authors' own elaborations based on National Institute of Statistics data

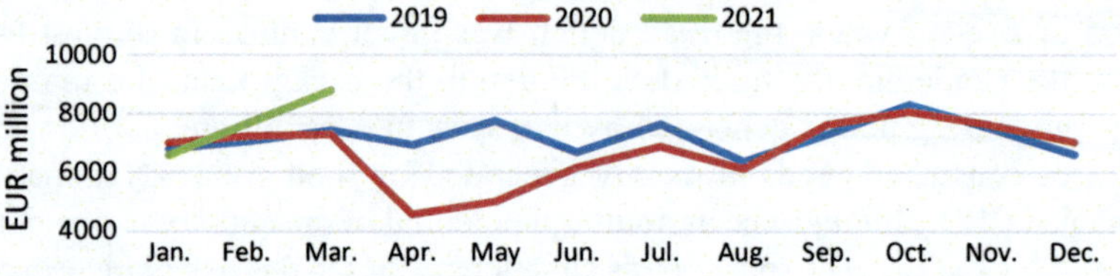

Fig. 3 Romania's monthly imports, 2019-March 2021. *Source* Authors' own elaborations based on National Institute of Statistics data

largest trade partner. After this month, exports started to raise again at the value level in 2019, in December even surpassing by 5% the previous year's value. The start of the year was again weaker than in 2020 in January and February, with values almost similar for 2019. However, a surge of 20.1% was registered for March as compared to the previous year, which could be a good sign for exports' recovery.

A similar evolution, in which a shock generated by the restriction measures during pandemics is noticed, was registered for imports (Fig. 3). The first two months saw a higher volume of imports than the one in 2019, when imports were larger by 3.3% in January and 2.6% in February. The introduction of restriction measures in March brought a brief decline (−1.9%), but the significant drop in imports was recorded for April and May, when the volume was 34% and 35.3% respectively lower on a year-on-year basis. Romanian imports recovered faster than exports. The gap stabilized at around 7.9–9.9% in June and July. After that, it started to return to the values in 2019 or to surpass them, with the exception of August and October. We notice a larger drop in exports of goods than in imports in Romania, which could point towards a decrease of the foreign demand for Romanian goods, meaning that the other economies were harder hit by the crisis than Romania.

4 Comparison with the 2008–2009 Financial Crisis

At the beginning of the pandemic, studies envisaged already that its impact on international trade might be higher than that of the Great Recession in 2008–2009. Yagi and Managi (2021) estimated an economic damage up to 1.4 higher than that of the financial crisis, by analyzing the global supply constraints. Very soon after the implementation of the lockdown policies, studies started to point that there is a major difference as compared to the pattern followed by the crisis a decade ago, as the channels of transmission were different. While the financial crisis affected firstly the demand in developed countries which further led to negative impact on production, the pandemic distorted the supply by generating a massive closure of factories and thus altering the production networks (Baldwin 2020; Vidya and Prabheesh 2020). Now, all authors agree that the impact induced by the actual crisis caused by the pandemic was more significant than the one following the financial crisis in 2008–2009 (Kejžar et al. 2021). Recent analysis confirms the expectations,

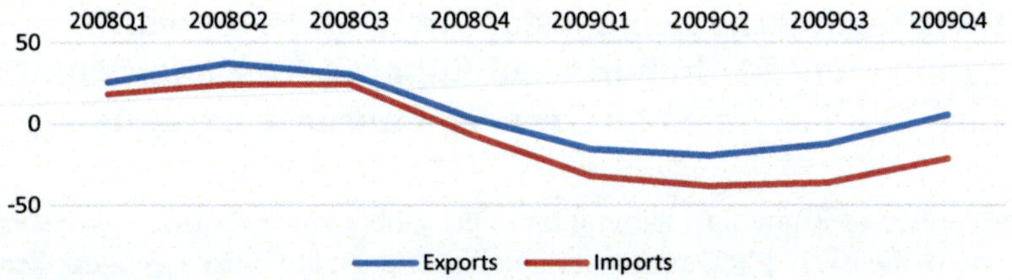

Fig. 4 Year-on-year change in the volume of trade in goods during the financial crisis, Romania. *Source* Authors' own elaborations based on Eurostat data

showing that trade in merchandise dropped by more than 20% in the second quarter of 2020 as compared to the same quarter of 2019 (UNCTAD 2020), when the extent of the decline was only half (10.2%) during the recession at the end of 2008 and the beginning of 2009 (Minodo 2021).

Romania experienced nine months of recession, from the fourth quarter of 2008 until the second quarter of 2009. Figure 4 shows that both exports and imports of merchandise registered a gap as compared to the volumes in the similar period of the previous year starting with the last months of 2008. The decrease has worsened in the second quarter of the crisis, hitting an export reduction of 15.7% in the first part of 2009 and 19.7% in the second quarter of 2009 as compared to the situation in the year before. The reduction in imports was even higher, and was felt since the first quarter of crisis when, at the end of 2008, imports dropped by 6.8% as compared to the similar period a year before. The gap increased significantly, being of 32.1% and 38.3% respectively in the following two quarters of the crisis.

Taking into account the general reduction in trade of goods during the quarters of recession in 2008 and 2009 as compared with the similar period of the previous year, we could notice a drop by 11.2% in exports and 26.3% in imports. Therefore, exports suffered the most drastic reduction during the lockdown months of 2020 than during the financial crisis, but imports had a different evolution. Moreover, if we look at the reduction in imports of goods in the two periods, we can notice a more severe drop in the second quarter of 2009 (38.3%) than during March–May 2020 (23.7%). In addition, imports had a difficult recovery after the financial crisis, the first quarter of growth being in the first part of 2010, and at a slower pace than the restoration of exports.

How is it possible that the magnitude of the impact in imports to be lower than during the financial crisis? Comparing Romania's international trade evolution from 2008 until 2019, Davidescu et al. (2021) point that Romania became an intermediary in the production network between manufacturing countries, like China, and final destinations, such as developed countries in the EU. A stronger integration of Romania in global value chains after the financial crisis could be partially an explanation for the discrepancy in the evolution of imports during the financial crisis in 2008–2009 versus the one during 2020. Imports for the production of goods restarted once with the relaxation of restrictions, therefore imports had to be resumed, while such a pressure was not obvious back in 2009, or it was only in preliminary phases.

5 Investigating the Relationship Between Romanian Exports and EU Imports and Exports. An Empirical Investigation Based on Granger Causality Analysis

In the context of Romania's integration in the global value chains, high trade dependence with the EU market, and increasing importance of China's as a supplier, which represent major factors characterizing Romania's trade before the pandemic, an important research interest is to assess the way in which Romania's trade is integrated in that of the EU. Therefore, we are interested into investigating the relationship between Romanian exports and EU imports and exports of goods and services using the Granger causality analysis. This approach builds on a previous research, in which Davidescu et al. (2021) have used panel data gravity models for the 2008–2019, in order to identify the dependency level of Romanian exports to China. The authors have stated that the most important channels that could affect Romania's exports in case of crises such as the one generated by the pandemic were the following:

- The decrease of the demand on the markets of Romania's main EU trade partners;
- The increase of the domestic demand, which reconfigures the distribution of the products that would have otherwise been exported;
- The decrease of Romania's imports from China, either because China partially closed its production, or due to import restrictions, reductions in the transport activity etc.;
- The decrease of the EU member states' exports to China, due to import restrictions, reductions in the transport activity, etc.
- The decrease of Romania's imports from the rest of the world, as a result of restrictions (isolation, reduction of transport activity, decrease of orders, etc.).
- The decrease of the EU member states' exports to the rest of the world, due to the same causes mentioned above.

Starting from these results, it is worth to analyze the nature of the relationship between Romanian exports of goods and services and EU-28 exports and imports of goods and services using VAR/VECM models for the period 2000–2019, based on quarterly data. Therefore, the main aim is to investigate if Romanian exports bring their contribution to the total EU imports as well as to the total EU exports, highlighting the long-run equilibrium relationship.

The graphical evolution of both Romanian exports and EU exports as well Romanian exports and EU imports revealed a positive relationship between variables, very high in intensity, which hits a value of 0.93 for Romanian exports and EU exports and 0.87 for Romanian exports and UE imports, respectively (Fig. 5).

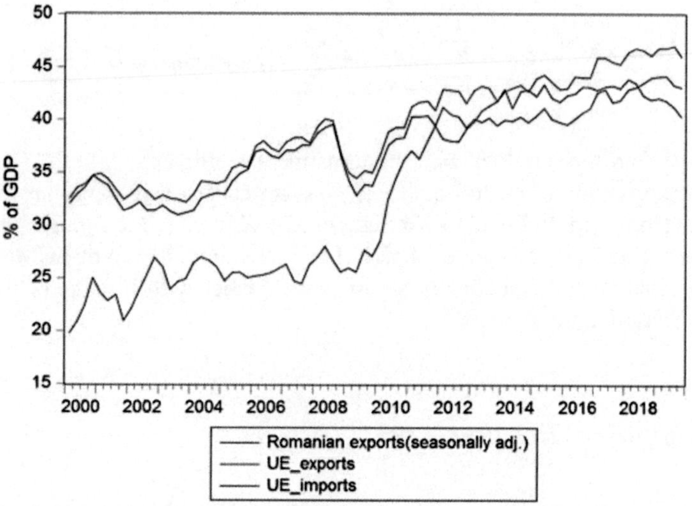

Fig. 5 The evolution of Romanian exports, EU exports and EU imports, 2000–2019, quarterly data. *Source* Authors' own elaborations based on Eurostat data

5.1 Methodology and Data

The data used in the research covers the period 2000:Q1–2019:Q4, with a total number of 80 observations. The variables used are as follows: Romanian exports of goods and services (expressed in % of GDP), EU imports of goods and services (% of GDP) and EU exports of goods and services (% of GDP). The Romanian exports have been seasonally adjusted using Census X-13 method. The main source of the data was the Quarterly National Accounts Database of Eurostat.

The methodology we have followed started with the stationarity analysis based on unit root tests (ADF and PP tests), cointegration analysis based on Johansen methodology, estimation of VAR/VECM models based on the decision regarding the presence of a long-run relationship, the Granger causality analysis on long run or/and short run term together with the impulse response function capturing the effect of a shock in the Romanian exports on both EU imports and exports.

Since most of the time the series exhibit a non-stationary pattern, if the both variables are I(1) and cointegrated, then the Granger causality test will be run under VECM (t-ratio of ECM and F-test should be statistically significant). Therefore, the Granger causality will take into account the results of co-integration. It becomes necessary to augment the simple Granger causality test with the error correction mechanism (ECM), derived from the residuals of the appropriate co-integration relationship to test for causality:

$$\Delta Y_t = C_0 + \sum_{i=1}^{k} \beta_i Y_{t-i} + \sum_{i=1}^{k} \alpha_i X_{t-i} + p_i ECT_{t-1} + u_t \tag{1}$$

$$\Delta X_t = C_0 + \sum_{i=1}^{k} \gamma_i X_{t-i} + \sum_{i=1}^{k} \zeta_i Y_{t-i} + \eta_i ECT_{t-1} + \varepsilon_t \quad (2)$$

where: Y, X are the variables, p_i is the adjustment coefficient while ECT_{t-1} expresses the error correction term. In Eq. (1), X Granger causes Y if α_i, p_i are significantly different from zero. In Eq. (2) Y Granger causes X if ζ_i, η_i are significantly different from zero. F-test alone is not enough to have causation; t-ratio of ECM term should be also negative and statistically significant together with F value of the model to have causation in the models.

5.2 *Empirical Results*

Based on the empirical results of unit roots tests applied for all series, we can state that all our time series are non-stationary in level and they become stationary in first differences, being therefore integrated of the same order, I(1). As a result, we will apply Johansen and Juselius cointegration approach in order to investigate if there is a long run relationship between both relationships.

In order to do that, two VAR models in levels have been developed, and the optimal number of lags have been identified to be one (according to LR, FPE, AIC, HQ, SC criterions) for both models, assuming a maximum number of 4 lags.

The results of the co-integration tests based on trace statistics and maximum eigenvalues pointed out the existence of a unique long run relationship in the case of both models. We have found a long run equilibrium relationship between, on one hand, Romanian exports and EU imports, and on the other hand, between Romanian exports and EU import. Therefore, we have built two VECM models in order to determine the direction of causality. The results of the VECM models are presented in Tables 1 and 3.

The long-run relationship proved its validity, the Romanian exports exhibiting a long run statistically significant and positive impact on the EU imports. The long-run coefficient is strongly significant inferring that a 1% increase of Romanian exports would imply an estimated increase of 0.44% in UE imports.

The estimated speed of adjustment to disequilibrium (error correction term ECT) indicates how fast equilibrium is restored. The significance of the error correction term shows causality in at least one direction. The lagged error term in our results is negative and highly significant.

The error correction term for EU imports is −0.11, indicating that the deviation from the long-term equilibrium is corrected by almost 12% over each quarter.

On the short run, the empirical results infirmed any Granger causality due to the lack of statistical significance of the lagged coefficient.

Table 1 The empirical results of VECM model supporting the relationship between Romanian exports and UE imports

Sample (adjusted): 2000Q3 2019Q4		
Included observations: 78 after adjustments		
Standard errors in () & t-statistics in []		
Cointegrating Eq:	CointEq1	
UE_IMPORTS(-1)	1.000000	
RO_EXPORTS_D11(-1)	**0.439817*** **	
	(0.09902)	
	[4.44160]	
C	23.08650	
Error Correction	D(UE_IMPORTS)	D(RO_EXPORTS_D11)
CointEq1	**-0.117777*** **	−0.031511
	(0.05172)	(0.07046)
	[−2.27722]	[−0.44725]
D(UE_IMPORTS(-1))	**0.231141***	0.058274
	(0.11778)	(0.16044)
	[1.96254]	[0.36321]
D(RO_EXPORTS_D11(-1))	0.064581	0.116166
	(0.09217)	(0.12556)
	[0.70065]	[0.92515]
C	0.078542	0.209253
	(0.09825)	(0.13384)
	[0.79940]	[1.56342]
R-squared	0.128241	0.023059
Adj. R-squared	0.092899	−0.016547
S.E. equation	0.839907	1.144175
F-statistic	3.628617	0.582213
Akaike AIC	2.538869	3.157166
Schwarz SC	2.659726	3.278023

Note All series used in the models are I (1). The models we estimated assume one cointegrating equation. ***, **, * indicates significance at 1, 5, 10% level
Source Authors' own elaborations

The results of VECMs support that Romanian exports explains about 13% of the variation in EU imports, while the model is well specified and the residuals satisfied the conditions of non-autocorrelation and homoscedasticity.

Table 2 reports the F-statistics and t-statistics for error correction term defined for the null hypothesis of no-causality. We can conclude that we have a Granger causality that runs from Romanian exports to EU imports (t-ratio of ECT and F-ratio are statistically significant at 1 and 5% levels, and the ECT is negative).

Table 2 Granger causality analysis of the relationship between Romanian exports and EU imports

Null hypothesis	Lag level	1	Results
		F-stat t_{ECT} F-statt_{ECT}	
Romanian exports and UE imports			
RO exp does not Granger cause UE_imp	3.62*	−2.27***	Ro exports => UE imports

Source Authors' own elaborations

Table 3 The empirical results of VECM model supporting the relationship between Romanian exports and EU exports

Sample (adjusted): 2000Q3 2019Q4		
Included observations: 78 after adjustments		
Standard errors in () & t-statistics in []		
Cointegrating Eq:	CointEq1	
UE_EXPORTS(-1)	1.000000	
RO_EXPORTS_D11(-1)	**0.570024*** **	
	(0.07868)	
	[7.24444]	
C	20.59462***	
Error Correction:	D(UE_EXPORTS)	D(RO_EXPORTS_D11)
CointEq1	**-0.149823*** **	−0.011386
	(0.05905)	(0.07853)
	[−2.53702]	[−0.14500]
D(UE_EXPORTS(-1))	0.155008	0.074983
	(0.11661)	(0.15506)
	[1.32929]	[0.48359]
D(RO_EXPORTS_D11(-1))	0.084179	0.119067
	(0.09433)	(0.12543)
	[0.89238]	[0.94926]
C	0.107214	0.202980
	(0.10134)	(0.13476)
	[1.05791]	[1.50626]
R-squared	0.129674	0.022532
Adj. R-squared	0.094391	−0.017095
S.E. equation	0.860709	1.144484
F-statistic	3.675218	0.568607
Akaike AIC	2.587800	3.157705
Schwarz SC	2.708657	3.278562

Source Authors' own elaborations

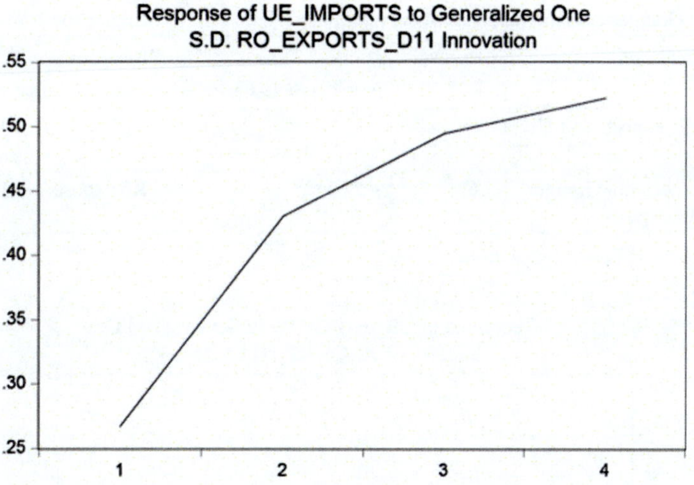

Fig. 6 Generalized impulse response functions (GIRFs) for the VEC Model. *Source* Authors' own elaborations

In order to quantify the effects of a shock in Romanian exports in the magnitude of EU imports, we have applied the generalized impulse response functions (GIRFs) proposed by Pesaran and Shin (1998). The results suggest that an increase of 1% in the Romanian exports will increase the EU imports with 0.50% at the level of fourth quarter (Fig. 6).

The relationship between Romanian exports and EU exports exhibited a long-run equilibrium, the Romanian exports having a long run statistically significant and positive impact on the EU exports. The long-run coefficient is strongly significant inferring that a 1% increase of Romanian exports would imply an estimated increase of 0.57% in UE exports.

The estimated speed of adjustment to disequilibrium (error correction term ECT) is −0.149, indicating that the deviation from the long-term equilibrium is corrected by almost 15% over each quarter. The negative sign of the ECT and the high significance of the coefficient reveals the existence of a long-run Granger causality from Romanian exports to EU exports.

However, on the short run, the empirical results infirmed any Granger causality due to the lack of statistical significance of the lagged coefficient.

The results of VECMs support that Romanian exports explains about 13% of the variation in EU imports, while the model is well specified and the residuals satisfied the conditions of non-autocorrelation and homoscedasticity.

Table 4 reports the F-statistics and t-statistics for error correction term defined for the null hypothesis of no-causality. We can conclude that we have a Granger causality that runs from Romanian exports to EU exports (t-ratio of ECT and F-ratio are statistically significant at 1 and 5% levels, and the ECT is negative).

The effect of a shock in Romanian exports in the magnitude of EU exports, evaluated based on the generalized impulse response functions (GIRFs) of Pesaran

Table 4 Granger causality analysis of the relationship between Romanian exports and UE exports

Nuli hypothesis	Lag level	1	Results
		F-stat t_{ECT} F-stat t_{ECT}	
Romanian exports and UE exports			
RO_exp does not Granger cause UE exports	3.67*	−2.53***	Ro exports => UE exports

Source: Authors' own elaborations

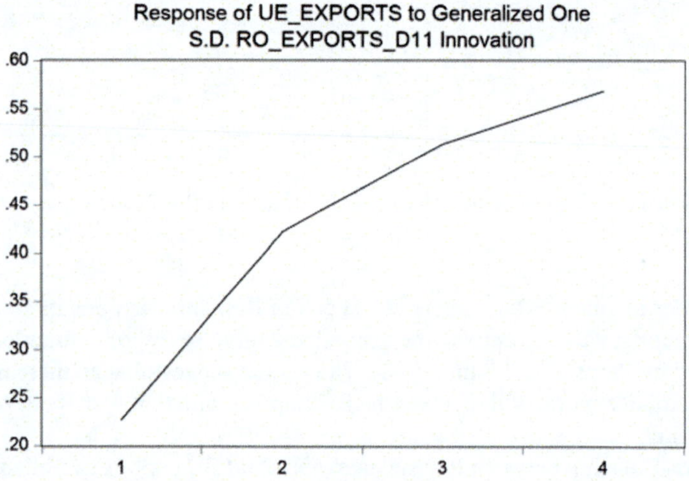

Fig. 7 Generalized impulse response functions (GIRFs) for the VEC Model. *Source* Authors' own elaborations

and Shin (1998), suggest that an increase of 1% in the Romanian exports will increase the EU exports with at most 0.55% at the level of fourth quarter (Fig. 7).

6 Conclusions

Covid-19 crisis was devastating for Romania's international trade, causing one of the largest drop in both trade of goods and services in the last years. In addition, the economic recovery which was enhanced by the increase of exports after the crisis in 2008–2009 is hard to be replicated, due to the specific of the actual crisis, which generated a shock crisis in both supply and demand, which was spread all over the global production networks.

Based on the analysis of monthly data since the start of pandemic, we conclude that exports of goods saw a larger drop than imports, while the decrease in imports of services surpassed the reduction of exports both during the whole year 0f 2020 and during the lockdown months, as compared to the similar periods in the previous year. As indicated in literature, exports and imports of Machinery and transport equipment and Miscellaneous manufactured articles were the most affected during March–May 2020. Another significant mutation was noticed in Romania's trade partners. The total values of exports and imports carried out with EU Member States started to drop in the favour of non-EU countries, which hit unprecedented levels in the last decade, especially during the months when the emergency state was imposed. This could be a consequence of the fact that the EU countries were among the most hit by the pandemic, enhancing restriction measures for a longer period, and thus experiencing at the same time low levels of demand. For Romania, it could the start for diversifying international trade partners, for reducing the high EU dependency. We also confirm that the Covid-19 crisis had a larger impact on Romania's international trade than the one felt during the economic crisis during 2008–2009.

In this context of strong dependency on the EU and integration in global value chains where China is an important supplier, we have also investigated the causality relationship between Romanian exports, EU imports and exports, expressed as % of GDP using Granger causality tests. Our results indicate that there exists a direct long-run relationship statistically significant between Romanian exports and EU exports and imports. The analysis leads to the finding that a 1% increase in Romanian exports contributes to an increase in the EU exports and imports to about 0.55% over the next four quarters. Although this analysis is only a starting point for more in-depth studies regarding the role and place of Romania's trade with the EU, it is a preliminary confirmation of the strong connections between these countries, that could further exacerbate vulnerabilities or enhance a common recovery. Romania should take into account such interconnectedness, given the actual proposals related to shortening and diversifying the global value chains, and creating a sustainable pool of competitive advantages for attracting the location of important industries.

References

Baicu, C.G., Gârdan, I.P., Gârdan, D.A., Epuran, G.: The impact of COVID-19 on consumer behavior in retail banking, evidence from Romania. In: Management & Marketing. Challenges for the Knowledge Society, vol. 15, No. Special Issue, pp. 534–556. https://doi.org/10.2478/mmcks-2020-0031 (2020)

Baldwin, R.: The Greater Trade Collapse of 2020: Learnings from the 2008–09 Great Trade Collapse. VoxEu CEPR. https://voxeu.org/article/greater-trade-collapse-2020 (2020)

Baldwin, R., Tomiura, E.: Thinking Ahead About the Trade Impact of COVID-19. https://cepr.org/sites/default/files/news/COVID-19.pdf (2020)

Bonadio, B., Huo, Z., Levchenko, A. A., Pandalai-Nayar, N.: Global Supply Chains in the Pandemic. National Bureau of Economic Research, w27224 (2020)

Brinca, P., Duarte, J.B., Faria-e-Castro, M.: Is the COVID-19 Pandemic a Supply or a Demand Shock?, vol. 31. Economic Synopses (2020)

Davidescu, A.A., Popovici, O.C., Strat, V.A.: An empirical analysis using panel data gravity models and scenario forecast simulations for the Romanian exports in the context of COVID-19. Econ. Res. Ekon. Istraživanja (2021). https://doi.org/10.1080/1331677X.2021.1907205

ECLAC: The Effects of the Coronavirus Disease (COVID-19) Pandemic on International Trade and Logistics, vol. 6. https://repositorio.cepal.org/bitstream/handle/11362/45878/1/S2000496_en.pdf (2020)

Eurostat data. https://ec.europa.eu/eurostat/data/database

Fonseca, L., Azevedo A.: COVID-19: outcomes for global supply chains. In: Management & Marketing. Challenges for the Knowledge Society, vol. 15, No. Special Issue, pp. 424–438. https://doi.org/10.2478/mmcks-2020-0025 (2020)

Friedt, F.L., Zhang, K.: The triple effect of Covid-19 on Chinese exports: first evidence of the export supply, import demand and GVC contagion effects. Covid Econ. **53**, 72–109 (2020)

Gruszczynski, L.: The COVID-19 pandemic and international trade: temporary turbulence or paradigm shift? Eur. J. Risk Regul. **7**, 1–6 (2020). https://doi.org/10.1017/err.2020.29

IFC: When Trade Falls-Effects of COVID-19 and Outlook. https://www.ifc.org/wps/wcm/connect/78f10cad-7e00-440d-b6fd-da210e5a6d1e/20201023-Trade-and-COVID-19-Note-1.pdf?MOD=AJPERES&CVID=nllE81b (2020)

IMF: World Economic Outlook: International Monetary Fund, p. 2020. DC, Washington (2020)

Kejžar, K.Z., Velić, A., Damijan, J.: Covid-19, trade collapse and GVC linkages: European experience. GROWINPRO Working Paper 38/2021 (2021)

Milea, C.: Consequences of covid-19 on the international trade in goods and services: forecasts, developments, restrictions. Financ. Stud. Victor Slăvescu Cent. Financ. Monet. Res. Buchar. 24, **4**(90), 29–40 (2020)

Minodo, A.: Impact of COVID-19 on the trade of goods and services in Spain. Appl. Econ. Anal. **29**(85), 58–76 (2021). https://doi.org/10.1108/AEA-11-2020-01562021

National Bank of Romania: Raport Asupra Inflatiei, February 2018. https://www.bnr.ro/Publicatii-periodice-204.aspx (2018)

National Institute of Statistics, Romania. http://statistici.insse.ro:8077/tempo-online/

OECD: COVID-19 and International Trade: Issues and Actions. https://www.oecd.org/coronavirus/policy-responses/covid-19-and-international-trade-issues-and-actions-494da2fa/ (2020)

Păunescu, C., Mátyus, E.: Resilience measures to dealing with the Covid-19 pandemic. In: Evidence from Romanian Micro and Small Enterprises. Management & Marketing. Challenges for the Knowledge Society, vol. 15, No. Special Issue, pp. 439–457. https://doi.org/10.2478/mmcks-2020-0026 (2020)

Pesaran, M., Shin, Y.: Generalized impulse response analysis in linear multivariate models. Econ Lett **58**(1), 17–29 (1998)

Saif, N.M.A., Ruan, J., Obrenovic, B.: Sustaining trade during COVID-19 pandemic: establishing a conceptual model including COVID-19 impact. Sustainability **13**, 5418 (2021). https://doi.org/10.3390/su13105418

Staszkiewicz, P., Chomiak-Orsa, I., Staszkiewicz, I.: Dynamics of the COVID-19 contagion and mortality: country factors, social media, and market response evidence from a global panel analysis. IEEE Access. **8**, 106009–106022 (2020)

UNCTAD: Global Trade Impact of the Coronavirus (COVID-19) Epidemic. https://unctad.org/en/PublicationsLibrary/ditcinf2020d1.pdf (2020)

UNCTAD: Key Statistics and Trends in International Trade 2020. United Nations, Geneva. https://unctad.org/system/files/official-document/ditctab2020d4en.pdf (2021)

Vidya, C.T., Prabheesh, K.P.: Implications of COVID-19 pandemic on the global trade networks. Emerg. Mark. Financ. Trade **56**(10), 2408–2421 (2020). https://doi.org/10.1080/1540496X.2020.1785426

World Bank: World Development Report 2020. World Bank Publications, The World Bank, 32437 (2020)

Yagi, M., Managi, S.: Global supply constraints from the 2008 and COVID-19 crises. Econ. Anal. Policy **69**, 514–528 (2021). https://doi.org/10.1016/j.eap.2021.01.008

Impact of COVID-19 Crisis on Banking Sector in Romania

Dumitru Ionut, Dumitrescu Bogdan-Andrei, Cepoi Cosmin Octavian, Pop Ionut Daniel, Barnea Dinu, Kubinschi Matei-Nicolae, and Tatarici Luminita

1 The Impact of the Moratorium on Loans for Individuals on the Banking System in the Context of the COVID-19 Pandemic

1.1 Research Objectives

The present research aims to assess the impact of the law of postponing bank rates from the perspective of general liquidity of the Romanian banking system for 2020, amid the non-collection of annuities for the suspension period, and from the perspective of the overall net result of the banking system for 2020 given the payments facilities granted to debtors.

The analysis will evaluate both the impact related to Government Emergency Ordinance (GEO) no. 37/2020, currently in force, and the impact of the Law approving it voted by the Parliament (hereinafter referred to as the Law), but declared unconstitutional on 6 May 2020. This approach is justified on the one hand by the possibility of resuming the legislative process for the law recently rejected by the Constitutional Court, with the correction of the deficiencies reported and, on the other hand, by

D. Ionut (✉) · D. Bogdan-Andrei · C. C. Octavian · P. I. Daniel · B. Dinu · K. Matei-Nicolae · T. Luminita
Bucharest University of Economic Studies, Bucharest, Romania
e-mail: ionut.dumitru@fin.ase.ro

D. Bogdan-Andrei
e-mail: bogdan.dumitrescu@fin.ase.ro

C. C. Octavian
e-mail: cosmin.cepoi@fin.ase.ro

P. I. Daniel
e-mail: ionut.pop@fin.ase.ro

A. M. Dima et al. (eds.), *Economic Recovery After COVID-19*, Springer Proceedings in Business and Economics, https://doi.org/10.1007/978-3-030-86641-9_7

the significant differences of impact on the overall net result of the banking system generated by the two normative acts.

The most important aspects that differ between the two normative acts and are likely to affect the results of this analysis are as follows:

(i) *the scope of eligibility of debtors who can apply for a moratorium* is much wider in the case of the *Law*, including both individual debtors who have arrears and those whose income is not directly or indirectly affected by the situation generated by the COVID-19 pandemic. In addition, debtors who are in the process of enforcement, payment procedure, judicial reorganization or any other judicial or extrajudicial proceedings that tend to suspend the effects of credit agreements are also eligible. In the case of legal entity debtors, the threshold regarding diminished incomes or receipts is at least 15% compared to the average of the last two months compared to 25% in the case of GEO no. 37/2020. In addition, the Law eliminates the maximum period of 45 days from the entry into force of GEO no. 37/2020 for submitting the request for suspension of payment rates.

(ii) *interest for deferred payments*: GEO no. 37/2020 establishes the capitalization of interest on consumer loans and those granted to non-financial companies, and in the case of mortgage loans, the deferred interest will represent a separate claim and will be repaid in 60 months at an interest rate of 0%. *The Law* establishes that the interest due by debtors and the related commissions corresponding to the suspended instalments are not capitalized at the balance of the existing loan, at the end of the suspension period.

(iii) *period of application*: *The Law* extends the period of application of the public moratorium for debtors who have been affected by the drought as follows: payment rates are suspended at the request of the debtor for up to 18 months, but not more than 31 October 2021.

Although, both GEO no. 37/2020 and the law approving it from the Parliament refer to the possibility of postponing the rates for both individuals and non-financial companies, the present analysis, for reasons of data availability, will consider an impact assessment only for loans granted to individuals. It is expected that large companies, usually those with a high degree of bankability and capitalization, will be able to better cope with the negative economic effects generated by the COVID-19 pandemic and, therefore, will only use to a small extent the facilities offered by the law of postponement of rates, as they have the possibility to renegotiate directly with the banks the conditions of the loans they have in progress. On the other hand, small- and medium-sized enterprises will be more affected and therefore more tempted to use this facility. According to the press release from 24.04.2020 issued by the Romanian Banking Association (RBA),[1] only 10,000 of the 270,000 applications submitted for the suspension of monthly payment obligations came from non-financial companies. Given the greater resilience of large corporations to shocks, we appreciate that most of the impact of the rate deferral law will be based on loans deferred by individuals

[1] https://www.arb.ro/wp-content/uploads/Comunicat-de-presa-ARB-24.04.2020.pdf.

and SMEs, respectively. Assessing the impact of the moratorium on the latter is not possible at this time due to the lack of granular information on the residual maturity of the loans and the interest rate, given the high heterogeneity of the contractual conditions for these credit agreements. In addition, it is expected that SMEs will resort to a credit restructuring that better reflects the particular financial situation of the company, as well as to programmes specifically created for this segment (e.g. SME Invest). However, the absence of an assessment of the impact generated by the postponement of rates by companies is a limitation of the analysis and is likely to underestimate the results.

1.2 Short Presentation of Moratoriums on Loans in Other European Countries

Various forms of moratoriums on loan repayments have been introduced in many other European countries:

a. In **Austria**, individuals and microenterprises are exempted from paying instalments on loans from 1 April to 30 June, with the terms of the loan agreements being extended by 3 months.
b. In **Belgium**, payments to banks and insurance companies may be deferred until 31 October 2020 at no additional cost to:

o Non-financial corporations, small- and medium-sized enterprises and self-employed workers who either had no delays in payment or were in arrears of up to 30 days on 29 February 2020 are not in a process of credit restructuring and whose capacity to reimbursement was reduced by the COVID-19 crisis.
o mortgage contractors who encounter difficulties in repayment, the deferral covering both the interest and the principal of the loan;

- Also, people in temporary unemployment schemes benefit from the automatic extension of the insurances offered by the employer. Also, companies with financing problems during this period are protected from enforcement by a moratorium on bankruptcies in the non-financial sector.

c. In **the Czech Republic**, non-financial corporations adversely affected by the epidemiological crisis may suspend payment of their loans until the end of October 2020.
d. In **Cyprus**, the rates for all performing loans to individuals, self-employed persons and companies may be deferred for a period of nine months until the end of the year.
e. Recommendations have been issued in **Croatia** for leasing and factoring companies to postpone collections in the event of payment delays caused by the COVID-19 crisis to high-performing customers.

f. In **Estonia**, the measures aimed at amending bankruptcy law so that companies have more flexible deadlines to avoid such situations. Banks were also encouraged to judge the need and terms of deferred payments for loans to individuals and legal entities on a case-by-case basis.
g. In **Germany**, individual borrowers whose livelihoods are endangered by the loss of income caused by the COVID-19 crisis have the right to suspend the payment of instalments on consumer loans for a period of up to three months. In addition, individuals and microenterprises can opt for the suspension of utility payments, also for a maximum period of three months.
h. In **Greece**, credit institutions shall grant the option to defer repayment for:

   - legal entities directly affected by the COVID-19 crisis, by suspending the payment of instalments (except interest) until September 30 this year, provided that they have been successful by the end of 2019;
   - directly affected individuals, who have the option of suspending the instalments for a period of up to three months, with the same condition of performance.

i. In **Ireland**, the largest commercial banks have implemented moratoriums of up to six months to support companies and individuals whose incomes have been reduced by the COVID-19 crisis, with the possibility of extension if the situation dictates. In addition, non-bank creditors have agreed to these deferral schemes.
j. In **Iceland**, operating firms whose revenues have been temporarily eroded by the health crisis may require deferred payments on loans by up to six months.
k. In **Italy**, the moratorium provides for the freezing of credit lines granted to SMEs, thus preventing creditors from withdrawing or reducing them and postponing repayments until the end of the moratorium.
l. In **Lithuania**, the Association of Financial Institutions has agreed to defer payments on loans to companies for up to six months, provided that the value of the loans does not exceed EUR 5 000 000 per group; the participation of credit institutions in this agreement is voluntary. In addition, some banks have introduced the possibility for borrowers to suspend payments on mortgages for up to one year and for consumer loans for up to half a year, during which time they only have to pay interest.
m. In **Luxembourg**, some banks have decided to suspend the repayment of loans to companies that are temporarily experiencing liquidity problems.
n. In **Malta**, a central bank decision introduced a six-month moratorium on the payment of instalments (principal and interest) for borrowers adversely affected by the COVID-19 crisis.
o. In **the Netherlands**, commercial banks have decided to offer the possibility of deferring payments for six months in the case of small companies with loans of up to EUR 2 500 000; some banks have increased this ceiling to EUR 50 000 000 in loans.
p. In **Portugal**, the moratorium is imposed for a period of six months, until the end of September 2020, and covers both the principal and interest on

primary residence mortgages to the population, all loans to non-financial institutions, and some loans to entities with social purposes. The conditions to be met include delays in payment of no more than 90 days, registered office in Portugal for companies, residence in Portugal and employment contract suspended/reduced/concluded as a result of the COVID-19 pandemic.

q. In **Slovenia**, the law exempts all companies, self-employed workers and farmers from paying debts to banks for a period of 12 months. In addition, the government provides them with facilities to pay tax obligations, such as deferrals or the possibility of payment in instalments.

r. In **Hungary**, the government, on the recommendation of the central bank, imposed moratoriums on the payment of credit obligations for consumers, non-financial companies, but also for financial institutions (including interbank exposures) and investment funds by the end of 2020. The central bank subsequently recommends credit institutions extending the repayment term so that monthly instalments do not exceed those previously established in the contract.

1.3 Data and Assumptions

The data used are from March 2020 and refer to the balance, the average residual maturity and the interest rate for mortgage and consumer loans, considered separately for lei and foreign currency loans. The category of consumer loans was obtained by summing the two components, respectively secured and unsecured consumer loans, and for the average residual maturity a weighted average of the two categories was calculated. The input data are presented in the table.

An important element in estimating the impact on the banking system of the rate deferral law is the hypothesis regarding the suspension period. Considering the entry into force of GEO no. 37/2020 on 30.03.2020 and the deadline of 31.12.2020 until which one can benefit from the postponement of the instalments results in a maximum application period of 9 months. It is expected that the vast majority of borrowers who will use this facility will initially opt for the maximum period. This decision is supported by the current high uncertainties about the future economic outlook, which will most likely prompt borrowers to exercise caution. However, as some borrowers will have a less uncertain outlook on their economic situation, it is expected to resume payment of instalments before 31.12.2020. The latter argument is stronger in the case of GEO no. 37/2020 compared to a variant of the law close to the one adopted by the Parliament since in the case of GEO no. 37/2020, the postponement implies costs for debtors while the Law approving GEO no. 37/2020 does not involve costs for borrowers. In view of these arguments, as well as the fact that the deferral becomes operational from the moment of the request from the debtor, the present analysis will be based on the hypothesis of a period of suspension of bank rates equal to 6 months, stating that if the final option of the law will be closer to the one voted by the Parliament, most likely, the suspension period will be longer.

1.4 Methodology

In estimating the impact on the banking system of the rate deferral law, we will consider a scenario-based analysis of the number of borrowers who will use the facility. From the information publicly available at this moment, having as source the commercial banks, at the beginning of May about 16% of the debtors had requested the deferral of payment in the conditions in which the deadline set by GEO no. 37/2020 expires in mid-May. In this context, it is reasonable to assume a level of at least 25% of the number of borrowers who will use this facility. Also, in case of continuing the application of the moratorium according to the provisions of GEO 37/2020, we consider it unlikely that more than 50% of borrowers will request the postponement of bank rates given that not all were significantly adversely affected financially by the effects of the COVID-19 pandemic. Thus, several scenarios of impact on the banking system will be presented as a result of the call for the rate deferral facility, considering a number of beneficiaries between 25 and 50% of debtors.

In order to determine the impact on the liquidity of the banking system at the level of 2020 generated by the call to the facility to postpone the instalments and implicitly by not collecting the principal and interest for the suspension period, an "aggregate" repayment schedule will be developed for mortgages and consumer loans. Each category will be considered separately, both for the lei and the foreign currency component. Also, this exercise is resumed for each scenario considered regarding the number of debtors who use the facility, respectively 25%, 35%, 50%. To illustrate the methodology, the case of mortgage loans in lei will be considered, with a percentage of borrowers requesting the deferral of instalments of 25%, and then the results obtained for all loan categories will be presented, as well as at the aggregate level. From the perspective of the impact on the liquidity of the banking system in 2020 generated by the call to the facility to postpone rates, things are not very different if the final form of the law will be the one in force now or will be closer to the one adopted in Parliament. However, the latter will probably lead to the materialization of a scenario in which a higher number of debtors use the facility.

Thus, starting from an existing balance of mortgages denominated in national currency of 60,176 million lei, characterized by an average interest rate of 5.57% and an average residual maturity of 22.9 years and considering a percentage of borrowers who postpones the payment of instalments for 6 months of 25% results in an annuity of about 97 million lei and implicitly a cash loss of the banking system at the level of 2020 of approximately 582 million lei for debtors who postpone their rates. In order to separate this impact in principal and interest rates, as well as for other objectives of this analysis, it is necessary to draw up the "aggregate" repayment schedule at the level of the entire banking system for mortgage loans denominated in lei. This is briefly presented below:

Month	Unpaid balance	Principal rate	Interest	Annuity
1	15,016.9	27.1	69.8	97.0
2	14,989.6	27.3	69.7	97.0
…	…	…	…	…
274	96.5	96.1	0.9	97.0
275	0.0	96.5	0.4	97.0
Total	–	15,044.0	11,621.3	26,665.4

Source own calculations
Note sums are expressed in mil. lei

Resuming the calculations described above and for the percentages of 35 and 50% of the debtors requesting the deferral of bank rates, for mortgage loans in foreign currency, for consumer loans in lei, as well as for consumer loans in foreign currency, we obtain the results described in the tables.

Cash losses at the level of the banking system in 2020 from mortgage loans in lei (million lei)				Cash losses at the level of the banking system in 2020 from mortgage loans in foreign currency (million lei)			
Percentage of moratorium debtors	*25%*	*35%*	*50%*	*Percentage of moratorium debtors*	*25%*	*35%*	*50%*
Annuities	581.8	814.5	1,163.6	Annuities	219.1	306.8	438.2
Principal rates	164.7	230.6	329.4	Principal rates	112.8	157.9	225.5
Interest	417.1	583.9	834.2	Interest	106.4	148.9	212.7
Cash losses at the level of the banking system in 2020 from consumer loans in lei (million lei)				*Cash losses at the level of the banking system in 2020 from consumer loans in foreign currency (million lei)*			
Percentage of moratorium debtors	*25%*	*35%*	*50%*	*Percentage of moratorium debtors*	*25%*	*35%*	*50%*
Annuities	1,472.4	2,061.4	2,944.9	Annuities	128.2	179.4	256.4
Principal rates	983.2	1,376.4	1,966.3	Principal rates	69.9	97.9	139.8
Interest	489.3	685	978.6	Interest	58.3	81.6	116.6

Cash losses at the level of the banking system from loans granted to individuals (million lei)			
Percentage of moratorium debtors	*25%*	*35%*	*50%*
Annuities	2,401.5	3,362.1	4,803.0
Principal rates	1,330.5	1,862.7	2,661.1
Interest	1,071.0	1,499.4	2,142.0

Source own calculations

Thus, the negative impact on the liquidity of the banking system at the level of 2020 is between 2.4 and 4.8 billion lei related to a percentage of debtors who call for the postponement of rates between 25 and 50%. It can be noted that most of the impact, respectively about 61.3%, comes from the consumer loans component which, although they have a share in total loans granted to individuals of about 37.3%, are characterized by higher monthly repayments, mainly attributable to a much lower average maturity, but also to higher related interest rates. It can also be noted that the impact is located in proportion of over 85% at the level of liquidity in national currency, in the context in which the share of loans in national currency exceeds 75%, amid the orientation of commercial banks mainly to lending in lei. It should also be noted that this loss of cash at the level of the banking system does not have per se a negative impact on interest income, banks continuing to record in the income account the accumulation of interest, even if their actual payment will take place later. A negative impact on the result will have, as described below, the granting of advantages to debtors by granting facilities to the payment of the accrued interest for the remaining life of the loan.

However, it is expected that the effect on the liquidity indicator at the level of the banking sector will not be high, given the following: (i) the liquidity indicator was at a value of 2.3 in February 2020, and the liquidity coverage ratio (LCR) at 257.2, well above the 100 threshold, and (ii) the demand for new loans will most likely be reduced in this economic context marked by uncertainty. The effect of postponing cash inflows from the population sector is insignificant in terms of the impact on the indicator of coverage of the liquidity requirement for 30 days—LCR (about 1% in the scenario of resorting to the deferral facility of 50% of individual debtors, ceteris paribus).

In order to determine the impact on the result (loss) of the banking system at the level of 2020 generated by the call for the rate deferral facility, the difference between the net present value of the loans before and after the suspension of monthly payments will be determined. According to IFRS international accounting standards, a restructuring of a loan that generates a decrease in net present value will generate a loss equal to the decrease in net present value, a loss that will be fully recorded in the year of restructuring.

In general, the net present value of a loan, repayable monthly in constant annuities, is determined according to the relation:

$$NPV_{loan} = \sum_{i=1}^{n} \frac{A_i}{\left(1 + \frac{r}{12}\right)^i}$$

where NPV_{loan} it designates the net present value of the loan, A_i the annuity in month i, r is the effective interest of the loan, n designates the last month of payment of the loan.

Thus, the net present value is equal to the discounted value of all remaining annuities, the discount being made at the effective interest rate of the loan. It is important to point out that before the restructuring the present value of the loan is equal to the credit balance.

In a restructuring, the present value of a loan is adversely affected only if facilities are granted related to the payment of the accrued interest. If the interest for a suspension period is capitalized, the formula presented above will provide the same result, namely a market value of the loan equal to its balance at the time of valuation.

GEO no. 37/2020 provides some facilities for the payment of interest but only in the case of mortgages. Therefore, the net present or market value of consumer loans does not change. In the case of mortgages, the interest accrued for the suspension period shall not be capitalized, but shall be paid in equal instalments within 60 months of the resumption of payments. Thus, there will be a net present impairment loss that reflects that the interest has not been capitalized or, alternatively, the effective interest rate on the loan is now lower.

Under these conditions, the "aggregate" repayment schedule presented above changes as follows: for 6 months nothing is paid, for months 7–66 the previous annuity of about 97 million lei is paid, to which is added about 7 million. lei, representing the 60th part of the accrued interest for the suspension period, following that from month 67 until month 281 (the maturity of the loan was extended accordingly by 6 months) to return to the previous annuity of 97 million lei. The table below briefly illustrates the modified repayment schedule:

Month	Unpaid balance	Principal rate	Interest	Annuity
1	15,044.04	0	0	0
2	15,044.04	0	0	0
…	…	…	…	…
6	15,044.04	0	0	0
7	15,016.9	27.1	76.8	103.9
8	14,989.6	27.3	76.7	103.9
…	…	…	…	…
66	13,171.6	35.7	68.3	103.9
67	13,135.7	35.8	61.1	97
68	13,099.7	36	61	97
…	…	…	…	…
281	0	96.5	0.4	97
Total	–	15,044.0	12,040.3	27,084.3

Source own calculations
Note sums are expressed in mil. lei

Under these conditions, the new net present value of the mortgage loans becomes:

$$NPV_{loans} = \frac{103,9}{\left(1+\frac{5,57\%}{12}\right)^{7}} + \frac{103,9}{\left(1+\frac{5,57\%}{12}\right)^{8}} + \ldots + \frac{103,9}{\left(1+\frac{5,57\%}{12}\right)^{66}} + \frac{103,9}{\left(1+\frac{5,57\%}{12}\right)^{67}} + \frac{103,9}{\left(1+\frac{5,57\%}{12}\right)^{68}} + \ldots + \frac{103,9}{\left(1+\frac{5,57\%}{12}\right)^{281}} = 14.986,7 \text{ mil.lei}$$

As a consequence, there is a loss of net present value equal to 15,044 million lei (current balance)—14,986.7 million lei = 57.3 million lei or 0.38% of the current value of mortgages in lei.

Resuming the calculations described above and for the percentages of 35 and 50% of borrowers requesting the deferral of bank rates, as well as for foreign currency mortgages, the results described in the tables below are obtained:

Net present value losses at the level of the banking system in 2020 from mortgage loans in lei (million lei)				Net present value losses at the level of the banking system in 2020 from mortgage loans in foreign currency (million lei)			
Percentage of moratorium debtors	*25%*	*35%*	*50%*	*Percentage of moratorium debtors*	*25%*	*35%*	*50%*
Loss (mil. lei)	57.3	80.2	114.6	Loss (mil. lei)	10.2	14.3	20,0.4
Loss (%)	0.38%	0.38%	0.38%	Loss (%)	0.18%	0.18%	0.18%

Net present value losses at the level of the banking system in 2020 from mortgage loans (million lei)

Percentage of moratorium debtors	*25%*	*35%*	*50%*
Loss (mil. lei)	67.5	94.5	135.0
Loss (%)	0.32%	0.32%	0.32%

Source own calculations

Thus, the impact on the result of the banking system at the level of 2020 is between −67.5 million lei and −135 million lei or about 0.32% of the market value of mortgages. Most of the impact, respectively about 85%, comes from the component of mortgages in lei, both as a result of their higher share, respectively about 72% of the total, and as a result of the higher sensitivity generated by the higher interest rate. Considering as a reference the profit registered at the level of the banking system in 2019 of about 6.4 billion lei, it can be estimated that the impact on the banking result generated by the loss of net present value of loans granted to individuals caused by the postponement of rates under GEO no. 37/2020 is not significant.

However, in case of resumption of the legislative process for the law approving GEO no. 37/2020 adopted by the Parliament while maintaining the provisions related to the absence of interest capitalization for all types of deferred loans, the impact on the loss of the banking system would be greatly amplified. According to the law approving GEO no. 37/2020, the crediting period is extended with the suspension period, the debtor owing the same annuity when resuming payments. This equates to zero interest on the balance of loans during the period of suspension of instalments, a reduction in the effective interest on loans and a decrease in net present value that will be recognized as a loss in 2020.

Under these conditions, the "aggregate" repayment schedule presented above changes as follows: for 6 months nothing is paid, for months 7–281 the previous annuity of about 97 million lei is paid. The new net present value of loans becomes:

$$NPV_{loans} = \frac{97}{\left(1+\frac{5,57\%}{12}\right)^7} + \frac{97}{\left(1+\frac{5,57\%}{12}\right)^8} + \ldots + \frac{97}{\left(1+\frac{5,57\%}{12}\right)^{281}}$$
$$= 14.631, 8 mil.lei$$

As a consequence, there would be a loss of net present value equal to 15,044 million lei (current balance)—14,631.8 million lei = 412.3 million lei or 2.74% of the current value of mortgages in lei.

Resuming the calculations described above and for the percentages of 35 and 50% of the debtors requesting the deferral of bank rates, for mortgage loans in foreign currency, for consumer loans in lei, as well as for consumer loans in foreign currency, the results are described in the table:

Net present value losses at the level of the banking system in 2020 from mortgage loans in lei (million lei)				Net present value losses at the level of the banking system in 2020 from mortgage loans in foreign currency (million lei)			
Percentage of moratorium debtors	*25%*	*35%*	*50%*	*Percentage of moratorium debtors*	*25%*	*35%*	*50%*
Loss (mil. lei)	412.3	577.2	824.5	Loss (mil. lei)	106.1	148.5	212.1
Loss (%)	2.74%	2.74%	2.74%	Loss (%)	1.85%	1.85%	1.85%
Net present value losses at the level of the banking system from consumer loans in lei (million lei)				*Net present value losses at the level of the banking system in 2020 from consumer loans in foreign currency (mil. lei)*			
Percentage of moratorium debtors	*25%*	*35%*	*50%*	*Percentage of moratorium debtors*	*25%*	*35%*	*50%*
Loss (mil. lei)	495.2	693.2	990.3	Loss (mil. lei)	58.2	81.4	116.3
Loss (%)	4.98%	4.98%	4.98%	Loss (%)	2.42%	2.42%	2.42%
Net present value losses at the level of the banking system in 2020 from mortgage loans (million lei)				*Net present value losses at the level of the banking system in 2020 from consumer loans (million lei)*			
Percentage of moratorium debtors	*25%*	*35%*	*50%*	*Percentage of moratorium debtors*	*25%*	*35%*	*50%*
Loss (mil. lei)	518.3	725.7	1036.6	Loss (mil. lei)	553.3	774.6	1106.6
Loss (%)	2.49%	2.49%	2.49%	Loss (%)	4.48%	4.48%	4.48%

Net present value losses at the level of the banking system in 2020 from loans granted to individuals (million lei)			
Percentage of moratorium debtors	*25%*	*35%*	*50%*
Loss (mil. lei)	1071.6	1500.3	2143.3
Loss (%)	3.23%	3.23%	3.23%

Source own calculations

Thus, the impact on the result of the banking system at the level of the year 2020 would have been between −1,071.6 million lei and −2,143.3 million lei or about 3.23% of the market value of loans granted to individuals. The loss would be distributed relatively balanced between consumer loans, which are responsible for about 51.6% of the negative result, and between mortgage loans, the latter being responsible for the remaining 48.4%. Although consumer loans have a share of only 37.3% in total loans to individuals, the decrease in market value in their case would be much higher, respectively about 4.48%. This result is explained by the higher interest rate for this category of loans, which is converted into a discount rate when determining the net present value. It can also be noticed the higher value loss of mortgage/consumer loans for the national currency component, this being also explained by the higher interest rates in lei compared to foreign currency loans. Considering as a reference the profit registered at the level of the banking system in 2019 of about 6.4 billion lei, it can be estimated that the impact on the banking result generated by the loss of net present value of loans granted to individuals caused by the deferral of instalments of a law close to the version adopted in Parliament would be significant. This impact would have been between 16.7 and 33.5% of the aggregate profit of the banking system in 2019, being at the same time about 15.9 times higher compared to the impact of GEO no. 37/2020.

According to the European Banking Authority (EBA),[2] the application of legislative and non-legislative moratoriums that respect its principles is not likely to lead to the classification of restructured loans as non-performing if the difference between the current net present value and the one resulting after the application of a moratorium is less than 1%.[3] The latter provision is to enter into force on 1 January 2021. Therefore, in the context of a the final form of the law close to the version adopted by Parliament, which implies a net present loss of restructured loans of more than 3%, it may be necessary that they be included in the category of non-performing loans and implicitly provisioned with 100%, which significantly complicates the situation.

1.5 Conclusions and Proposed Measures

Postponing debt payment in the context of closing down significant parts of the economy arising from the need to control the COVID-19 pandemic is a logical and beneficial step for all parties involved. However, it is essential that the solution adopted, on the one hand, ensures the necessary protection for debtors in difficulty

[2] European Banking Authority, *Guidelines on legislative and non-legislative moratorium on loan repayments applied in the light of the COVID-19 crisis*, 2 April 2020, the application of moratoriums on a large scale and without producing other contractual changes, except for the maturity lag.

[3] According to the information provided by EBA (*Guidelines on the application of the definition of default under Article 178 of Regulation (EU) No 575/2013*), in the event of a restructuring in the event of financial distress of the debtor (distressed restructuring), the value change threshold Net present of financial obligations may not be higher than 1%. These specifications come into force on January 1, 2021.

and, on the other hand, does not jeopardize the stability of the banking sector and its ability to lend to the real economy, This is more even important in the particular case of Romania where financial intermediation is at the lowest level in the European Union.

A first conclusion that can be drawn from the present analysis is that, from the perspective of the liquidity of the banking system, the solutions proposed both by GEO no. 37/2020 and the Law approving it are not likely to significantly affect the liquidity position of commercial banks, as they are able to absorb the shock. The cash loss caused by the non-collection of annuities can be supported on the one hand, as a result of a very comfortable initial liquidity position of the banking system and, on the other hand, as a result of the decrease in credit demand from economic agents after the emergence of the pandemic.

In addition, uncertainty about the final version of the rate deferral law is a negative element for all stakeholders, adding to the major uncertainties caused by the COVID-19 pandemic.

It is also essential that the final form of the law to take into account the alignment with European regulations regarding the classification of loans into performing/non-performing category. Thus, a possible reclassification of restructured loans in the non-performing category has severe implications for the banking system and its ability to lend to the real economy, supplementary to the impact already determined in the present research.

2 The Evolution of Non-Performing Loans in the Romanian Banking System in the Context of the COVID Pandemic—19

2.1 Evolutions of the Banking System in the Period 2008–2019

Banking risk represents the total loss that a bank or the entire system can experience during negative events influencing the debtors' ability to pay, or cause changes in market developments. Thus, banking risk can arise via operational problems, but also as a result of contagion. The latter is generally visible in developing economies, such as Romania. Starting from this definition, credit risk is the most important component of banking risk management. It arises as a result of the inability of debtors to honour their credit obligations, and the reasons may be macroeconomic or microeconomic. To investigate the effects on credit risk caused by COVID-19 pandemic, we analyse the non-performing loans which are quantified for Romanian banking system in line with European Banking Authority (EBA). The non-performance rate that is used in this analysis represents the share of loans that are over 90 days due, with contamination at the level of the debtor in the case of individuals, in total loans granted to the population and non-financial companies. This analysis aims to conduct a study

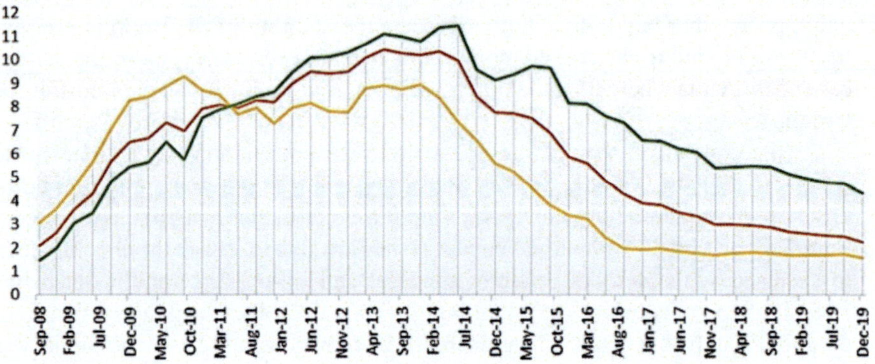

Fig. 1 NPL evolution for individuals, in red, NPL for individuals; in yellow, NPL for loans in RON; in green, NPL for loans in EUR. *Source* National Bank of Romania

using historical data on the rate of non-performing loans in the period between the third quarter of 2008 and the end of 2019, in conjunction with a forecast of the evolution of this indicator for the next two years, including economic effects of the COVID-19 pandemic. In what follows we propose an analysis of the evolution of the non-performing loans rate.

At the beginning of the analysed period, the loans in RON experienced a steeper evolution of the non-performance rates, the average of the period 2008 Q3—2010 Q4 being of 5.38%, while for those granted in foreign currency was of 4.57% (Fig. 1). During the recession, there was a depreciation of the national currency against EUR, USD or CHF, which led to higher rates in RON for those who had borrowed in foreign currency. Against the background of rising unemployment in Romania and the economic decline and taking into account those presented above, the ability to repay debtors decreased, generating more losses from non-repayment of loans. After the third quarter of 2014, with the economic recovery and the exit from the recession, the rate of non-performing loans experienced a decrease One year later, there is a return of credit growth in the Romanian economy, while the downward trend in the rate of non-performing loans is maintained until the end of the analysis period (Fig. 2).

Taking into account these developments for the period 2008 Q3 and 2019 Q4, the expectations regarding the evolution of the non-performing loans rate for 2020 and 2021 is not so optimistic and depends on how long the pandemic will continue to exist.

The effects of the non-performing loans rate on the financial results and the capitalization of the banking sector are expected to be less severe compared to the 2008 period. First, banks are now better prepared in terms of capitalization and liquidity to face adverse shocks than in 2008. Second, this time banks started the process of restructuring the loans at a much earlier stage. The Romanian banking sector is relatively well positioned to cope with the uncertain economic situation generated by the onset of the COVID-19 pandemic. Compared to the period after the burst of

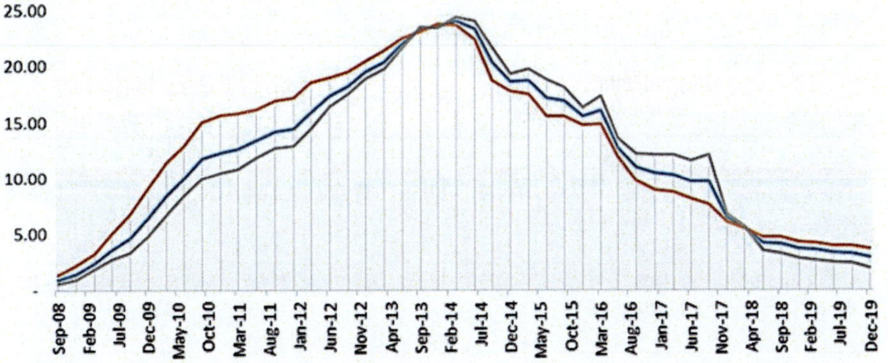

Fig. 2 NPL evolution for non-financial institutions, in blue, NPL for non-financial institutions; in orange, NPL for loans in RON; in grey, NPL for loans in EUR. *Source* National Bank of Romania

Table 1 Outstanding loans and interest rate for households as of March 2020

	Mortgage loans balance (million lei)	Balance of consumer loans (million lei)	Average residual maturity of mortgages (years)	Average residual maturity consumer loans (years)	Mortgage interest rate (%)	Consumer loan interest rate (%)
Total	83,113	49,421	21.5	5.8	–	–
Lei	60,176	39,810	22.9	4.2	5.57	10.25
Currency	22,937	9,611	18.0	12.6	3.74	4.91

Source NBR, Central Credit Register, Credit Office,[4] own calculations

the 2008–2009 financial crisis, the banking sector can now use the capital buffers,[5] and most prudential and financial indicators are at an appropriate level compared to the risks and above the EU average (Table 1). In addition, the measures adopted by the NBR[6] are likely to contribute to provide the necessary liquidity in the system to ensure a proper access to finance for the real economy.

Between January 2008 and March 2020, although private sector bank lending (non-financial corporations and the population) increased significantly, the degree of financial intermediation remained among the lowest in the region, with 55% of lending oriented towards the households sector. There have been positive developments in the financing of the banking sector, with the ratio between loans granted

[4] For the interest rate on foreign currency loans, the interest rate on euro loans was used as a proxy. For the interest rate on consumer loans, the interest rate on consumer loans and other purposes was used as a proxy.

[5] https://www.ecb.europa.eu/press/pr/date/2020/html/ecb.pr200312~45417d8643.en.html.

[6] https://bnro.ro/Masurile-BNR-in-contextul-situa%c8%9biei-generate-de-epidemia-COVID-19-21312.aspx.

Table 2 Banking sector risk indicators

Risk indicators	EBA defined prudential range	Romania[a]						EU average 2019
		2015	2016	2017	2018	2019	Mar. 2020	
Solvency								
Tier 1 capital ratio	>15% [12%–15%] <12%	16,72	17,55	17,95	18,64	20,05	18,52	**16,6**
CET1 capital ratio	>14% [11%–14%] <11%	16,72	17,55	17,95	18,64	19,95	18,42	**15,0**
Asset quality								
Non-performing loan ratio	<3% [3%–8%] >8%	13,51	9,62	6,41	4,96	4,09	3,94	**2,7**
Non-performing loan coverage by provisions	>55% [40%–55%] <40%	57,72	56,34	57,68	58,51	60,75	60,88	**44,7**
Ratio of restructured loans and advances	<1,5% [1,5%–4%] >4%	8,43	4,80	6,36	4,80	3,26	2,49	**1,8**
Profitability								
ROE	>10% [6%–10%] <6%	11,89	10,10	11,80	13,77	11,06	10,90	**5,8**
Cost-to-income ratio	<50% [50%–60%] >60%	58,46	53,19	55,30	53,81	55,32	61,42	**64,0**
Balance sheet structure								
Loan-to-deposit ratio for households and non-financial corporations	<100% [100%–150%] >150%	78,18	74,34	73,21	71,89	69,48	68,81	**116,1**

[a]Includes only banks, Romanian legal entities, according to EBA methodology

best bucket

intermediate bucket

worst bucket

Source NBR, EBA

and deposits attracted from the private sector declining steadily and remaining sub-unitary (Table 2). In addition, the portfolio quality has improved during the recent years, but the trend is likely to be affected by current developments; however the non-performing loan coverage by provisions is adequate and above the European average.

However, in the current context, a risk factor may come from the significant share of claims on the government sector and among the highest in the EU (21.8 share of government exposures in banking assets, December 2019). Thus, the important link between the banking and the public sector can contribute to the transmission of unfavourable developments on the banking sector in the event of the deterioration of sovereign risk. At the same time, the prolongation of this period of economic uncertainty, doubled by the legislative uncertainty at national level, generated by the existence of several normative acts that can lead to substantial losses in the banking sector, requires careful monitoring, but also better coordination with supervisors in order to identify as accurately as possible the implications of the current situation on the banking sector.

2.2 *Macroeconomic Shock Impact on Non-Performing Loans*

The COVID-19 pandemic impact will focus on measuring the effects of various macroeconomic scenarios on the banking sector through projecting NPL rates, based on a methodology using in an IMF Working Paper (Grigoli et al. 2016, Macro-Financial Linkages and Heterogeneous Non-Performing Loans Projections: An Application to Ecuador, Working Paper No. 16/236), adapted to the macrofinancial context in Romania and extended in order to ensure a high degree of robustness.

1. Defining the Macroeconomic Scenarios and Forecasting Real Credit Growth

We define 2 macroeconomic scenarios—baseline (based on the European Commission Spring Forecast for economic growth in Romania and the Euro Zone) and **adverse** (sluggish recovery in 2021). The scenarios are defined over the 2020–2022 period (8 quarters) by using the following macroeconomic variables:

- Economic growth Romania (YoY % change)
- Economic growth Euro Zone (YoY % change)
- EURRON exchange rate (YoY % change)—average forecast, Bloomberg
- Short-term interest rate (ROBOR 3 M, level)—average forecast, Bloomberg.

In the baseline scenario, Romania will record a 6% contraction in 2020, followed by a swift recovery in 2021, estimated at 4.2% (Fig. 3). The adverse scenario starts at the baseline figures, but deepens the drop in 2020 to 7% and assumes a significantly slower recovery in 2021 (−0.3%) simulating a long-lasting impact of the pandemic on the macroeconomic environment.

In the case of the Euro Zone, European Commission forecasts point to a contraction of 7.7% in 2020, partially compensated by an expansion of 6.3% in 2021. The adverse scenario was constructed by assuming an additional contraction of 1 percentage point in 2021, followed by a slow recovery in 2021 (3.5%), a similar hypothesis applied in Romania's case (Fig. 4).

Due to the intrinsic macroeconomic nature of the COVID-19 pandemic shock, the macroeconomic scenarios are used to forecast the impact on the financial sector, through the real credit channel. Consequently, the set of variables selected to describe

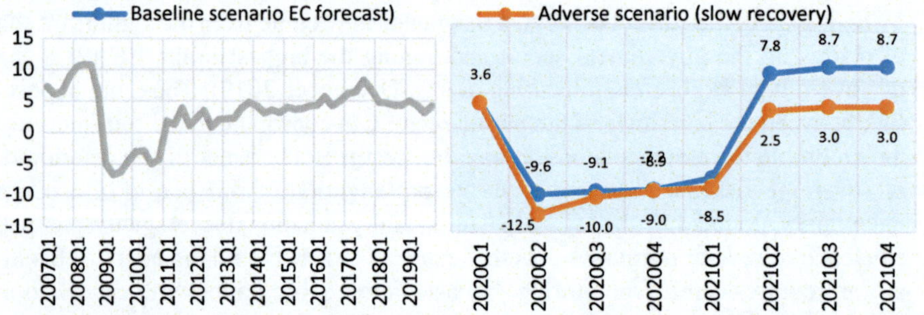

Fig. 3 Baseline and adverse scenarios for economic growth—România. *Source* European Commission and own estimation

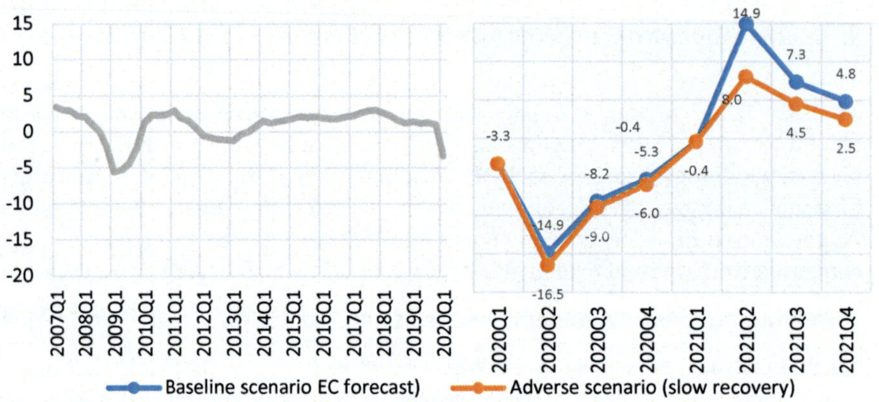

Fig. 4 Baseline and adverse scenarios for economic growth—Euro Zone. *Source* European Commission and own estimation

a reduced-form macroeconomic model is extended with the annual real growth rate of credit, with the goal to capture the interactions between the financial sector and the real economy.

In order to conditionally forecast real credit dynamics on the basis of the macroeconomic scenarios defined previously, a structural VAR model is chosen, estimated using Bayesian techniques—Minnesota prior with optimized hyperparameters using a grid search technique (2000 simulations). The model is identified using a Cholesky decomposition, by ordering the variables according to exogeneity.

Formally, the SVAR model is described by the following relation:

$$A_0 z_t = a + \sum_{j=1}^{p} A_j z_{t-j} + \varepsilon_t$$

where z_t is the vector of variables (economic growth, real credit, exchange rate and interest rate) and ε_t is the vector of shocks. Taking into account the relatively

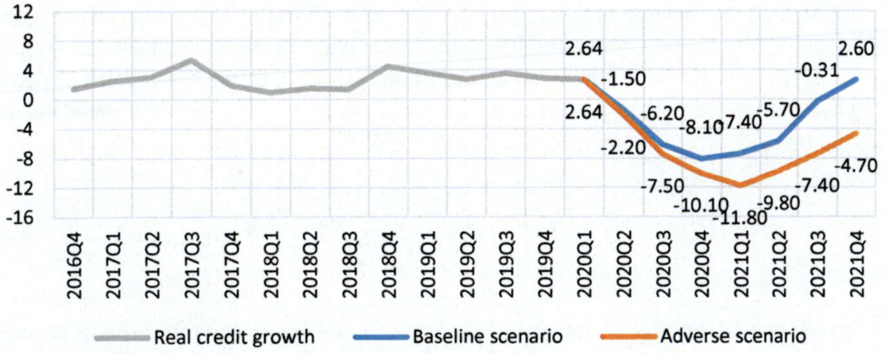

Fig. 5 Conditional forecasts for real credit growth, under the baseline and adverse scenarios. *Source* own estimation

low number of observations, 3 lags were used for the SVAR model (p = 3). The estimation results show that the model is stable—all the roots are inside the unit circle—and capable of closely reproducing the empirical dynamics.

Running the conditional forecasting exercise under the macroeconomic scenarios, the results highlight a significant impact of the macroeconomic shock in 2020, annual growth rates turning negative for the first time in the last 5 years. In the baseline scenario, the rate reaches a minimum value of -8% in the last quarter of 2020, followed by a positive trajectory and finishing 2021 in positive territory (Fig. 5). Conversely, the negative impact is significantly larger in the adverse scenario (−11.8% in 2020 Q4), while recovery is much slower compared to the baseline scenario (reaching −4.7% at the end of the forecast horizon).

2. An ARDL Model to Forecast NPL Rates Based on the Macrofinancial Scenarios

NPL rates will be forecast on the basis of the conditional projections obtained for the macrofinancial variables from the structural VAR model. In this context, it is necessary to derive elasticities between NPL rates and the aforementioned macrofinancial variables in order to capture the transmission mechanism and feedback loops stemming from macroeconomic shocks, such as the shock induced by the COVID-19 pandemic. Building on the idea that there can be significant delays (lags) between the onset of an economic contraction episode and tightening financial conditions leading to an increase in non-performance rates, defining and econometric framework capable of including lagged information would be recommended. Therefore, we resort to an Autoregressive Distributed Lag (ARDL) model in order to adequately capture the gradual impact of economic shock transmission to the financial sector.

Taking into account the limited time series tracking NPL dynamics in Romania (the longest quarterly time series starts from 2005, using the NBR definition of loans with payment delays of over 90 days), the model cannot incorporate a high number of regressors in order to avoid potential over identification issues. Furthermore, to overcome any potential endogeneity problems, contemporaneous interactions between the dependent variable and regressors have been omitted, taking also into account lagged transmission effects on NPL rates in the banking sector. Finally, the first lag of NPL rates[7] has been included in the model to account for the empirical persistence associated with this indicator. The ARDL model is described by the following equation:

$$NPL_t = a_1 NPL_{t-1} + \sum_{i=1}^{p} b_i X_{t-i} + u_t$$

where X_t are the regressors included in the model (economomic growth and real credit growth) and u_t are the idiosyncratic errors. Lag selection is done by iteratively estimating all combinations up to three lags and comparing informational criterion values (in this case, the Akaike information criterion was used to optimally choose the final specification between the 64 candidate models presented in Fig. 7). Additionally, to avoid autocorrelation or heteroscedasticity issues, a Newey–West correction was applied (test results for the presence of autocorrelation are presented in the Annex, Table 4). The results for the optimal specification, on the basis of the lag selection procedure, are the following:

Selected model—ARDL (1, 1, 2, 1)				
Variable	Coefficient	Std. Err	T-stat	Prob
NPL rate (t–1)	0.98	0.01	105.49	0.00
Economic growth RO (t–1)	0.01	0.01	0.99	0.33
Economic growth RO (t–2)	−0.02	0.01	−2.06	0.04
Economic growth EZ (t–1)	−0.08	0.03	−2.50	0.02
Economic growth EZ (t–2)	0.10	0.04	2.17	0.04
Economic growth EZ (t–3)	−0.06	0.03	−2.22	0.03
Real credit (YoY growth rate, t–1)	−0.01	0.00	−1.85	0.07
Real Credit (YoY growth rate, t–2)	0.01	0.00	2.95	0.01
R-squared				0.991
R-squared adj				0.990
Std. err. regression				0.116
Durbin-Watson stat				1.956

Source Own estimation

Estimation results confirm the persistent behaviour of NPL rates (the autoregressive coefficient is close to 1) but also the lagged transmission of macroeconomic shocks stemming from both Romania and the Euro Zone. In order to validate the estimated coefficients' stability, given the high uncertainty degree associated with limited

[7] The NPL rates enter the model under a logistic transformation to avoid any potential issues with restrictions in the [0, 1] interval or the violation of the error normality hypothesis—the approach is common in related literature, for example, see Vazquez et al. (2012) or Wezel et al. (2014).

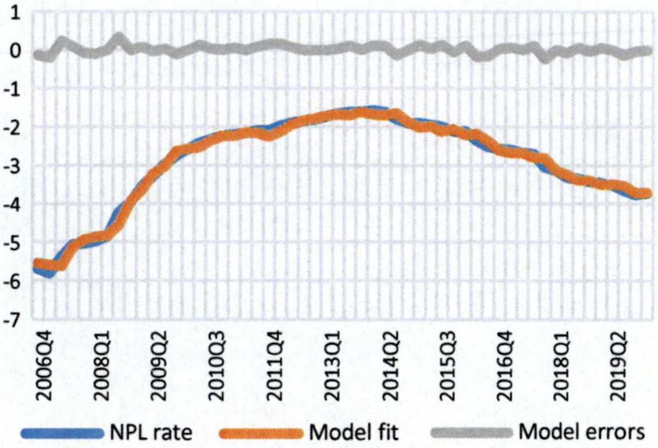

Fig. 6 ARDL model results for the NPL rate fit (logistic transformation) and associated errors. *Source* own estimation

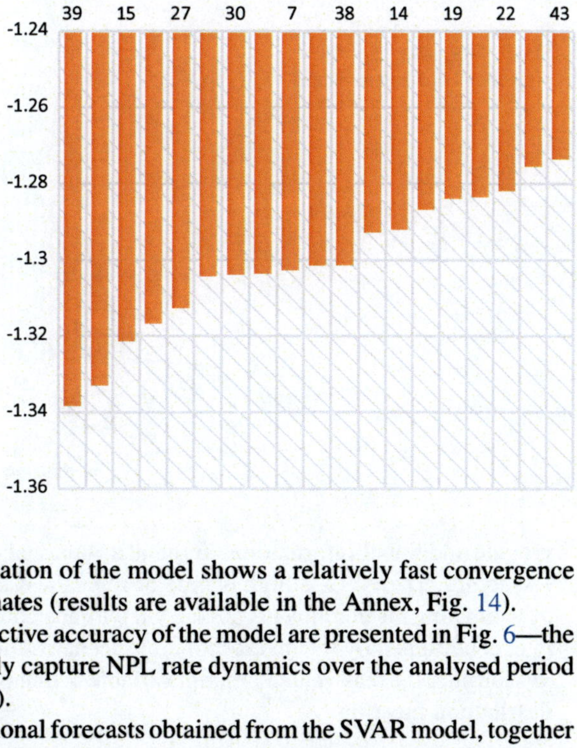

Fig. 7 Lag selection results based on the AIC value

data length, a recursive estimation of the model shows a relatively fast convergence towards the full sample estimates (results are available in the Annex, Fig. 14).

Results related to the predictive accuracy of the model are presented in Fig. 6—the model is capable to adequately capture NPL rate dynamics over the analysed period (2006 Q4—2020 Q1) (Fig. 7).

In the final step, the conditional forecasts obtained from the SVAR model, together with the macroeconomic variables, are used to estimate NPL rate projections based on the elasticities estimated by the ARDL model. In the baseline scenario, the NPL rate climbs rapidly to 8.9% at the end of the forecast horizon, while in the adverse scenario the rate reaches a level close to 12% at the end of 2021 (Figs. 8 and 9).

3. A Quantile Regression Approach

While the previous section uses the historical evolution of macroeconomic variables to construct non-performing loan rate projections, the quantile regression will

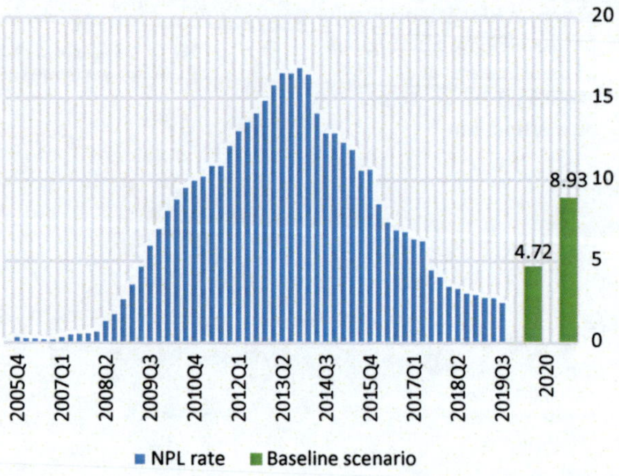

Fig. 8 NPL rate projection—baseline scenario. *Source* own estimation

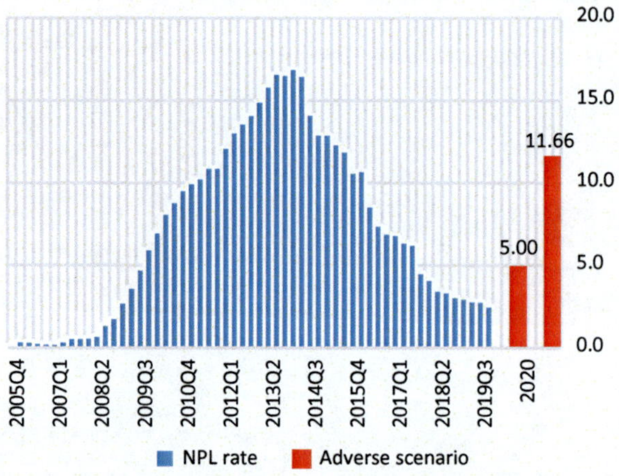

Fig. 9 NPL rate projection—adverse scenario

provide additional information on the distributional characteristics of the estimated elasticities. Therefore, a high degree of robustness of the final estimates is ensured by estimating the coefficients associated with the conditional distribution of the NPL rate, conditioned by the macroeconomic scenarios described in the first section.

Consider the real-valued random variable Y that is characterized by the following distribution function:

$$F(y) = \Pr(Y \leq y).$$

In this context, for any quantile τ, the τ'th quantile of Y is defined as the inverse function:

$$Q(\tau) = inf\{y : F(y) \geq \tau\},$$

where $\tau \in (0, 1)$.

The conditional quantile function, $Q(\tau|X = x) = X_i\beta(\tau)$ can be computed based on the algorithm given below:

$$\hat{\beta}(\tau) = arg \min_{\beta\in\mathbb{R}} \sum_{i=1}^{n} \rho_\tau (Y_i - X_i\beta)^2,$$

for any quantile τ. In Eq. (4), the term ρ_τ is the loss function defined by:

$$\rho_\tau(u) = u(\tau - I(u > 0)),$$

with I being an indicator function.

Variables	Model 1	Model 2	Model 3	Model 4	Model 5
NPL(-1)	1.098***	1.101***	0.960***	0.998***	0.980***
Economic growt_Euro(-1)		−0.133**	−0.202*	−0.118	−0.135
Economic growt_Romani (-1)		-0.030	−0.060*	−0.062**	-0.011
Unemployment (-1)			0.207**	0.096*	0.276
ROBOR3M(-1)				0.047**	0.081
EURIBOR3M(-1)					0.144
LIBOR3M_CHF(-1)					−0.599
EUR/RON(-1)					−0.214
CHF/RON(-1)					−0.110
Pseudo R-squared	76.66%	85.06%	91.09%	91.39%	92.39%

Coefficients are statistically significant at: ***(1%); **(5%); *(10%)

In this case, given that significant increases in NPLs due to the COVID 19 pandemic are expected, we estimated several regressions for the upper quantiles—0.8, 0.85, 0.9 and 0.95. The results of the estimates are summarized in the table above. The coefficients for Models 1–5 are given in the mean values. Given the small size of the sample, a fairly high volatility of the estimated coefficients can be observed, especially in the case of economic growth and unemployment. We decided to go with Model 4 as the basic representation because the NPL variation is explained in a fairly high proportion (pseudo R-squared >90%), and, except for the economic growth in the Euro Zone all the coefficients generated are significant from statistically.

Under these conditions, the previous results regarding the persistent character of the non-performing loans rate (the autoregressive coefficient is close to 1) but also the delayed transmission of the effects from the real economy, especially that of Romania are confirmed. The forecasts for 2020 and 2021 are presented in the graphs above. It can be seen, comparatively Figs. 8 and 9 versus Figs. 10 and 11 that the results and especially the trend of NPLs remain robust to the estimation method, the differences between them being quite small regardless of the chosen scenario.

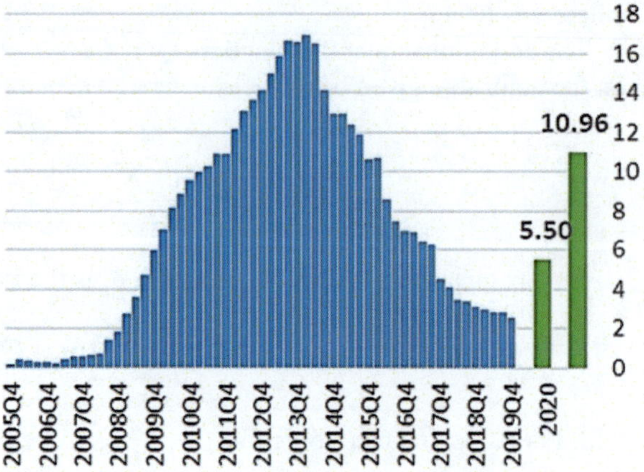

Fig. 10 NPL forecast—baseline scenario. *Source* own calculation

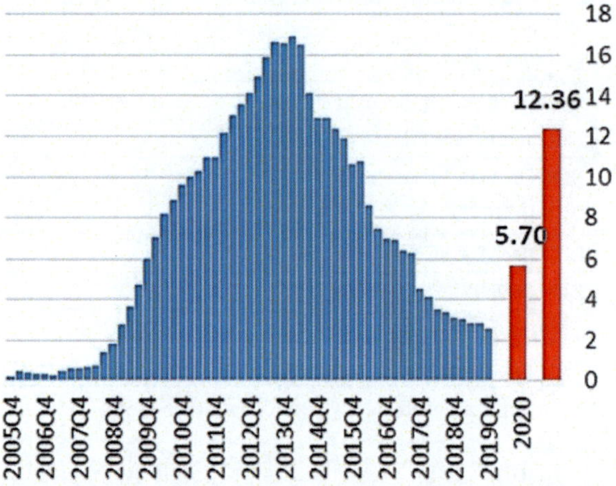

Fig. 11 NPL forecast—adverse scenario

4. Counterfactual Scenario Regarding the Banking Sector Capacity to Support the Real Economy During the COVID-19 Pandemic

In the last stage of the analysis, we conduct a counterfactual scenario regarding the potential cushioning effect of maintaining a stable provision of credit towards the real economy. By considering a positive trajectory for the annual growth rate of real credit, similar to the observed rates throughout 2019, we run a conditional forecasting exercise for economic growth, employing the same SVAR model described in the previous sections (Fig. 12).

Figure 13 plots the results for the economic growth conditional forecasting exercise, in a stable credit flow scenario, which could significantly contribute to dampening the impact of the macroeconomic shock. The simulation highlights the conclusion according to which the banking sector can substantially mitigate the economic

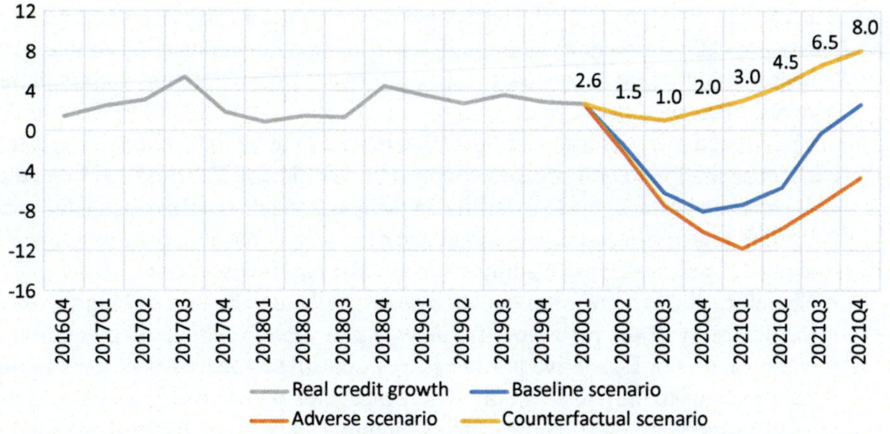

Fig. 12 Counterfactual scenario regarding real credit dynamics (2020 Q2—2021 Q3). *Source* own estimation

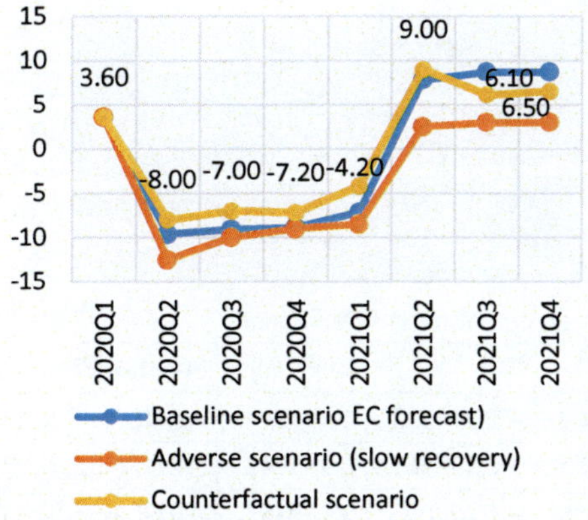

Scenario	Baseline	Adverse	Counterfactual
2020Q1	3.6	3.6	3.6
2020Q2	-9.6	-12.5	-8
2020Q3	-9.1	-10	-7
2020Q4	-8.9	-9	-7.2
2021Q1	-7.2	-8.5	-4.2
2021Q2	7.8	2.5	9
2021Q3	8.7	3	6.1
2021Q4	8.7	3	6.5
Difference in Real GDP (vs. baseline)	-	-3.19%	+1.41%

Fig. 13 Economic growth conditional forecast for Romania using the counterfactual scenario. *Source* own estimation

contraction in 2020 and 2021 and, consequently, dampen the volatility of the business cycle. In the counterfactual scenario, economic growth is approximately 1.4 percentage points higher compared to the baseline scenario.

3 Conclusions and Policy Recommendations

1. The non-performing loans rate is dependent on macrofinancial conditions, and an unforeseen macroeconomic shock may lead to a significant increase in the volume of non-performing loans, with subsequent negative effects on the banking sector's ability to lend to the real economy.

2. In the context of the COVID-19 pandemic, the reduced-form stress testing exercise indicates a potential increase in the NPL rate in Romania, up to a level of approximately 12% in the adverse scenario, over a 2-year horizon. The results are robust to the methodology used (autoregressive model or quantile estimation).
3. The simulations performed indicate that the banking sector can make a substantial contribution to limiting the economic contraction of 2020 and 2021 and thus to reducing business cycle volatility. In the counterfactual scenario in which real lending registers a positive dynamic over the next 2 years, economic growth is about 1.4 percentage points higher than in the baseline scenario.
4. Therefore, the main recommendation concerns the use, by the banking sector, of the flexibility of the regulatory framework and avoiding the implementation of any measures or legislative initiatives that may affect the ability of the banking sector to lend to the real economy. These measures are necessary because, in this difficult macrofinancial context, bank lending can be a key factor in alleviating the recession and fostering further economic recovery.

4 Annex

See Tables 3 and 4.

Table 3 Results for the optimal specification selection of the ARDL model

Model	LogL	AIC	BIC	HQ	R-sq. adj.	Specification
39	44.132292	−1.338233	−1.043569	−1.224593	0.989954	ARDL(1, 1, 2, 1)
31	42.988202	−1.332896	−1.075065	−1.233461	0.989742	ARDL(1, 2, 0, 1)
15	43.675914	−1.32133	−1.026666	−1.20769	0.989783	ARDL(1, 3, 0, 1)
23	44.550076	−1.316669	−0.985172	−1.188824	0.989889	ARDL(1, 2, 2, 1)
27	43.441137	−1.312635	−1.01797	−1.198994	0.989694	ARDL(1, 2, 1, 1)
47	41.215519	−1.304278	−1.08328	−1.219048	0.989274	ARDL(1, 1, 0, 1)
30	43.203589	−1.303837	−1.009172	−1.190196	0.989603	ARDL(1, 2, 0, 2)
35	44.198669	−1.303654	−0.972157	−1.175809	0.989756	ARDL(1, 1, 3, 1)
7	45.170682	−1.302618	−0.934287	−1.160567	0.989894	ARDL(1, 3, 2, 1)
11	44.13752	−1.30139	−0.969892	−1.173544	0.989733	ARDL(1, 3, 1, 1)
38	44.133624	−1.301245	−0.969748	−1.1734	0.989731	ARDL(1, 1, 2, 2)
63	39.905245	−1.292787	−1.108622	−1.221762	0.988971	ARDL(1, 0, 0, 1)
14	43.882326	−1.291938	−0.960441	−1.164092	0.989635	ARDL(1, 3, 0, 2)
55	41.741966	−1.286739	−1.028908	−1.187304	0.989258	ARDL(1, 0, 2, 1)
19	44.665685	−1.283914	−0.915584	−1.141864	0.989703	ARDL(1, 2, 3, 1)
26	43.653373	−1.283458	−0.951961	−1.155613	0.989547	ARDL(1, 2, 1, 2)

(continued)

Table 3 (continued)

Model	LogL	AIC	BIC	HQ	R-sq. adj.	Specification
22	44.611454	−1.281906	−0.913575	−1.139855	0.989682	ARDL(1, 2, 2, 2)
29	43.438419	−1.275497	−0.944	−1.147651	0.989464	ARDL(1, 2, 0, 3)
43	41.386405	−1.273571	−1.015739	−1.174135	0.989115	ARDL(1, 1, 1, 1)
10	44.340807	−1.271882	−0.903551	−1.129831	0.989578	ARDL(1, 3, 1, 2)
37	44.305765	−1.270584	−0.902254	−1.128533	0.989565	ARDL(1, 1, 2, 3)
46	41.232129	−1.267857	−1.010025	−1.168421	0.989053	ARDL(1, 1, 0, 2)
6	45.231123	−1.267819	−0.862656	−1.111564	0.989682	ARDL(1, 3, 2, 2)
34	44.203235	−1.266786	−0.898456	−1.124736	0.989525	ARDL(1, 1, 3, 2)
3	45.193355	−1.266421	−0.861257	−1.110165	0.989667	ARDL(1, 3, 3, 1)
59	40.012156	−1.259709	−1.038711	−1.174479	0.988786	ARDL(1, 0, 1, 1)
13	43.9843	−1.258678	−0.890347	−1.116627	0.98944	ARDL(1, 3, 0, 3)
62	39.913862	−1.256069	−1.035071	−1.170839	0.988745	ARDL(1, 0, 0, 2)
25	43.812953	−1.252332	−0.884001	−1.110281	0.989373	ARDL(1, 2, 1, 3)
21	44.787028	−1.251371	−0.846208	−1.095116	0.989511	ARDL(1, 2, 2, 3)
18	44.760852	−1.250402	−0.845239	−1.094146	0.989501	ARDL(1, 2, 3, 2)
54	41.745329	−1.249827	−0.955163	−1.136187	0.989026	ARDL(1, 0, 2, 2)
51	41.742271	−1.249714	−0.955049	−1.136073	0.989024	ARDL(1, 0, 3, 1)
45	41.409836	−1.237401	−0.942737	−1.123761	0.988888	ARDL(1, 1, 0, 3)
42	41.398153	−1.236969	−0.942304	−1.123328	0.988884	ARDL(1, 1, 1, 2)
33	44.393538	−1.236798	−0.831634	−1.080542	0.989357	ARDL(1, 1, 3, 3)
9	44.393195	−1.236785	−0.831622	−1.080529	0.989357	ARDL(1, 3, 1, 3)
5	45.297276	−1.233232	−0.791236	−1.062772	0.989462	ARDL(1, 3, 2, 3)
2	45.241516	−1.231167	−0.789171	−1.060707	0.98944	ARDL(1, 3, 3, 2)
32	39.189313	−1.229234	−1.008236	−1.144003	0.988439	ARDL(1, 2, 0, 0)
58	40.024761	−1.223139	−0.965308	−1.123704	0.988552	ARDL(1, 0, 1, 2)
17	44.963931	−1.220886	−0.77889	−1.050426	0.989331	ARDL(1, 2, 3, 3)
61	39.922242	−1.219342	−0.961511	−1.119907	0.988509	ARDL(1, 0, 0, 3)
53	41.775018	−1.21389	−0.882392	−1.086044	0.988794	ARDL(1, 0, 2, 3)
50	41.745442	−1.212794	−0.881297	−1.084949	0.988782	ARDL(1, 0, 3, 2)
48	37.716547	−1.211724	−1.027559	−1.140699	0.98804	ARDL(1, 1, 0, 0)
56	38.64851	−1.209204	−0.988206	−1.123974	0.988205	ARDL(1, 0, 2, 0)
41	41.534199	−1.20497	−0.873473	−1.077125	0.988694	ARDL(1, 1, 1, 3)
28	39.510122	−1.204079	−0.946247	−1.104643	0.988332	ARDL(1, 2, 1, 0)
40	39.454251	−1.202009	−0.944178	−1.102574	0.988308	ARDL(1, 1, 2, 0)
60	37.398928	−1.19996	−1.015795	−1.128935	0.987898	ARDL(1, 0, 1, 0)
16	39.311401	−1.196719	−0.938887	−1.097283	0.988246	ARDL(1, 3, 0, 0)
1	45.298574	−1.196243	−0.717414	−1.011578	0.989205	ARDL(1, 3, 3, 3)

(continued)

Table 3 (continued)

Model	LogL	AIC	BIC	HQ	R-sq. adj.	Specification
57	40.059771	−1.187399	−0.892735	−1.073758	0.988319	ARDL(1, 0, 1, 3)
24	39.97702	−1.184334	−0.88967	−1.070694	0.988283	ARDL(1, 2, 2, 0)
44	37.829257	−1.178861	−0.957863	−1.093631	0.987841	ARDL(1, 1, 1, 0)
49	41.775024	−1.176853	−0.808522	−1.034802	0.988539	ARDL(1, 0, 3, 3)
52	38.691789	−1.17377	−0.915939	−1.074335	0.987973	ARDL(1, 0, 3, 0)
12	39.629945	−1.171479	−0.876815	−1.057839	0.988131	ARDL(1, 3, 1, 0)
36	39.615132	−1.170931	−0.876267	−1.05729	0.988125	ARDL(1, 1, 3, 0)
20	40.218735	−1.156249	−0.824752	−1.028404	0.988129	ARDL(1, 2, 3, 0)
8	40.060339	−1.150383	−0.818886	−1.022537	0.988059	ARDL(1, 3, 2, 0)
4	40.219113	−1.119226	−0.750896	−0.977176	0.987859	ARDL(1, 3, 3, 0)

Source Own estimation

Table 4 ARDL model autocorrelation test results

Lag	AC	PAC	Q-Stat	Prob*
1	0.011	0.011	0.0066	0.935
2	−0.003	−0.003	0.0072	0.996
3	−0.075	−0.075	0.3374	0.953
4	−0.113	−0.112	1.1086	0.893
5	0.275	0.281	5.7761	0.329
6	0.145	0.143	7.1091	0.311
7	0.109	0.096	7.8797	0.343
8	−0.062	−0.045	8.1335	0.421
9	−0.088	−0.013	8.6492	0.47
10	−0.058	−0.101	8.8779	0.544
11	−0.063	−0.145	9.1574	0.607
12	−0.048	−0.169	9.3203	0.675
13	0.098	0.087	10.026	0.692
14	−0.002	0.02	10.026	0.76
15	−0.082	−0.043	10.545	0.784
16	−0.099	−0.03	11.325	0.789
17	−0.048	0.087	11.511	0.829
18	−0.007	−0.024	11.516	0.871
19	0.009	−0.056	11.522	0.905
20	−0.02	−0.06	11.557	0.93
21	−0.098	−0.063	12.434	0.927
22	−0.069	−0.079	12.879	0.936

(continued)

Table 4 (continued)

Lag	AC	PAC	Q-Stat	Prob*
23	−0.021	−0.031	12.921	0.954
24	0.084	0.106	13.634	0.954

Source own estimation

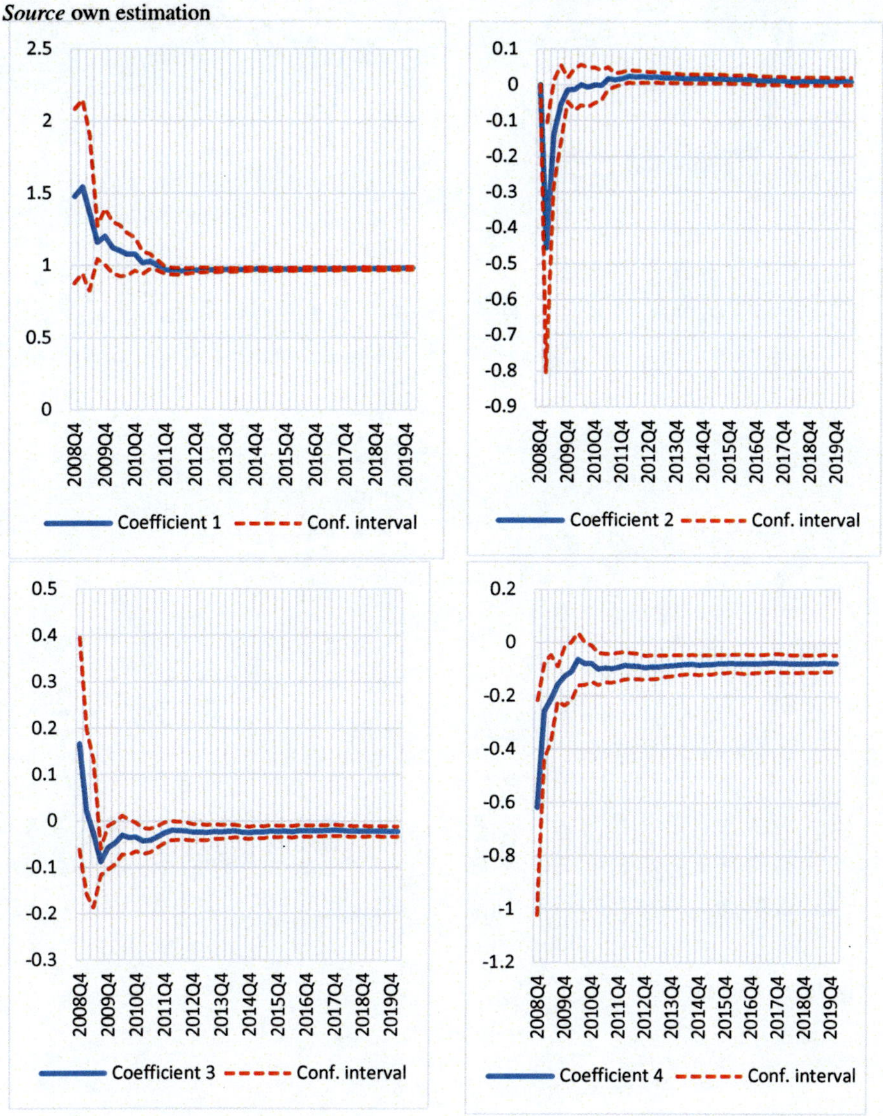

Fig. 14 Iterative coefficient estimation results for the ARDL model. *Source* own estimation

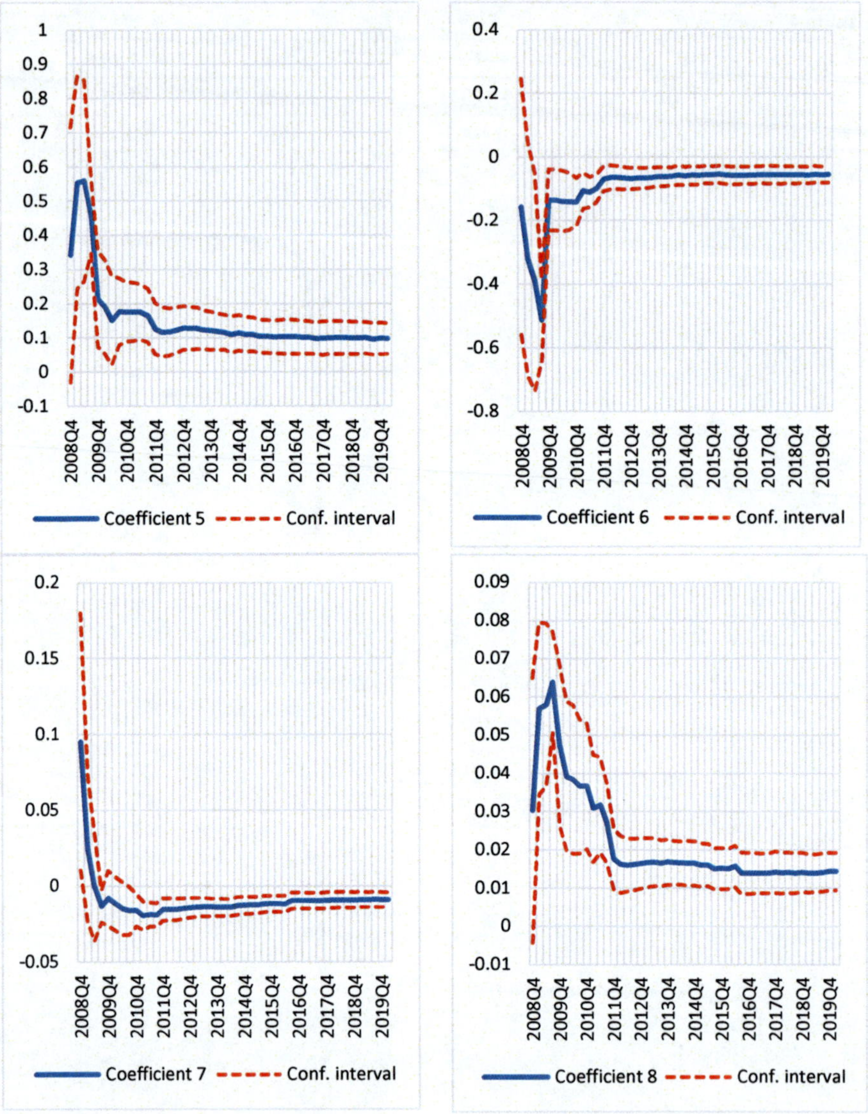

Fig. 14 (continued)

References

[Government Emergency Ordinace no. 37/2020] Ordonanța de urgență nr. 37/2020 privind acordarea unor facilități pentru creditele acordate de instituții de credit și instituții publicată în Monitorul Oficial din 30.03.2020

[The law for approval of the Government Emergency Ordinance no. 37/2020] Lege pentru aprobarea Ordonanței urgentă nr. 37/2020 privind acordarea unor facilități pentru creditele acordate de instituții de credit și instituții adoptată de Parlament în 23.04.2020

https://www.zf.ro/banci-si-asigurari/criza-coronavirusului-banking-tot-multi-romani-cer-amanarea-ratelor-19098960

https://www.arb.ro/wp-content/uploads/Comunicat-de-presa-ARB-24.04.2020.pdf

Chohan, U.W.: Reprieve and mercy: debt relief for the developing world during coronavirus (2021)

Demmou, L., Franco, G., Calligaris, S., Dlugosch, D.: Liquidity shortfalls during the COVID-19 outbreak: assessment and policy responses (2021)

European Banking Authority: guidelines on legislative and non-legislative moratoria on loan repayments applied in the light of the COVID-19 crisis

European Banking Authority: guidelines on the application of the definition of default

Grigoli, F., Mansilla, M., Saldias, M.: Macro-financial linkages and heterogeneous non-performing loans projections: an application to ecuador. IMF Working Paper, No. 16/236 (2016)

Higham, N.J.: Analysis of the Cholesky decomposition of a semi-definite matrix. Oxford University Press, pp. 161–185 (1990)

Liu, Y., Garrido, J., DeLong, C.: Private debt resolution measures in the wake of the pandemic. In: IMF Special Series on COVID-19, International Monetary Fund, Washington, DC (2020)

Reinhart, C.M., Rogoff, K.: The coronavirus debt threat. Wall Str. J. **26** (2020)

Vazquez, F., Tabak, B.M., Souto, M.: A macro stress test model of credit risk for the Brazilian banking sector. J. Financ. Stab. **8**(2), 69–83 (2012)

Wezel, T., Canta, M., Luy, M.: A practical example of the nonperforming loans projection approach to stress testing. In: A Guide to IMF Stress Testing: Methods and Models, pp. 473–483 (2014)

The Impact of COVID-19 on the Building Industry and on Real Estate Transactions in Romania

Anghel Ion, Simion Cezar-Petre, Ciora Costin, Ionaşcu Elena, and Dumitru Ovidiu

1 Introduction

The building industry and real estate transactions represent one of the major economic sectors both in Romania and across Europe. The building sector accounts for 10% of the GDP in Europe and supports about 20 million jobs, mainly in small and medium-sized enterprises. Although in the period of economic growth of 2007–2008, the building sector accounted for more than 10% of the GDP in Romania, in 2019 it dropped to only 6.4% of the Romanian GDP, but showed a good growth potential. Despite its relatively low share in the Romanian GDP, the building sector has been a major driver of economic growth in Romania in the past three years, similar to other EU member states (Pâslaru 2019; Residential real estate market report 2020a, b; Statistical Yearbook of Romania 2008–2019).

Similar to the past, the building sector may be a catalyst of economic growth in Romania. Although it is a field with an average added value, it is highly valuable from an economic perspective, since it can significantly influence both the economic growth and the overall economic performance of the country (Pâslaru 2019). Altogether, the building industry and real estate transactions make one of the major consumers of intermediate products (raw materials, chemical products, equipment

A. Ion · S. Cezar-Petre (✉) · C. Costin · I. Elena · D. Ovidiu
Bucharest University of Economic Studies, Bucharest, Romania

A. Ion
e-mail: ion.anghel@cig.ase.ro

C. Costin
e-mail: costin.ciora@cig.ase.ro

I. Elena
e-mail: elena.ionascu@cig.ase.ro

D. Ovidiu
e-mail: ovidiu.dumitru@cig.ase.ro

A. M. Dima et al. (eds.), *Economic Recovery After COVID-19*, Springer Proceedings in Business and Economics, https://doi.org/10.1007/978-3-030-86641-9_8

and machinery) and of related services (engineering, technical assistance, consulting, etc.). The analysis and quantification of COVID-19 impact on this field are an absolute must, given the role that it plays in overall economic activity as well as its links with the other economic fields, mainly dealing with the manufacturing of building materials and products (EIC 2020; Proposals for FPSC measures 2020).

The complexity of the processes implemented in the building industry is given by the huge volumes of building works which, in turn, require just as high volumes of materials, labor and machinery operation time. It is common to operate with bills of quantities that include over 40,000 items or over 10,000 aggregated items, with about 150,000 standardized sizes for materials, 150 different professions and over 200 classes of equipment (Radu and Curteanu 2020). The production cycle in the building sector is typically long (several months of even years). Under the circumstances, values (as translated in materials and unfinished production) are immobilized for much longer in the building industry that in manufacturing. The natural elements do force building activities to be seasonal, i.e., between November 15 and March 15 work is significantly reduced and even discontinued for most entities.

All the features outlined above argue in favor of selecting the field of the building industry and real estate transactions for the study of the COVID-19 impact, both from a quantitative and a qualitative perspective, in order to develop a plan of adequate actions that would support this sector during the pandemic as well as in the post-pandemic period. The analysis of the impact of COVID-19 on the construction of buildings and real estate transactions focused on those activity segments where we could identify this impact fairly quickly and describe it from a quantitative perspective (Proposals for FPSC measures 2020; OUG no. 30/2020 2020). In addition to that, when the quantitative description was not readily available, such as for civil engineering and special building works, we obtained a series of data by conducting interviews with the representatives of the related employers'/professional associations.

The article represents a first important contribution regarding the study of the effects of the COVID-19 pandemic on the construction and real estate sector in Romania. It contains a multidimensional analysis on the effects of COVID-19 on the main types of construction works, the demand and supply in the real estate field but also on the price dynamics in this field. It is, at the time of its completion, one of the few comprehensive studies conducted in this field. Only a few other studies (few in the region of Romania) addressed similar issues and not at the same level of completeness.

The structure of the article includes, in addition to the introductory part, the following sections: literature review, research methodology, presentation of the main research results, discussions and conclusions.

2 Literature Review

After March 2020, a series of studies appeared in the literature that considered the impact of COVID-19 on the economy and the price of assets in the economy. However, most studies have focused on the impact of COVID-19 on the price of financial assets. There have been fewer studies on the impact of COVID-19 on the construction and real estate sectors, although European International Contractors estimates in 2020 that this pandemic has affected the construction sector globally in the following areas:

- health and safety of construction workers;
- delays in the supply processes with construction materials;
- the emergence of new legal and administrative issues;
- distortion of demand and financial problems.

Qian et al. (2021) used monthly data on cases confirmed with COVID-19 in China and monthly data on house prices to investigate the impact of the pandemic on the real estate sector. These researchers concluded that real estate prices in communities with COVID-19 confirmed cases decreased by 2.47% and this impact persisted for three months with an upward trend after this period (Qian et al. 2021).

Hu et al. (2021) conducted research on the impact of the pandemic on the real estate sector in Australia but also on the effect of government measures (lockdown) on prices in this sector. Following research by Hu et al. (2021), they found a reduction in revenue with each doubling of COVID-19 cases in the five capitals of the Australian regions analyzed. On the other hand, the effect of government measures to mitigate the effects of the pandemic was reduced according to the results of this study (Hu et al. 2021).

Tanrıvermiş (2020) analyzed the possible effects and impact of the COVID-19 outbreak on real estate development and management processes. The global effects of the pandemic have negatively affected the development of projects in the real estate sector, sales operations of existing buildings, cost estimates, values and rates of return on existing buildings during operation. The launch of new policies and precautions have the following effects: narrowing the volume of real estate transactions, such as retail facilities, residential transaction offices, significantly increasing operating costs, lower demand, lower rental income, lower net income from investment exploitation (Tanrıvermiş 2020).

Gan and Koh (2021) analyzed the effects of the pandemic on construction workers in Singapore and the effects of government measures to reduce the effects of the pandemic on the workforce in this area. Government measures to reduce the effects of the pandemic have had the effect of reducing the incidence of COVID-19 on construction workers (Gan and Koh 2021).

3 Research Methodology

The research was used using three data sources: official statistical data from the monthly bulletins of the National Institute of Statistics, data collected and / or provided by construction companies / real estate development / real estate consulting and analysis and data from interviews with representatives of employers' associations in the field (focused mainly on those aspects of the impact of COVID-19 on the construction and real estate sector for which there were no official data or provided by organizations in the economic environment).

Official statistics and those provided by private organizations were centralized and analyzed using descriptive statistics. The impact of COVID on new construction works, current and capital repairs but also on the real estate sector was analyzed. Regarding the real estate field, the effects of COVID-19 on demand, supply and price dynamics were analyzed. The three elements analyzed in the real estate field were taken into account as they represent the most important characteristic elements followed by the analyses in this field.

Semi-structured interviews were conducted with a representative sample consisting of five members of the management of employers' associations in the field. The selection criterion used for the position held in the management of the employers' association (in the first two hierarchical levels). The interviews were conducted between April 15 and May 7, 2020, in successive two-hour sessions with each interviewee.

4 The Impact of COVID-19 on the Works Related to New Buildings, Refurbishments and Current Repairs

The impact of COVID-19 on the works related to new buildings, refurbishments and current repairs was analyzed in the light of construction work indicators (as percentage of 2015 as the baseline year, adjusted by the number of working days and seasonality).

In the first half of 2020, the total volume of construction works expressed as an adjusted series rose by 21% compared with the same period of the previous year, an increase which is reflected in the growth of maintenance and current repairs works (+56.8%), of refurbishment works (+44.7%) and of new construction works (+8.9%) (Fig. 1). The upward trend in the volume of construction works, which emerged as early as December 2019, became a slightly downward slope as soon as the pandemic was formally acknowledged in March 2019.

In June 2020, the total volume of construction works, as adjusted by number of working days and seasonality, dropped by 4.8% compared with May 2020, a decrease which is reflected in maintenance and current repairs works (−17.2%), in refurbishment works (−9.0%) and new construction works (−7.5%).

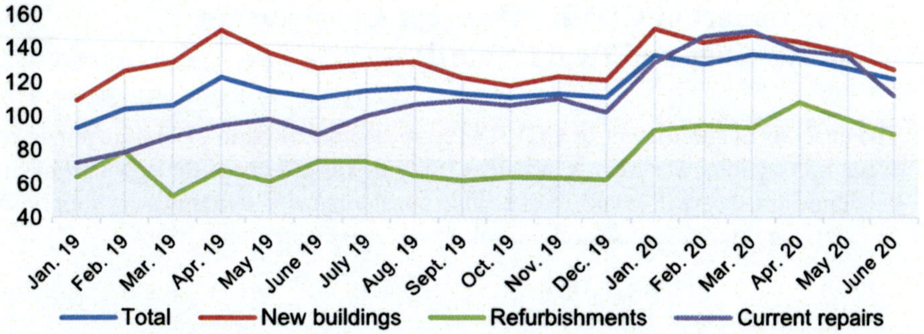

Fig. 1 Monthly dynamics of construction works by structural elements—January 2019–June 2020 (series adjusted by number of working days and seasonality, 2015 = 100). *Source* own elaborations based on the National Institute of Statistics (NIS) data

Table 1 Comparative analysis of the monthly construction work indicators by structural elements (adjusted series)

	March 2020 versus		June 2020 versus		Percentage
	February 2020	March 2019	May 2020	June 2019	H1 2020 versus H2 2019
Constructions—total	104.2	128.6	95.2	110.3	121.0
– By elements of structure					
New constructions	103.0	112.5	92.5	99.4	108.9
Refurbishments	98.5	177.5	91.0	122.3	144.7
Maintenance and current repairs	102.0	171.5	82.8	125.7	156.8

Source own elaborations based on the NIS data

Table 1 shows the comparison of the construction work indicators by structural elements in the first and second quarters of 2020 in comparison with the same period of the previous year.

Although at the end of March 2020, the volume of construction works by all structural elements was higher both in comparison with the previous month (excepting refurbishment works) and March 2019, at the end of the second quarter, irrespective of their type, construction works evince a significant drop from one month to the next, i.e., in June–May 2020. This drop is also visible for new constructions carried out in June 2020 in comparison with June 2019. Considering that the lockdown was instated in the second half of March, the effects of the pandemic were still not visible by the end of the first quarter. Consequently, the indicators signal the first negative influences of the COVID-19 pandemic on the building industry, notably on new constructions, only starting with the second quarter.

5 The Impact of COVID-19 on the Construction of Buildings and Real Estate Transactions

The analysis of the impact of COVID-19 on the construction of buildings and real estate transactions was mainly aimed at studying the effects of the new coronavirus pandemic on the real estate market and considered the dynamics of supply and demand, the price response and the concluded real estate transactions.

5.1 The Response on the Real Estate Demand Side

Under the circumstances of the restrictions that the authorities resorted to in order to curb the spread of the new coronavirus, the demand for new apartments and houses plummeted during the lockdown, when the bottom point was reached in the week of March 23–29, with an average demand indicator of 29% in the week of February 3–9 (Residential real estate market report 2020a, b) (Fig. 2).

As soon as the first COVID-19 cases were recorded in Romania, the demand for apartments and houses in Bucharest showed a steep drop, an effect that was also felt in the other cities, although it was not as marked as in the capital of the country (Fig. 3).

The buyers' interest was moderate in March–April 2020, mainly under the influence of the limited freedom of movement that came with the lockdown instated all over Romania and evinced a slight comeback with the relaxation of the protection measures.

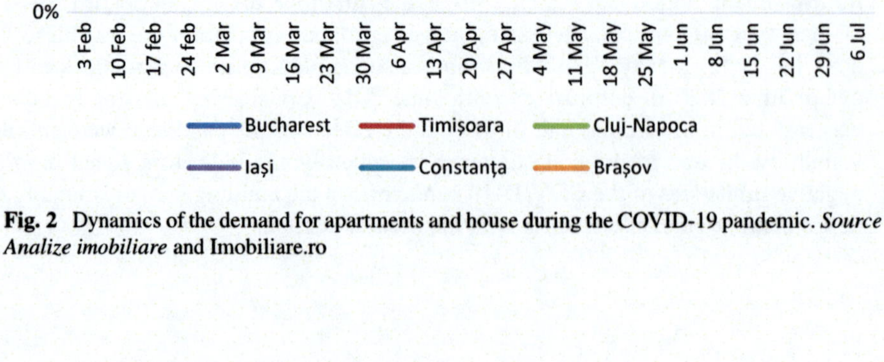

Fig. 2 Dynamics of the demand for apartments and house during the COVID-19 pandemic. *Source Analize imobiliare* and Imobiliare.ro

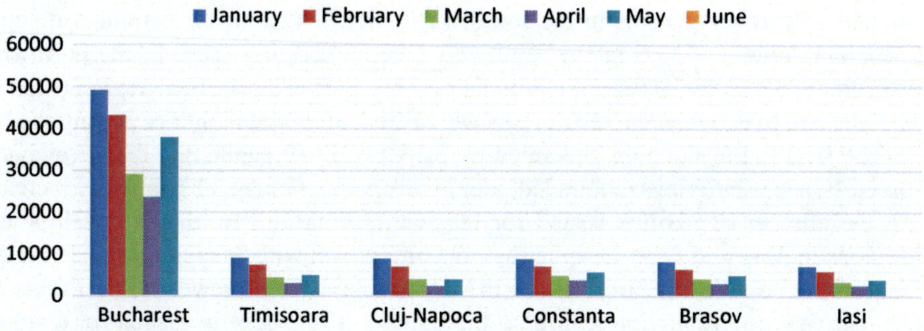

Fig. 3 Buyers' interest in purchasing apartments and houses during the COVID-19 pandemic. *Source* own elaborations based on the data provided by *Analize Imobiliare* and Imobiliare.ro

5.2 *The Response on the Real Estate Supply Side*

The dynamics of the monthly construction work indicators by construction type for the period January 2019–June 2020 (adjusted series by number of working days and seasonality) is shown in Fig. 4. The chart shows that the curve of the residential buildings is clearly superior to the curves corresponding to the non-residential buildings and construction engineering. The end of 2019 was marked by an increase in the volume of new residential buildings, but starting January 2020, the indicators evinced a downward trend which deepened with the pandemic. The dynamics of non-residential buildings and construction engineering are relatively similar, with a slight drop at the beginning of the pandemic.

At the level of Romanian regions, the number of building permits issued for residential use dropped significantly in April, when, compared with March, authorities

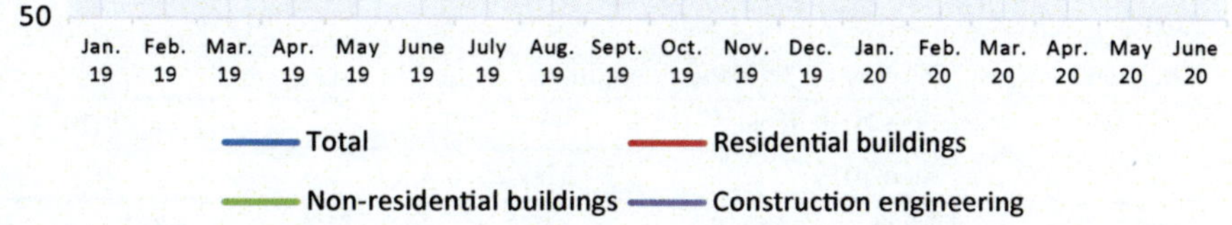

Fig. 4 Monthly dynamics of construction works by construction type—January 2019–June 2020. Adjusted series by number of working days and seasonality, 2015 = 100. *Source* Own elaboration based on NIS data

issued 42% fewer permits in the southeast region, −41% in the central and south Muntenia region, - 33% in the southwest Oltenia region, −28% in the northwest region, −23% in the northeast region and −11% in Bucharest–Ilfov region (Fig. 5).

Starting May, when the restrictions were lifted, after one month of getting the lay of the land in the situation generated by the COVID-19 pandemic, the developers' interest in new buildings rebounded, judging from the average 30% monthly increase in the number of permits issued for residential buildings in all the development regions in May and June. Despite that, in comparison with May and June 2019, the authorities issued 26% fewer permits in May and about 0.18% fewer in June (Table 2).

The described situation regarding the number of the permits issued for residential buildings is relatively similar with the number of permits for non-residential buildings, as shown in Table 3.

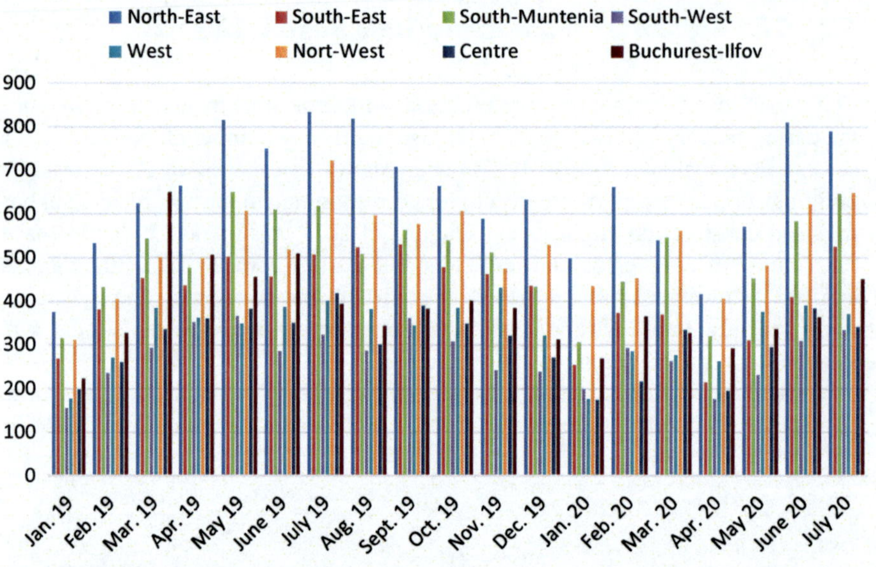

Fig. 5 Monthly distribution of the building permits issued for residential use, by development regions. *Source* Own elaboration based on NIS data

Table 2 Comparative situation of the number of building permits for residential use issued in June 2020

Location	Permits for residential buildings				
	June 2020 versus June 2019		June 2020 versus May 2020		June 2020
Total	3,874	0.18%	3,062	26.75%	3,881
Urban areas	1,335	9,96%	940	27,87%	1,202
Rural areas	2,539	5,51%	2,122	26,25%	2,679

Source own elaborations based on the NIS data

Table 3 Comparative situation of the number of building permits for non-residential use issued in June 2020

Location	Permits for non-residential buildings					
	Administrative buildings			Other buildings		
	June 2019	May 2020	June 2020	June 2019	May 2020	June 2020
Total	27	11	18	657	483	663
Urban areas	10	4	15	274	172	250
Rural areas	17	7	3	383	311	413

Source own elaborations based on the NIS data

The number of building permits issued for non-residential use reached the lowest point in May, followed by a significant increase in the last month of the second quarter of 2020. This trend is apparent both for administrative buildings and other types of buildings, irrespective of their location (urban or rural).

5.3 *The Response at the Level of Real Estate Prices and Concluded Real Estate Transactions*

On the background of the entire 2008–2020 period, in the first quarter of the year, the monthly price dynamics for new apartments followed the general upward trend featured by the large urban centers in the three previous years. Starting with the second quarter, however, the asking prices for residential properties showed a slight 1.7% decline in comparison with the previous quarter.

Still, according to the data aggregated by *Analize Imobiliare*, the asking prices for residential real estate in Romania were 7.1% higher in the second quarter in comparison with the previous year, whereas the sales prices went up by 8.1% in the first quarter, according to the INS and Eurostat data (Imobiliare.ro, 2020).

All the major urban centers in Romania (Brașov, Bucharest, Cluj-Napoca, Constanța, Timișoara) recorded slight monthly drops in the asking prices for new and existing apartments, which reflected the effects of the COVID-19 pandemic on the Romanian residential market (Figs. 6 and 7).

Market rents for residential properties are a significant influence in the formation of their prices, which is why we followed the monthly market rent dynamics in Romania during the pandemic period (Fig. 8).

The analysis of the monthly market rent dynamics in 2008–2020 shows the following:

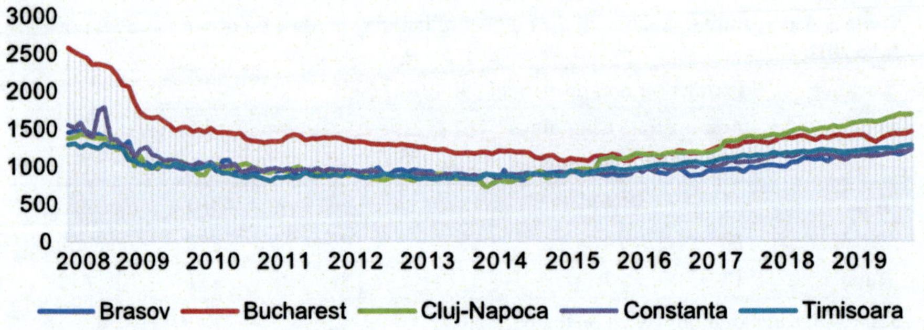

Fig. 6 Monthly dynamics of the asking prices for new apartments (euro/sq.m.) in large urban center in 2008–2020. *Source* Own elaboration based on Imobiliare.ro

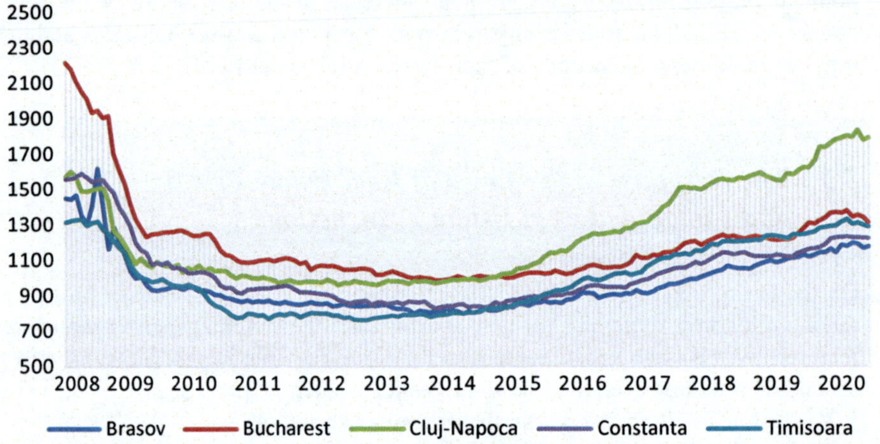

Fig. 7 Monthly dynamics of the asking prices for old apartments (euro/sq.m.) in large urban center in 2008–2020. *Source* Own elaboration based on Imobiliare.ro

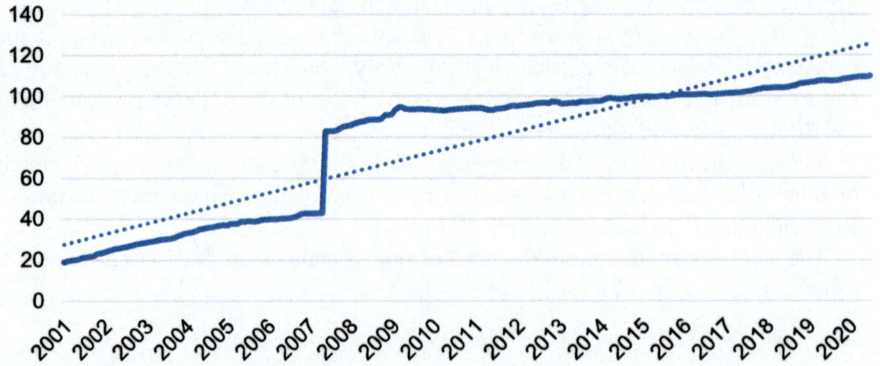

Fig. 8 Monthly market housing rents dynamics in 2008–2020 (2015 = 100). *Source* Own elaboration based on the Eurostat data

- rents generally follow a constant upward trend;
- in the first two quarters of 2020, the rent levels quarterly appreciated by 2% in comparison with the same period of 2019, a period when the leased real estate market was fairly dynamic.

The fact that the effects of the COVID-19 pandemic were not felt in the Romanian real estate market in the first quarter of 2020 was also apparent in the number of real estate transactions concluded in the same period. The comparative analysis of the data related to the number of land-and-building properties that changed hands in March 2020 in comparison with March 2019 shows that most of the Romanian counties had not yet been affected by significant mutations that could have been associated to the global COVID-19 pandemic at the time (Fig. 9).

At country level, the effects of the COVID-19 pandemic on real estate sales started to reflect in the data about the sales that were concluded in April and May, in comparison with the same period of the previous year, as shown in Fig. 10. The number of properties sold in May was 28% lower than in the same period of the previous year, but sales returned to the upward trend pattern in June, when they

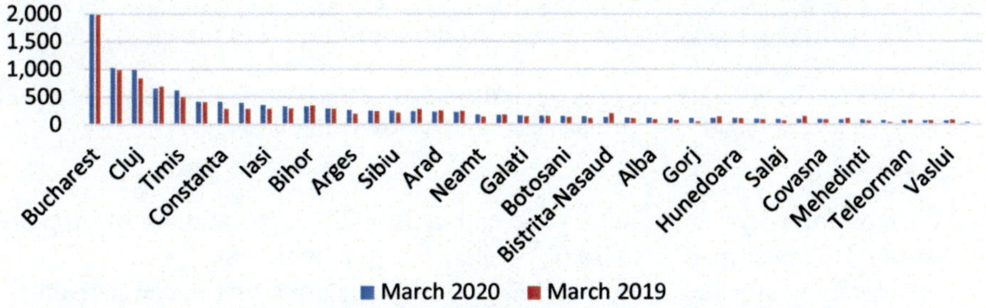

Fig. 9 Number of land-and-building properties sold in March 2020 in comparison with March 2019. *Source* own elaborations based on the ANCPI data

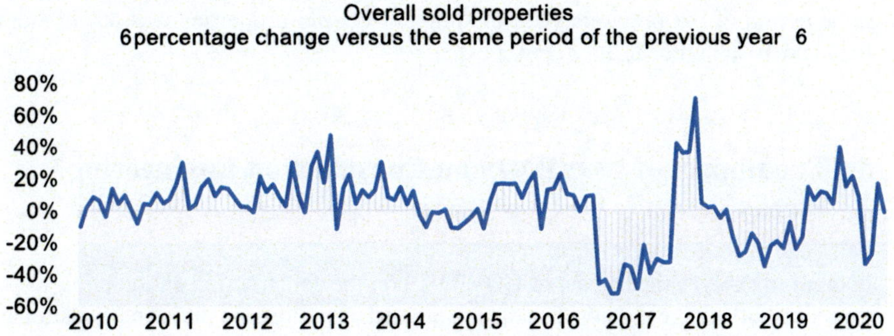

Fig. 10 Dynamics of the percentage change in overall sold properties versus the same periods of the previous year. *Source* own elaborations based on the ANCPI data

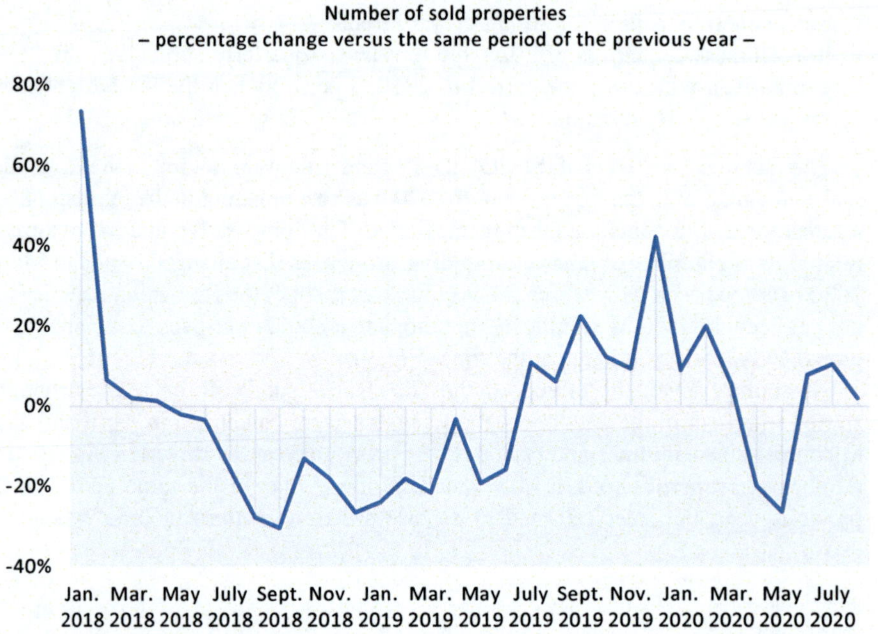

Fig. 11 Dynamics of the percentage change in the number of sold properties versus the same period of the previous year. *Source* own elaborations based on the ANCPI data

accounted for a 16% increase. By the end of July 2020, the number of properties sold was 1% lower than in the same period of the previous year.

By detailing on categories of buildings, it is noteworthy that in comparison with the same period of the previous year, the number of buildings sold was 20% lower in April and 26% lower in May. Starting May, as soon as the curfew was lifted, the number of real estate transactions picked up every month, so 5% more buildings were sold in May, 28% more in June and 27% more in July. In comparison with the same period of the previous year, the number of sold properties was 8% higher in June and 10% higher in July (Fig. 11).

6 The Impact of COVID-19 on Construction Engineering Works

In order to analyze the impact of COVID-19 on the construction engineering works, we relied both on the quantitative data published on national institutions websites and the data that we collected and processed from the interviews with representatives of the employers'/professional associations in the field. For construction engineering, the series adjusted with the number of working days and seasonality indicate a higher

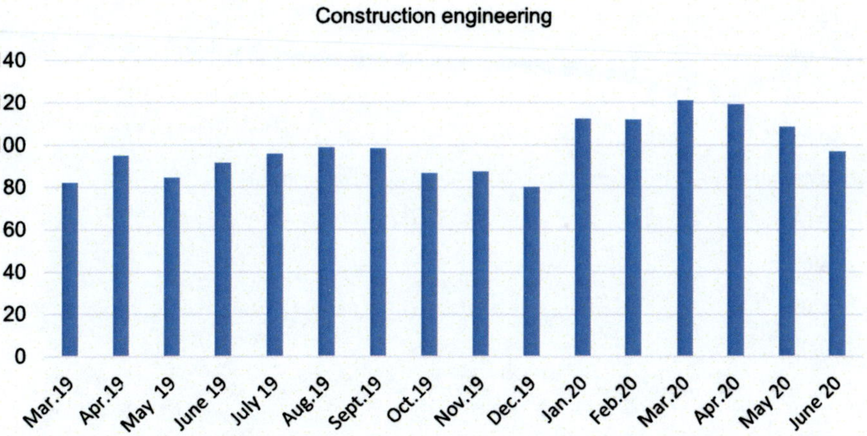

Fig. 12 Evolution of construction engineering monthly indicators – adjusted series. *Source* own elaborations based on the INS data

volume of construction engineering projects in January–June 2020 in comparison with the same period of the previous year (Fig. 12), which is explained by the fact that works are resumed at the beginning of spring.

With regard to the aspects related to the impact of COVID-19 on construction engineering works, the interviews with the representatives of the employers'/professional associations revealed the following:

- Works continued for most of the projects.
- Part of the funds that the county councils earmarked for road works in 2020 were channeled to the fight against COVID-19.
- Large projects were discontinued because of the shortage of funds across clients such as local authorities and SMEs.

7 The Impact of COVID-19 on Human Resources in the Building Industry

In order to analyze the impact of COVID-19 on human resources working in the building industry, we relied both on the information provided by the Ministry of Labor regarding the number of cancelled labor contracts and the information emerging from the interviews with the representatives of the employers' associations.

One of the first important effects of COVID-19 on the field of constructions was the cancellation of a large number of labor contracts. The data presented in Fig. 13 show a high (over 12% on March 30, 2020) and continuously growing share of the cancelled labor contracts in the field of constructions (over 14% at the beginning of May) in the total number of cancelled contracts across the country.

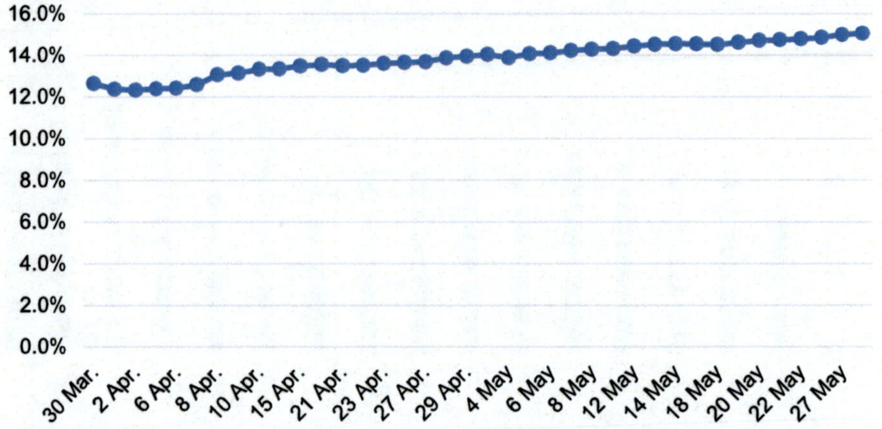

Fig. 13 Share of the cancelled contracts in the field of constructions in overall cancelled contracts at national level in March 30–May 8, 2020. *Source* own elaborations based on Ministry of Labor and Social Protection data

In the field of constructions, the fixed base growth rate (March 30 as baseline) of the cancelled labor contracts is higher than the national growth rate (Fig. 14).

With regard to the fixed base growth rate (March 30 as baseline) of the cancelled labor contracts in the field of constructions and at national level, it is noteworthy that the upward trend in the field of constructions is much higher than the national rate. Moreover, the gap between the situation in the field of constructions and the national one (including all the economic sectors) tends to widen in May.

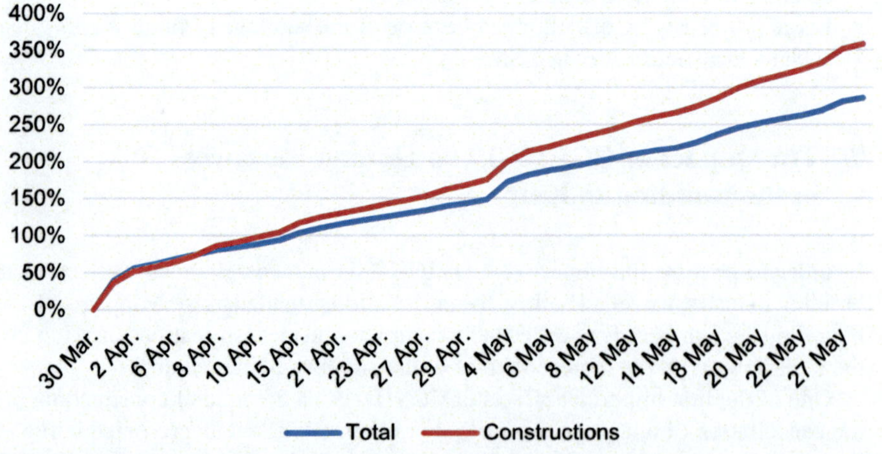

Fig. 14 Fixed base growth rate (March 30 as baseline) of the cancelled labor contracts in the field of constructions and at national level. *Source* own elaborations based on Ministry of Labor and Social Protection data

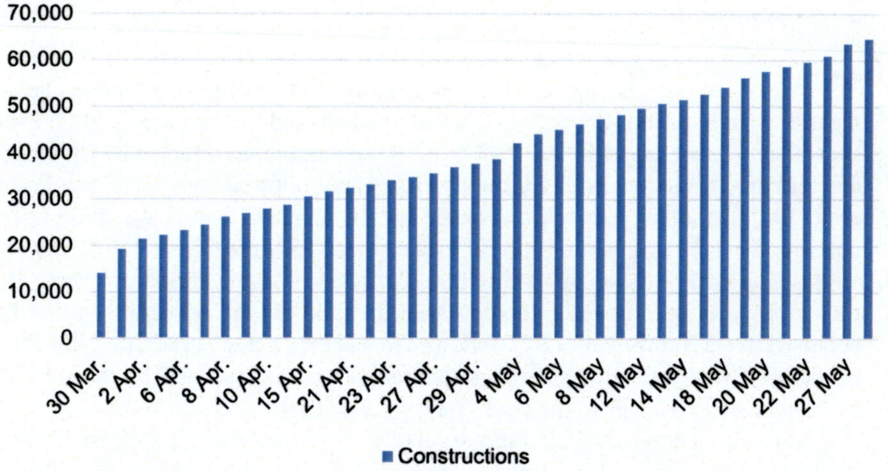

Fig. 15 Evolution of the labor contracts in the field of constructions in March 30-May 28, 2020. *Source* own elaborations based on Ministry of Labor and Social Protection data

Figure 15 describes the actual evolution of the cancelled individual labor contracts in the field of constructions.

The analysis of the data presented in the graph above yields that the total number of the cancelled individual labor contracts in the field of constructions went up by 60% in May in comparison with the previous month. The cancellation of such a high number of contracts in May stems from the deferred launch of the new building projects (both in the private and public sectors) for the third and fourth quarters of 2020.

In the building industry, over 95% of the different types of building works suppose the physical presence of the workers on site throughout the working hours. Telework is only possible for some of the ancillary staff. The impact of COVID-19 on the human resources in the field of constructions was also apparent as:

- cases of absenteeism because of the associated phobias (the "fear" of returning to the workplace);
- the stay of some projects (or delays caused by the postponement of certain critical activities because of the absenteeism of a number of "key" employees).

The particulars of work in the field of constructions result in an amplified effect of COVID-19 on the human resources when activities are supposed to be carried out in a closed space (finishes, inside partitions, plumbing and electrical works) and a lower impact when works are performed in the open (road and railway works, artworks, thermal rehabilitation, structural resistance works).

8 Discussions

The case of the construction and real estate sector in Romania is not a singular one regarding the impact of COVID-19. Research conducted by Qian et al. (2021) China showed that house prices fell by 2.47% in local communities affected by COVID-19 and that this impact persisted for three months and followed an upward trend (Qian et al. 2021). Another research conducted by Hu, Lee and Zou in Australia (2021) confirmed a 1.26% reduction in real estate prices for every doubling of COVID-19 cases in each Australian state (Hu et al. 2021). These authors also showed in their study that government intervention in the field did not necessarily have only positive effects. Tanrıvermiş (2020) showed that in the case of Turkey, the COVID-19 pandemic severely affected the real estate sector, having as main effects the reduction of demand and revenues in the field (Tanrıvermiş 2020).

The research conducted by Tanrıvermiş (2020), Qian et al. (2021), by Hu et al. (2021) confirms some of the results obtained in the research conducted on the real estate market in Romania regarding an initial decline in prices as a result of the COVID-19. However, at least at the beginning of the pandemic, the decline in the real estate market in Romania seems to have been much more severe compared to other states.

Gan and Koh (2021) investigated in Singapore the effect of government measures on the safety of construction workers during the 2020 COVID-19 pandemic led to the decline of COVID-19 cases in the construction sector (determined as an incidence per 100,000 inhabitants) in October 2020 compared to the situation in May of the same year (Gan and Koh 2021). The research conducted by Gan and Koh confirms the results of this study conducted in Romania on the ability of the construction sector to have a relatively rapid return and resumption / continuation of work on most construction projects.

Although there are relatively few published studies on the impact of COVID-19 on the construction sector, they confirm the results obtained in the case of research on the construction sector and the real estate market in Romania. In all research, the effect of COVID-19 on the real estate market was significant and the construction sector was one in which workers were able to resume work on ongoing projects relatively quickly.

9 Conclusions

The impact of COVID-19 on the building industry and real estate transactions was determined both through the analysis of the existing data (for buildings and real estate transactions) and interviews with the representatives of the related professional organizations. The analysis of the impact of COVID-19 on the building industry and real estate transactions revealed a series of elements that are typical of this field: There was a clear drop in the demand for new buildings and real estate transactions starting with the beginning of March 2020; the price per square meter of housing units was relatively constant one month after the first cases of COVID-19 were detected in Romania; the human resources in the building industry and real estate transactions were among the most affected, i.e., the field of constructions accounted for more than 18% of the overall cancelled individual labor contracts at national level.

The effects of COVID-19 on real estate transactions started to reflect in the data on the transactions concluded in April and May in comparison with the same period of the previous year. In May, the number of sold buildings dropped by 28% in comparison with the same period of the previous year, but sales regained an upward trend in June, so by the end of July 2020, the number of real estate sales was only 1% lower than the same period of the previous year (Residential real estate market report 2020a, b).

In the first months after the occurrence of COVID-19 cases, works continued for most of the projects, but there were also major projects that were postponed because of the shortage of funds for clients such as local authorities and SMEs. In the first months of the pandemic, part of the funds earmarked for investment by local authorities were rechanneled to the measures taken to curb the spread of COVID-19.

The research has a number of limitations that stem from the fact that it has been going on since the first months of the pandemic and is not based solely on definitive official statistics because they are not yet available. In the case of human resources, some information from the semi-structured interviews can only represent the perception of the respondents regarding some trends manifested at the beginning of the COVID-19 pandemic in Romania, then confirmed by official statistical data. However, these limits are not likely to significantly affect research results that are in line with those on the effects of the pandemic on the residential sector in other regions.

Future research directions will focus on analyzing the effects of the pandemic on the construction and real estate sectors in 2021. Another future research direction will be related to the effects of the COVID-19 pandemic on human resources in the construction sector in 2021. The relationship will be studied between the duration of the COVID-19 pandemic and the concluded / suspended employment contracts in the field of constructions and real estate transactions.

References

COVID-19 and global construction business, EIC (2020)

Gan, W.H., Koh, D.: COVID-19 and return-to-work for the construction sector: lessons from Singapore. Saf Health Work **12**(2), 277–281 (2021)

Hu, M.R., Lee, D.A., Zou, D.: COVID-19 and Housing Prices: Australian Evidence with Daily Hedonic Returns, Finance Research Letters, 101960 (2021)

H.G. no. 264/2003 regarding the establishment of actions and categories of expenses, criteria, procedures and limits for making advance payments from public funds

Law no. 263 of December 30, 2019 for the amendment of Law no. 227/2015 regarding the Fiscal Code

Law no. 227/2015 regarding the Fiscal Code
Law no. 146/30.04.2013 for the amendment and completion of Law no. 153/2011 on measures to increase the architectural-environmental quality of buildings
Law no. 153/05.07.2011 on measures to increase the architectural-environmental quality of buildings
Law no. 10/1995 regarding the quality in constructions
National Competitiveness Strategy (SNC) 2015–2020, approved by Government Decision no. 775/2015
OUG no. 30/2020 for amending and supplementing some normative acts, as well as for establishing measures in the field of social protection in the context of the epidemiological situation determined by the spread of the SARS-CoV-2 coronavirus
O.U.G. no. 114/2018 regarding the establishment of some measures in the field of public investments and of some fiscal-budgetary measures, the modification and completion of some normative acts and the extension of some terms
Proposals for FPSC measures, Annex to Letter 1131/15.04.2020
Pâslaru, S.: Capitalul financiar românesc, 4th edn. Everest, Bucharest (2019)
Qian, X., Qiu, S., Zhang, G.: The impact of COVID-19 on housing price: Evidence from China, Finance Research Letters, 101944 (2021)
Regulation (EC) No 305/2011 of the European Parliament and of the Council of 9 March 2011 laying down harmonized conditions for the marketing of construction products and repealing Council Directive 89/106/EE
Residential real estate market report—first quarter 2020, prepared by Imobiliare.ro.
Residential real estate market report—second quarter 2020, prepared by Imobiliare.ro
Radu, V., Curteanu, D.: Managementul proiectelor de construcţii, Editura Economică, Bucharest (2002)
Simion, C.P., Radu, V.: Difficulties of romanian construction organizations in context of economic crisis. Rev. Int. Comparative. Manag. **1**, 666–671 (2010)
Strategy for mobilizing investments in the renovation of the fund of residential and commercial buildings, both public and private, existing at national level - Version 2/2017
Statistical Yearbook of Romania (2008–2019)
Tanrıvermiş, H.: Possible impacts of COVID-19 outbreak on real estate sector and possible changes to adopt: a situation analysis and general assessment on Turkish perspective. J Urban Manag. **9**(3), 263–269 (2020)

The Evolution of Romania's International Trade in Services During the COVID-19 Crisis

Paraschiv Dorel Mihai, Popovici Oana Cristina, Davidescu Adriana AnaMaria, Manea Daniela, Gerard Cazabat, and Birol Ibadula

1 Introduction

International trade was among the most affected by the COVID-19 pandemic, the drop in the global trade in goods being worse than the one during the financial crisis of 2008. The COVID-19 pandemic is a very complex phenomenon because it generated unexpected crises in the economic systems, national health systems, educational systems, social systems and cultural systems (Bratianu 2020). Global trade was affected by the restrictions on free trade and the closure of the productive activity, whose consequences further reverberated in economies all around the world. We can consider international trade as one of the most important channels through which

P. D. Mihai (✉) · P. O. Cristina · D. A. AnaMaria · M. Daniela · B. Ibadula
Bucharest University of Economic Studies, Bucharest, Romania
e-mail: dorel.paraschiv@ase.ro

P. O. Cristina
e-mail: oana.popovici@rei.ase.ro

D. A. AnaMaria
e-mail: adriana.alexandru@csie.ase.ro

M. Daniela
e-mail: daniela.todose@csie.ase.ro

B. Ibadula
e-mail: ibadula.birol@fin.ase.ro

P. O. Cristina
Institute for Economic Forecasting, Romanian Academy, Bucharest, Romania

D. A. AnaMaria
National Research Institute for Labor and Social Protection, Bucharest, Romania

G. Cazabat
EDC Paris Business School, Courbevoie, France
e-mail: gerard.cazabat@edcparis.edu

A. M. Dima et al. (eds.), *Economic Recovery After COVID-19*, Springer Proceedings in Business and Economics, https://doi.org/10.1007/978-3-030-86641-9_9

economies were affected, due to the actual scale of globalization and interconnection. Exports and imports were affected by a double shock, of both demand as supply, as compared to twelve years ago, when the financial crisis came as a demand shock (Baldwin 2020). However, studies signal a different behavior for the trade in goods as compared to the one in services. While the first category was strongly affected by the economic and financial situation, the evolution of trade in services was mostly resilient (Ariu 2016; Shingal 2020; Tomé 2020).

The COVID-19 pandemic came with a change, since the actual crisis is not only an economic, but also a health crisis. The social isolation enhanced by the health measures for the containment of the virus has affected a large part of the services. The restrictions and border lockdown negatively impacted travel, tourism, accommodation, transport or logistics services, which were suspended all around the world to a smaller or larger extent, depending on the medical situation inside the domestic borders. The interconnection between economies at international level also affected the production and trade in services in the rest of locations. However, the outcome was uneven. In the category of the most affected services, there are those requiring proximity and interaction between the consumer and the producer, such as tourism and international travel (Maliszewska et al. 2020). Gruszczynski (2020) states that the most visible impact of the pandemic is in the international service sector, since "international tourism, passenger air travel and container shipping" (p. 338) are the most affected. On the other hand, other types of services had better evolutions or managed to recover faster, such as the information and telecommunication sector.

This paper takes a deep overview on the evolution of Romania's exports and imports of services during the COVID-19 crisis. In this aim, monthly data since the beginning of 2020 are used. Romania is not as developed as other European countries as regards financial services, rather international trade in services is relying on telecommunication and transport. Both of them were under the strong influence of the measures enhanced during the pandemic, but were affected in opposing ways. Therefore, our aim is to evidence the impact of the crisis for trade in both exports and imports of services and to identify potential risks and opportunities of development.

We start by looking at the characteristics of services that might be under the influence of the measures taken with the aim of preventing the spread of the pandemic. We also survey the previous literature regarding the impact of other epidemics on services in order to extract the expected behaviors in international trade with services. We further analysis the state and evolution of Romania's trade in services, from the sights of both exports and imports. Our purpose is to identify if the observed evolutions are similar to the ones in other countries. Finally, we comparatively look at the evolution of the international trade in services during the financial crisis in 2008 and the actual one, for assessing whether and when a restoration in their evolution would be possible.

2 Impact of Pandemic on Services

The literature points to several characteristics that make services different in nature as compared to goods: inseparability, intangibility, heterogeneity, perishability (Wolak et al. 1998; Moeller 2010). Inseparability states for the fact that the delivery and consumption of services takes place at once. For example, goods are produced before they are brought to market and traded, while services are produced at the very moment of their consumption. Intangibility is related to the fact that services cannot be evaluated qualitatively by consumers before they are purchased. Heterogeneity looks at the difficulties to standardize services, due to their high complexity. Even in the case of standardization, their production cannot be repeated identically, because the same service has different providers, whose performance is different from one to another or during time. Perishability refers to the fact that services are consumed at the time of their production, which is why they cannot be stored for later consumption. The newest frameworks for the description of services, such as the one proposed by Moeller (2010), suggest a high involvement of the customer and his experience in the consumption of services.

Most of the ways in which services are traded at international level require proximity between the buyer and the seller (Busu et al. 2020). Shingal (2020) states that, among the four modes in which the services are transacted, three of them are based on this proximity (the "consumption abroad," the "commercial presence," and the "movement of natural persons"). The fourth one, even if it implies "cross-border services trade," is still quite often related to proximity. Since two-quarters of the trade-in services is based on the three modes that imply proximity (Shingal 2020), a large negative effect on trade in services is expected. Previous studies investigating the impact of other epidemics on services showed unequal consequences due to these characteristics of services. Lee and McKibbin (2004), for example, exposed the negative impact of SARS infection on the global economy, seen as a decrease in demand for services such as travel and retail sales, while Adegun (2014) pointed toward the decreases in the transport services sector. Sanda et al. (2015) identified that trade, tourism, construction, and financial services were the most affected following Ebola outbreak.

The impact of pandemic in services generated two opposing consequences, at least on the short and medium terms: losses and opportunities. In the first category, there are similar services as the ones already suffering following different other outbreaks. COVID-19 has a large impact on the demand for services that require proximity when consumed (such as transport, tourism, accommodation, restaurants, or other recreational services) and the restriction on travel. McKibbin and Fernando (2020) emphasize the bad consequences for all types of transport services, such as air, sea, and land transport, while Coates et al. (2020) indicate the negative impact for the hospitality sector. Javed (2020) confirms the negative impact for transport, hospitality, and tourism for Pakistan. These are, in fact, the services' sectors the most sensitive to health security (Burkle 2006). On the other hand, expenses are to be increased in order to prevent the spread of the disease (Lee and McKibbin

2004). Obviously, the cancelation of production has indirectly affected the services accompanying the manufacturing of those goods (Stramge 2020). In a simulation regarding the impact of COVID-19 on GDP and trade, Maliszewska et al. (2020) show that domestic and tourist services are prone to suffering the biggest negative shock due to pandemics.

However, for other sectors of services, there are some large opportunities. The same lockdown measures have transformed homes into offices, thus enforcing digitalization and leading to the modernization of the economy. This measure was applied by both the business environment in the case of the insurance or banking sectors, even in the most traditional ones, such as medical services where the use of telemedicine increased (Gilson and Muramatsu 2020), but also in providing public services. This is why the question is how fast the recovery in services could take place, with positive impact on the recovery of the economies.

3 The Evolution of International Trade in Romania During the COVID-19 Pandemic

3.1 The Situation in Romania's International Trade Before the COVID-19 Crisis

Romania's international trade in services saw an increasing trend starting with the 2000s (Fig. 1), although the total values could not reach the levels registered for trade in goods. Services exports hit EUR 27 billion at the end of 2019, while imports amounted at EUR 18.4 billion. In addition, there is a trade surplus that managed to be maintained in the last 20 years, with a better evolution of export and not large fluctuations in imports until 2016.

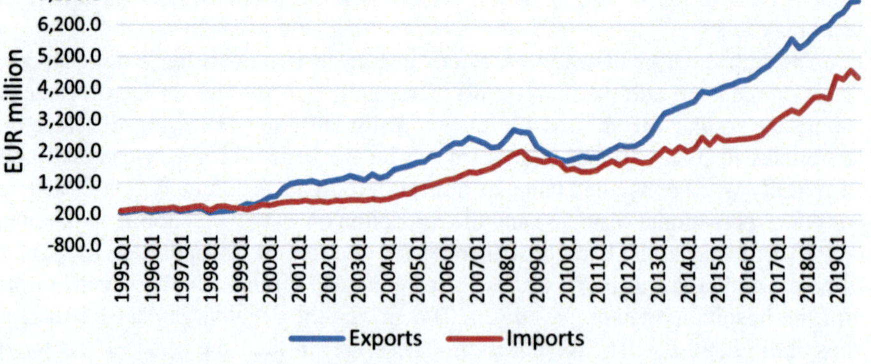

Fig. 1 Romania trade in services, quarterly data, 1995–2019. *Source* Authors' own elaborations based on Eurostat data

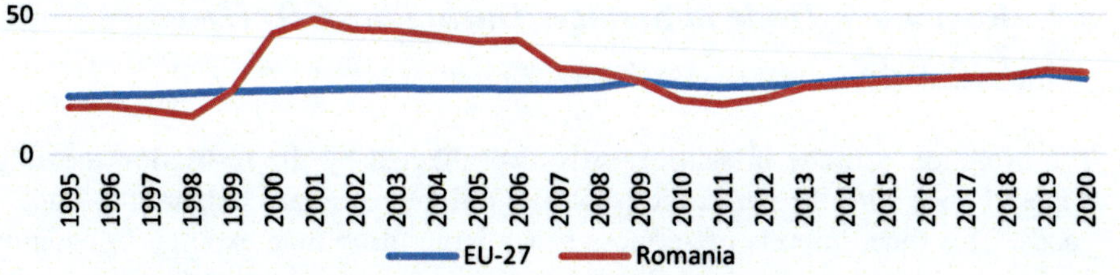

Fig. 2 Annual share of exports of services in total exports of goods and services, Romania and EU. *Source* Authors' own elaborations based on Eurostat data

The exports of services represented 29.2% of the total value of exported goods and services in Romania in 2020, in a slow decrease as compared to 2019 (30%). In the last years, the importance of services in Romania's exports increased above the average value in EU. Figure 2 shows the evolution in the shares of exports in services in Romania and EU, pointing to the high importance of services in Romania's international trade.

The situation of imports is completely different. Imports represented only 15.7% of the total value of imported goods and services in Romania, suffering a higher decrease than exports as compared to 2019 (18.5%). Moreover, they are well below the EU average. Usually, imports account for 27–28% of the total value imported, almost double than the values in Romania. Besides, we can notice in Fig. 3 that there were years in which the gap between Romania and the UE widened. We can conclude that exports of services are more important than imports for Romania, as compared to other European countries; therefore, Romania would be more affected by a drop in exports than in imports.

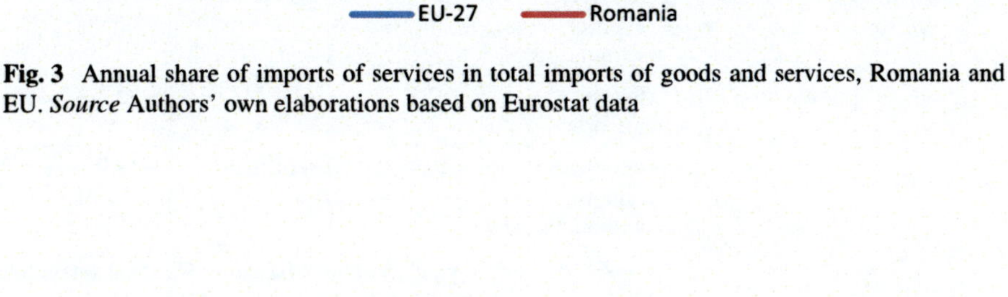

Fig. 3 Annual share of imports of services in total imports of goods and services, Romania and EU. *Source* Authors' own elaborations based on Eurostat data

3.2 *Romania's Trade in Services During the COVID-19 Pandemic*

The evolution of trade in services was also affected by the restriction measures imposed once with the pandemics, but in a different way as compared to trade in goods. This time, imports of services saw a larger drop than exports. In addition, for the export of services there is a lower gap as compared to the levels scored in the previous year in the most exposed months (March–May 2020), while imports of services were more severely affected than the drop in the imports of goods. Tourism services sector is among the ones in which the shock in demand could be best seen, the consumption of such services depending on the transport measures and the opening of the hospitality industry (Saif et al. 2021). For Romania, based on the data available for last year, we could notice that the drop in exports of good was larger than in imports, while the decrease in imports of services surpassed the reduction of exports of services (Table 1) both during the whole year and during the lockdown months. The magnitude in the reduction of trade in services remains high even if we exclude the impact on travel and tourism. Such an evolution is expected given the interconnectedness in services (e.g., air transport and travel and tourism or other cultural and recreational activities) (Milea 2020).

The decline in the export of services started in March 2020, when the value was 5.3% lower than in the same month of 2019. The drop became more acute in April, scoring a gap of 23.1% on a year-on-year basis, and it was the largest in May, as the difference reached 29.3% (Fig. 4). However, although the year-on-year gap in the value of export services was lower than that in goods during these months, the recovery of export services did not register a similar pace. The value of exports

Table 1 Year-on-year change in the volume of exports and imports

	2020 versus 2019	March–May	March–August
Goods exports	−9.9	−32.4	−21.0
Goods imports	−6.6	−23.7	−15.8
Services exports	−12.2	−18.5	−17.5
Services exports without travel	−5.7	−11.9	−10.0
Services imports	−22.1	−34.5	−32.2
Services imports without travel	−10.4	−21.3	−19.0

Source Authors' own elaborations based on National Institute of Statistics and National Bank of Romania data

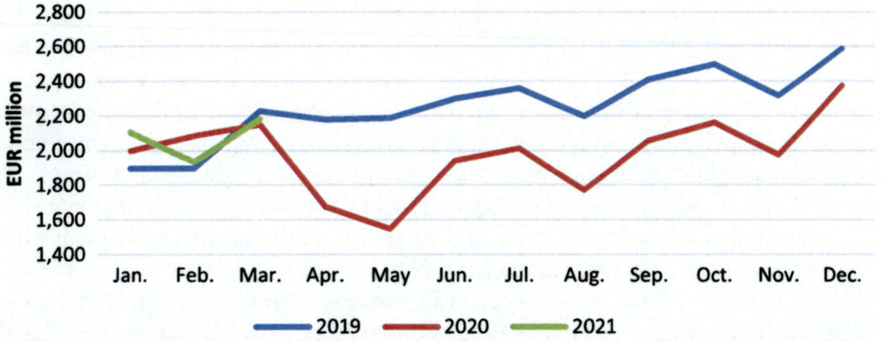

Fig. 4 Romania's monthly export of services, 2019–March 2021. *Source* Authors' own elaborations based on National Bank of Romania data

continued to be lower than in the same month of 2019, with differences between 8.3% (in December) and 19.3% in August.

Although such an evolution could be caused by one important branch of services, namely the tourism, Fig. 5 shows that the remaining important sectors did not manage to recover, as compared to exports in goods. The impact was uneven. The telecommunications, computer, and information services is the only one having a better evolution than in 2019 (excepting the month of May 2020, when it had a drop of 1.8%), as a result of working from home activities and online trade (Milea 2020). A lasting decrease could be seen in travel, as expected, which experiences the strongest decline and the hardest recovery. The values continue to be 65% lower than in 2019 even at the end of 2020. Travel and tourism was one of the most affected sectors, strongly depending on the confinement measures and the restrictions related to limitation of passenger transport, the closure of the borders and severely limited openness of the

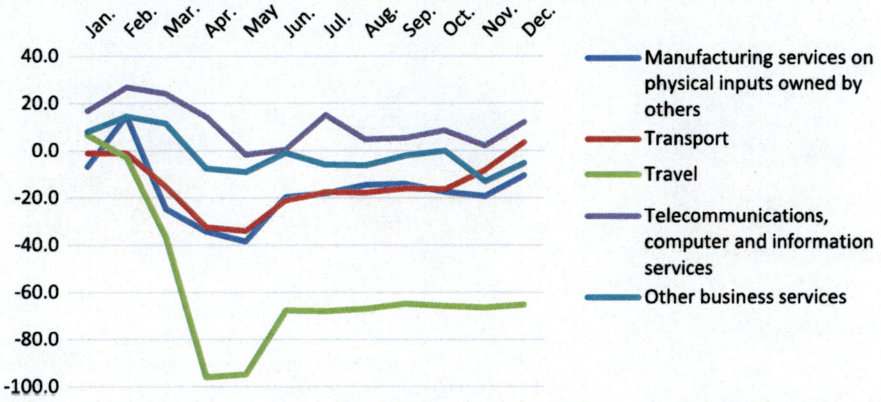

Fig. 5 Year-on-year change in the volume of exported services, per branches. *Source* Authors' own elaborations based on National Bank of Romania data

foodservice and hotel industries. Travel and tourism is among the sectors which will have the longest recovery, which will be determined by the vaccination pace in each country and the capacity of governments to enhance social distancing measures. For both sectors, their evolution in foreign trade was strongly influenced by the measures under the emergency and alert states that imposed working for home and implied therefore a higher use of telecommunications systems, while the free movement was limited. The export of manufacturing services on physical inputs owned by others, transport and other business services did not return to full capacity, but the tendencies in the last part of 2020 show an improvement.

The exports in these five categories of services represent around 93.5% of the total value of services exports in Romania; therefore, they impose the trend in the evolution of trade in services. There are only two sectors whose importance has significantly changed in the last two years as compared to 2013. We can observe in Fig. 6 a narrowing of the exports in manufacturing services from 16.9% in 2013 to 10.3% in 2020, a trend imposed in the last years and therefore not affected by the crisis. On the contrary, the share of exports in telecommunications, computer, and information services increased from 14% in 2013 to 20.7% in 2019 and was even higher in 2020 (25.9%), as a consequence of the crisis. The share in the export of services is almost similar during these years for other business services and transport, while the most significant drop, which is certainly caused by the pandemic, is that of travel.

Imports of services dropped significantly, being 30.6%, 36.4% and 37.2% lower in March, April, and May 2020, respectively, as compared to the same period in 2019. In addition, they continued to be almost one-third lower than in the corresponding month of 2019 until August (Fig. 7). The recovery is slow, but continues at the beginning of this year.

When looking at the most important branches for import (Fig. 8), tourism and travel is the hardest hit, while telecommunications, computer, and information services generally had better evolutions than in 2019 almost all the year (except

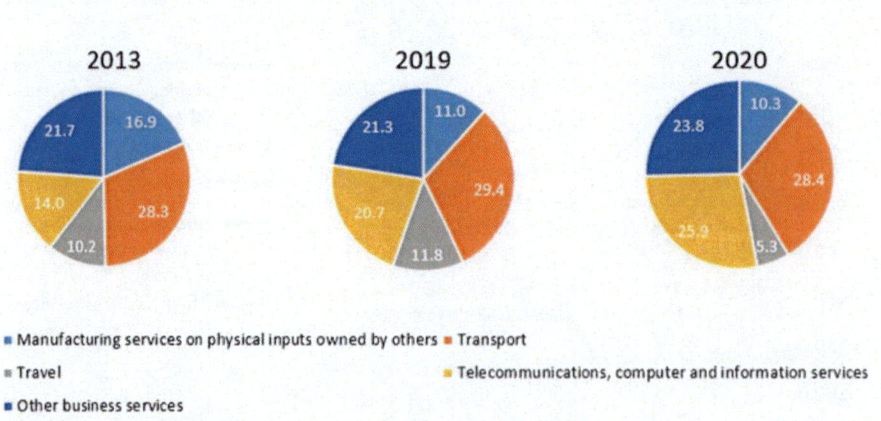

Fig. 6 Share of exports in the most important services sectors in Romania. *Source* Authors' own elaborations based on National Bank of Romania data

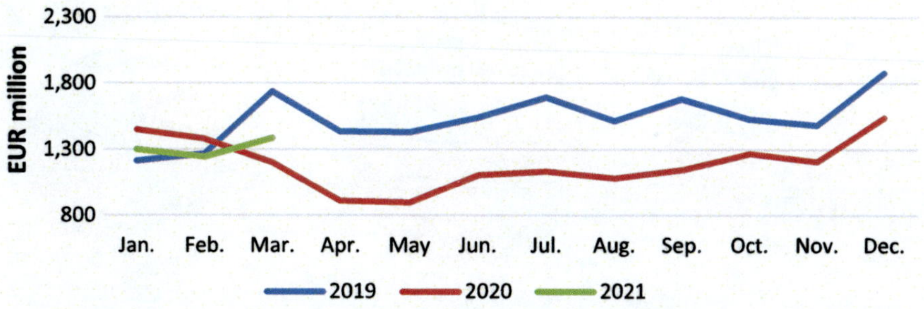

Fig. 7 Romania's monthly import of services, 2019–March 2021. *Source* Authors' own elaborations based on National Bank of Romania data

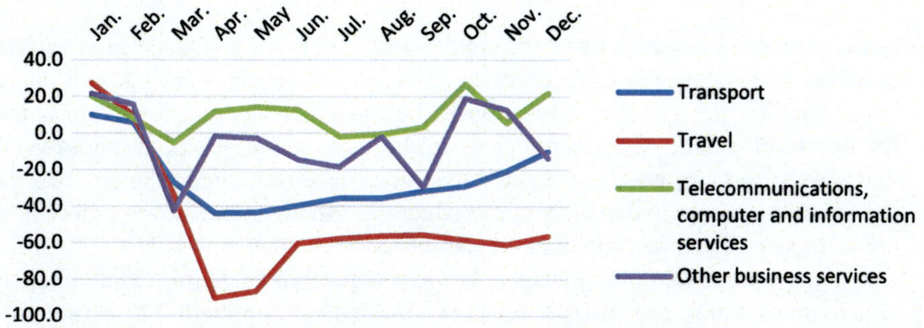

Fig. 8 Year-on-year change in the volume of exported services, per branches. *Source* Authors' own elaborations based on National Bank of Romania data

for March, July, and August). Transport import services were severely affected, and, on the background of restrictions all over Europe, the recovery was stagnant. The imports of other business services remained highly volatile.

These four sectors of services account for around 88% of total imports of services. We can also notice steady increase in the share of imported telecommunications, computer, and information services, from 10.3% in 2013 to 13.6% in 2019 and 19.2% in 2020 and the negative impact on travel services, although not as high as for the exports of these services (Fig. 9). Transport and other business services do not show large fluctuations in the years under observation.

4 Comparison with the 2008–2009 Financial Crisis

Shingal (2020) states that services were more resilient during the financial crisis in 2008 due to the fact that they were less impacted by the demand shock and not very dependent on supply finance. Borchert and Mattoo (2009) identified several characteristics of the behavior for the trade in services. They indicate that the decrease

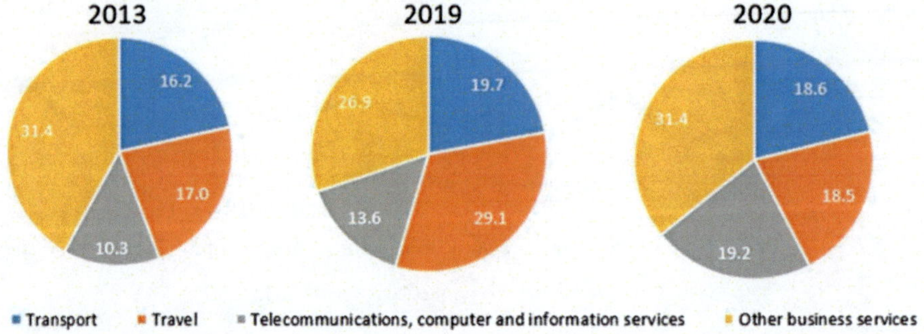

Fig. 9 Share of exports in the most important services sectors in Romania. *Source*: Authors' own elaborations based on National Bank of Romania data

in financing which was a form of supply shock did not affect trade in services as much as trade in goods. Companies in services are usually working with clients, being paid for the services they provide, but no other external funds are needed for the development of the services as in the case of the goods. In addition, the demand for services was less affected than that for goods, due to the fact that they cannot be stored or not dependent on production. Moreover, the development of the crisis imposed the expansion of new types of services, such as debt processing. Ariu (2016) also shows that only transport services registered decreases, while financial, telecommunication, and business services continued their growth. The authors state that services are behaving like fixed costs for companies, which cannot continue the production without them, especially in what concerns management, accounting or legal services. As a consequence, the exports of services in Belgium decrease 5% less than that of goods.

The COVID-19 crisis, however, imposed social distancing measures and closing borders, which significantly affected trade in services, due to the fact that one of their major characteristics is the proximity of the customer and the producer. This is why, a large drop in international trade in goods was also signaled. Minodo (2021), for example, indicates that for Spain, the decrease in services in the three months affected by the general lockdown was larger than the general decrease during the recession in 2008–2009.

In Romania, services, with or without the impact on travel, were less affected during the financial crisis (Fig. 10), at least during the recession period. Quantifying the total decrease of exports in services in the period starting from the fourth quarter of 2008 until the second quarter of 2009 as compared to the previous period, we obtain a gap of 6.2%, while the drop in imports of services was only 1.6%. The impact was felt in the second quarter of the official declared economic crisis, when exports decreased by 9.3%. However, the decrease in exports was not stopped by the economic recovery; on the contrary, it worsened until the end of 2009, when hitting a record of 30.6% reduction as compared to the same quarter in 2008. Hardly the last months of 2010 brought a restauration at higher levels than before. Imports of services had a milder decrease than exports throughout the crisis, dropping by

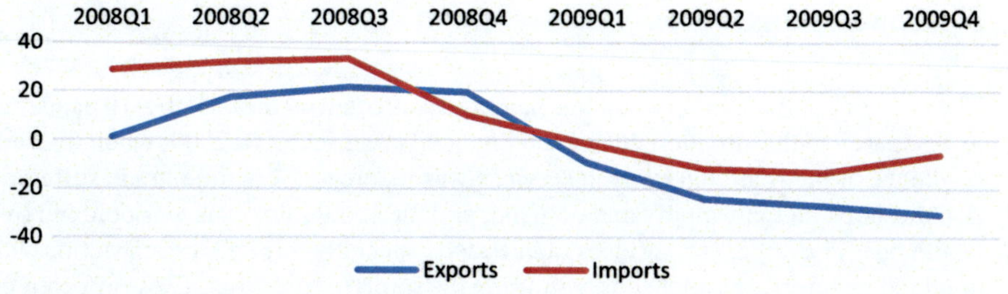

Fig. 10 Year-on-year change in the volume of trade in services during the financial crisis, Romania. *Source* Authors' own elaborations based on Eurostat data

only 1.4% in the first instance, but continued to decrease until 13.2% in the third quarter. Although there were signs of recovery, the values remained below those in the previous years until the beginning of 2011.

During the pandemic, the largest drop in the exports of services was recorded in the second quarter of 2020 as compared to the same period in 2019, of −21.8%. This time, the imports of services were the most affected, having the largest drop of 33.8% in the second quarter of 2020 (Fig. 11). Both of them are on increasing trend starting with the third quarter.

If we compare the evolution of exports and imports during the financial crisis with the actual one, we can state that services were severely affected in 2020. The drop of exports was of 12.1% in 2020 as compared to the previous period, almost double than the one registered in the quarter affected by the crisis in 2008–2009, as previously shown. The decrease of imports was even larger, of 21.8%. However, we should take into account the fact that, even after the GDP growth was restored and the crisis period was officially over, the evolution of trade in services was hardly rebuilt. We draw the attention that we do not have yet a full picture of this situation.

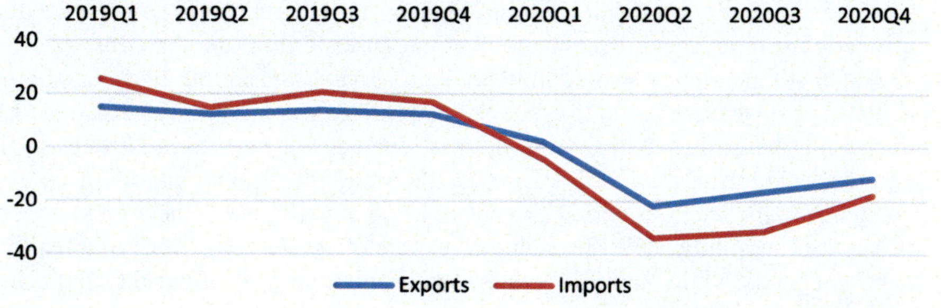

Fig. 11 Year-on-year change in the volume of trade in services during 2019–2020, Romania. *Source* Authors' own elaborations based on Eurostat data

5 Conclusions

The behavior of trade in services was negatively affected by the COVID-19 pandemic as compared to the situation during the financial crisis in 2008–2009, when a certain resilience of international trade in services was recorded. This time, trade suffered a double shock, in both supply and demand, and the economic crisis was doubled by a health one. The impact on services manifested especially through the restrictions and containment measures imposed for limiting the spread of the virus. These affected the very nature of services: the proximity of consumption and production, intangibility, heterogeneity, and perishability. As a result, trade in services was hardly hit than 12 years ago, while the main sectors affected were those of travel, tourism, hospitality, and accommodation.

In this context, we have assessed the impact of COVID-19 on Romania's international trade in services, using monthly data in order to trace the evolution of both exports and imports during 2020 as compared to the previous year. Imports of services had a larger drop than exports of services and experienced a stronger decrease than imports in goods during the most exposed months (March–May 2020). Exports of services were less affected than those of goods. The impact on the economy is, still, moderate, since exports of services represented 29.2% of total exports of goods and services in Romania, while imports were almost half, registering 15.7% of total imports in 2020.

However, the impact on services was uneven. The telecommunications, computer, and information services is the only one having a better evolution than in 2019, as a result of working from home activities and online trade, while travel and tourism was the most negatively affected due to restriction and lockdown measures. We have evaluated the behavior of the major groups of traded services, and we can conclude that the increase in traded telecommunications, computer, and information services as a share of total exports and, respectively, imports is the result of a steady evolution, not only the influence of the pandemic. Other sectors had marginal changes in the share of traded services, while tourism was the most affected and its negative drop is clearly the influence of the containment measures for limiting the virus.

When comparing the evolution of trade in services during the financial and the actual crises, we have found that imports of services saw a larger drop than exports during the pandemic. Quantifying the total decrease of exports in services in the period starting from the fourth quarter of 2008 until the second quarter of 2009 as compared to the previous period, we obtain a gap of 6.2%, while the drop in imports of services was only 1.6%. In addition, export of services was less affected than export in goods, while imports of services were more severely affected than the drop in the imports of goods. Travel and tourism was the most affected, while the rest of the most important other sectors show a certain recovery at the end of 2020. The drop in the exports of services in 2020 was double than the one registered during the crisis quarters in 2008–2009, and even higher for imports. Data for Romania show that the drop of exports was of 12.1% in 2020 as compared to the previous period, while the decrease of imports was even larger, of 21.8%, in the same period.

References

Adegun, O.: The effects of ebola virus on the economy of West Africa through the trade channel. IOSR J. Humanit. Soc. Sci. **19**(10) (2014)

Ariu, A.: Crisis-proof services: why trade in services did not suffer during the 2008–2009 collapse. J. Int. Econ. **98**, 138–149 (2016)

Baldwin, R.: The Greater Trade Collapse of 2020: Learnings from the 2008–09 Great Trade Collapse, VoxEu CEPR, April 2020. https://voxeu.org/article/greater-trade-collapse-2020 (2020)

Borchert, I., Mattoo, A.: The crisis-resilience of services trade. Serv. Ind. J. **30**(14), 1–20 (2009)

Bratianu, C.: Toward understanding the complexity of the COVID-19 crisis: a grounded theory approach, Management & Marketing. Chall Knowl Soc **15**, 410–423. https://doi.org/10.2478/mmcks-2020-0024 (2020)

Burkle, F.M.: Globalization and disasters: issues of public health, state capacity and political action. J. Int. Aff. **59**(2), 231–265 (2006)

Busu, M., Vargas, M.V., Gherasim, I.A.: An analysis of the economic performances of the retail companies in Romania, management & marketing. Chall. Knowl. Soc. **15**(1), 125–133 (2020). https://doi.org/10.2478/mmcks-2020-0008

Coates, B., Cowgill, M., Chen, T., Mackey, W.: Shutdown: estimating the COVID-19 employment shock. GRATTAN Institute (2020)

Gilson, I., Muramatsu, K.: Health services trade and the COVID-19 pandemic. World Bank Group (2020)

Gruszczynski, L.: The COVID-19 pandemic and international trade: temporary turbulence or paradigm shift? Eur. J. Risk Regul. **11**(2), 337–342 (2020). https://doi.org/10.1017/err.2020.29

Javed, A.: Impact of COVID-19 on Pakistan's services sector. Jurnal Inovasi Ekonomi **5**, 107–116 (2020)

Lee, J.W., McKibbin, W.J.: Globalization and disease: the case of SARS. Asian Eco Papers **3**(1), 113–131 (2004)

Maliszewska, M., Mattoo, A., van der Mensbrugghe, D.: The potential impact of COVID-19 on GDP and trade: A preliminary assessment. World Bank Group, Policy Research Working Paper 9211 (2020).

McKibbin, W., Fernando, R.: The global macroeconomic impacts of COVID19: Seven scenarios. Australian National University, CEPAR (2020)

Milea, C.: Consequences of covid-19 on the international trade in goods and services: Forecasts, developments, restrictions. Financial Studies, Victor Slăvescu Centre for Financial and Monetary Research, Bucharest, 24, 4 (90), pp. 29–40 (2020)

Minodo, A.: Impact of COVID-19 on the trade of goods and services in Spain. Appl. Econ. Anal. **29**(85), 58–76 (2021). https://doi.org/10.1108/AEA-11-2020-01562021

Moeller, S.: Characteristics of services–a new approach uncovers their value. J. Serv. Mark. **24**(5), 359–368 (2010)

National Institute of Statistics, Romania (2021). http://statistici.insse.ro:8077/tempo-online/

Saif, N.M.A., Ruan, J., Obrenovic, B.: Sustaining trade during COVID-19 pandemic: Establishing a conceptual model including COVID-19 impact. Sustainability **13**, 5418 (2021). https://doi.org/10.3390/su13105418

Sanda, I., Kedir, A., Ngonze, C., Ikome, F.: Socio-economic impacts of Ebola on Africa. United Nations Economic Commission for Africa (2015)

Shingal, A.: Services trade and COVID-19 (2020). https://voxeu.org/article/services-trade-and-covid-19

Stramge, R.: The 2020 Covid 19 pandemic and global value chains. J. Indust. Business Econ. **47**, 455–465 (2020)

Tomé, E., Gromova, E., Hatch, A.: Did the bubble burst? the portuguese economy during COVID-19", management & marketing. Chall. Knowl. Soc. **15**, 477–495. https://doi.org/10.2478/mmcks-2020-0028 (2020)

Wolak, R., Kalafatis, S., Harris, P.: An investigation into four characteristics of services. J. Empir. Gen. Mark. Sci. **3**, 22–43 (1998)

The Impact of COVID-19 Crisis on Fiscal Environment in Romania

Sobolevschi David Maria Iulia, Petcu Monica Aureliana, Țâțu Lucian, Catarамă Delia, Ciobanu Radu, Jinga Gabriel, Gavril (Moldovan) Ioana Andrada, Balaban Geeorgiana, and Avram (Zamfir) Mădălina

1 Introduction

The 'shutdown' effect imposed by the COVID-19 pandemic has given to the current economic crisis an element of novelty. In contrast to the previous crisis, now the global economy is not facing a liquidity crisis and governments around the world have allocated considerable amounts to reduce the negative effects of the pandemic. The situation in the case of Romania is not exactly favorable, from a fiscal-budgetary perspective, because the fiscal room for maneuver is limited due to the fact that in the previous period of economic expansion the fiscal-budgetary policy had a pro-cyclical character.

S. D. M. Iulia · P. M. Aureliana · Ț. Lucian · C. Delia · C. Radu (✉) · J. Gabriel · G. I. Andrada · B. Geeorgiana · A. Mădălina
Bucharest University of Economic Studies, Bucharest, Romania
e-mail: radu.ciobanu@fin.ase.ro

S. D. M. Iulia
e-mail: maria.sobolevschi@cig.ase.ro

P. M. Aureliana
e-mail: monica.petcu@cig.ase.ro

Ț. Lucian
e-mail: lucian.tatu@fin.ase.ro

C. Delia
e-mail: delia.catarama@fin.ase.ro

G. I. Andrada
e-mail: ioana.moldovan@economie.ase.ro

B. Geeorgiana
e-mail: georgiana.balaban@economie.ase.ro

A. Mădălina
e-mail: madalina.avram@economie.ase.ro

A. M. Dima et al. (eds.), *Economic Recovery After COVID-19*, Springer Proceedings in Business and Economics, https://doi.org/10.1007/978-3-030-86641-9_10

Although Romania has a relatively low public debt compared to other Member States, the current fiscal-budgetary position puts pressure on the costs of financing the budget deficit, in a context where Romania's financing needs have increased significantly as a result of the additional expenditures imposed by the COVID-19 pandemic.

Strictly from a fiscal-budgetary perspective, Romania must take action for a medium-term fiscal adjustment even though the fiscal rules have been temporarily suspended by the European Commission and the fiscal impact of the measures implemented in the context of the pandemic will not be taken into consideration within the excessive deficit procedure in which Romania stands. On the other hand, the fiscal impulse is vital for the health and satisfaction of people's needs and for the support of the business environment. Thus, the measures adopted must be strategically thought out and directed in such a way as to avoid situations of moral hazard and to bring maximum benefits to the most affected sectors.

Romania has quickly adopted a series of measures that are comparable to those applied in other European countries, in order to support the business environment and the population. However, given that the room for maneuver is limited (as a result of the budget deficit recorded in 2019, of 4.4% of GDP—the highest in the EU), the amounts allocated by Romania are much lower compared to those allocated by the other states. In Romania, the cumulative value of the fiscal-budgetary measures adopted in 2020 to combat the effects of the pandemic amounts to 4.4% of GDP (European Commission 2020).

Although the business environment was supported by the fiscal facilities and by the subsidies granted by the state in the context of the pandemic, many entrepreneurs considered equally important the measures that would improve the administrative capacity of the state (a computerized administrative system and the reduction of bureaucracy).

Therefore, from a macroeconomic perspective, beyond the stabilization of the health situation, Romania's short-/medium-term priority should be achieving a coherent plan of structural reforms and public investments, in accordance with the Recovery and Resilience Facility, so that these projects be financed by the non-reimbursable funds made available to Romania by the European Commission and to ensure the sustainable development of the economy, based on digitalization and investments in 'green' projects, which would contribute to a 'fair transition' (The European Commission 2020).

2 The Analysis of the Fiscal-Budgetary Framework

Romania has registered a robust economic growth in recent years, among the highest in the European Union, a development favored by the expansionary fiscal-budgetary policy, which took into account both tax and fee reductions and the increase of expenditures (especially personnel expenditures and those on social security as permanent expenses). Romania has registered a significant deviation from the medium-term objective (MTO), starting with 2016, in the context of the discretionary measures applied. According to this, the structural budget deficit should not be higher than 1% of GDP. In the period up to and including 2018, the general consolidated budget deficit was kept below the threshold of 3% of GDP, imposed by the Stability and Growth Pact, but in 2019 this target was exceeded and the budget deficit registered by Romania reached 4.4% of GDP. Thus, the European authorities started the Excessive Deficit Procedure against Romania at the beginning of March 2020 (Ministry of Public Finance 2020a).

If prior to the onset of the COVID-19 pandemic, it was estimated that in 2020, Romania will achieve a budget adjustment to a deficit of 3.6% of GDP, in the context of measures implemented to combat the effects of the crisis, the budget deficit for 2020 amounted to 9.2% of GDP, given that GDP contracted by 3.9% in real terms (Ministry of Public Finance 2020b).

The European Commission (EC) launched the 'general escape clause' of the Stability and Growth Pact (SGP) on 20th of March, in the context of the pandemic. This implies that the budgetary impact of the measures taken to combat the COVID-19 pandemic and its negative social and economic effects will not be taken into account in the Commission's assessments of the deficit target in the excessive deficit procedure. At the same time, the impact of these measures will not influence the structural deficit and the clause will allow the extension of the deadline until which Romania will be able to correct its excessive budget deficit, provided that the implemented measures are effective (National Commission for Forecasting and Strategy 2020).

Although Romania enjoys this flexibility, both in 2020 and in the medium-term, fiscal-budgetary policy must face significant challenges, imposed by the fiscal position registered before the crisis caused by COVID-19 on the one hand and the budgetary efforts needed to combat the social and economic effects of the pandemic on the other hand. Therefore, in the short term (in 2020), the fiscal-budgetary policy is intended for stabilization and economic recovery, while in the medium-term, the challenge is to consider effective measures to support the economy simultaneous with the entering on a path of budget deficit adjustment (Fiscal commission 2020).

Strictly from a fiscal-budgetary perspective, Romania is in a situation similar to that of 2009, in 2020, even though the triggering events are not comparable: the onset of the COVID-19 crisis found us in the context in which the fiscal space for action is limited, after several years of applying some pro-cyclical fiscal-budgetary policies and accumulating increasing deficits.

After the budget slippage registered in 2019, the significantly higher deficit in 2020, amplified by the effects of the COVID-19 pandemic, puts pressure on the need for financing and implicitly on the dynamics of public debt. Romania's public debt increased significantly by 12 percentage points, to 47.3% of GDP in 2020. The fiscal room for maneuver that could have stimulated economic growth was very limited in the context of a sharp economic decline expected for this year. The fiscal space was depleted due to the pro-cyclical nature of fiscal policy, which created an increasingly tense budget construction in previous years, by significantly increasing the permanent spending in the context of the approved legal framework (unitary wage law and pension law). The fiscal-budgetary policy should have helped reduce the volatility of economic growth by increasing public investment, along with private investment, which would have led to a more balanced growth structure, so that it cannot be predominantly based on consumption (which would implicitly improve the predictability of budget revenues).

The increasing of the funding need as a result of the coronavirus pandemic prompted the consideration of all possibilities for access to financial resources. Among the possibilities of financing the optimal order of prioritization of the instruments is the following: European funds, loans through the issuance of public securities in lei on the domestic market, loans from international financial institutions, loans through the issuance of euro bonds. In the last resort, Romania can use conditional funding sources from international financial institutions, such as loans from the European Investment Bank, the European Bank for Reconstruction and Development or the International Monetary Fund (stand-by arrangement). However, these loans may involve severe correction programs and a recurrence of events during the previous economic and financial crisis.

3 Measures Implemented by Romania in Order to Reduce the Effects of COVID-19

The appearance and development of COVID-19 infection in Romania required the state intervention, including by taking measures in the taxation field, but also by taking some economic and social measures. The purpose of these measures was to diminish the COVID-19 effects on Romania's economy.

As main measures in the fiscal field taken by Romania in order to reduce the effects of COVID-19, we summarize the extension of the payment term for taxes and fees, granting bonuses for the timely payment of fiscal obligations, granting facilities to pay the annual building tax or monthly tax on buildings, in the case of non-residential buildings, non-application of interest and late payment penalties for tax obligations due between March 21 and October 25, 2020, postponement of VAT customs payments for certain categories of imported goods. Application of reverse charge for imports of medicines, medical equipment, etc., which can be used to treat COVID-19, VAT refund with subsequent control. VAT exemption was also granted for deliveries of personal protective masks and medical ventilators for intensive care as well as for deliveries to legally constituted associations and foundations of medicine, protective equipment, other medical devices and equipment and sanitary materials that may be useful in preventing, limiting, treating and combating COVID-19.

Among the main measures taken by Romania in the economic and social field in order to effectively reduce COVID-19, we can list ensuring liquidity in the economy by guaranteeing loans and lines of credit through the SME Invest Romania program, postponing the plate for utility services - electricity, natural gas, water, telephone and Internet services, as well as the postponement of the payment of rent for the building intended for the registered office and secondary offices. With a special impact in supporting the activity of companies, we consider it to be a measure supported by the state at an indemnity of 75% of the basic salary, but not more than 75% of the average gross salary offered by the Law of the state social insurance budget for 2020 and bearing the allowance from the state budget for other professionals. As an active measure of financial support was granted a support allowance of 41.5% of the basic salary, subsidies for employers who employ people over 50 years of age or people between 16 and 29 years of age.

The analysis of the measures taken by Romania both in the taxation field and in the economic and social field in order to reduce the effects of COVID-19 must be carried out taking into account the increased need for budgetary resources manifested during this period, simultaneously with the existing limited financing possibilities.

4 Business Environment Perception of the Impact of the COVID-19 Pandemic on Business

4.1 Methodology, Description of Statistical Research and Characteristics of Respondents

For analyzing the business environment perception of the impact of the COVID-19 pandemic on the measures imposed and on the measures that should have been taken further, we conducted two surveys. We addressed these to the business environment (companies, authorized individuals, other entities that carry out lucrative activities) in various fields of activity (production, services, construction, consulting, industry, education, etc.).

The first survey was sent during the pandemic, and the answers were received during the period May 3–8, 2020. A number of 328 respondents answered the first survey. They are mainly entrepreneurs or company managers (64.94%) working in companies with less than 250 employees (89.63%). From the perspective of the fields of activity of the companies in which the respondents of the first survey operate, the largest share is that of the various services (44.21% of the total), followed by the organization of events (16.77% of the total) and industry (10.37% of total). From the point of view of the financial stability of the companies in which the respondents operate, most of the responding entities (85.06%) present a positive financial situation (positive profit and equity), which shows a sound management of the business and the prerequisites for a lower risk of bankruptcy.

We have analyzed further the business environment perception by the second survey, addressing it to the business environment (companies, authorized individuals, other entities that carry out lucrative activities) in various fields of activity (production, services, construction, consulting, industry, education, etc.). We received the answers during the period July 20–26, 2020. A number of 295 respondents answered the survey. They are mainly entrepreneurs or company managers (61.69%) working in companies with less than 250 employees (92.20%). We asked the respondents to indicate exactly the field of activity in which they work, respectively the main CANE code, in order to perform a more detailed analysis by fields of activity. The classification of the fields of activity included in the study presents the area of professional services in the first place (36.95%), followed by trade (10.51%) and constructions (7.46%). The percentage of 3.39% of the total respondents belong to the HORECA field (hotels and restaurants). By geographical distribution, most respondents are located in Bucharest–Ilfov (58.31%), followed by those in the south (16.61%), northwest-center (15.25%) and northeast (9.83%).

4.2 The Interpretation of the Surveys' Results

4.2.1 Business Environment Perception Regarding the Impact of the COVID-19 Pandemic on Business During the State of Emergency

As shown by the processing of data collected during the pandemic, 60% of SMEs participating in the survey recorded decreases in activity of more than 25%, in March–April 2020, which makes their opinion relevant in the context of understanding the impact of measures taken to protect the business environment, precisely to prevent the negative effect of this decrease in activity. When asked about the opinion on the activity that will take place throughout the year 2020, SMEs were cautious, 77.14% of them appreciating that they will record decreases in income. We then asked respondents to assess which of the presented measures would be most likely to help them maintain the activity or to help the development of the company in which they operate in the context of the crisis. We have included in the response options both financial measures applicable through the company's internal decision (reduction of expenses, deferrals to suppliers), and financial measures that would be applicable only if the state decides to promote them (tax facilities, subsidies), as well as an administrative/qualitative measure, which cannot be considered as having an impact on the company's immediate financial results (a computerized state administrative apparatus, functional in conditions of respect, trust and less bureaucracy). The results were surprising, the ranking made by the respondents being presented in Table 1.

As shown in Table 1, faced with a choice between financial measures that can be taken by a company (cost reductions, deferrals), financial measures that can be taken by the state (tax facilities and subsidies) and administrative measures that can be taken by the state, SMEs considered that a computerized state administrative apparatus, functional in conditions of respect, trust and less bureaucracy, would have helped them the most. The fiscal measures that should have been taken by the state (fiscal facilities, subsidies) were on the second place and finally the financial measures that would have been taken by the company itself (cost reductions, deferrals) were on the third place. The results of the survey confirm the literature (Slemrod 2002), namely that trust in the administrative apparatus is a key element both in reducing

Table 1 The respondents' perception regarding the measures that could help them maintain/develop the activity, including measures at state level and company level

Measure that could help the company maintain/develop the activity	Number of respondents who appreciated that this would help them much and very much	Percentage of total
A computerized state administrative apparatus, functional in conditions of respect, trust and less bureaucracy	241	73.48%
Fiscal facilities	202	61.59%
Subsidies	201	61.28%
Reduction of company expenses	114	34.76%
Deferrals to suppliers	68	20.73%

Source Own processing based on the data from the survey

tax evasion (with positive effects on the public budget) and increasing the prosperity of society as a whole. On the second place in the choice of SMEs in Romania are the measures offered by the state, namely tax facilities and subsidies, which are considered by a larger share of respondents as more helpful than those such as reducing company expenses and postponing the payment of suppliers. Thus, our study shows that Romanian SMEs preferred foreign aid to the company in a time of crisis, being less willing to take company's internal measures. This could also be explained by the low rate of financial education in Romania [according to Batsaikhan and Demertzis 2018]. Romania is on the last place in the European Union in terms of the percentage of population with financial education (22%), the European Union average being 50%), companies preferring 'someone else' to solve the crisis, and not themselves. One explanation could be the perception that this economic crisis was caused by the state by declaring a state of emergency and therefore it must take responsibility for resolving it.

Given the perception of Romanian SMEs on the importance of the state aid measures, we continued to focus on measures taken by the state to mitigate the impact of the COVID-19 crisis and we asked respondents to give a grade in the form of a whole number between 1 and 5 (1 being minimum and 5 being maximum) of the measures adopted. The classification of the measures taken by the authorities, carried out by the responding SMEs, is (Table 2).

The perception regarding the measures taken by the government is positive at the level of the entire group of respondents, the average being 3.89 out of 5. Once again, on the first place is a non-financial measure, 'Electronic communication with public institutions', which confirms the pressing need of the Romanian business environment for a supple, communicative administrative apparatus that respects its taxpayer partner and is trustworthy. This measure has been strongly demanded by the business environment, and now the need has worsened. Further, there are the financial measures, on the second place being 'Non-collection of interests and penalties for non-payment/postponement of tax liabilities' (the grade 4.35 out of 5 - the measure was perceived as coming to support businesses, to cope with the decrease of

Table 2 The first five measures taken by the government, in the perception of Romanian SMEs

Government measure	Grade received (1 the minimum grade, 5 the maximum grade)
Electronic communication with public institutions	4,50
Non-collection of interest and penalties for non-payment/postponement of tax liabilities	4,35
The bonus for paying the profit tax/microenterprises' income tax on term	4,15
Full payment of technical unemployment from the budget, with the payment postponement of the related fiscal obligations until after the collection of the amounts from the budget	4,14
Exemption from the payment of the specific tax applicable in the HORECA industry	3,95
The average of all the measures	3,89

Source Own processing based on the data from the survey

liquidity in terms of reduced activities) and, almost tied, 3–4 'The bonus for paying the profit tax/microenterprises' income tax on term' and 'Full payment of technical unemployment from the budget, with the payment postponement of the related fiscal obligations until after the collection of the amounts from the budget'. From these four measures, the first can be considered a proactive measure, intended to help the state and the taxpayer communicate in the best possible conditions. The other measures are caused by the crisis, and their application must be made limited in time and with discernment; otherwise, these could lead to unethical behaviors and non-assumption of responsibilities by the taxpayer.

We have proceeded to structure the responses by subgroups to identify the top measures by company size, how it was affected by the crisis or field of activity, in order to make an analysis as relevant as possible from the perspective of the need for measures taken by the government. The results are similar on all the groups made. Therefore, even if the business environment wants the support of the state through various active measures, what it wants most is to communicate effectively and correctly with the state, regardless of the size of the company or how it has been affected by the crisis. Consequently, we can appreciate that the first measure that should be taken by the state, in any field, is to improve the relationship between public institutions and citizens. The following question concerns the applicability of the measure at the company level, grouping the first five measures that were used in most cases (Table 3).

We mention that the measures considered by the companies to be the best were also the most applied.

However, it is interesting that, even if 'Non-collection of interest and penalties for non-payment/postponement of tax liabilities' was considered the second best measure after 'Electronic communication with public institutions', only 39.94% of the responding SMEs have chosen to postpone the taxes payment at the due dates,

Table 3 The first five measures applied by SMEs from those prorogued by the government

Government measure	Percentage of respondents who applied the measure
Electronic communication with public institutions in ways and situation that weren't applicable/possible before the crisis	75,30%
The bonus for paying the profit tax/microenterprises' income tax on legal term	52,44%
Efficient and operative communication in relation to the tax administration staff	51,52%
Technical unemployment paid from the budget	48,48%
Postponement of the taxes payment at the due dates	39,94%

Source Own processing based on the data from the survey

confirming once again that the leniency measures also have a compliance effect. Also, 86% of them called for the postponement of the payment of taxes and fees due to cash flow difficulties, while only 14% did so as a protection measure for possible future difficulties.

From the perspective of the measures extended by the government, we have centralized the first five measures already taken by the government and wanted by the business environment in the future, but also a list of the requested measures that are not currently implemented (Table 4).

The first three measures are noteworthy: electronic communication, bonuses for good payers and the SME Invest program. All of these are measures addressed to companies with appropriate fiscal behavior.

Finally, we asked respondents what other measures they would take to stimulate the economy in the future. Respondents received a list of proposals, but were also invited to propose measures. There was an effervescence of the proposed measures, which proves that the business environment is the best source for the measures that can be taken. The result of centralizing the answers to this question can be found in Table 5.

It can be seen that, almost entirely, the fiscal solutions recommended by the questionnaire received a significant number of validations. Also, a number of 34 respondents proposed other measures to revive the economy.

By processing the data provided by the first questionnaire, it turned out that over 50% of SMEs estimated that their income will decrease by over 25% in 2020 compared to 2019. Faced with choosing between financial measures that can be taken by a company (expenditure reductions, deferrals), financial measures that can be taken by the state (fiscal facilities and subsidies) and administrative measures that can be taken by the state, SMEs considered that an administrative apparatus of the computerized state, functional in conditions of respect, trust and less bureaucracy. In second place were the measures given by the state (fiscal facilities/subsidies), followed by those that could be taken by the company (cost reductions/deferrals).

Table 4 The first five measures prorogated that should be maintained in the future

The measure currently taken by the government which is intended to be maintained	Number of respondents who want it in the future	Percentage of total
Electronic communication with public institutions	171	52.13%
The bonus for paying the profit tax/microenterprises' income tax on legal term	153	46.65%
SME Invest program	147	44.82%
Full payment of technical unemployment from the budget, with the payment postponement of the related fiscal obligations until after the collection of the amounts from the budget	146	44.51%
Non-collection of interest and penalties for non-payment/postponement of tax liabilities	140	42.68%

Source Own processing based on the data from the survey

The first 5 measures taken by the authorities to combat the effects of the COVID-19 crisis were: electronic communication with public institutions, non-collection of interest and penalties, bonus for paying corporate income tax, support for technical unemployment, exemption from specific tax in HORECA. The top remains about the same, regardless of the size of the company, the degree to which it has been affected by the crisis or the field of activity. Also, 52.44% of the companies applied the bonus for the timely payment of the profit / income tax of the microenterprises, 48.48% of the companies accessed the ethnic unemployment. At the same time, 39.94% of companies applied the deferral of tax payments. Of these, 86% called for the payment of taxes to be postponed due to cash flow difficulties, while only 14% did so as a protection measure for possible future difficulties. The first three measures implemented by the government and wanted to be maintained in the future were: electronic communication, bonuses for good payers, the SME Invest program, all measures addressed to companies with appropriate fiscal behavior. The first three measures proposed for the future are: granting subsidies for jobs maintained after returning from technical unemployment, reducing social contributions due to wage income, introducing simplified pay-as-you-go measures for deferred payment obligations.

Table 5 Measures that should be applied in the future for the economic recovery

Newly proposed measures	Number of positive opinions	Percentage of respondents
Subsidies for jobs maintained after returning from technical unemployment	258	78,66%
Reducing the social contributions due for the salary incomes	249	75,91%
The need to introduce simplified payment arrangements for deferred payment obligations	219	66,77%
Compensation for allowances for sick leave to be recovered with the contributions due in the current month and the following months, but also with other fiscal obligations	211	64,33%
Compensation of tax liabilities with trade receivables from state institutions	195	59,45%
Granting tax reductions to both individuals and legal entities for the acquisition of software and IT technology	165	50,30%
Granting technical unemployment benefits, borne by the state until the end of 2020	163	49,70%
Increasing the threshold for the application of the VAT collection system	104	31,71%
Modification of the contribution period of minimum 12 months in the last 24 months prior to the date of registration of the application in order to benefit from the unemployment indemnity, for the period 2020–2021	104	31,71%
Eliminating the threshold for the application of social contributions for incomes other than those from salaries and payment of social contributions to the realized income	102	31,10%
Increasing tax on dividends	27	8,23%
Other response	34	

Source Own processing based on the data from the survey

4.2.2 The Business Environment Perception Regarding the Impact of the COVID-19 Pandemic on Business After the State of Emergency

The economic agents wanted to return to the normality of life before the COVID-19 crisis as soon as possible, after the end of the state of emergency. This normality was long overdue, Romania still being on alert at the time of writing this study, with lower restrictions but still with companies that have suspended their activity (event organizers, restaurants serving the interior, etc.). A new cause of suspension of economic activity also appeared: the illness of an employee with COVID-19, which can lead to the closure of the company's activity until the elimination of health risks. However, at this time, economic agents had a more realistic picture of the impact the pandemic had on their businesses, but also on the future evolution of these businesses.

From the point of view of the financial stability of the companies in which the respondents operate, most of the responding entities (84.41%) present a stable financial situation (positive profit and equity), which shows a healthy business management and the prerequisites for a lower risk of bankruptcy. Thus, we find that the profile of the respondent to the post-emergency-situation survey is the same as that of the respondent from the survey addressed during the emergency situation, which allows a comparability of the results. As a result, the first question answered by the interviewees was similar to the one in the survey addressed during the emergency situation and referred to the impact that the state of emergency had on the company's activity. Therefore, if in May 2020 over 60% of respondents said that the pandemic had a large and very large impact on the activity of the companies in which they operate, in July 2020 only 37% had this perception. In the authors' opinion, the measures taken by the government to support the business environment played an important role in changing this perception, as we will see further in the study. It is also gratifying that the percentage of respondents who claimed that the activity of the companies in which they operate was not affected by the pandemic doubled, increasing from 11% in May 2020 to 23% in July 2020. This trend is also reflected in the following question, in which respondents were asked to assess whether from June 2020 the company has recovered.

There is also a significant change in the July 2020 survey compared to May 2020 in terms of the perception of the business environment on the results of the whole year 2020. Thus, the business environment has now a clearer perspective on the evolution of the activity of the companies in which it operates. If in May 2020 a percentage of 12.50% of respondents could not make an estimate on the evolution of revenues in 2020, in July 2020 only 5.42% kept this uncertainty. In addition, if in May 2020 a percentage of 77% of respondents believed that 2020 will generate lower revenues than in 2019, in July 2020 this perception has changed significantly, in the sense that only 55% believe that revenues will decrease in 2020 compared to 2019. We believe that the governmental measures taken have significantly contributed to improve this perception, but given the high percentage of those who believe that 2020 will have lower revenues than 2019, we believe that these measures should continue and contribute to compensating for the decrease in income.

Analyzing the measures that the business environment has applied to deal with the crisis caused by the COVID-19 pandemic, we found that the most used measure was a non-financial one, namely electronic communication with public authorities, a measure that was used by 91% of respondents, as shown in Table 6.

The companies resorted in particular to measures that allowed them to intervene and take direct action (reducing costs, obtaining the bonus for the payment of profit tax/microenterprises' income tax) or to measures considered by them as measures they should have always applied: electronic communication with public institutions, timely reimbursement of amounts not reimbursed by the National Health Insurance House for sick leave. This is somewhat contrary to the image created by the survey conducted in May 2020. Thus, the companies indicated at that time that the types of measures they would find most useful were (in order): a computerized state administrative apparatus, fiscal facilities, subsidies, reduction of company expenses, deferrals to suppliers, image that suggested that the business environment sees the state as its 'savior'. In fact, the companies resorted to a lesser extent to subsidies and fiscal facilities, compared to the measures related to the functional administrative apparatus of the state and the reduction of the company's expenses.

We have analyzed further the behavior of the companies regarding the two main measures promoted by the decision-makers during the state of emergency: granting technical unemployment benefits from the budget and the SME Invest program. Regarding the granting of technical unemployment benefits, the implementation of the measure was not accompanied by sanctions in case of non-payment of social security contributions and income tax for the benefits received by the employer from the budget. Furthermore, by not applying interest and penalties for non-payment of contributions and income tax due in the period from March 21, 2020 to October 25, 2020, the taxpayers wouldn't have had any incentive to pay these amounts to the budget, thus being able to use these amounts collected from the budget, without additional costs and without the risk of criminal liability. Analyzing the behavior of the respondents to our survey, we find that the business environment was a fair and serious partner of the state, as 92% of those who received from the budget the gross value of technical unemployment benefits, also paid social contributions and taxes on salary income to the budget. Regarding the SME Invest program, although the respondents of our study are 92% SMEs, only 20% accessed the SME Invest program.

Another measure taken by the legislator, after the survey conducted by the authors of the study in May 2020, is the granting of subsidies for the return of employees from technical unemployment, but also for the employment of unemployed from the records of unemployment agencies. This type of measures was considered the most important by the survey's respondents from May 2020. Thus, at that time 78% of companies considered it essential to implement a job subsidy mechanism. Thus, at that time 78% of companies considered it essential to implement a job subsidy mechanism. Therefore, we wanted to check to what extent the respondents will use these

Table 6 The degree to which the business environment has used various measures to deal with the crisis caused by the COVID-19 pandemic

Measure	To a very large extent (%)	To a large extent (%)	To some extent (%)	To a lesser extent (%)	Not at all (%)	Total (%)
Reduction of salaries and/or dismissal of personnel	3,73	5,76	13,90	21,02	55,59	100,00
Reduction of the company expenses, other than salary expenses	12,54	20,68	32,54	21,36	12,88	100,00
Deferred payment of debts to suppliers and of bank loans	5,08	5,08	16,27	16,61	56,95	100,00
Deferred payment of tax liabilities	7,80	3,05	13,90	9,49	65,76	100,00
Requesting technical unemployment benefits from the budget	16,95	7,80	9,83	9,15	56,27	100,00
Requesting the amounts for the days off granted to parents from the budget	7,46	4,75	5,76	9,83	72,20	100,00
Requesting the reimbursement of the amounts from sick leave that were not reimbursed until the moment of the pandemic appearance	18,64	10,17	10,51	11,19	49,49	100,00
Requesting the bonus for paying the profit tax/microenterprises' income tax for the first quarter	44,41	8,47	11,86	8,81	26,44	100,00
Electronic communication with public institutions	51,19	14,92	16,27	8,81	8,81	100,00
The postponement of the deadline for submitting the annual financial statements	19,32	6,78	9,15	11,19	53,56	100,00

Source Own processing based on the data from the survey

Table 7 The intention of the respondents who had employees in technical unemployment to resort to the subsidy of 41.5% related to employees returning from technical unemployment

Will you apply/ did you apply for the 41.5% subsidy for employees returning from technical unemployment?	Number of respondents	Percentage of total
YES	82	46.33%
NO	85	48.02%
I DON'T KNOW	10	5.65%
Total	177	100,00%

Source Own processing based on the data from the survey

Table 8 The intention of the respondents to apply for the subsidy for the employment of unemployed people aged between 16 and 29 years or over 50 years old

Will you apply/ did you apply to benefit of unemployed people aged between 16 and 29 years or over 50 years old	Number of respondents	Percentage of total
YES	39	13,22%
NO	159	53,90%
I DON'T KNOW	97	32,88%
Total	295	100,00%

Source Own processing based on the data from the survey

measures. Regarding the subsidy for employees returning from technical unemployment, as 40% of respondents did not have employees in technical unemployment, we consider it relevant to analyze the percentage of those who have accessed/will access the subsidy for employees returning from technical unemployment out of the total respondents who have had employees in technical unemployment (Tables 7 and 8).

Although 78% of the respondents to the May 2020 survey requested measures to subsidize jobs maintained or created during this period, only 46% of those who had employees in technical unemployment will resort to the 41.5% subsidy to maintain employees returning from technical unemployment, and only 13% intend to obtain the subsidy for the employment of the unemployed. In the authors' opinion, the explanation is also given by the perception of the business environment on the administrative apparatus as dysfunctional and unfriendly, companies fearing that these subsidies have 'hidden elements' that they cannot identify and because of which they may be needed to return these subsidies.

We then analyzed the extent to which the respondents have resorted/will resort to the bonus system for the timely payment of the profit tax/microenterprises' income tax. The results show that 84% of respondents have applied or intend to apply to benefit from the 10% bonus for the timely payment of the profit tax/microenterprises' income tax. We must remind here that this bonus is obtained only if the tax is actually paid to the budget within the legal term by the taxpayer. The huge percentage of taxpayers who want to benefit from such a bonus is relevant. This reconfirms the position of taxpayers, their desire for active and fair measures, which remunerate those with appropriate tax behavior.

The desire of the respondents to have a correct fiscal behavior is also reflected by the very small percentage of those who choose to postpone the tax obligations, in the context in which for the obligations maturing after March 21, 2020 no interest and penalties are calculated until October 25, 2020. Thus, the measure of non-application of interest and penalties was among those required by the business environment to be maintained even after the end of the emergency situation (42% of respondents to the May survey requested it), being on the fifth place among the measures desired to be maintained. However, as the respondents of our survey show, only 18% want to apply it, and 82% want to pay their tax obligations on time, even if they do not have sanctions for non-payment. This confirms once again that, fundamentally, taxpayers want fair tax behavior.

Another measure taken at the end of the emergency situation, which was intended to support taxpayers, was to support tenants by paying the outstanding rent by ANAF. We analyzed the applicability of this measure and found that no more than 3% of respondents applied it. The result of the questionnaire is that such a measure is not considered appropriate by the business environment and the legislator should consider to what extent it is necessary in the future to apply such measures that have no appeal to the business environment.

We further analyzed the measures, other than the existing ones, that the business environment would want in the future. The most desirable measure of the business environment (with a percentage of 100% of respondents) is the compensation of the sick leave allowances that employers have to recover from National Health Insurance House with the current tax obligations. The business environment is showing once more maturity in calling for measures to ensure fairness and balance in the relations between the taxpayer and the state. On the third place, desired by 51% of the respondents, is the measure of compensation of fiscal obligations with other receivables from state institutions. Thus, it is obvious that the main demand of the business environment is to no longer be obliged to make various payments to the state, while there are debts to be recovered from the state. On the second place in the top of the agreed measures, desired by a percentage of 58% of the respondents, is the elimination of the threshold for the application of social contributions for incomes other than salary incomes. Although counterintuitive, as it would lead to an increase in taxpayers' payment obligations to the budget, it is a measure that promotes equity. Likewise is the following measure, agreed by 35% of respondents, namely the taxation of global income and the application of social contributions to global income, to ensure equity again.

The results of the research conducted in July 2020 show that if in May 2020 over 60% of respondents said that the pandemic had a large and very large impact on companies, in July 2020 only 37% had this perception. The percentage of respondents who consider that their activity was not affected by the pandemic has doubled, increasing from 11% in May 2020 to 23% in July 2020. If in May 2020 a percentage of 12.50% of respondents could not make an estimate on the evolution of revenues in 2020, in July 2020 only 5.42% kept this uncertainty. The main measure applied by companies during the pandemic remains electronic communication with public institutions (applied by 91% of respondents). It is reconfirmed that the Romanian business environment needs first of all a functional, computerized administrative mechanism.

5 Conclusions and Recommendations

Romania's economy was hit by the COVID-19 pandemic after a period of robust economic growth, which was supported, among other things, by an expansionary, pro-cyclical fiscal policy, which led to the depletion of the fiscal space and, worse, led to the entry into the excessive deficit procedure (after the fact that in 2019 the budget deficit was 4.3% of GDP, exceeding the 3% limit imposed by the Stability and Growth Pact). Moreover, in a context where the pandemic significantly affects tax revenues, caution must be exercised in budgetary expenditures, given that the need for financing is growing and may put pressure on the cost of financing, on the one hand, and on the sustainability of public debt, on the other hand. In the current context, however, the fiscal impulse is vital for the health and satisfaction of people's needs and for the support of the business environment. Thus, the measures adopted must be strategically thought out and directed in such a way as to avoid situations of moral hazard and to bring maximum benefits to the most affected sectors.

Romania has quickly adopted a series of measures that are comparable to those applied in other European countries, in order to support the business environment and the population. Although the business environment has been supported by the measures taken, many entrepreneurs consider equally important the measures that would improve the administrative capacity of the state (a computerized administrative apparatus and reduce bureaucracy), in line with the European Commission's recommendations on reform and digital public administration.

From a macroeconomic perspective, beyond the stabilization of the health situation, Romania's short-/medium-term priority should be achieving a coherent plan of structural reforms and public investments, in accordance with the Recovery and Resilience Facility, so that these projects be financed by the non-reimbursable funds made available to Romania by the European Commission and to ensure the sustainable development of the economy, based on digitalization and investments in 'green' projects, which would contribute to a 'fair transition'. At the same time, in the medium term, an efficient fiscal-budgetary adjustment plan must be considered, which will ensure the sustainability of public finances and implicitly the compliance with the fiscal rules imposed by the Stability and Growth Pact.

The main measures in the taxation field, taken by Romania in order to reduce the effects of COVID-19, aimed at fiscal facilities granted to taxpayers in order to reduce the tax burden and leave liquidity at the business level to overcome this crisis. At the same time, the economic and social measures implemented by Romania in order to reduce the effects of COVID-19 aimed at providing financial support to taxpayers for job retention and economic support in order to revive the economy after the state of emergency period.

References

Batsaikhan, U., Demertzis, M.: Financial Literacy and Inclusive Growth in the European Union, Policy Contribution, Vol. 8, May 2018, pp. 1–18 (2018)

European Comission: Spring Forecast 2020: A deep and unevean recession, an uncertain recovery. https://ec.europa.eu/info/business-economy-euro/economic-performance-and-forecasts/economic-forecasts/spring-2020-economic-forecast-deep-and-uneven-recession-uncertain-recovery_ro (2020)

Fiscal comission: Opinion of the Fiscal Council on the draft rectification of the general consolidated budget for 2020. http://www.consiliulfiscal.ro/Opinie%20Rectificare%20I%202020.pdf (2020)

Ministry of Public Finance: Note on the implementation of the general consolidated budget. https://www.mfinante.gov.ro/pagina.html?pagina=buletin&categoriebunuri= (2020a)

Ministry of Public Finance: Indicative program for issuing government securities for 2020. https://www.mfinante.gov.ro/static/10/Mfp/emisiuni/programindicativ (2020b)

National Commission for Forecasting and Strategy. https://cnp.ro/user/repository/prognoze/Prognoza_2020_2021_varianta_vara_2020.pdf (2020)

Slemrod, J.: Trust in Public Finance. NBER Working Paper No. 9187 (2002)

The European Comission: The 2020 Stability and Convergence Programmes. https://ec.europa.eu/info/sites/info/files/economy-finance/ip131_en_0.pdf (2020)

Macroeconomic Policies, Economic Revitalization

Huru Dragoș, Roman Mihai Daniel, Manafi Ioana, Paraschiv Anca Maria, and Ștefan George

1 The Economic Situation at the Beginning of the Pandemic

The economic situation from before the pandemic highlighted the emergence of a series of complex systems of economic creation with added value, linked through a complex network of economic, administrative, political, geopolitical relations. Romania stands out as a European Union country whose economy, immediately after overcoming the 2007–2009 crisis, registered an ongoing economic growth process. The phenomenon of development in Romania was seen with distrust because it took place under the conditions described here and not as a result of a completely integrated production development in the national territorial space but as an integrated component in international production chains. The acceptance of such a development strategy marked our economic policy, regardless of the nature of government's politics (with different formulas and degrees of manifestation) and highlighted us as a particular case in the EU, in the sense that we are probably the most sensitive economy compared to the way that the strong EU economies will react in response to the foreseeable post-pandemic economic crisis. The transformation of the Romanian economy, from Europe's microeconomic with the highest degree of closure,

H. Dragoș (✉) · R. M. Daniel · M. Ioana · P. A. Maria · Ș. George
Bucharest University of Economic Studies, Bucharest, Romania
e-mail: dragos.huru@economie.ase.ro

R. M. Daniel
e-mail: mihai.roman@ase.ro

M. Ioana
e-mail: ioana.manafi@csie.ase.ro

P. A. Maria
e-mail: anca.gherman@economie.ase.ro

Ș. George
e-mail: george.stefan@economie.ase.ro

A. M. Dima et al. (eds.), *Economic Recovery After COVID-19*, Springer Proceedings in Business and Economics, https://doi.org/10.1007/978-3-030-86641-9_11

was a response to the globalization of the world economy formed by the explosion of borders that led to the disappearance of competitive advantages of spatial positioning and changing competitiveness in the direct relationship between the providers of goods and services and the final consumer which led to the accentuation of the behaviour through which the probabilities of occurrence of the economic phenomenon are evaluated counterintuitively.

During the pandemic, in the field of macroeconomic policies, it is preferable to formulate solutions starting from the idea that it is preferable to aspire for a revitalization of the economy because returning to the economic conditions from before the pandemic (as it happened in the case of the previous economic crises experienced by the current population) is highly unlikely; an orientation on the coordinates of a new economic world, which does not consider only the economic aspects is foreseen.

Also, we cannot talk about restarting the economy because it never stopped, it only works slower. Designing solutions can only be achieved in forecasting conditions and not from the requirement of predictability manifested by the economic agents in the economy's efficient functioning conditions.

2 The Economic Policy Trends Adapted to the Pandemic Situation

After a long time, the global economic space is facing an unprecedented situation of territorial segregation, especially given that cross-border economic integration trends have been adapted as strategies to increase economic efficiency at company level. Economic individualism is based on conventionality, tradition, and goodwill and is therefore relative and can lead, for the general public, to the creation of an image in which the economic world is dominated by the principle of adversity—the world as a whole is imagined as made out of different parts that are in opposition to each other.

This fragmented interpretation of the economic behaviour's perspectives is confusing regarding the present situation, which explains the unrealistic expectations of breaking the economic ties made based on state suzerainty concessions. Until today, people have lived much better than in the past, so it is difficult for them to accept that there is a growing distance between what they seem to know and what is happening in the world around them, which makes economic policies, regardless of their nature, to be viewed with suspicion. The popular support for the economic policies is strange because during the COVID-19 pandemic, for the first time, governments become responsible for the medical policies; compared to the past, the causes of the disease are identified and can be controlled through adaptive medical policies, not only restrictive ones, so the idea of managing the risks of social insecurity through large-scale austerity policies does not seem to be feasible, generating boomerang effects in the governance.

The current economic situation is notable because a medical crisis generates and is complemented by the expectations for an economic crisis. This fact forces an approach of the economic policies in two phases: First—Financing the economy—Ensuring a liquidity-solvency system until overcoming the medical pandemic crisis; Second—Revitalizing the economy—Creating the opportunity to consolidate private capital. The alternatives of economic policies taken into account, in different hypostases conditioned by the level of stopping the economy and the orientation into the doctrinal vision and the tradition for social policies, are oriented towards a help offered to economic agents by increasing public expenditures. Comprehensive policies to increase public spending are being adopted, making the austerity policies used in the previous crisis, from 2008, seem not feasible in the current type of economic policy.

For the two hypostases, we identify that the necessary hypotheses for the economic policy conception are: (i) the need to perform for each sector, analysis that can successfully identify directions and solutions, justifiable in the short term that will guide the public spending on the principle of efficiency and limiting the inflationary impact. The level of public expenditure must consider the different financing possibilities in each national state, the level of economic integration in cross-border production chains, and the integration channels in these chains. This approach's limitation arises from the emergence of economic sectors whose survival must be ensured due to the total cessation of their activities. (ii) Elaborating a broad plan for revitalizing the economy with long-term strategies, strategies aimed at economic reconfiguration at a national level and framing in a world development strategy dictated by the adaptation to the new directions of production and productivity opened by online integration systems labour and the widespread adoption of artificial intelligence in production.

As an example of this type of behaviour, we estimate a relaxation in EU's state aid policy restrictions and budget deficit restrictions, which will allow the use of aid models based on the granting of subsidies to vulnerable sectors; this will also constitute the pillars of a new system of economic operation, meaning everything that involves the latest technologies and the new economies based on the production of goods and services.

On the other hand, we must keep in mind that the balances on the money–banking–foreign exchange markets will suffer, which will require anti-inflationary measures. We can anticipate that the focus will be on punctual fiscal relaxation policies and not raising taxes or cutting wages. It should be noted that the prolongation of the medical crisis will force the transition from the system of technical unemployment to mass layoffs, which will lead to constant revisions of the public policies during the revitalization period. At the same time, we can notice that an extensive discussion has been opened, and the elaboration of a strategy in terms of medical, social and civic security is pursued, which will lead to a new type of approach of the economic policies, much more integrated with the social and educational ones, which implies the need for a much more flexible public policy management structure.

In terms of transnational economic relations, must be considered a different political approach, such as political and military suzerainty in trade relations with China, and those related to the design of relations within the EU. At this point, analysis is difficult to make, because a reaction is expected, because of the political inter-state "negotiations", given that the need of a new design for the economic system for goods and services that meet security needs (medical, food, military, and educational, in particular) is a clear issue; these negotiations will be triggered when the end of the medical crisis can be predicted.

In the development of the economic policies, the risks arising from the public debate environment must be considered, especially since it generously provides "dreadful" views regarding the evolution of the economy, views that seem to serve the interest of certain sectors of activity to obtain faster the "we are needed as soon as possible in order not to fall into the abyss" type of situations.

3 Macroeconomic Impact. Fiscal Multipliers and the Potential Effect of Macroeconomic Policies

From a macroeconomic perspective, the impact of COVID-19 is manifested both on the demand and on the supply side, the two shocks being interconnected. Obviously, in the short term, the hotel industry, restaurants, tourism, and transport sectors are among the first to be influenced as public social distancing actions are implemented. Also, low demand and reduced confidence are factors that determine the decrease of companies' investments.

In Romania's case, the most problematic sectors will be industry (with a contribution of almost 22% to the GDP in 2019) and trade (including HORECA and transport, with a share of 18% of the GDP in 2019). These sectors are expected to decline due to declining domestic demand (especially in the private sector), reductions in external demand, rising unemployment, and COVID restrictive measures. However, this decline can be offset by the growth of the public sector, due to increased government intervention in the economy and the allocation of more resources to the health and home affairs sectors, but also through the influence of two other factors:

(1) The suspension of the Stability and Growth Pact provisions at the European Union level, which removes the restrictions on public spending and macrostability provisions.
(2) The central bank's expansionary decisions destined to stimulate growth and access to liquidity for both the banking sector and the state. The ICT sector can also make a favourable contribution due to the more intensive use of software, data transfer, the Internet, and of remote work solutions with effects of increasing the speed of currency rotation.

3.1 The Impact on the Romanian Economy

We consider three scenarios determined mainly by the evolution of industry and trade and by the state's ability to mobilize resources and support the economy. They seek mainly to quantify the effects of declining production in the sectors that contribute to GDP formation, starting from the share each sector of activity has in the Romanian economy from 2019.

In Romania, the most important sectors of activity that contribute to the GDP formation are Industry, Trade and Public Administration (approximately 55% of the total).

In the baseline scenario, the most substantial negative impact on the GDP real growth rate comes from industry and trade, while the agricultural sector is decreasing significantly due to the droughts registered this year. Simultaneously, the construction sector is expected to have a slightly positive contribution, below 0.5%, to the economic growth. In addition to construction, the public sector and the information and communications sector will also positively contribute. The "Other services" sector, which includes professional, scientific and technical activities, administrative service activities and support service activities, but also entertainment, cultural and recreational activities, repairs of household products and other services, will also have a negative contribution, of about half a percentage point. Considering all of this, in the basic scenario, the Romanian economy would decrease by 4.4%.

In the second scenario, the most pessimistic, the decline in external demand and the inability to produce due to the restrictive measures, would further lower the results from the industrial sector, while the ones from construction would decrease by 10%. Real estate transactions and the trade sector, including HORECA and transport, would also register a sharp fall, while financial intermediation and insurance would significantly decline, pulling down the real GDP growth rate by more than 1.5%. As in the baseline scenario, the public sector and the ICT would positively contribute to the growth.

The third scenario, the most optimistic, estimates a more moderate decline in industry (10%) and a smaller decline in trade (5%), while the government and the ITC sectors will make a positive contribution to growth. Also, real estate transactions and construction will stagnate, while financial intermediation decreases less than in previous scenarios. This scenario envisages a temporary decline in activity in the second quarter and then a gradual recovery by the end of 2020 (Figs. 1 and 2).

Another way to analyse the economic impact is through the working hours of individuals. According to National Institute of Statistic (NIS) data, in the last five

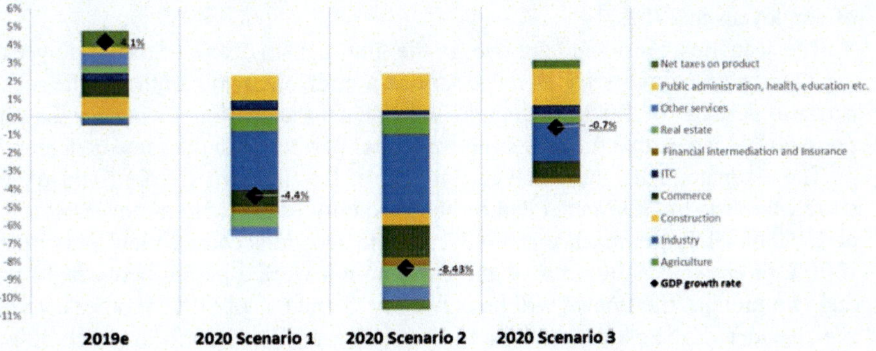

Fig. 1 GDP growth scenarios. *Source* Author's calculation

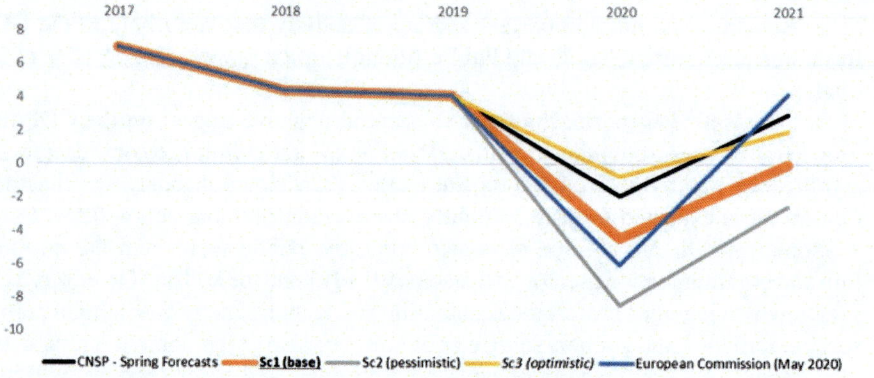

Fig. 2 GDP forecasts 2020 and 2021. *Source* Author's calculation

years, the structure of the number of hours worked by the employed population of Romania has remained relatively unchanged, with industry and trade cumulating approximately 60% of the total number of hours. They are followed by the public sector activities, with a share of 17.3% of the total. If the effects of COVID-19 will be strong, the most affected sectors in terms of volume of worked hours will be those with significant shares in the total number of hours worked—industry and trade, including HORECA activities and transport.

At a preliminary calculation, the first 14 days of inactivity of the workers from these sectors can significantly negatively impact the economy. Obviously, the longer the period of inactivity, the more significant the impact. In the figures below, some simulations are presented depending on the sector of activity, the number of employees affected, and a period of inactivity of up to two months. The three sectors of activity considered were industry, trade, and other activities, including entertainment, cultural and recreational activities, and the repair of household products and other services. The values are expressed as a share in the nominal GDP of 2019 and were calculated starting from the average hourly productivity per person employed in each sector (the latest data available dating from 2018) and the average number of employees in 2019.

The scenarios considered are two: in the first scenario, 50% of the employees of each sector cannot work for 14 days, for one month, and two months; in the second scenario, a share of 70% of the employees of each sector cannot work for the same periods. We can extend the reasoning for longer periods with the same benchmarks.

The estimated data show that in the case of the first two sectors (industry and trade), the loss of GDP generated by the inactivity of 50% of employees can start at 1.1% of GDP and reach up to 4.3%. In the second scenario, more pessimistic, if 70% of employees in industry and trade do not work a period between 14 days and two months, the impact will be between 1.5 and 6% of GDP. If other activities are considered, the estimates show that in the case of a scenario in which 50% of employees are inactive, the loss is between 1.1 and 4.6% of GDP, and in the second scenario, the negative impact is between 1.6 and 6.4% of GDP (Fig. 3).

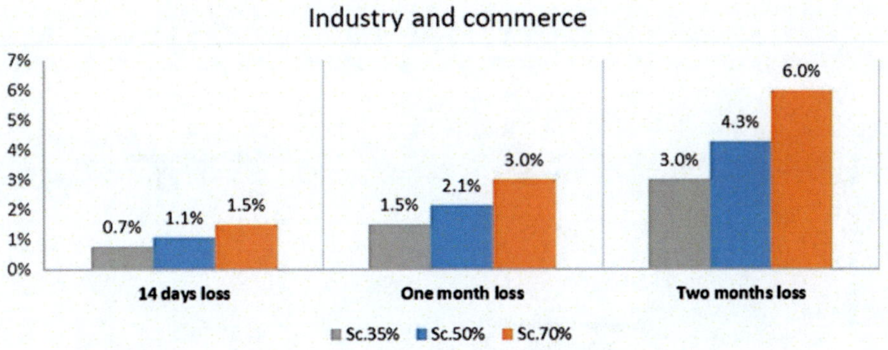

Fig. 3 GDP losses generated by employee inactivity. *Source* Author's calculation

4 Impact on the Budget Deficit

The economic downturn will be reflected both on the revenue side (which will decline because of the slowdown in activity and as a result of the fiscal facilities provided by the government) and on the expenditure side (by increasing the unemployment spending and the investment and support programmes dedicated to companies, announced by the government).

The amount of revenues collected to the state budget is also influenced by the inflation rate, a general price index (GDP deflator) of 4% being considered for the three scenarios. Considering the three scenarios regarding GDP's evolution, Romania's budget deficit may reach in 2020 values between 6.8 and 9.9% of the estimated GDP (Fig. 4).

4.1 Estimation of Tax Multipliers

Regarding the determinants for the size of tax multipliers, studies show that there are several types. On the one hand, are the structural factors that characterize an economy in the long term and how it responds to fiscal shocks in periods considered normal. On the other hand, there are cyclical factors (IMF 2014). These two categories of factors will be presented in the next.

Structural determinants influence the economy's response to fiscal shocks in periods considered normal. At the same time, empirical studies show that multipliers' values vary, even if the incremental effect of structural factors on multipliers is, to a large extent, unknown.

The structural features include:

- The degree of trade openness—a lower propensity to import leads to higher tax multipliers because the demand for imported goods is lower (Barrell et al. 2012; IMF 2008).

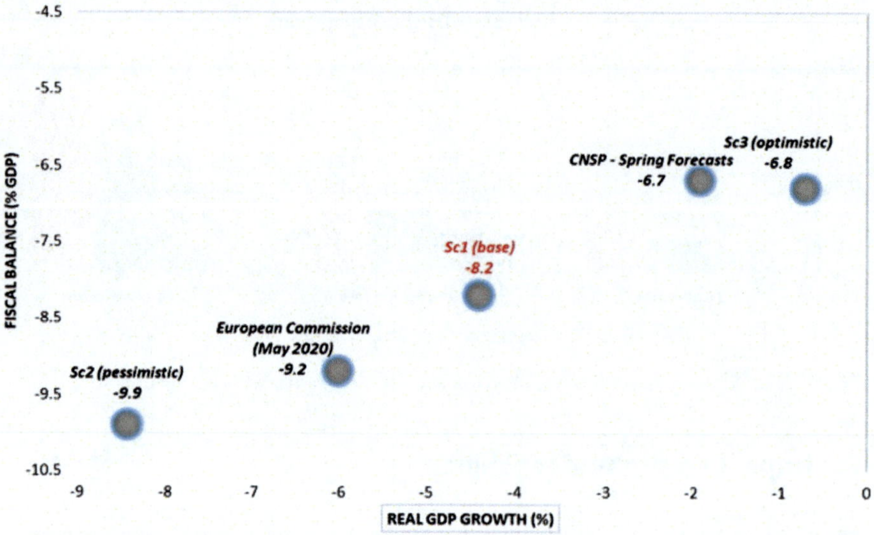

Fig. 4 Estimated real GDP growth rate and public balance in 2020. *Source* Author's calculation

- Labour market—Countries with more rigid labour markets due to strong unions or stricter labour market regulations have higher tax multipliers in the context where these rigidities imply less wage flexibility. Cole and Ohanian (2004) show that rigid wages tend to amplify the production's responses to the shocks on the demand).
- The size of automatic stabilizers—Larger automatic stabilizers reduce fiscal multipliers because the automatic, mechanical response of the transfers and taxes partially compensates for the initial fiscal shock, thus reducing its effect on GDP (see Dolls et al. 2012).
- Exchange rate regime—Different authors (Born et al. 2013; Ilzetzki et al. 2013) show that countries with a flexible exchange rate tend to have lower tax multipliers since the exchange rate movements can cancel out the impact of the discretionary fiscal measures on the economy.
- Level of public debt—Countries with high public debt have lower multipliers because fiscal consolidation may have higher credibility and reliable effects on private demand as well as on interest rates (Kirchner et al. 2010). Therefore, the fiscal stimulus can be negatively perceived and can damage private companies' confidence, and lead to the increasing interest rates due to rising risk premiums.
- Public expenditure management and revenue administration—the multipliers are expected to be lower if the government registers difficulties in collecting taxes and inefficiencies in public spending. They can limit the impact of the fiscal policy on production.

Conjectural factors tend to impact multipliers and may increase or decrease their magnitude compared to regular periods. In this regard, the literature analysing multipliers identifies two main categories of factors, as presented below.

(i) Business cycle phase—in most cases, tax multipliers are higher in the recession than in the expansion phase. This is true both when implementing expansionist (stimulating the economy) and restrictive (fiscal consolidation) policies. On the one hand, stimulus measures are considered less effective in an expansion because when the economy is above potential, an increase in public sector demand generates an eviction effect on private demand, leaving production unchanged but with higher prices. On the other hand, fiscal consolidation is much more expensive in a phase of a recessionary gap because households/companies—constrained from the perspective of liquidity and credit—cannot borrow to maintain their consumption/investments.

Moreover, a decrease in economic activity has a stronger effect on the multipliers than an increase in activity. Multipliers increase more in a recession period than they decrease in an expansion phase. One reason for this may be that supply reacts asymmetrically: if in an increase the impact of fiscal policy is limited by the inelasticity of available resources (and possibly zero when the economy reaches its productive potential at full employment), these constraints no longer exist when there is a decline in the economy, and the additional resources provided or extracted by the government have a more direct impact on production.

(ii) The degree of monetary accommodation to fiscal shocks—An expansionary monetary policy and interest rate cuts can cushion the impact of restrictive taxation on demand. In contrast, multipliers can be potentially higher when the use or transmission of monetary policy is difficult—such as the situation of zero-interest rates (Erceg and Lindé 2010; Woodford 2011).

Thus, the literature shows that a temporary increase in government demand has a significantly higher multiplier in zero-interest rates compared to "normal" periods. Erceg and Lindé (2010) show that the size of the shock matters in these periods: the higher the discretionary increases in spending, the less the economy will be in the zero-interest area and, therefore, the tax multiplier will be lower.

Christiano et al. (2011) show that lags in implementation reduce the multiplier in periods of zero interest; for the multiplier to be significantly higher than in periods considered "normal", the zero-interest period must be still present when the fiscal (expenditure) shock affects the economy (Table 1).

Given the above, a fiscal multiplier has been built that aims to quantify the impact that government spending could have on the economy, starting from determining the structural data of the Romanian economy presented by the literature, such as: the propensity to tax (change in tax revenue due to change in income/production), marginal propensity to consume (change in consumption due to change in income), but also marginal propensity to import, given that import is a function of income from the economy (the other key factor being the real exchange rate).

The determined multiplier is a Keynesian one, starting from the hypothesis that, at equilibrium, the level of production is equal to the aggregate demand (CA), and a change in government spending will lead to a change in GDP based on the following formula:

Table 1 Impact of structural invoices on fiscal multipliers

Structural factors	Romania
Degree of commercial openness	Positive—low degree of trade openness compared to other EU Member States
The size of the automatic stabilizers	Negative—weak, small-sized automatic stabilizers
Labour market	Positive—rigid labour market with low internal mobility, active labour market policies inefficient, poorly used
Exchange rate regime	Negative—flexible exchange rate, under the supervision of the central bank
The level of public debt	Positive—a low share of public debt in GDP

$$\Delta Y = \beta x \, \Delta G, \, and \, \beta = 1/(1 - c\prime(1 - t) + m) \quad (1)$$

where β is the government expenditure multiplier, c' the marginal propensity to consume, t the tax rate (share of tax revenues in GDP), m the marginal propensity to import; ΔY the absolute change in GDP, and ΔG the absolute change in government spending.

The determination of the coefficients included in the multiplier formula was made based on quarterly data from 1995Q1-2019Q4, for each of the composing indicators, respectively: household expenditure (C), tax revenue (T) from budget execution, imports (M), and quarterly gross domestic product(Y). The data source was Eurostat and the Ministry of Public Finance, and the processed data presented in millions of lei.

To capture the evolution over time of the multiplier and to see if cyclically there were also some fluctuations in terms of its value, the analysis took into account several time intervals: 1995–2019; 2000–2010; 2000–2019; 2010–2019; 2013–2019; 2015–2019; 2008–2012.

In addition, to see the changes following the recession in 2008, the period 2008Q3-2013 was also considered. The values of the coefficients used in the calculation of the tax multipliers were determined based on the following formulas (Table 2).

$$c\prime = \partial C/\partial Y; t = \partial T/\partial Y; \; m = \partial M/\partial Y \quad (2)$$

5 The Capacity to Mitigate the Effects of COVID as a Result of the Fiscal-Budgetary Measures Announced in Romania

Depending on the scenarios considered regarding the evolution of GDP, it is found that the gross value added in Romania can decrease significantly, with values between 41 and 122 billion lei, in the context of a decrease in the number of employees with

Table 2 Fiscal multiplier in Romania in different periods

	1995–2019	2000–2010	2000–2019	2010–2019	2013–2019	2015–2019	2008Q4—2012Q4
MG(t1)	1,29	1,75	1,58	1,43	1,42	1,43	1,63
MG(t2)	1,40	1,92	1,73	1,54	1,54	1,58	1,73

Source Authors' processing based on INS and Ministry of Public Finance data; Note: MG (t1) refers to the multiplier calculated on the basis of budget revenues, while MG (t2) is the multiplier calculated on the basis of fiscal revenues

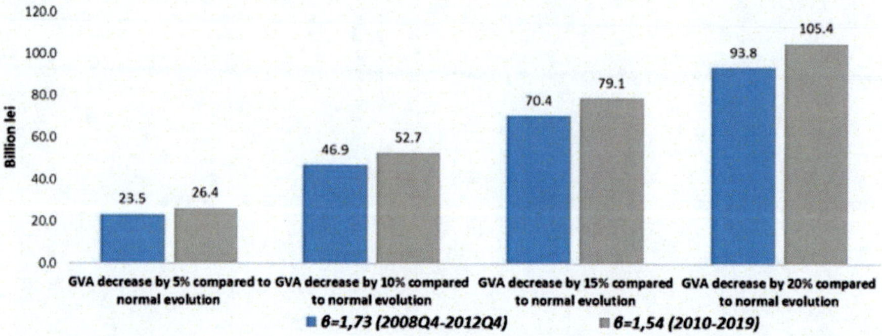

Fig. 5 Public expenditure needed to mitigate GDP decline (Billion lei). *Source* Author's calculation

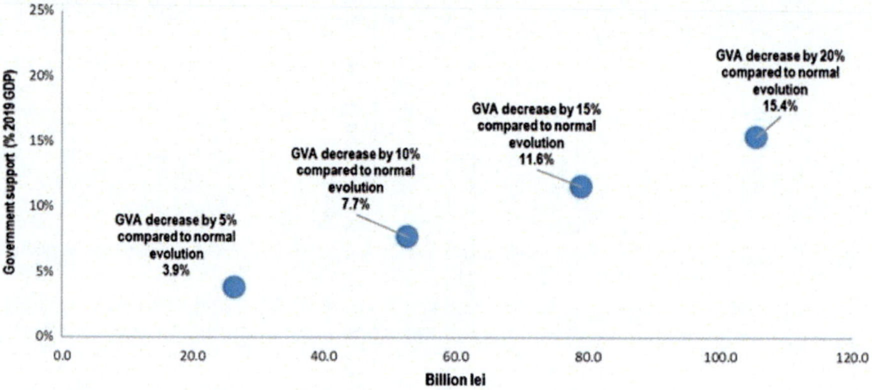

Fig. 6 Public expenditure needed to mitigate GDP decline (% 2019 GDP). *Source* Author's calculation

values between 5 and 20% compared to the value recorded in 2019. Based on the multipliers estimated above (using the multipliers obtained for the period 2008Q4-2012Q4 and 2010Q1-2019Q4), it can be considered that the absorption of this GDP loss because of the effects of the crisis can be achieved in the context of significant governmental intervention.

Estimates show that the additional government injection that should be made would be between 23.5 billion and 93.8 billion (when $\beta = 1.73$) or between 26.4 and 105.4 billion lei (when $\beta = 1.54$). In the last recession period (2008Q4-2012Q4), the estimated multiplier is equal to that of the period 2000–2019 (Figs. 5 and 6).

5.1 A Coherent Industrial Policy in the COVID Pandemic 19

The article by Reda Cherif and Fuad Hasanov outlines an interdisciplinary strategy of state support for market failures. On the one hand, epidemiological investigations are targeted to allow further economic activity, and on the other hand, the type of appropriate industrial policy to support production is analysed.

The authors of the article created a model that demonstrates that testing and isolating according to a series of logical criteria called Smart Testing is much more effective in terms of impact on the economic activity than random testing. Of course, the economic costs generated by such a strategy have to be taken into account, but the subsequent economic plus fully compensates for these costs and generates a significant positive result. The cost of a total lockdown is enormous, and the phenomenon, in turn, causes subsequent economic and social costs that will be very difficult to address.

At the same time, the authors demonstrate that a cumulative effort on the part of both the state and the private sector, and also of the general population, can mitigate the impact generated by the negative evolutions of some industries such as HORECA (hotels, restaurants, and catering sector), tourism, etc. Thus, the manufacturing industry could take on new dimensions.

There is a common voice of renowned economists (Romer 2020a and 2020b; Siddhartha and Weyl 2020; Baldwin 2020; Berger et al. 2020, Brotherhood and others 2020; Eichenbaum et al. 2020a; Bethune and Korinek 2020, Acemoglu et. al. 2020; Piguillem Shi 2020) who argue that mass testing, in addition to a number of other measures, is the only viable strategy to combat the pandemic and its economic effects. However, there is no consensus on how much should be tested and what the complementary measures should be so that the negative economic and social effects of the SARS-CoV-2 virus would be minimal.

The authors' detailed analysis shows that social distancing reduces the transmission rate of infection by 50%. At the same time, depending on the type of profession, certain activities can be very efficiently carried out also by working in isolation, this being true for of approximately 37–40% of the total professions. At the moment, despite all these measures, the spread rate of the infection remains exponential.

The cost of massive and repeated testing in order to continue the economic activity safely is determined to be 3.5–4 times lower than the cost of the economic lockdown.

In the consulted literature, we have identified a series of simulations aimed at various possible measures to combat the pandemic with minimal negative economic and social effects. At the same time, these simulations also provide the optimization of the testing process both in number and in samples, etc.

5.2 Analysis of the Evolution of the Labour Market

Productivity and wages are closely linked to the level of education (Becker 2009; Pompeii and Selezneva 2015; Brunello 2001); employees with a higher level of education can cope more easily with the imbalances caused by economic crises because they are able to better adapt to changes. Several studies (Kumhof et al. 2015; Cheong 2001; Martins 2011) have shown that economic crises have as an effect the increase of inequality in income distribution. During economic crises, the return to school rate increases, as a lower level of education implies a higher chance of losing a job or earning less (Dey and Loewenstein 2020). Although agricultural workers are less affected by economic crises, there is evidence that COVID-19 has caused considerable damage to the incomes of less-educated workers (Richards Rickard 2020).

Part-time employment contracts are also affected by the economic cycles, their number increasing in times of recession. Although it involves lower wages and less favourable work conditions, recent research on the US labour market suggests that such a solution is more advantageous than unemployment (Borowczyk-Martins 2017) and less expensive (Abraham and Houseman 1994). Although it may be difficult to ask workers to reduce their working hours, they still accept (Cahuc 2019). Using short-term compensation schemes (kurtzarbeit - unilateral reduction of working time), employees can reduce their working hours without a proportional diminution in income, the cost difference being supported by both the employer and the state. In countries like Austria, Belgium, Denmark, Finland, such schemes were used successfully even before the 2008 crisis (Cahuc 2019). Pavlopoulos and Chkalova (2017) analyse the effect of kurtzarbeit policies on the Dutch labour market during the crisis of 2009–2011. Nuno (2020) mentions that all sectors will be affected by the crisis caused by COVID-19, but special problems will be in the tourism-related sectors.

In 2018, the Romanian labour force has an approximately even distribution by sex, the highest percentage of employed people (21%) being registered in agriculture, followed by the manufacturing industry (20%) and wholesale and retail trade repair of motor vehicles and motorcycles (14%). Cumulatively, the first three sectors of activity absorb about 55% of the total labour market. The HORECA sector, one of the sectors most affected by the crisis generated by COVID-19, employs about 3% of the total workforce and constructions about 8%. Considering the different fields of activity, in 2018, approximately 21.7% of the total workforce are employed in agriculture, 30.1% in industry, and 48.2% in services. In the last decade, the highest unemployment rate was recorded at the beginning of 2010, following a downward trend with slight fluctuations manifested until the end of the analysed period.

In 2019, the highest unemployment rate (5.86%) is registered among the people with secondary education; higher education graduates are the category most protected from unemployment (1.57%). 21% of the employed population graduated from higher education, 3% have post-secondary education, 40% high school, 18% come from vocational, complementary, and apprenticeship education, 16% graduated (as the last form) gymnasium, and 2% only primary education. The largest share of the employed population belongs to the age group 35–49 years (43%). Young people under 35 represent 28% of the employed population. Only 3% of the employed population is 65 years old. In the case of higher education graduates, the structure of the employed population is the same. Between 2008 and 2018, the total number of Romania employees varied, decreasing by almost 14% during the last economic crisis.

5.3 *The Influence of the Health Crisis on the Labour Market*

The number of unemployed (as defined by the International Labour Office, ILO) increased in just five months from a minimum of 337,858 persons, registered in January 2020 to 466,583 persons in June 2020 (representing an increase of 38.1%) (Fig. 7).

The unemployment rate followed the same trend in the analysed period, increasing from a minimum of 3.7% in January 2020 to 5.2% in March of the same year. Another negative aspect is the number of suspended employment contracts. The cessation of activity in a very short time in many sectors of activity has led to the suspension of over one million employment contracts (out of the approximately five million employees in the economy) and to the termination of over 300,000 individual employment contracts (given that the number of unemployed registered in March 2020 was around 250 000). On 4 May 2020, more than 20% of all employees in the national economy were affected, either by the termination of their employment contract or by its suspension, by the crisis caused by the COVID-19 virus. This unprecedented economic shock on the labour demand, in time of peace, has created an imbalance that seems to have been overcome with the return to activity of most sectors (except HORECA). Thus, from a maximum of 1,046,527 (over one million) suspended contracts registered in April 2020, a number of 102,830 (just over one hundred thousand) suspended contracts at the level of the national economy was reached on 3 July 2020 (data provided by MMPS). Regarding the manufacturing industry, the share of suspended employment contracts varied between 20 and 30% of the total, the lowest percentage being recorded in June (Fig. 8).

Among the most affected sectors of the economy were HORECA, the retail sector (excluding foodstuffs), and the SME sector.

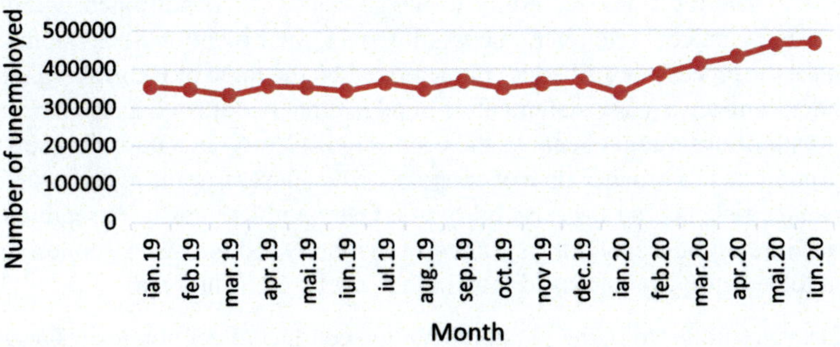

Fig. 7 Evolution of the number of unemployed in the period January 2019–June 2020. *Source* INSS

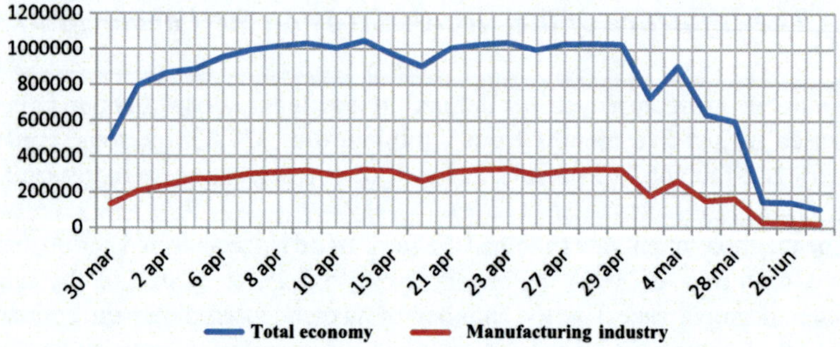

Fig. 8 Evolution of the number of suspended individual employment contracts

6 Measures for Economic Revitalization

In order to be able to assess a path to follow in the decision-making process regarding investments, we must consider that in the vicinity of a health crisis event, the economic systems do not react according to a set of rules that could have been analysed before the pandemic.

It is necessary to consider an adaptation of the sale and purchase decisions dictated by reactions of adaptation from the decision-makers to what they understand to be a new system of economy, in the sense of an economic system that works with rules adapted to the sanitary crisis and post-crisis conditions, but also to adapt the rules of valorization in the economic calculation and to assess the efficiency of the economic agents natural persons / welfare of the private persons.

This adaptation is dynamic at the moment and will continue for a long time after the end of the human crisis of a medical nature. Under these conditions, we can only state the rules according to which trends are conditioned without being able to mention concrete phenomena; moreover, their mention does not make sense because the process described is characterized by the logic of Heisenberg's principle of indeterminacy, so any statement of trend is already outdated at the moment of its observation/formulation because the economy is already in a new situation.

In addition to a broader state of economic risks, the economic agents with capacity to manage risk, having the possibility of a faster and less costly economic recovery because the national economic systems, individually and as a macroeconomic system, seem to be better characterized than in the past by the following:

- The rules imposed in the pandemic on the conduct of economic acts and on individuals seem to emphasize the importance of discussing the role and position of the state in the economy. All the rules imposed on this occasion with the intention to limit the effects of the pandemic lead to the limitation of personal freedoms and diminished the individual's joy of living. Paradoxically, the situation seems to be similar to that of societies and economies from 200–300 years ago when, historically speaking, the current system of individual and collective economic and social freedoms was set in place. Undoubtedly, although the role of these rules is (to some degree) understood, it is difficult to accept, and we expect some form of opportunism by which some economic agents will try to avoid adopting these rules, reacting in the same manner in which, metaphorically speaking, smugglers reacted to various state prohibitions. That is why it is important for each measure of intervention in the economy to demonstrate its reasonableness in order to avoid reaching the paradox of the predominance of the negative effects of the good intentions; the perverse, eviction effect of economic policies is much stronger;

- The economic networks are damaged in several directions: stigma is more perceivable, namely the tendency to avoid transactions based on territoriality criteria—considering the different intensities of the pandemic; the level of aggression towards the public authority (state or in the system of a non-governmental organization) increases the regularization of the transaction systems that seems to suffer; the state of asymmetric information and the degree of reaching moral hazard are increasing; these phenomena lead to a reorientation of the economic networks, of the domestic/international chains of creation of economic value. We do not appreciate that the economy tends to collapse by breaking economic ties but that it tends to orient towards those transactions that prove more reliable than others in relation to the manifestation of the pandemic, and therefore to redefine the importance and role of its presence in different types of commercial agreements (e.g. Schengen);
- Not all people have been affected in the same way by the pandemic; the differences can be quantified, depending on the number of infections in one area or another, but can also be analysed in connection with a person's appurtenance to a vulnerable group. The labour market will be impacted differently considering the different occupational groups/areas of activity /age groups. We appreciate that special attention will have to be paid to frictional unemployment with ad hoc decisions and interventions. We should keep in mind that the effects of unemployment will be lower for sectors considered essential, that not only have not ceased their activity, but are experiencing increasing employment needs (e.g. the medical sector) and also in the case of certain age groups; paradoxically, although the unemployment rate had a slightly higher growth in the case of young people, given their greater ability to adapt to new conditions and new social situations, the return will be faster and easier than in the case of other age groups. For such identifiable categories, we appreciate that new jobs will emerge, different from the existing ones at least through the way they are practised. Even if the development of online economic activities is the obvious formula for orienting economic efficiency, now only fastened by the pandemic, the next kind of trend is different, and is that of personalization/adaptation of business standardization for different partners in this process, that of increasing the interaction between business partners with considerable logistic flow distances in the absence of new technologies. This phenomenon in the economy is important not only for the labour market but, remarkably, it is the trend unaffected by social distancing, the economy does not slowdown in these sectors not being affected by the phenomenon of social dystopia.

On the other hand, we appreciate long-term negative effects on the labour market for the sectors in which the activity contracted during the pandemic and for the vulnerable categories of people that are currently difficult to identify given that the economy is still operating in a pandemic blockage.

- Due to the state of personal anxiety, we appreciate that the transactions for certain categories of goods will reduce differently: (1) purchases of durable goods up to 25–40% (for all these data, we considered the evolution of consumption as it is reported by EU countries and North America); the current decrease will return to a strong increase in 1–2 years after the state of risk of infection will be resolved; the fields to which it applies are varied, and it includes the purchase of new cars, houses, etc.; (2) purchases of goods that presupposed a great social behaviour (tourism, luxury clothing products, etc.) up to 35–65%; in this case, it is difficult to appreciate the rapidity of the return; given that the total consumption seems to have not changed in value we can say that we are witnessing an adaptation of the consumption trends, probably in those directions imposed by the need to adapt the lifestyle to the new isolation conditions (e.g. changing preferences for single-family or multi-room dwellings where work can be arranged; explosive increase in demand for individual leisure products, etc.). As long as we cannot appreciate that the changes in the current lifestyle will evolve towards the previous trends, we cannot appreciate the return for these sectors either. Compared to the classic economic crises, it is not possible to draw a temporal differentiation between crisis and recovery, this being another argument for using the term economic revitalization.

7 Pandemic Investment Policy

For this period, we should bear in mind that most economists and organizations/companies with demonstrable expertise in the field anticipate a decrease of the international flows of investment funds by about 30%.

Another relevant aspect is that the high value of utility of public investments compared to private ones that can bring a 1.5 times greater effect for revitalization is questioned, because: (a) the vast majority of public expenditures are conditioned by the imperative need to cover the needs of the medical crisis (e.g. sanitary materials) and (b) the multiplication effect is neutral for the restart of the economy and has an effect especially in the recovery phase of its revitalization. For the economic recovery stage, public expenditures are in a fragile balance between the need for liquidity insurance and the pressure to trigger inflation. This balance is difficult to assess because economic systems no longer react naturally—by price increases to the increase in liquid money, but is conditioned by a huge increase in preferences for liquidity provisions in the face of the lack of a medical remedy to the pandemic.

In supporting private investments, facilitating the links/contacts between economic agents is of major importance in the short term, but these measures exceed the range of economic measures, so we will only focus on the interesting importance that public investments have at this moment on a long term. A change in the companies' preferences for investments is expected, for preferences grouped according to geographical criteria. The current pandemic has shown companies that ignoring sunk costs (generated by the impossibility of explicitly and completely representing them in accounting) can lead to major security crises (being also the case of this current crisis) to increased risks of bankruptcy. A change in investment preferences in geographical areas with increased security and opportunities for labour management, production, in general, is expected. At the same time, the criterion of the lowest possible production cost as a basis for the current profit is rather interpreted in terms of opportunity cost, in which the acceptance of higher production costs ensures the long-term sustainability of profit and especially in times of security crises.

Globally, Romania falls into the category of areas that are becoming more interesting after the crisis, and therefore, the investment policy must take into account the support of further business development through smart and strategic infrastructure development. We use the term "smart" in the sense that the geopolitical redefinition of the economy space implies the need to think the investment strategies in an interdisciplinary system.

In terms of the dynamics of public spending, in order not to witness a broad crisis of public funds, or worse, a major liquidity crisis, we must keep in mind that, considering the natural passing of the time, it is anticipated that the return of the economy and international capital flows to normal will be affected by the entry of the northern hemisphere in the autumn–winter period, a period in which doctors expect an increase in the volume of medical problems and a new slowdown in the economy.

It is noteworthy, analysing a wide range of predictions of economic evolution considered relevant using scientific methods and the elimination, to a large extent, of emotions, that even the most alarming assessments do not consider a long-term economic crisis. For revitalization, it is important to wait for the end of the winter period in the northern hemisphere to assess the state of the Romanian economy in relation to the possibilities of economic recovery. However, throughout this period, it is expected that the reinvested rate will decrease, and the number of acquisitions and mergers will be extremely low.

In terms of taxation, it would be advisable to eliminate profit taxes because the existing liquidity will be reinvested later in companies to ensure their sustainability even if for small companies it is expected that for the H3 2020-H1 2021quarters, profits will be transferred to private provisions.

In the optimist scenario, the public health and safety measures that have been taken manage to control the spread of the virus in the next 2–3 months; better treatments that reduce the number of deaths and the serious illnesses caused by the virus are identified; testing continuous in an extended system. The economic policy interventions are effective and avoid serious structural damage to the economy by considering the changes in economic behaviour, including those sectors of the economy that are most affected. In this scenario, the economic growth is resumed in the second half of the year, and it returns to pre-crisis levels by the end of 2020.

Revenues are projected to start rising in the second half of 2020 and return to pre-crisis levels by the end of 2021, as the economy recovers; the share that direct investors choose to reinvest will return and even exceed historical levels. There will be a period of decline in the medium term due to the reorientation by geographical areas of interest. We must mention that the current pandemic /momentary economic blockade overlaps with a global trend of decreasing foreign direct investment flows manifested worldwide since 2015, a trend in which Romania has been in a happily atypical situation due to constant economic growth over a period of several years. The economic recovery will be unequal in areas, and it will consider the change in economic behaviour and the ability to reconnect in economic flows.

Under the reserved scenario, public health measures were initially successful in combating current outbreaks, but there are future outbreaks, so strict public health measures will be required until a vaccine is developed and widely administered at the end of 2021. The economic policy interventions are palliative, and therefore, the economic recovery is uneven and weak.

Also, in this scenario, the economic recovery will be uneven. While the incomes from some sectors will recover, others will remain below the level registered before the economic blockade. Equity flows will be diminished not only by the lack of new projects negotiated during the pandemic but also by a continuous decline in new business opportunities. However, there will be some acquisitions because financially stronger firms could buy assets at prices that have become attractive through other companies' bankruptcy.

Under the alarmist scenario, current public health measures are not able to fully control the virus, which requires strict measures to be maintained for a long time. Economic policy interventions are unable to compensate for economic damage and economies are in a persistent recession; bankruptcies and unemployment are more common than in the other scenarios.

We did not call the last scenario pessimistic, but we considered the term alarmist to be more appropriate because the state of panic contributes significantly to the economic blockade and the postponement of revitalization.

Earnings would remain low and depressing in most sectors, as would the share of reinvested earnings. Capital flows would be significantly reduced since many of the pending transactions and announced projects would be cancelled because they no longer make strategic sense, or the investor is facing financial pressures. Companies will be strategically oriented towards obtaining and managing liquidity. In general, investment flows would decrease by more than 50% in 2020 and with more than 70/80% by the end of 2021, when the introduction of a vaccine could finally allow economic revitalization.

It should be noted that the current situation overlaps an international situation with developments outside the trends; we already had the uncertainty generated by Brexit, questions about the future of the EU, the atypical political situation of the USA, etc.

Companies were already rethinking their production chains in response to consumer demand and were moving towards more sustainable and inclusive production methods; the introduction and expansion of digital technologies was the focus. Companies were adapting for the introduction of electronic solutions and the dematerialization and automation of the production processes. Reducing dependence on long-term contracts and fixed assets were the other two strategic directions. Strengthening e-commerce by improving the existing networks and reducing moral hazard are solutions for new investments and for reducing the impact of future shocks. The widespread of advanced technologies made usage it possible to redistribute capital to the areas where the development of infrastructure in the field (as in the case of Romania) makes it possible to conduct business in this spectrum, illiteracy for the workforce is redefined in relation to the empathic ability to work through technologies. Advanced: Personal incomes (especially wages) increased especially in emerging economies, with higher rates than in developed economies.

The pandemic will accentuate these trends. Short-term economic policy trade-offs, compromises dictated by medical and social requirements, must be carefully assessed to avoid dramatic and prolonged financial disruptions in a context where international economic policy coordination seems impossible to achieve. Related to the international aspect, there is a great deal of unknown about the future intentions regarding the current economic measures in the field of policy relaxation such as: monetary policy facilities, increasing liquidity, the introduction of fiscal incentives, relaxation of prudential policies, increasing tolerance towards regulation in various fields.

In this context, it is necessary to follow how future flows of direct foreign investments and investments from national capitals will be oriented because the economic policies from different countries correspond to the pandemic requirements, not to the positioning interests at its end. The adaptation of governments to the current situation has led to the imposition of restrictions decided by medical criteria, which has led to a reduction in the non-discriminatory treatment of investors, some obligations to guide production, restricted employment, or total closure in certain sectors. Although such decisions are necessary, it must be considered that with the expected disappearance of the medical danger, all these adaptations lose their rationality and become cost-generating. The effective response of governments to the pandemic requires not only restrictive actions but requires great attention to non-discriminatory measures, especially since any necessary decisions are frequently the subject of different interpretations for the government regulatory space. A regulatory solution must be found to enable governments to respond effectively to the pandemic and take vital measures such as rapid access to essential goods and services. The political answer to this problem is delayed.

International production and value chains are essential beyond the immediate response to the crisis. Not only will they be recovered post-pandemic, but they will also be rethought. The current medical crisis has exposed economic weaknesses, political dependencies, and geopolitical blockages tacitly accepted due to the economic efficiency they generated. Stopping them due to the pandemic will lead to the reconfiguration of the economy in a shape that has not yet been completed as it is an ongoing adaptation to the evolution of the pandemic, but the international economic positioning remains vital that is adequate in the interest of strong supply chains and production, resistant to threats. Security: The links between companies and intercompany will allow a better absorption of future shocks and risks resulting from economic crises, pandemics, or climate change, by strengthening the general research capacity, disseminating new business directions and more creative management techniques.

The investment policy becomes a component and is also the responsibility of the general state policy. Romania's investment policy must consider the slightly higher vulnerability of our economy compared to other EU countries because the need for support (manifested mainly through the mechanism of the common cohesion funds) encounters the tendency to prioritize national interests, so additional incentives are needed to attract foreign or domestic investments. Private investments become vital in the equation of development financing since both capital, and private investments will focus in the short term on financing the overall economic revitalization. The flattening of the current economic relations will evolve into an economic system with increased mutual responsibilities for those who will agree to accept each other as members of the same production and value chain; the probability to see a major return of the geostrategic role of national states (or groups of states following the model of the European Union) in the configuration of the transnational systems of companies is extremely high.

8 Proposed Measures to Improve the Capacity to Manage the Economic Activity

Learning from other crises and pandemics that happened over time, also considering that they do not entirely look alike, the common denominator that has always worked in concerted government actions has had three directions:

1. Reducing risk and uncertainty for the private sector;
2. The roles of coordinating the economic activity and securing financing (European grants, state guarantees, etc.) must be linked to the private sector's productive capacity.
3. Adapting key state institutions and agencies so they can function optimally (e.g. digitization process, etc.)

From a macroeconomic perspective, the government's capacity to influence the economy manifests itself in two directions of action—the first being that of macrostabilization through the fiscal-budgetary policy and the second being the macrostructural one, with medium- and long-term effects. Macroeconomic guidance in times of recession—a natural stage of the economic cycle that follows a period of growth of almost ten years, respectively, a period of stimulating economic growth, especially in times of recession, is related to a combination of structural, specific factors that should be considered.

We are talking, first, about the management of public expenditures and about the share of fiscal revenues in the GDP, which is the lowest in the European Union. It is imperative to reduce tax evasion and digitize public services to increase the voluntary compliance of individuals and private companies and to free up resources (time, money, staff) for other public activities (e.g. prevention and counselling/information services).

From a public expenditure perspective, prioritizing and allocating funds where the ex ante analysis shows significant spill-over effects are essential. In addition, to do this, it is valuable to increase the analysing capacity of the post-implementation impacts of investment projects, regardless of their financing source (state budget, European non-reimbursable funds, funds from international financial institutions, etc.).

Also, the size of automatic stabilizers contributes to the adjustment of economic imbalances, other than through the implementation of discretionary measures. These automatic stabilizers are correlated with the taxation system (single taxation, progressive taxation), the size of government intervention, and the degree of trade openness of a country with a specific, small, and open economy. Depending on its size, the latter may expose the national economy more or less to the influences of the global/regional business cycle and the transmission of potential external shocks.

On the labour market, although the labour force's flexibility from the perspective of the labour contracts is relatively high, the internal mobility of the labour force is low, the predisposition of workers for external migration being obvious. The properly prepared human resource plays the most important role in optimizing the proper functioning of the labour market, but this goal can only be achieved in the medium and long term. Active policies on the labour market can play an important role in the short term. Although they have been used in recent years, including supporting mobility over distances of 15, 30 or 50 km, they had limited effects, the number of beneficiaries being under the target proposed by the Ministry of Labour and Social Protection, and relatively small as percentage from the total number of unemployed persons.

Therefore, optimizing and intensifying the use of active labour market policies and measures to stimulate mobility can help increase the economy's resilience to current challenges and potential future shocks.

Additional measures to revitalize the labour market.

- Reducing bureaucracy;
- Amending the legislation so that work from home/telework is easier to implement;

- Encouraging the participation of young people in the labour market (the highest unemployment rate is registered among young people, over 18% at the end of 2019);
- Providing tax facilities for companies in areas severely affected by the crisis;
- Supporting exports in order to relaunch employment;
- Ensuring a more permissive legislative framework for seasonal work and agricultural activities.

Annexes

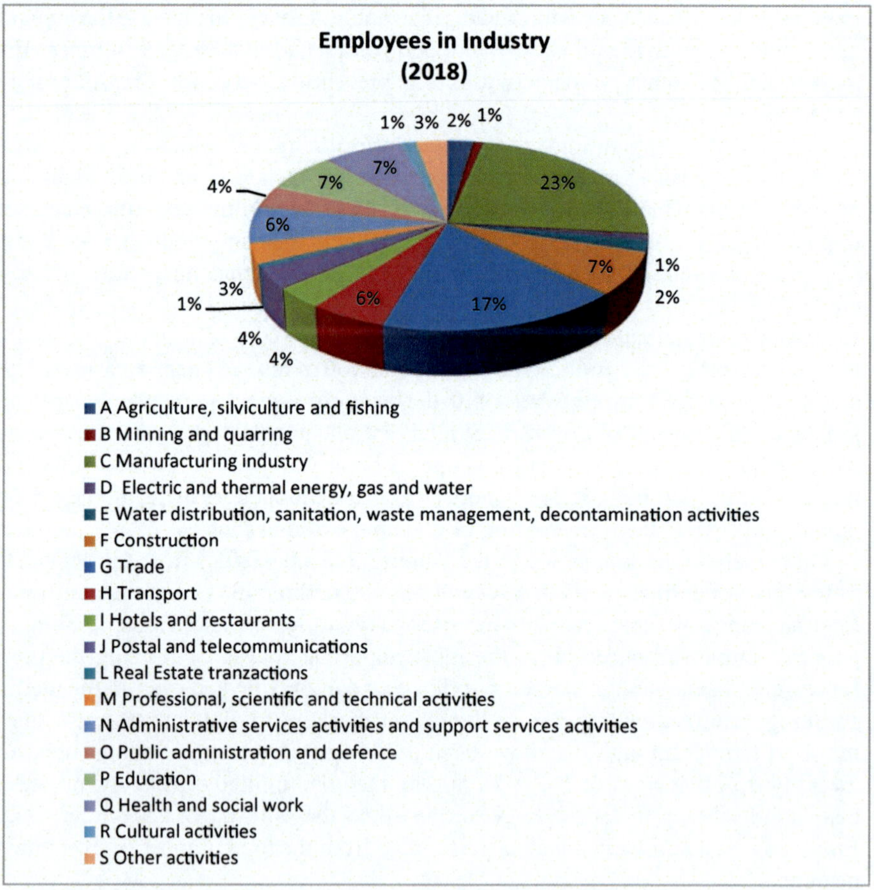

Source INSSE

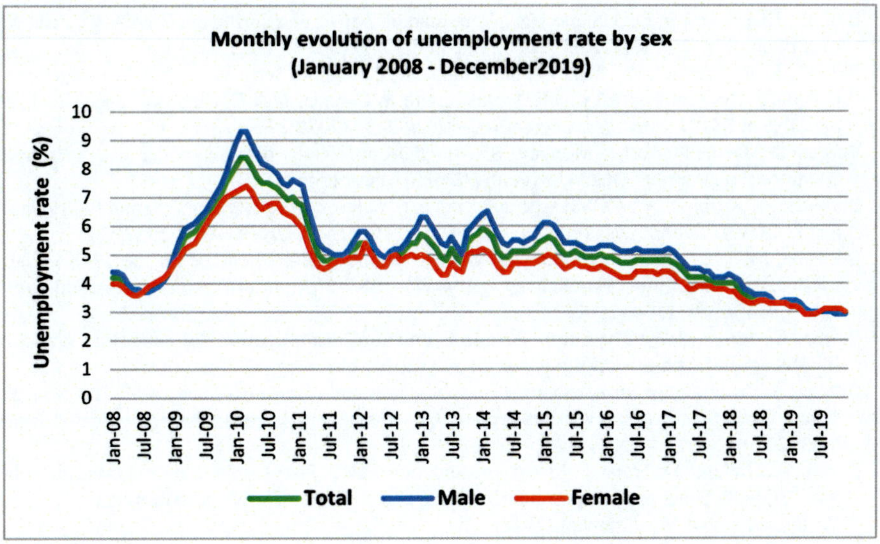

Source INSSE

References

Abraham, K., Houseman, S.: Does employment protection inhibit labor market flexibility? Lessons from Germany, France, and Belgium In: Blank, R. (ed.). Social Protection versus Economic Flexibility: Is There a Trade-Off? Chicago, IL: University of Chicago Press (1994)

Acemoglu, D., Chernozhukov, V., Werning I., Whinston, M.D.: A multi-sir model with optimally targeted lockdown. NBER Working Paper 27102 (2020)

Adam, D.C., Cowling, B.J.: Just Stop the Superspreading. The New York Times. June 2. https://www.nytimes.com/2020/06/02/opinion/coronavirussuperspreaders.html (2020)

Afelt, A., Roger, F., Devaux, C.: Bats, coronaviruses, and deforestation: toward the emergence of novel infectious diseases? Front. Microbiol. **9**, 702 (2018)

Alon, U., Milo, R., Yashiv, E.: "10–4: How to reopen the economy by exploiting the coronavirus's weak spot. The New York Times, May 11. https://www.nytimes.com/2020/05/11/opinion/coronavirus-reopen.html (2020)

Azmeh, S.: The perverse economics of ventilators. Project-Syndicate. April 16. https://www.project-syndicate.org/commentary/ventilator-shortage-reflects-profitdriven-innovation-by-shamel-azmeh-2020-04 (2020)

Baldwin, R.: COVID-19 Testing for Testing Times: Fostering Economic Recovery and Preparing for the Second Wave. VoxEU, March 26. https://voxeu.org/article/testing-testing-times (2020)

Barro, R., Ursua, J., Weng, J.: The coronavirus and the great influenza pandemic: Lessons from the 'Spanish Flu' for the coronavirus's potential effects on mortality and economic activity. NBER working paper 26866, March (2020)

Batini, N., Eyraud, L., Weber, A.: A simple method to compute fiscal multipliers, FMI, WP/14/93, June (2014)

Becker, G.S.: Human capital: A theoretical and empirical analysis, with special reference to education. University of Chicago press (2009)

Bell, D., Blanchflower, D.: US and UK labour markets before and during the Covid-19 Crash. Natl. Inst. Econ. Rev. **252**, R52–R69 (2020). https://doi.org/10.1017/nie.2020.14

Béland,, L.-P., Brodeur, A., Mikola, D., Wright, T.: The Short-Term Economic Consequences of Covid-19: Occupation Tasks and Mental Health in Canada. IZA Discussion Paper No. 13254, available at SSRN: https://ssrn.com/abstract=3602430 (2020).

Berger, D., Herkenhoff, K., Mongey, S.: An SEIR infectious disease model with testing and conditional quarantine. Duke University, March, Manuscript (2020)

Bethune, Z., Korinek, A.: COVID-19 infection externalities: Pursuing herd immunity or containment? COVID Economics, Vetted and Real-Time Papers 11, CEPR, April 29 (2020)

Bootsma, M.C.J., Ferguson, N.M.: The effect of public health measures on the 1918 influenza pandemic in U.S. Cities. PNAS, May 1, **104**(18): 7588–7593. https:// doi.org/https://doi.org/10.1073/pnas.0611071104 (2007)

Bossie, A., Mason, J.W.: The Public Role in Economic Transformation: Lessons from World War II", Roosevelt Institute working paper, March (2020)

Bradley, J.: In scramble for coronavirus supplies, rich countries push poor aside. The New York Times, April 9. https://www.nytimes.com/2020/04/09/world/coronavirus-equipment-rich-poor.html (2020)

Barrell, R., Holland, D., Hurst, I.: Fiscal consolidation: Part 2. Fiscal multipliers and fiscal consolidations", OECD Economics Department Working Paper No. 933. Paris: Organization for Economic Co-operation and Development (2012)

Borowczyk-Martins, D.: Why does part-time employment increase in recessions?, IZA World of Labor (2017)

Born, B.F., Mueller, J.G.J.: Exchange rate regimes and fiscal multipliers. J. Econ. Dyn. Control **37**(2), 446–465 (2013)

Brunello, G.: Unemployment, education and earnings growth (2001)

Brotherhood, L., Kircher, P., Santos, C., Tertilt, M.: An Economic Model of the COVID-19 Epidemic: the importance of testing and age-specific policies. working paper (2020)

Brunet, G.: 5 Lessons From World War II For the Coronavirus Response", Vox. April 10. https://www.vox.com/2020/4/10/21214980/coronavirus-economy-jobsppe. (2020).

Budish, E.: R < 1 as an economic constraint: can we 'expand the frontier' in the fight against Covid-19? April 1. University of Chicago, working paper (2020)

Cleevely, M., Susskind, D., Vines, D., Vines, L., Wills, S.: A workable strategy for Covid-19 testing: stratified periodic testing rather than universal random testing. COVID economics, vetted and real-time papers 8, CEPR, April 22

CDC: Historical reference of seasonal influenza vaccine doses distributed. https://www.cdc.gov/flu/prevent/vaccine-supply-historical.htm (2019)

Cerra, V., Fatas, A., Saxena, S.: Hysteresis and business cycles. CEPR Discussion Paper No. DP14531 (2020)

Christiano, L., Eichenbaum, M., Rebelo, S.: When is the government spending- multiplier large? J. Polit. Econ. **119**(1), 78–121 (2011)

Cole, H.L., Ohanian, L.E.: New deal policies and the persistence of the great depression: a general equilibrium analysis. J. Polit. Econ. **112**(4), 779–816 (2004)

Cahuc, P.: Short-time work compensation schemes and employment. IZA World of Labor. https://doi.org/10.15185/izawol.11.v2 (2019)

Cheong, K.S.: Economic crisis and income inequality in Korea. Asian Econ. J. **15**(1), 39–60 (2001)

Cherif, R., Hasanov, F., Zhu, M.: Breaking the Oil Spell, IMF (2016).

Cherif, R., Hasanov, F., Zhu, M. (eds): Breaking the oil spell: The Gulf Falcons' path to diversification. Washington, DC: IMF Press (2016)

Cherif, R., Hasanov, F.: The return of the policy that shall not be named: principles of industrial policy. IMF Working Paper 19/074 (2019)

Corman, V., Bleicker, T., Brunink, S., Drosten, C., Landt, O., Koopmans, M., Zambon, M.: Diagnostic Detection of 2019-nCoV by Real-Time RT-PCR", January 17, World Health Organization. https://www.who.int/docs/default-source/coronaviruse/protocol-v2-1.pdf?sfvrsn=a9ef618c_2 (2020)

Correia, S., Luck, S., Verner, E.: Pandemics Depress the economy, public health interventions do not: Evidence from the 1918 Flu. March, working paper (2020)

de Walque, D., Friedman, J., Gatti, R., Mattoo, A.: How two tests can help contain COVID-19 and revive the economy. Research and Policy Briefs, The World Bank, April 8 (2020)

Demirgüç-Kunt, A., Lokshin, M., Torre, I.: The sooner, the better: the early economic impact of non-pharmaceutical interventions during the COVID-19 Pandemic. May. World Bank working paper (2020)

Denworth, L.: How the COVID-19 pandemic could end. Scientific American, April 28. https://www.scientificamerican.com/article/how-the-covid-19-pandemic-could-end/ (2020)

Dingel, J., Neiman, B.: How many jobs can be done at home? NBER, Working Paper 26948 (2020)

Dolls, M., Fuest, C., Peichl, A.: Automatic stabilizers and economic crisis: US vs. Europe. J. Public Econ. **96**, 279–294 (2012)

Dey, M., Loewenstein, M.A: How many workers are employed in sectors directly affected by COVID-19 shutdowns, where do they work, and how much do they earn? Monthly Labor Review, pp. 1–19 (2020)

Egilmezer, E., Walker, G.J., Bakthavathsalam, P., Peterson, J.R., J., Gooding, J., Rawlinson, W, Stelzer-Braid, S.: "Systematic Review of the Impact of Point-of-care Testing for Influenza on the Outcomes of Patients with Acute Respiratory Tract Infection", Reviews in Medical Virology 28(5). Available: https://doi.org/10.1002/rmv.1995 (2018).

Eichenbaum, M.S., Rebelo, S., Trabandt, M.: The macroeconomics of testing and quarantining. CEPR Working Paper 14688, May (2020a)

Eichenbaum, M.S., Rebelo, S., Trabandt, M.: The macroeconomics of epidemics. NBER Working Paper 26882, April. (2020b)

Erceg, C.J., Lindé, J.: Is There a Free Lunch in a Liquidity Trap? International Finance Discussion Papers 1003. Washington: U.S. Federal Reserve System (2010)

Fearnow, B.: Wuhan tested nearly 7 million people in 12 days to prevent second coronavirus wave, health officials say. Newsweek, May 26. https://www.newsweek.com/wuhan-tested-nearly-7-million-people-12-days-prevent-secondcoronavirus-wave-health-officials-say-1506537 (2020)

Fernandes, N.: Economic effects of coronavirus outbreak (COVID-19) on the World Economy. SSRN: https://ssrn.com/abstract=3557504 or http://dx.doi.org/https://doi.org/10.2139/ssrn.3557504 (March 22, 2020)

Ferretti, L., Wymant, C., Kendall, M., Zhao, L., Nurtay, A., Abeler-Dörner, L., Parker, M., Bonsall, D., Fraser, C.: Quantifying SARSCoV- 2 transmission suggests epidemic control with digital contact tracing. Science 368 (6491), May 8. https://science.sciencemag.org/content/368/6491/eabb6936 (2020)

Gollier, C., Gossner, O.: Group testing against Covid-19. COVID, Economics, Vetted and Real-Time Papers 2, CEPR, April 8 (2020)

Hatchett, R.J., Mecher, C.E., Lipsitch, M.: Public health interventions and epidemic intensity during the 1918 influenza pandemic. PNAS, May 1, **104**(18): 7582–7587. https://doi.org/10.1073/pnas.0610941104 (2007)

Hellewell, J., Abbott, S., Gimma, A., Bosse, N.I., Jarvis, C.I., Russell, T.W., Munday, J.D., Kucharski, A.J., Edmunds, W.J., Funk, S., Eggo, R.M.: Centre for the Mathematical Modelling of Infectious Diseases COVID-19, Working Group. Feasibility of Controlling COVID-19 Outbreaks by Isolation of Cases and Contacts. The Lancet Global Health **8**(4), April: E488-E496. https://www.thelancet.com/journals/langlo/article/PIIS2214-109X(20)30074-7/fulltext (2020)

Hill, A., Levy, M., Xie, S., Sheen, J., Shinnick, J., Gheorghe, A., Rehmann, C.: Modeling COVID-19 spread vs. healthcare capacity. Accessed 15 April 2020. https://alhill.shinyapps.io/COVID19seir/?fbclid=IwAR2aXJT79M2AmZxMdy8jsiEuSC4i7ijU8Av6oB4dmlZIeJ2VQgL7Tt3QGxA (2020)

Ilzetzki, E., Mendoza, E.G., Vegh, C.A.: How big (small?) Are fiscal multipliers? J. Monet. Econ. **60**, 239–254 (2013)

International Monetary Fund, World Economic Outlook, October, Chapter 5, Fiscal Policy as a Countercyclical Tool. (Washington) (2008)

Kirchner, M., Cimadomo, J., Hauptmeier, S.: Transmission Of government spending shocks in the Euro area: Time variation and driving forces. ECB Working Paper Series 1219. Frankfurt: European Central Bank (2010)

Kumhof, M., Rancière, R.: Winant, P. Inequality, leverage, and crises. American Economic Review, **105**(3), 1217–1245 (2015)

Martins, N.: Globalisation, inequality and the economic crisis. New Polit. Econ. **16**(1), 1–18 (2011)

Pavlopoulos, D., Chkalova, K.: Short-time work: A bridge to employment security or a springboard to unemployment?. Economic and Industrial Democracy, 0143831X19890674 (2019)

Pompei, F., Selezneva, E.: Education mismatch, human capital and labour status of young people across European Union countries (2015)

Richards, T.J., Rickard, B.: COVID-19 impact on fruit and vegetable markets. Canadian Journal of Agricultural Economics/Revue canadienne d'agroeconomie (2020).

Woodford, M.: Simple analytics of the government expenditure multiplier. Am. Econ. J. Macroecon. **3**(1), 1–35 (2011)

Assessment of the Impact of COVID-19 Pandemic on the Romanian Transportation and Storage Sector

Hurduzeu Gheorghe, Lupu Radu, Cioc Mihai, and Ciora Costin

1 Introduction

The transportation and storage sector (section H, NACE code) is an essential sector for the proper functioning of an economy, being a communication link between several sectors of activity. In the new created context by the effects of COVID-19, this sector was exposed to an extreme shock by the closure of economies, but at the same time ensured the continuation of activities, by finding solutions for freight transport, by ensuring the return of citizens to the country, by continuing the services of post and courier that limited the movement of people. While governments are making scenarios for the transition from isolation to pandemic management, the main priority of companies in the transportation and storage sector has been to continue to provide services and goods and at the same time stop the spread of the virus.

In terms of its strategic importance for the national economy, the transportation and storage sector is among the five main industries dominated by domestic private capital (Ziarul Financiar 2019), along with trade, agriculture, construction and agri-food industry. At the same time, the transportation and storage sector generates a gross value added of 46 billion lei annually, the highest of all economic sectors in Romania, followed by the construction industry, with 42 billion lei, and the IT&C, with 36 billion lei. However, in terms of the share of gross value added in turnover, the transportation and storage sector is only in 13th place, with 43%. In fact, in

H. Gheorghe (✉) · L. Radu · C. Mihai · C. Costin
Bucharest University of Economic Studies, Bucharest, Romania
e-mail: gheorghe.hurduzeu@rei.ase.ro

L. Radu
e-mail: radu.lupu@rei.ase.ro

C. Mihai
e-mail: mihaicioc@man.ase.ro

C. Costin
e-mail: costin.ciora@cig.ase.ro

A. M. Dima et al. (eds.), *Economic Recovery After COVID-19*, Springer Proceedings in Business and Economics, https://doi.org/10.1007/978-3-030-86641-9_12

correlation with labour productivity, Romania ranks second to last in the European Union in terms of gross value added per employee in the transportation and storage sector, with a level of 14.4 thousand euros per employee, well below the European average of 47 thousand euros per employee (Eurostat 2020a, b).

Also, at the level of industry there is a high share of domestic private capital in the land transport and transport via pipeline (67%), respectively, in the air transport sector (64%). In fact, with over 57 billion lei of total turnover in 2017 and 67% local private capital, the land transport and transport via pipeline sector is, after Wholesale and retail trade, the third-largest economic sector in which dominates the Romanian capital. Moreover, the data provided by the Trade Register show that the share of Romanian capital is increasing at the level of the analysed sector (from 66% in 2016 to 67% in 2017). Another important feature of the sector is the important share of public capital, mainly in the air transport (29%) and postal and courier activities (28%). The only industry dominated by foreign capital is warehousing and support activities for transportation.

Transport and storage is one of the most dynamic economic sectors in Romania, including approx. 400 thousand individual employment contracts (PIAROM 2019), increasing by 18% in the last 3 years (2015–2018). More than 40% of the workforce at the sector level is concentrated in the freight transport by road industry, with over 160,000 employees, respectively, 4 times more employees than in any other industry in the sector.

The transportation and storage sector plays a strategic role at European level in terms of employment, given that 8.1% of employees in the European Union work in this sector (Eurostat 2020a, b). 36.1% of these employees are concentrated in small enterprises, 16.1% in medium-sized enterprises and 47.7% in large enterprises. Overall, 5.2% of companies registered in European Union countries are in the transport–logistics sector. According to the same statistics, in terms of the distribution of employees in the sector by enterprise categories, Romania has a specific structure, being included among the countries where employees are mainly employed in small enterprises (44.4%), while the number of employees in large companies (39.6%) is significantly below the average of the European Union or of countries such as France (67.7%), Denmark (50.6%) or Germany (47.6%). However, in Romania, the largest contribution to gross value added at sector level is made by large enterprises (47.2%), followed by small and micro-enterprises (35.1%) and medium-sized enterprises (17.7%).

Regarding labour productivity, the evolution of this indicator at the level of industries in the transportation and storage sector indicates a series of productivity gaps, both between industries and between Romanian and foreign companies. Thus, global labour productivity is by far the highest in the air transport sector, this sector being the most productive sector of all industries dominated by domestic private capital. At the same time, the authors' analysis reveals major gaps in relation to the productivity averages registered at the level of the European Union (Eurostat data), where the water transport and air transport sectors are characterized by a high labour productivity (112 thousand euro/employee/year, respectively, 80 thousand euro/employee/year), the sector of warehousing and support activities for transportation through an average productivity (67 thousand euro/employee/year), while at the level of the land transport sectors and postal and courier activities are registered lower productivity levels (39 thousand euro/employee/year, respectively, 32 thousand euro/employee/year). Other productivity gaps are also noticeable depending on the capital structure. At the level of 4 of the 5 industries analysed, labour productivity is higher in the case of foreign companies than in those with domestic private capital.

2 Analysis of the Evolution of the Transportation and Storage Sector in the Period 2008–2018

The analysis of this sector for the period 2008–2018 provides a dynamic picture of the specific activities and is a starting point for assessing the behaviour of this sector in crisis and outlining possible measures to overcome the situation and return to normalcy.

The main employer in the industry is the land transport and transport via pipelines sector (NACE 49). At the level of this sector, among the first 10 companies in terms of volume of activity, there are six state companies (CFR Călători, Transgaz, RATB, CFR Marfă, Metrorex and Conpet), two companies with local private capital (Aqula Park and Grup Feroviar Român) and two foreign companies (Carrion and Vos Logistics). The land transport and transport via pipelines sector have the most companies, their number tripling from 2008 to 2018 when it reached 42,666 registered companies. The number of companies tripled in the postal and courier activities sector (NACE 53) during this period, but the number of companies is much smaller (1,661 companies in 2018). There was also a small increase in the sector of warehousing and support activities for transportation (NACE 52), the maximum number of companies reaching 2,947 in 2018 from 2,543 in 2008. A large decrease (five times) in the number of companies registered in the water transport sector (NACE 50), which reached 68 in 2018 from 266 companies in 2008. In the case of the air transport sector (NACE 51), the number of companies decreased fourfold, from 266 companies in 2008 to only 68 companies in 2018.

With the exception of the water transport sector, in all other sectors of the transportation and storage sector, turnover in millions of euros increased compared to 2008. The largest increase, but also the highest values belong to land transport and transport via pipelines sector, which dominates the image for this indicator. The following values (but approximately three times lower for 2018) are recorded in the warehousing and support activities for transportation. The postal and courier activities grew slightly in the first five years of the period under review, but grew more sharply in the second half of the period, supported by the development of online commerce. In the air transport sector, turnover decreased in the first part of the period and recovered the loss in the second half, slightly exceeding in 2018 the value of 2008. In the case of water transport, the turnover fell by about 3.5 times in the first part of the period, and the recovery in the second part was more symbolic.

The air transport sector and the water transport sector remain the least represented in terms of the number of employees, with the same trend of reduction and moderate recovery in the case of air transport and a sharp decrease in the first part of the period and decrease more modest in the second part. Although the number of companies and the value of turnover has increased significantly in the case of land transport and transport via pipelines sector, this is not valid in the case of the number of employees, for which the growth is much more limited.

In the case of the warehousing and support activities for transportation, it is observed a reduction and then an increase in the number of employees, a development similar to that of the number of companies for this sector.

In the postal and courier activities, the number of employees increased modestly, while the number of companies tripled and the number of employees increased by approximately 65%, proving a decrease in labour intensity and an increase efficiency.

In the case of the turnover per employee indicator expressed in thousands of euros, the dominant position is that of the air transport sector, this being followed by the water transport sector, but where the maximum value (in 2018) is almost half that of air transport.

Both sectors have a decrease in the indicator in the first period and a significant recovery after 2013. In the case of the other three sectors, there is a gradual increase, stronger in the second part of the interval.

For 2018, the highest turnover of the top 10 companies is registered in the case of the air transport sector, where only 5 companies out of 68 (7.4% of companies) bring 90.7% of the turnover for this sector. Also, the sample represents 64.5% of the number of employees in the sector, a value of the turnover/employee indicator of 254 thousand euros and 64.9% of the profit margin. In the postal and courier activities, a sample of 10 companies out of 1,661 (0.6%) represents 73.6% of the market share, has 75.8% of the number of employees in the sector and represents 60,2% of the registered profit. The land transport and transport via pipelines sector is the most dispersed sector, with most registered companies. The first 14 companies (0.03% of the sector's total) have 16.3% of the turnover, 18.3% of employees and represent the only sample that records a loss compared to the rest of the sector.

Net investments in the transportation and storage sector decreased in 2009–2010, as did total investments in the economy as a result of the economic and financial crisis that arose during that period. A stronger growth was in 2011, and another peak was in 2015, and in the last years of the period, it is observed a moderate growth.

The structure of the transport activity by types of goods transported is relevant both for establishing correlations with other sectors of activity and in terms of the influence of transport on the competitiveness of these sectors, given that, depending on the specifics of each industry, transport costs have a greater or lesser share in the cost structure. Thus, in the case of road transport, over 60% of the transported goods is concentrated in three categories of goods: metal ores and other mining and quarrying products (26.71%), other non-metallic mineral products (18, 11%) and grouped goods (15.37%). The share of food, beverages and tobacco does not exceed 9% of the total goods transported by road. The railway transport activity is as polarized as in the case of road transport, in the sense that two categories of goods accumulate over 50% of the transported goods: coal and lignite, crude oil and natural gas (27.71%) and charred coal, refined petroleum products (24.32%). In the case of maritime transport, one-third of the volume of goods transported relates to agricultural, hunting and forestry products, fish and other fishery products.

Another particular aspect that needs to be taken into account in the context of any public policy with an impact on the transport sector is road safety. As mentioned, road transport has become in recent years the most important branch of the transport–storage sector in Romania, concentrating over 40% of the workforce in the sector, most of which is the drivers of heavy vehicles. Analysing the data provided by the National Institute of Statistics, there is a growing trend of freight transport with large vehicles (+24% thousand tons of goods transported by road in 2014–2018) much faster than road infrastructure (length of public roads has increased in the same period by only 1.23%, respectively from 85,184 to 86,234 km), which represents a major risk for road safety. Moreover, given that deaths and injuries from road accidents involve an estimated annual effective cost of approx. 100 million euros, but also a social cost that exceeds 48.5 billion euros every year, in the European Union there is a constant and growing concern about increasing road safety, embodied in a series of regulations such as fi Directive 2003/59/EC on the initial and regular training of certain categories of drivers for the carriage of goods and passengers or Directive 89/391/EEC on the health and safety of workers, but also in various national initiatives aimed at stimulating the increase of the level of professional training of drivers.

3 The Behaviour of the Transportation and Storage Sector Under the Impact of the New Coronavirus Pandemic Crisis

3.1 General Impact

The transportation and storage sector is under the direct influence of freight and passenger transport activities, therefore the crisis behaviour of this sector is a result of fluctuations in the number of passengers and the volume of goods transported in road transport, rail, air, sea and river.

The experience of the previous economic crisis shows a very slow return of transport activity. The analysis reveals the following relevant aspects of crisis behaviour in the transport and storage sector:

- cumulated at sector level, it is found that the number of transported passengers returned only in 2017 to the level of 2008, after registering consecutive decreases until 2011 inclusive;

- until 2018, the freight transport activity failed to return to the level registered in 2008; moreover, the period of decline of this sector was both longer (until 2012) in relation to passenger transport, and steeper (−39% compared to −18%);
- the air transport sector was the least affected by the economic crisis, registering increases almost every year, both in terms of the number of aircraft movements and in relation to the number of passengers and the amount of goods transported; practically, the analysis of the figures indicates a doubling of the volume of activity in this sector in the period 2008–2018;
- on the other hand, neither the rail transport sector nor the maritime and river transport sector managed to return to the levels recorded in 2008, registering consecutive contractions in the volume of activity for 6 years (2009–2014) as a result of the economic crisis;
- road transport registered decreases in the volume of activity in the period 2009–2012, and increased after that, reaching in 2018 a volume of goods transported approximately equal to that recorded in 2008; regarding the number of passengers, it exceeded in 2016 the level registered in 2008, the total increase in the period 2008–2018 being of approx. 22%.

Regarding the evolution of the sector in the context of the new coronavirus pandemic, although the actions of registration, suspension, dissolution or radiation in the first three months of the year cannot be directly attributed to the impact of COVID-19, but rather to a broader context that characterizes the sector in the medium term. Looking at the evolution of these actions can give us an image of the general and sectoral trend. According to the information provided by the National Trade Register Office, the registrations of individuals and legal entities in the field of transportation and storage decreased in the period 01.01.2020–31.03.2020 by 3.55% compared to the same period of the last year, in the context in which the decrease was 35.46% in the total economy. The suspensions decreased by 28.26% in the transportation and storage sector, while the general trend is slightly lower, respectively, a decrease by 33.79%. Dissolutions increased by 11.99%, and radiation decreased by 36.66%, a more modest percentage compared to the rest of the economy (decrease by 72.84%).

On 15 April 2020, the National Institute of Statistics, published in the press release no. 104 a document entitled "Assessment of the impact of COVID-19 on the economic environment in March and April 2020 (experimental statistics)" (Eurostat 2020a, b) which presented some estimates on the impact of COVID-19 on the most affected sectors of the economy. In the transportation and storage sector, 52.1% of the surveyed economic agents that could estimate the evolution of activities, considered that in April 2020 there would be a reduction in the volume of activity by more than 25%.

The World Bank stressed out during this period that this crisis has highlighted, globally, the vulnerabilities in the transport sector and complex problems that need to be addressed: state-owned air carriers that are heavily indebted and not financially sustainable; reorganization of public transport services; reducing the dependence of railway companies on subsidies.

In mid-March, the National Union of Road Hauliers from Romania made some clarifications on the effect of the epidemic on road transport companies in Romania.

According to their own estimates, the number of passengers on regular lines has decreased by 50%, and in the case of occasional transport, the decrease is 100%. Road transport of people with Romanian companies was stopped in relation to Italy, while for other foreign destinations the volume is very low compared to the situation in the same period last year. Occasional transport has also decreased by 100% in the case of external travel. In the case of domestic road freight transport, the activity was not affected, while in the case of road freight transport on international routes, the general decrease was between 15 and 30%, some companies not being affected.

In March, the National Union of Road Hauliers from Romania also asked the government for financial and fiscal compensatory measures for road transport companies whose drivers are sent for self-isolation in case of cancellations. It also requested the Government of Romania to take steps with the European Commission and the Government of Italy in order to apply a temporary derogation from the prohibition of carrying out the normal weekly rest in the motor vehicle, according to Reg. (EC) no. 561/2006 of the European Parliament and of the Council of March 15, 2006, on the harmonization of certain provisions of social legislation in the field of road transport.

At the beginning of May, the National Union of Road Hauliers from Romania estimated that 30% of companies operating in the road transport sector will not survive the crisis caused by COVID-19, and 50% of those that resist will leave Romania within 18 months as a result of views of the Mobility Package 1, approved by the Council of the European Union.

Although transport is important for the economy, the economic downturn caused by the limitation of activity as a result of COVID-19 will eventually have an impact on freight companies due to the decline in performance in many sectors of activity. An extension of the current context will put great pressure on smaller companies in the transport sector that does not have the resources for long-term survival. As in other sectors, we can expect market consolidations, through mergers and acquisitions.

Air passenger transport remains one of the most affected sectors. The immediate effects of COVID-19 on the aviation industry will materialize in the availability of airlines and ancillary personnel at airports, as well as in the slowdown in activity in related sectors. The sharp drop in demand and the far-reaching and long-term negative implications will affect the financial stability of airlines, with global bankruptcies expected.

With regard to national developments in the air transport sector in the light of the COVID-19 crisis, the following information is relevant:

- Air traffic decreased by 94% in Romania in March compared to the same month of the previous year;
- The evolution of the pandemic has led to a decrease in demand, and traffic restrictions and prohibitions to a decrease in the activity of companies. The TAROM company reduced its activity by approximately 95%, having only cargo or special flights (Financial Newspaper 2020);
- At the same time, the company sent over 1,100 employees into technical unemployment since April 27, 2020 (Doroftei 2020). Thus, the salaries of the pilots

reached from several thousand euros to less than 500 euros per month through the decision of the TAROM management to grant 75% of the average salary per economy for the staff sent to technical unemployment (Albu 2020);

- Blue Air announced in early April that 90% of employees are already technically unemployed (Oprea 2020);
- In February, TAROM received 36.7 million euros as state aid to pay aircraft leasing rates (Bonyhai 2020);
- In April, the Romanian Government approved a rescue loan to overcome the crisis for TAROM and Blue Air worth 130 million euros (Albu 2020).

3.2 *Social Impact*

The social impact at the level of the transportation and storage sector is important. Even if the economic activity in this sector was not blocked as a result of COVID-19, there is a continuity throughout the pandemic, the impact of the crisis is important as the transport industry plays a very important role in the Romanian economy. Thus, the transportation and storage sector is, along with trade and the administrative services and support services sector, among the three economic sectors that generated over 50% of the newly created jobs in the period 2015–2018 (61,5 thousand individual employment contracts, representing an increase of over 18%) (PIAROM 2019). According to Eurostat data (Eurostat 2020a, b), Romania ranks 4th in the European Union, after Lithuania, Latvia and Finland, in terms of the share of the number of employees in the transportation and storage sector in the total workforce. Along with the retail and construction sector, the transport sector is among the top 5 employing economic sectors belonging to the private sector, while the other two are mainly specific to the public sector (health and education). Also, the most important increases in the number of individual employment contracts among all economic sectors in Romania, in the period 2015–2018, were registered in the road freight transport sector (+39.5 thousand individual employment contracts, +32.6%).

Last but not least, the road freight transport sector is the third-largest economic sector in terms of labour force, with a 44% increase in the number of individual employment contracts, by sectors: contracting activities, on a temporary basis (+175.9%) and custom software development activities (+54.3%). Regarding the structure of the labour force by occupation groups, on 01.10.2018, the first 4 employing occupations included 2 occupations in the transport sector (truck/heavy truck driver and driver of cars and vans); also, among the first 10 employing occupations in Romania, there is an occupation specific to the logistics sector, namely that of merchandise handler (89.6 thousand individual employment contracts on 01.10.2018). At the same time, following the development of the transport–logistics sector, but also of trade, the share of the number of workers in the field of services in Romania continued to increase, exceeding the percentage of 16% on 01.10.2018.

3.3 Economic Impact

At international level, studies indicate the transport sector as one of the most affected economic sectors as a result of the COVID crisis, especially at the level of sub-sectors such as air or sea transport. Thus, according to a recent Coface study (Coface Economic Publications 2020), estimates show that the transport sector will not have the capacity to return, before 2022, to the level of turnover in the fourth quarter of 2019. According to the baseline scenario considered by Coface, the figure of companies in the transport sector will be 32% lower in the fourth quarter of 2020 and 5% lower in the fourth quarter of 2021 than in the fourth quarter of 2019. According to the same study, in the case of a second wave of pandemic, the decreases would be much more significant, respectively, by 57% in the fourth quarter of 2020 and by 27% in the fourth quarter of 2021.

In Romania, in the case of the transport–logistics sector, the economic impact of the COVID crisis was important especially for companies in the passenger transport sub-sector, given the restrictions on the movement of persons imposed both in Romania and at the level of the main international markets on which the Romanian passenger carriers operate. However, unlike other industries, the economic impact of the COVID crisis was more moderate in the freight and warehousing sub-sectors, as these sectors remained responsible for the delivery of consumer goods from producers to distributors from the retail sector. Moreover, as will be seen below, amid measures to isolate and intensify online commerce, the crisis has even had a stimulating effect on the postal and courier services sector.

According to the data provided by the Ministry of Labour, on 10.04.2020, in the transportation and storage sector there were 74,934 suspended employment contracts, of which over 68,000 were suspended due to the state of emergency, representing approx. 6.5% of the total suspended employment contracts in Romania, respectively, approx. 19% of the workforce employed at sector level. Therefore, in the case of the transportation and storage sector, the share of the number of suspended employment contracts was similar to that recorded in the wholesale and retail sector, slightly lower than in the national economy (21,9%) and significantly lower than in the most affected sectors, such as the hotel and restaurant sector (56.6%) or the manufacturing industry (25.8%).

Based on monthly data on the evolution of average gross and net earnings per sector, we conducted an assessment of the extent to which the analysed sub-sectors were affected by the pandemic. For this analysis, we employed the Holt-Winters methodology (Holt 2004) and (Winters 1960), which uses exponentially weighted averages for trends and seasonality measures. For each time series, we estimated the corresponding parameters for the period April 2017–January 2020 and generated predictions for the period February–April 2020. The differences between these predictions and the actual values of these salaries allow us to quantify the impact of this crisis.

Following a sector analysis, we can conclude that the impact is differentiated on the analysed sectors, but at the level of gross salary no significant changes can be identified. By comparison, the evolution of the net salary at the level of the entire economy was subjected to wider changes in February–April 2020, as can be seen in Fig. 1.

If for the gross salaries, the differences between the predicted and realized values are small for February and April 2020 and even negative for March, in the case of net salaries the values are slightly higher. This demonstrates that the impact is different if we analyse each sector separately.

For the transportation and storage sector, the evolution and impact at the level of gross wages are presented in Fig. 2.

It can be seen that the impact is significant for this sector as a whole. The differences for the three months of analysis (February–April 2020) are approximately 263, 285 and 499 lei, respectively, for gross salaries and 121, 126 and 257 lei for net salaries.

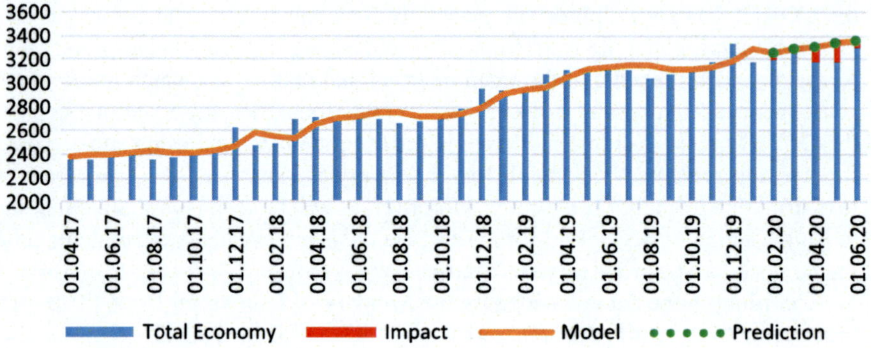

Fig. 1 Impact of the COVID crisis on the average net salary at the level of the entire economy. *Source* National Institute of Statistics data, authors' calculations

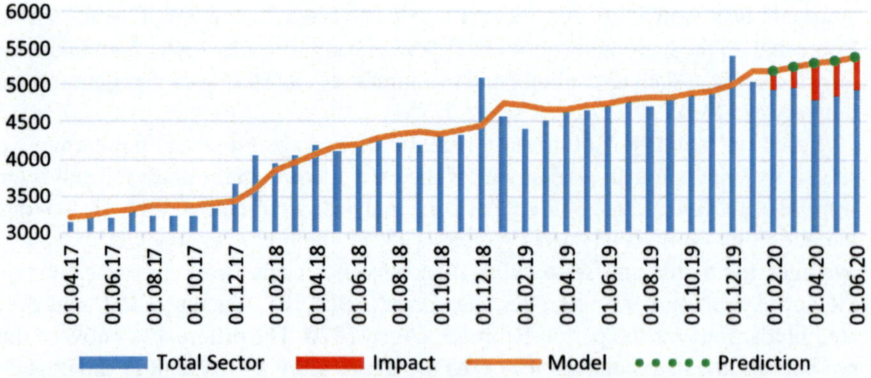

Fig. 2 Impact of the COVID crisis on the transportation and storage sector on the average gross salary. *Source* National Institute of Statistics data, authors' calculations

The model used in our analysis takes into account the seasonality of this time series, with higher levels in general in December (related to year-end bonuses) and lower values at the beginning of the year. This trend of increasing net wages throughout the period under review is particularly noteworthy, and we can see that the last three months have marked a significant deviation from this trend. An analysis on each sub-sector will make it possible to measure the impact differently and identify the contribution of each sector to these aggregate values.

The behaviour of the transportation and storage sector during the crisis caused by the pandemic COVID-19 is one that is directly related to the evolution of international trade, respectively, to the dynamics of exports and imports by different product groups. According to the data provided by the National Institute of Statistics (National Institute of Statistics 2020a, b), between 01.01–31.05.2020, exports decreased by 19% compared to the similar period of 2019, respectively, by approx. 5.5 billion euros. At the level of the same period, imports registered a slightly lower rate of decrease, respectively, by 13.5% compared to the period 01.01–31.05.2020, reaching 31,093.4 million euros. Compared to May 2019, exports in May 2020 decreased by 40.1%, and imports decreased by 35.4%.

3.4 Analysis Related to Sentiment Indicators

The European Commission publishes sentiment indicators on a monthly and quarterly basis using harmonized questionnaires (monthly questionnaires are completed in the first two to three weeks of the month, and quarterly questionnaires in the first two to three weeks of the first month of each quarter) conducted by authorized partners in European countries (Gelper and Croux 2010). In Romania, the surveys are conducted in partnership with the National Institute of Statistics and Gfk (for the consumer sector).

The information collected in this way complements the official statistical data published by the authorities, being available with high frequency and providing real-time information. In this way, turning points can be observed in advance in various areas of activity and appropriate measures can be taken (Soric et al. 2016). The economic sentiment indicator reflects the attitude and opinion of a large number of economic actors and consists of five different sectors, each with a specific share: industry (40%), services (30%), consumers (20%), construction (20%) and retail trade (5%). In the case of the composite indicator, values above 100 indicate an above-average economic sentiment, while values below 100 indicate a below-average position. The answers obtained from the surveys are subsequently aggregated in the form of "balances". These are constructed as the difference between the share of respondents who give positive answers and the share of those who give negative answers. For sub-sectors, confidence indicators are calculated in the form of an arithmetic mean of the answers to a given selection of questions (Tomic et al. 2020).

In the case of the services sector, the monthly survey presents evaluations of managers regarding the activity of their companies in the last three months (economic situation of the company, demand for services/turnover, evolution of the number of employees) and prospects for the next three months on turnover, employees and sales/billing prices; the answers are qualitative (e.g. will increase / will be approximately the same / will decrease). Regarding quarterly questions, managers appreciate which are the main factors that currently limit the activity: none/insufficient demand/lack of labour force/lack of space and/or equipment/financial problems/others. In addition, managers assess whether the volume of activity could be increased with present resources and, if so, by how much. According to the latest data published by the European Commission, we notice in the case of Romania small decreases in the values of indicators since February 2020, but the decrease is stronger in March (with a higher margin for the European Union) and steep in April. The value of the economic sentiment indicator increases slightly in May and more pronounced in June, but remains modest. In the case of the services sector, we have a decrease in May and a slight recovery in June, the value registered for Romania being a little better for the period March–June 2020, compared to the one related to the European Union as a whole (Fig. 3).

For example, at the level of NACE division 49—land transport and transport via pipelines sector, the monthly survey data show that in general the sentiment indicators have positive values for the analysed period, except for the two crisis periods, respectively, the one from 2009–2010 and the recent health crisis. An important element worth mentioning is that the impact on sentiment calculated according to the mentioned methodology is higher in the first months of 2020 compared to the situation of the previous economic crisis.

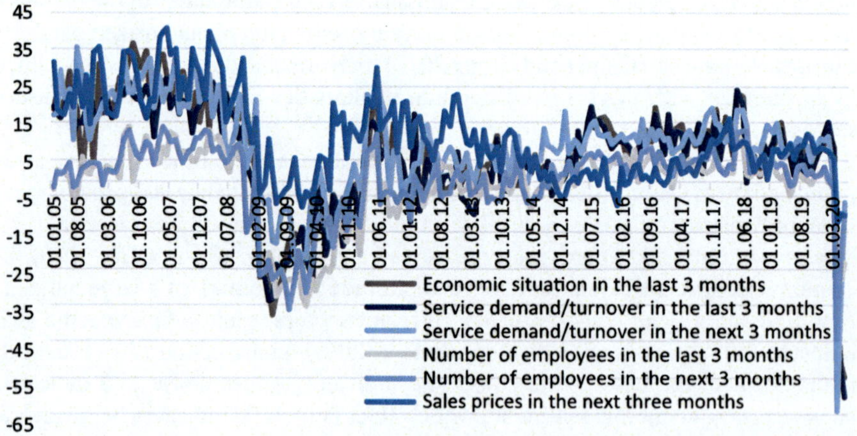

Fig. 3 Evolution of the monthly responses for NACE 49 in Romania, during January 2005–June 2020. *Source* European Commission data, Joint Harmonised EU Programme of Business and Consumer Surveys, Business and consumer survey results for June 2020, Subsector data, authors' representation

4 Conclusions and Recommendations

The transportation and storage sector is an essential sector for the Romanian economy, with a cumulative turnover of 57 billion lei, being also among the 5 main industries dominated by domestic private capital (about 67% of the capital of the over 42,000 companies registered at sector level). The transportation and storage sector generates the highest gross added value of all economic sectors in Romania, respectively, 46 billion lei, generating at the same time approx. 25% of Romania's service exports. In the transportation and storage sector, work approx. 400 thousand employees, Romania being on the 4th place in the European Union, after Lithuania, Latvia and Finland, in terms of the share of the number of employees at sector level in total labour force. In fact, the transport and storage sector is also among the top 5 employing industries in the private sector, while among the top 4 employing occupations in Romania are two specific to this sector (4 in the European Union, after Lithuania, Latvia and Finland, in terms of regarding the share of the number of employees).

In order to combat the effects of the COVID crisis, the main recommendations of the research team are mainly to optimize public policies, on the one hand by aligning strategic documents (National Competitiveness Strategy, Regional Development Policies, Intermodal Transport Strategy, etc.) to the requirements of business environment in the Transportation and storage sector, and, on the other hand, by updating the criteria for allocating non-reimbursable funds available under financing programmes (state aid scheme regulated by GD 807, Regional Operational Programme, investment grants, etc.) in a manner that ensures the non-discriminatory access of companies from this sector to non-reimbursable funds, intended for the development of their own infrastructure. Last but not least, the recommendations addressed to companies in the transportation and storage sector aim at increasing the volume of investments in the development and modernization of their own infrastructure, including by accessing investment grants, increasing the level of digitization, continuous staff development or building clusters of activity.

In line with the objectives of the study, some of the research team's recommendations to public authorities include the following:

- Revision of the National Strategy for Competitiveness by including the transportation and storage sector in the category of economic sectors with competitive potential. The proposal is based on the economic role and the influence on employment at sectoral level, given that transport and storage generate the highest gross value added in Romania, being also the third-largest economic sector employer, with approx. 400 thousand employees. A precedent in this regard is the construction sector, which in 2018 was included among the 11 economic sectors with competitive potential in the National Strategy for Competitiveness;
- Reviewing regional development policies (under the responsibility of Regional Development Agencies), in conjunction with the National Strategy for Competitiveness, by taking measures to develop the transportation and storage sector at regional level. The proposal takes into account the fact that the transportation

and storage sector has a higher economic and social impact in the case of certain development regions. Thus, approx. 45% of the specialized labour force is concentrated in two development regions: Bucharest-Ilfov (approx. 30% of the total) and north-west (approx. 15% of the total). Also, as shown in the analysis, in 8 counties (Ilfov, Mehedinți, Cluj, Timiș, Suceava, Alba, Dâmbovița and Călărași), the main employment occupation is specific to the transport and storage sector;

- Urgent review of government strategies in the transportation and storage sector, mainly the intermodal transport strategy. At the same time, it is recommended to integrate the objectives set out in the sectoral strategies with those assumed by the National Investment and Economic Recovery Plan (July 2020) for the transport sector, this proposal aiming at a unitary approach to the sectoral development strategy. More concrete and detailed source of funding needed for its implementation;
- Revision of the National Export Strategy by indicating much more concretely (strategic objectives, strategic options, etc.), the strategic role of the transportation and warehousing sector in supporting Romania's exports. The proposal considers the double role of this sector, on the one hand through the exports of services performed, directly, by the transport companies from Romania, and on the other hand, through the integration in value chains constituted at the level of other in-exporting industries, such as the automotive or food industries;
- Reassessment of the principles for allocating funds within state aid schemes (e.g. GD 807/2014). At present, state aid schemes do not encourage the implementation of investments for the development and modernization of infrastructures in the field, such as warehouses or other logistics spaces. In fact, in most companies in Romania, the level of automation of activity in logistics spaces is quite low, which creates problems in terms of competitiveness in the face of repeated increases in labour costs, but also due to low availability of labour (also accentuated by accessibility issues, given that most warehouses are located outside major cities). By correlating with the inclusion of the transport sector in the National Competitiveness Strategy, such incentive measures would amplify the degree of process automation, resulting in increased labour productivity and optimization of flow activities, including intermodal transport;
- Adoption of regulatory measures in the direction of professionalization of the main occupations in the transport–logistics sector. Such measures include, in the first instance, updates of the Classification of Occupations in Romania nomenclature at the level of sector-specific occupational groups, while defining new occupational standards in the field (including in the field of driver training);
- The implementation of standards and procedures for the training and certification of skills in the field, a special category of measures in this regard should target the activity of passenger transport;
- Development and implementation of an action plan on the development of the national system of safe and secure parking. This recommendation also comes in the context of the letter of delay addressed by the European Commission to Romania and 6 other countries, in May 2020, regarding the communication of information on safe and secure parking, regulated by Regulation (EU)

no. 885/2013. Moreover, in the context of the coronavirus epidemic, increased measures are needed to ensure the hygiene and endowment of these parking spaces;

- Development and implementation of a plan for the digitization of information on transport activity. The recommendation comes in the context of another 3 letters of formal notice sent by the European Commission in May 2020, aiming at the process of communicating traffic information related to road safety;
- Implementation of the electronic transport letter (e-CMR), ratified by Romania in 2019, thus facilitating both the efficiency of the carriers' activity and the monitoring of the flows of goods, simultaneously with the identification of fraud risks. The implementation of the measure needs to be accelerated in the context of the COVID pandemic, in order to eliminate paper documents and minimize interactions between shippers, carriers and recipients.

References

Albu, A.: Almost 1000 employees from Tarom are in technical unemployment. https://www.mediafax.ro/economic/aproape-1-000-de-angajati-tarom-sunt-de-azi-in-somaj-tehnic-ce-salarii-au-ajuns-sa-primeasca-pilotii-19100212 (2020a). Acceded 29 May 2020

Albu, A.: Government economic aid for Tarom and Blue Air, https://www.mediafax.ro/economic/ajutorul-de-salvare-pentru-tarom-si-blue-air-a-fost-aprobat-de-guvern-19094503 (2020b). Acceded 28 May 2020

Bonyhai, O.: Government approved credits for TAROM and Blue Air, https://boardingpass.ro/guvernul-a-aprobat-creditele-pentru-tarom-si-blue-air/ (2020). Acceded 30 May 2020

Coface Economic Publications: Global Transport: What does the future hold beyond COVID-19, 16 July (2020). https://www.coface.com/News-Publications/News/Global-Transport-What-does-the-future-hold-beyond-COVID-19

Doroftei, M.: Tarom employees in technical unemployment, https://www.aviatiamagazin.com/aviatie-civila/angajatii-tarom-au-intrat-in-somaj-tehnic-75-din-salariul-mediu-inclusiv-pentru-piloti-si-insotitori/ (2020). Acceded 22 May 2020

Eurostat: Apparent labour productivity by NACE Rev. 2, (2020a). https://data.europa.eu/euodp/ro/data/dataset/OSKVAqsn4IZAUZtTQqfDkg. Acceded 10 July 2020.

Eurostat, Statistics Explained: Transportation and storage statistics - NACE Rev. 2, (2020b) https://ec.europa.eu/eurostat/statistics-explained/index.php/Transportation_and_storage_statistics_-_NACE_Rev._2, updated March 2020. Acceded 14 July 2020

Financial Newspaper: https://www.zf.ro/zf-24/2-000-de-angajati-tarom-lucreaza-de-acasa-iar-compania-analizeaza-19091888 (2020). Acceded 24 May 2020

Gelper, S., Croux, C.: On the construction of the European Economic Sentiment Indicator. Oxford Bull. Econ. Stat. **72**, 1 (2010)

Holt, C.: Forecasting Trends and Seasonal by Exponentially Weighted Averages, Office of Naval Memorandum (1957), reprinted in International Journal of Forecasting (2004)

National Institute of Statistics: Press release no. 104, Assessment of the impact of COVID-19 on the economic environment in March and April 2020 (experimental statistics) (2020a)

National Institute of Statistics: Press release no. 181/10 July (2020b)

Oprea, A.: Blue Air announces technical unemployment for 90% of the employees, https://www.news.ro/social/blue-air-anunta-ca-90-dintre-angajati-sunt-in-somaj-tehnic-compania-are-nev

oie-de-un-sprijin-financiar-temporar-sub-forma-unui-credit-de-salvare-192240210722202004 1519327740 (2020). Acceded 29 April 2020
PIAROM: Study on labor market dynamics in the period 2015–2018 at the level of economic sectors representing the directions of industrial policy of Romania (2019)
Soric, P., Lolic, I., Cizmesija, M.: European economic sentiment indicator: an empirical reappraisal, Auality and Quantity, 50, (2016)
Tomic, D., Simurina, J., Jovanov, L.: The nexus between Economic Sentiment Indicator and Gross Domestic Product; a Panel Cointegration Analysis, Zagreb International Review of Economics & Business, vol. 23, No. 1 (2020)
Winters, P. R.: Forecasting Sales by Exponentially Weighted Moving Averages, Management Science (1960)
Ziarul Financiar: Romanian privat capital. 4th Edition (2019)

The Impact of COVID-19 on the Wholesale and Retail Trade—Repair of Motor Vehicles and Motorcycles Sector in Romania

Anghel Ion, Davidescu Adriana Ana Maria, Mosora Mihaela Hrisanta, Curea Stefania Cristina, and Achim Luminita Georgiana

1 Introduction

Trade is one of the most important industries in Romania and the second employer countrywide after the manufacturing sector. The SARS-CoV-2 outbreak will lead to changes in the consumer's behavior: He will work from home more, eat at home more often, try to spend more time at home or go for walks outside, try to consume more traditional products, be more rational and will try to replace traditional shopping with the online alternative; however, online shopping will not fully replace the physical alternative because shopping involves a strong personal component that the online experience cannot fully replace.

The food trade industry is one of the "winners" in this pandemic; however, the pre-COVID business model will have to change and adapt to fit the profile of the new consumer. The discount segment and the supermarkets will gain ground due to the proximity to the consumers. The non-food trade is at the opposite pole. The closing of commercial centers led to a drastic decrease in sales among these traders, and most workers are now in furlough. Practically, we will see in the entire trade sector a "new beginning" based on other values and principles.

A. Ion · D. A. A. Maria (✉) · M. M. Hrisanta · C. S. Cristina · A. L. Georgiana
The Bucharest University of Economic Studies, Bucharest, Romania
e-mail: adriana.alexandru@csie.ase.ro

A. Ion
e-mail: ion.anghel@ase.ro

M. M. Hrisanta
e-mail: mihaela.mosora@economie.ase.ro

C. S. Cristina
e-mail: stefania.curea@ase.ro

A. L. Georgiana
e-mail: achimluminita14@stud.ase.ro

A. M. Dima et al. (eds.), *Economic Recovery After COVID-19*, Springer Proceedings in Business and Economics, https://doi.org/10.1007/978-3-030-86641-9_13

The end of the crisis depends largely on the authorities' decision to support the economy, encourage consumerism, investments and the creation of new jobs. The state must support local entrepreneurship and production.

This paper is structured in five parts: In the first part, we present a review of the literature on the COVID-19 pandemic and trade, in the second, we show the role played by this sector in Romania's economy; in the third part, we identify the recovery time for this sector after the 2008 crisis, in order to anticipate how many years it will take the commerce sector to recover after this pandemic using the k-means algorithm; in the fourth part, we analyze the impact of COVID-19 on the trading sector during the state of emergency; and the last part presents our conclusions, as well as a set of proposed measures for re-launching this activity sector.

2 Literature Review

Due to the numerous studies related to the COVID-19 pandemic and trade, we proceed with a bibliometric analysis to capture the main issues.

At the time of our research, we found 436 articles indexed in Web of Science for this research area. We reviewed all these articles using a novel tool—VOS viewer software, checking the strong links with the most used words, focusing on "trade."

Figure 1 presents the graphical distribution of the number of occurrences and the links between the most used terms that are correlated with COVID and trade, when Web of Science indexed articles are used. The higher the bullets, the higher

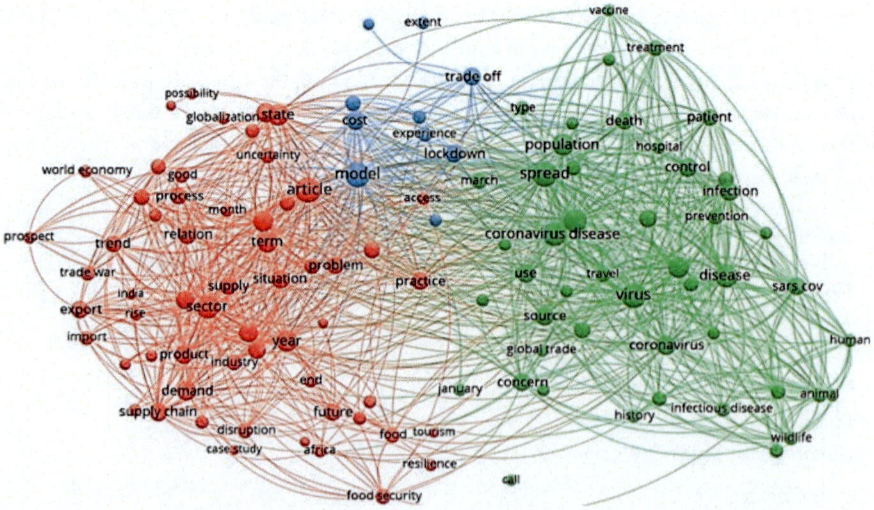

Fig. 1 Map of the occurrences and links regarding the terms COVID-19 and trade. *Source* Authors' processing in VOSviewer, using Web of Science indexed articles

the occurrences of terms and the stronger the links between terms. Different colors refer to different clusters corresponding to the way in which the links are realized. From Fig. 1, we can observe that there are three clusters:

- Cluster 1 (the red one) shows that COVID-19 is associated with many aspects related to trade activity such as: product, good, demand, supply, supply chain, disruption, trend, prospect, export, import, trade war, resilience, etc.;
- Cluster 2 (the green one) reports issues related to the impact of COVID-19 on the population mentioning the following terms: coronavirus disease, infection, spread, control, prevention, etc.;
- Cluster 3 (the blue and the smallest one) highlights the economic impact of COVID-19 on trade.

From Fig. 2, we find that the largest number of papers related to COVID-19 and trade is published in the USA (108 studies), followed by England (60 studies) and China (60 studies). Among European countries, Italy (24 studies), Germany (19 studies) and France (18 studies) published the highest number of papers on this topic. However, this number is far away from the first three mentioned countries.

On this background, our study intends to fill the gap in the literature by analyzing the role played by the Wholesale and retail—repair of motor vehicles and motorcycles sector in Romania's economy, identifying the recovery time for this sector after the 2008 crisis; in order to anticipate how many years, it will take the commerce sector to recover after this pandemic and highlighting the main measures proposed for diminishing the effects of COVID-19 and re-launching the sector.

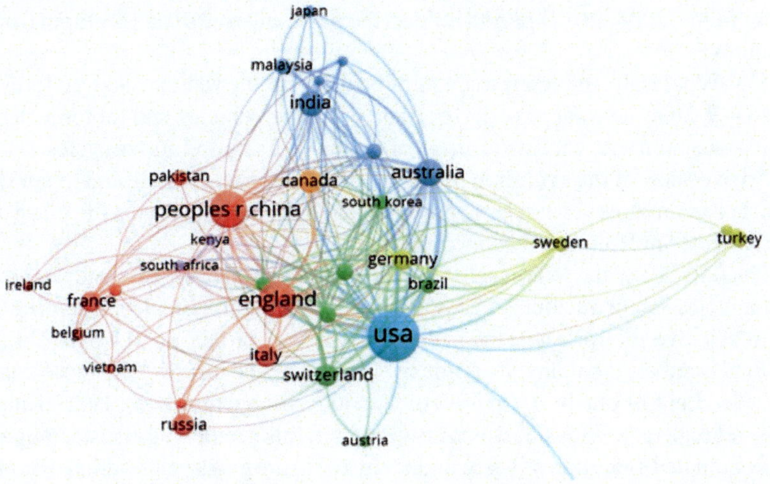

Fig. 2 Map of the occurrence studies on COVID-19 and trade, by countries. *Source* Authors' processing in VOSviewer, using Web of Science indexed articles

3 Methodology

The identification of the recovery period after the 2008 crisis was made by studying the sector behavior during the previous crisis from a multi-criteria perspective, taking into account dynamic indexes with a fixed basis calculated at the reference period 2008 = 100 and considering the first year after the recovery from the crisis to be the one in which a value higher than 100% was registered. To this end, the algorithm k-means was used for the purpose of detecting the years with similar performances by comparison to the reference year 2008, using as input the variables (Morard et al. 2014): turnover, gross result of the exercise, gross investments in tangible assets, the average number of employees and the number of active companies that operate in the sector Wholesale and retail trade—repair of motor vehicles and motorcycles.

The data source for the main indicators used in the analysis of retail sector has been the databases of Eurostat and National Institute of Statistics.

4 Place and Role of the Wholesale and Retail Trade—Repair of Motor Vehicles and Motorcycles in Romania's Economy

Wholesale and retail trade—repair of motor vehicles and motorcycles, according to the European classification of economic activities NACE REV 2, includes the divisions Wholesale and retail trade and repair of motor vehicles and motorcycles sector for the 2008–2018[1] period reflects the place and role of this sector in Romania's economy:

45—Wholesale and retail trade and repair of motor vehicles and motorcycles.

46—Wholesale trade, except for trade of motor vehicles and motorcycles.

47—Retail trade, except for trade of motor vehicles and motorcycles.

An overview of the evolution of the Wholesale and retail trade and repair of motor vehicles and motorcycles sector for the 2008–2018 period reflects the place and role of this sector in Romania's economy.

Thus, in 2018, the Wholesale and retail trade and repair of motor vehicles and motorcycles sector included 172,856 operational enterprises (representing 30% of the total active enterprises in the national economy), providing 914,396 jobs (18% of the total number of employed people in Romania). The turnover for these companies exceeded Lei 617 bln. in 2018 (40% of the total national turnover), 19.27% more than the level registered in 2008. Business growth in this sector was also accompanied by an accentuated evolution of value added. In 2018, the gross value added of companies

[1] The data processed in this chapter was taken from the site of the National Statistics Institute (INSSE) and was expressed in comparable prices. The comparability of data over time was achieved by adjusting value indicators for inflation (updating value indicators to the last year of the period used in the analysis).

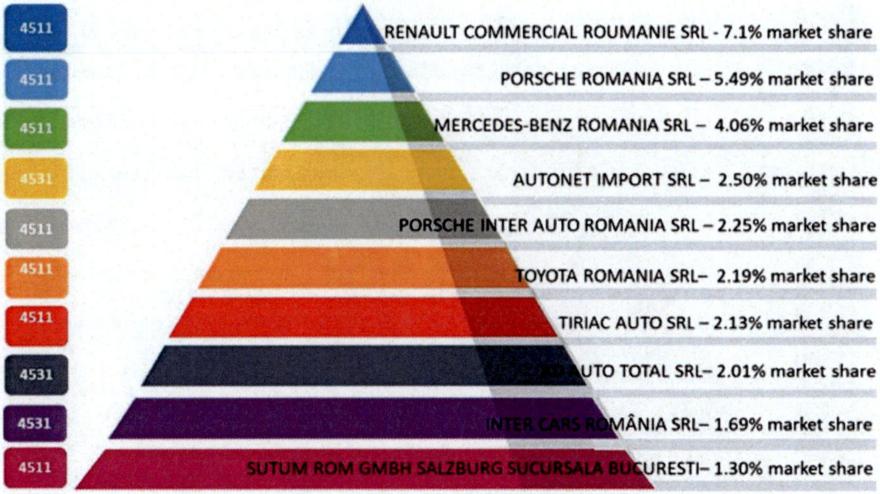

Fig. 3 Top 10 companies in division 45—Wholesale and retail trade, maintenance and repair of motor vehicles and motorcycles, in 2018. *Source* Top Firme Romania and INSSE

in the sector registered a growth of 38% by comparison to 2008, totaling over Lei 82 bln. (23% of the total gross value added of Romania's economy).

Gross investments totaled approximately Lei 18 bln. in 2018, a decrease by 42% from 2008, representing 14% of the total gross investments in Romanian 2018, and the gross result was Lei 28 bln. in 2018, 122% higher than the one registered in 2008.

The degree of market concentration is high. In 2018, the value of the sales of the top 10 companies in division 45—Wholesale and retail trade and repair of motor vehicles and motorcycles was Lei 17.68 bln. Their cumulative share for these sales was 30. 72% in total sales per sector in 2018 (Fig. 3). For division 46—Wholesale trade, except for trade of motor vehicles and motorcycles, the cumulated revenue of the top 10 companies was Lei 86.68 bln., generating over 26.5% of the total turnover of the division in 2018, and for division 47—Retail trade, except for trade of motor vehicles and motorcycles, the top 10 companies had cumulated sales of Lei 61.52 bln., generating over 20% of the total turnover of the division (Figs. 4 and 5).

5 Recovery Time for the Sector Wholesale and Retail Trade—Repair of Motor Vehicles and Motorcycles After the 2008 Crisis

The identification of the recovery period after the 2008 crisis was made by studying the sector behavior during the previous crisis from a multi-criteria perspective, taking into account dynamic indexes with a fixed basis calculated at the reference period 2008 = 100 and considering the first year after the recovery from the crisis to be the

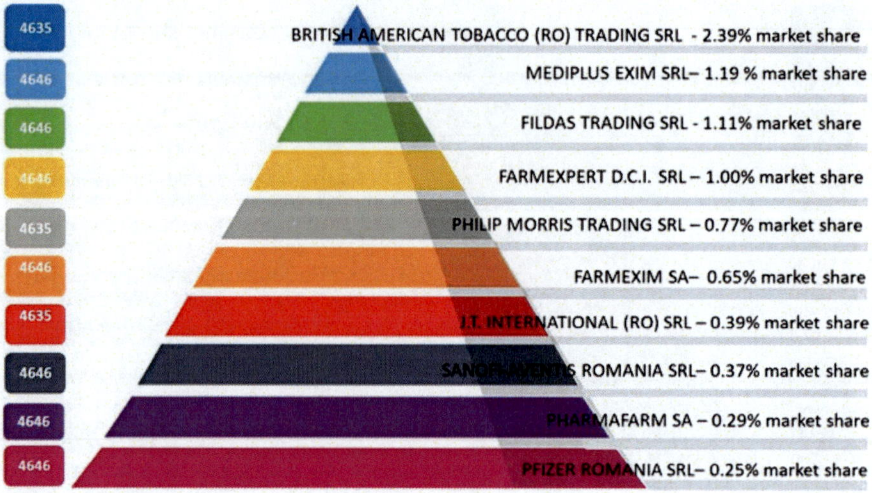

Fig. 4 Top 10 companies in division 46—Wholesale trade, except for trade of motor vehicles and motorcycles, in 2018. *Source* Coface Romania

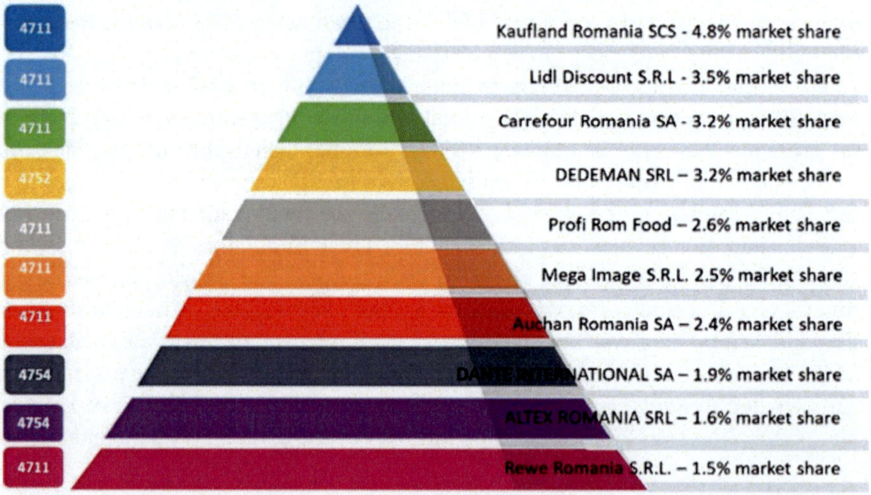

Fig. 5 Top 10 companies in division 47—Retail trade, except for trade of motor vehicles and motorcycles, in 2018. *Source* Coface Romania

one in which a value higher than 100% was registered. To this end, the algorithm k-means was used for the purpose of detecting the years with similar performances by comparison to the reference year 2008, using as input the variables (Morard et al. 2014; Lalou et al. 2020): turnover, gross result of the exercise, gross investments in tangible assets, the average number of employees and the number of active companies

ANOVA

	Cluster		Error			
	Mean Square	df	Mean Square	df	F	Sig.
TURNOVER	922.367	1	62.020	9	14.872	.004
GROSS_OUTCOME	41356.367	1	1214.020	9	34.066	.000
GROSS_INVESTMENT	8.445	1	301.829	9	.028	.871
GVA	3717.208	1	184.048	9	20.197	.002
AVERAGE_NUMBER_EMPLOYEES	1.718	1	29.385	9	.058	.814
ACTIVE_FIRMS	57.432	1	45.639	9	1.258	.291

Fig. 6 Section G—Wholesale and retail trade—repair of motor vehicles and motorcycles

that operate in the sector Wholesale and retail trade—repair of motor vehicles and motorcycles.

The empiric results of the k-means algorithm for determining the recovery time post-crisis (Figs. 6, 7, 8 and 9) have shown that only three of these variables are significant, gross result and gross value added.

ANOVA

	Cluster		Error			
	Mean Square	df	Mean Square	df	F	Sig.
turnover45	1920.003	1	68.909	9	27.863	.001
gross_outcome45	11634.575	1	288.401	9	40.342	.000
gross_investment45	1577.302	1	291.067	9	5.419	.045
GVA45	2577.536	1	88.496	9	29.126	.000
average_no_employees45	61.831	1	9.635	9	6.417	.032
active_firms45	324.208	1	45.492	9	7.127	.026

Fig. 7 Division 45—Wholesale and retail trade and repair of motor vehicles and motorcycles

ANOVA

	Cluster		Error			
	Mean Square	df	Mean Square	df	F	Sig.
turnover46	1019.394	1	145.259	9	7.018	.027
gross_outcome_46	23251.212	1	928.148	9	25.051	.001
gross_investment46	594.694	1	280.893	9	2.117	.180
GVA46	3560.776	1	155.348	9	22.921	.001
average_no_employeest46	30.912	1	37.959	9	.814	.390
active_firms46	2.048	1	44.459	9	.046	.835

Fig. 8 Division 46—Wholesale trade, except for trade of motor vehicles and motorcycles

ANOVA

	Cluster		Error			
	Mean Square	df	Mean Square	df	F	Sig.
turnover47	4674.436	1	186.133	9	25.113	.001
gross_outcome47	454512.148	1	10702.226	9	42.469	.000
gross_investment47	92.803	1	220.093	9	.422	.532
GVA47	9709.394	1	334.148	9	29.057	.000
average_no_employees4 7	.982	1	28.133	9	.035	.856
active_firms47	189.394	1	56.148	9	3.373	.099

Fig. 9 Division 47—Retail trade, except for trade of motor vehicles and motorcycles

The identification of the post-crisis recovery period, depending on the similarities and differences between these significant variables, is presented in Figs. 10, 11, 12 and 13, for the wholesale and retail trade overall and for each division separately.

As reflected in the Figures above, the recovery time for the previous crisis, from a multi-criteria perspective (turnover, gross profit, gross value added), was 6 years (2014) at the level of the entire wholesale and retail trade and of Division 47—Retail trade, except for trade of motor vehicles and motorcycles, whereas Division 46—Wholesale trade, except for trade of motor vehicles and motorcycles recovered at the level of the year 2008 in 7 year (2015), and Division 45—Wholesale and retail trade and repair of motor vehicles and motorcycles, in 9 years (2017).

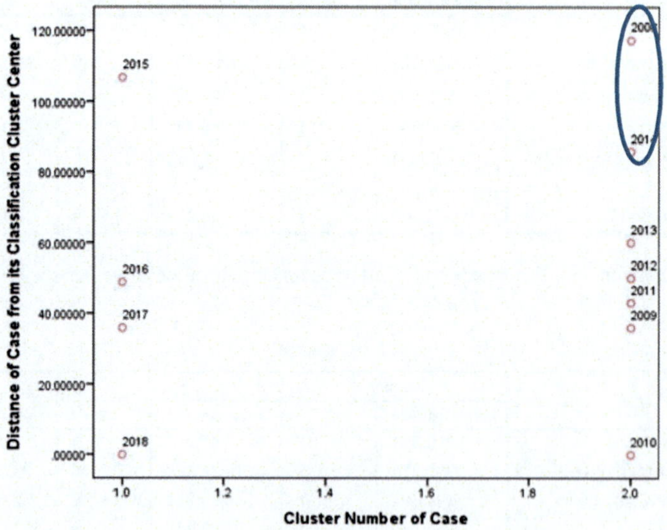

Fig. 10 Section G—Wholesale and retail trade—repair of motor vehicles and motorcycles

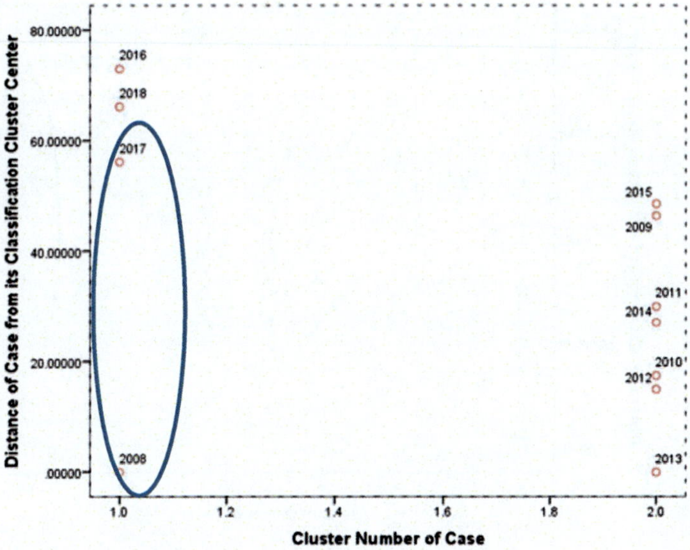

Fig. 11 Division 45—Wholesale and retail trade and repair of motor vehicles and motorcycles

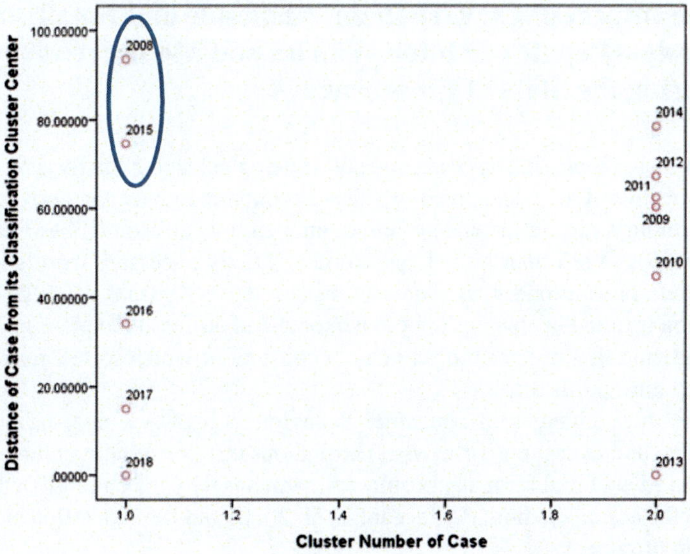

Fig. 12 Division 46—Wholesale trade, except for trade of motor vehicles and motorcycles

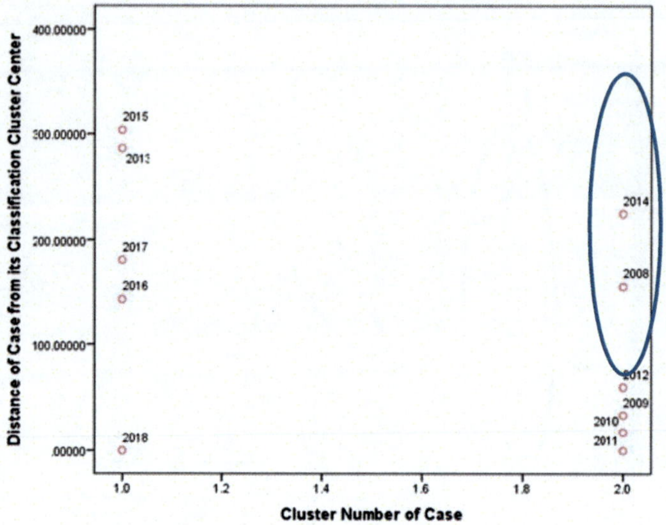

Fig. 13 Division 47—Retail trade, except for trade of motor vehicles and motorcycles

6 The Impact of COVID-19 on Wholesale and Retail Trade—Repair of Motor Vehicles and Motorcycles During the State of Emergency

COVID-19 is a topic that has been and still is being debated globally, especially from the perspective of the widespread social and economic impact it generated. Focusing on our country, during the state of emergency almost all Romanians changed their daily habits and left their homes only to take strictly necessary trips, taking all the appropriate precautionary measures (Abrihan 2020; Bolisani et al. 2020). Social distancing resulted in changes in both personal and professional plans and activities. The pandemic also affected the behavior of consumers, who resorted mostly to online shopping during this time.

Given these changes in consumer behavior, companies must be permanently responsive and adapt to their needs. Throughout this period, the online component proved to be essential for many businesses, which is why the emphasis will continue to be on the online medium (Vrânceanu et al. 2020) and the adaptation of businesses to this environment.

In Romania, according to INSSE, the turnover for the Retail trade except for the trade of motor vehicles and motorcycles increased during the period 01.01.2020–31.03.2020, compared to the same period of last year, by 9.4%. This increase was determined by: sales of food products, beverages and tobacco (+14.6%), sales of non-food goods (+7.5%) and by the retail trade of fuel for motor vehicles in specialized stores (+3.7%). Online commerce played a significant role in this increase.

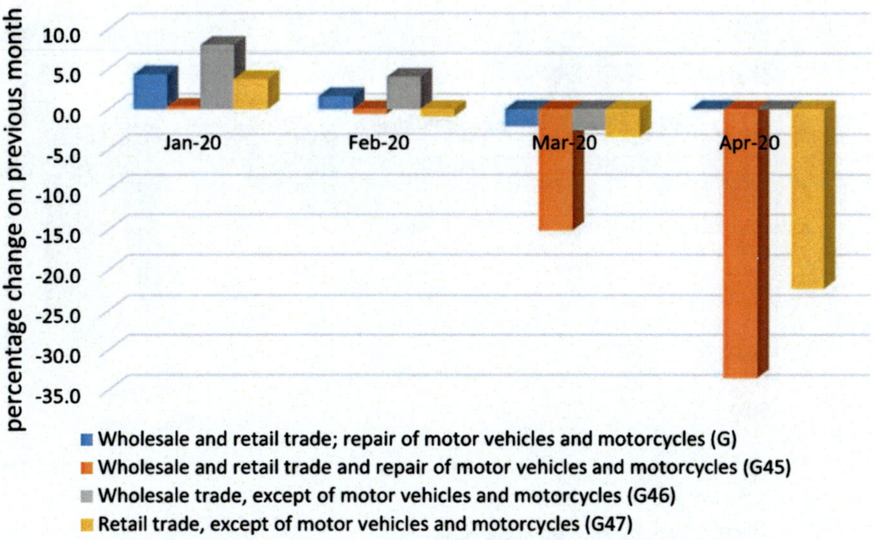

Fig. 14 Index of deflated turnover in retail trade; repair of motor vehicles and motorcycles compared to the previous month in Romania during January 2020–April 2020, seasonally adjusted time series. *Source* STS, Eurostat

According to the data published by Eurostat, in Romania, the sharpest drop is registered in April as opposed to March in division 45—Wholesale and retail trade and repair of motor vehicles and motorcycles (−33.5%), followed by division 47—Retail trade, except for trade of motor vehicles and motorcycles (−22.3%) (Fig. 14).

At the level of division 45—Wholesale and retail trade and repair of motor vehicles and motorcycles, Romania registers the sharpest drop in April compared to March 2020 for motor vehicle maintenance and repair (−43.4%), followed by motor vehicle sales (−39.3%) and by the sale of motor vehicle parts and accessories 35.5%). Only the sale, maintenance and repair of motorcycles and of related parts and accessories registered increases of almost 18% in April compared to March 2020 (Fig. 15).

At the level of division 46—Wholesale trade, except for trade of motor vehicles and motorcycles, there was a decrease of −2.6% in March from February 2020. By components, the sharpest drops were registered in March from February 2020 in the wholesale trade of food products, beverages and tobacco (−5.4%), followed by wholesale trade of agricultural feedstock and livestock (−3.8%). At the other end of the spectrum, increases were registered in the wholesale of home appliances (+3.9%) (Fig. 16).

In March 2020, the sale volume (turnover adjusted for price) of retail trading in the EU-27 dropped by 10.1% from 2020 and 7.6% from March 2019. In the Eurozone, the decline was 11.1% from February 2020 and 8.8% comparative to the previous year. The decrease in retail trade in the EU continued in April 2020. The volume of retail trade decreased by 11.1% from March 2020 and by 18% from April 2019. In

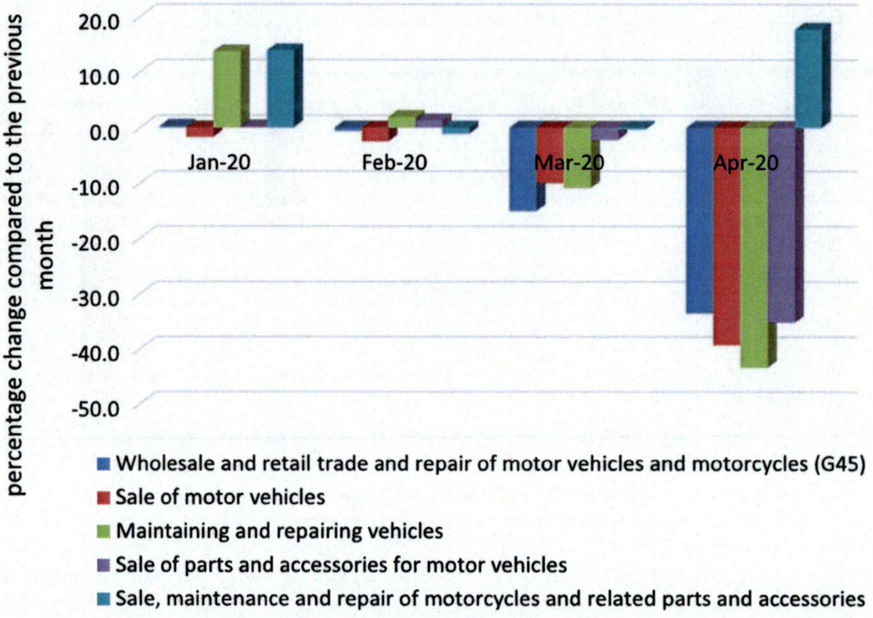

Fig. 15 Index of deflated turnover in wholesale and retail trade and repair of motor vehicles and motorcycles (45) compared to the previous month in Romania during January 2020–April 2020, seasonally adjusted time series. *Source* STS, Eurostat

the Eurozone, the decline was 11.7% from March 2020 and 19.6% from April 2019 (Fig. 17).

The volume of retail trade (division 47) in Romania decreased by 3.4% in March 2020 and by 22.3% in April 2020 as compared to the previous months. The sharpest drops of −71.1 and −54.2% were registered for textiles, clothing and leather products. In March and April 2020, purchases of automotive fuel decreased in Romania by 1.3% in March and by 18.5% in April 2020.

Since the isolation methods in response to COVID-19 differ from country to country with respect to timing and severity, it was to be expected that the effects on retail trade would differ. Table 1 presents the growth rates for April compared to February for 2010–2019 (average) and for the year 2020.

For food products (including beverages and tobacco), there was a decrease of 1.3% at the level of EU-27 between February and April. The country data varied considerably, varying from −13.2% (Romania) to +16.7% (Ireland). Purchase of non-food products (except for automotive fuel) decreased in all member states in March and April, and especially in Spain (−55.2%), Luxemburg (−51.1%), Ireland (−50.4%), Italy (−50.2%) and France (−49.8%). Romania also registered a decrease of 27.4% in April as compared to February 2020.

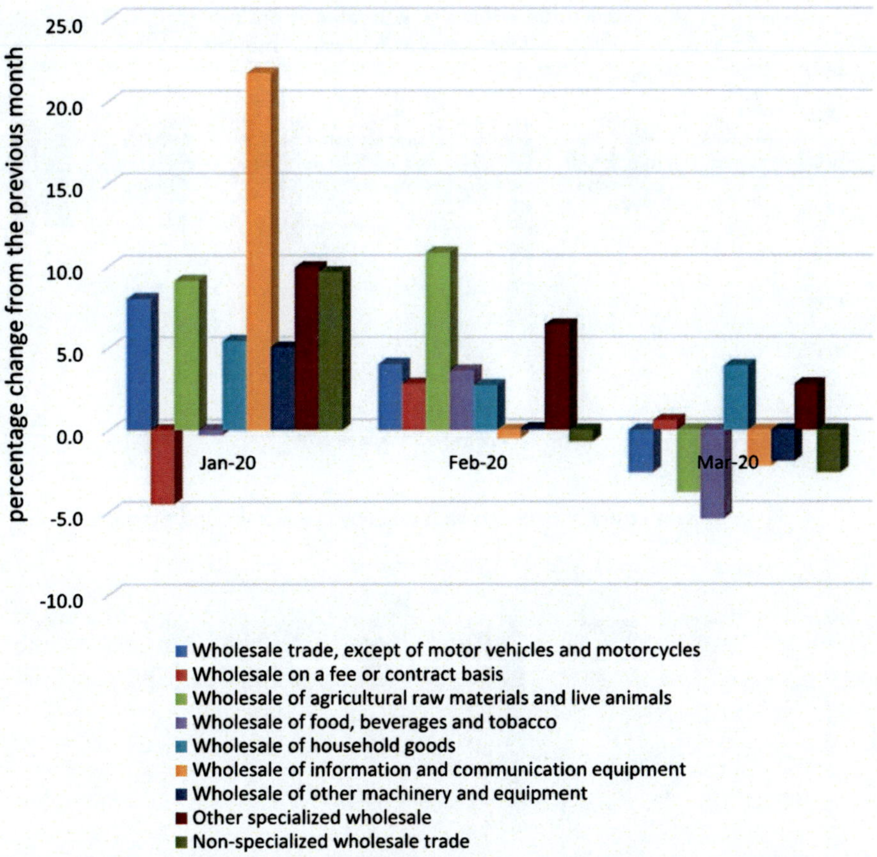

Fig. 16 Index of deflated turnover in wholesale trade, except for trade of motor vehicles and motorcycles (46) compared to the previous month in Romania during January 2020–March 2020, seasonally adjusted time series. *Source* STS, Eurostat

The automotive fuel consumption decreased in all member states in March and April, with the lowest drops registered in Italy (−66.2%), France (−64.7%) and Spain (−6.8%). Romania registered a drop of 42.5% in April 2020.

Starting from mid-March until the end of April or beginning of May 2020, many countries closed the stores that were not considered essential and in general only the supermarkets and pharmacies remained open. This had a clear impact on the volumes of retail trade for various distribution channels for March and April (Table 2).

In supermarkets (meaning general stores selling predominantly food products), sales grew from February until April by 0.8% in the EU. Supermarket sales remained unchanged or even decreased and in the countries that registered the strongest drops in total retail trade sales: Italy (−32% overall and not changed in supermarkets), Spain (−31.2% overall and −0.2% in supermarkets), Portugal (−27.2% overall and −

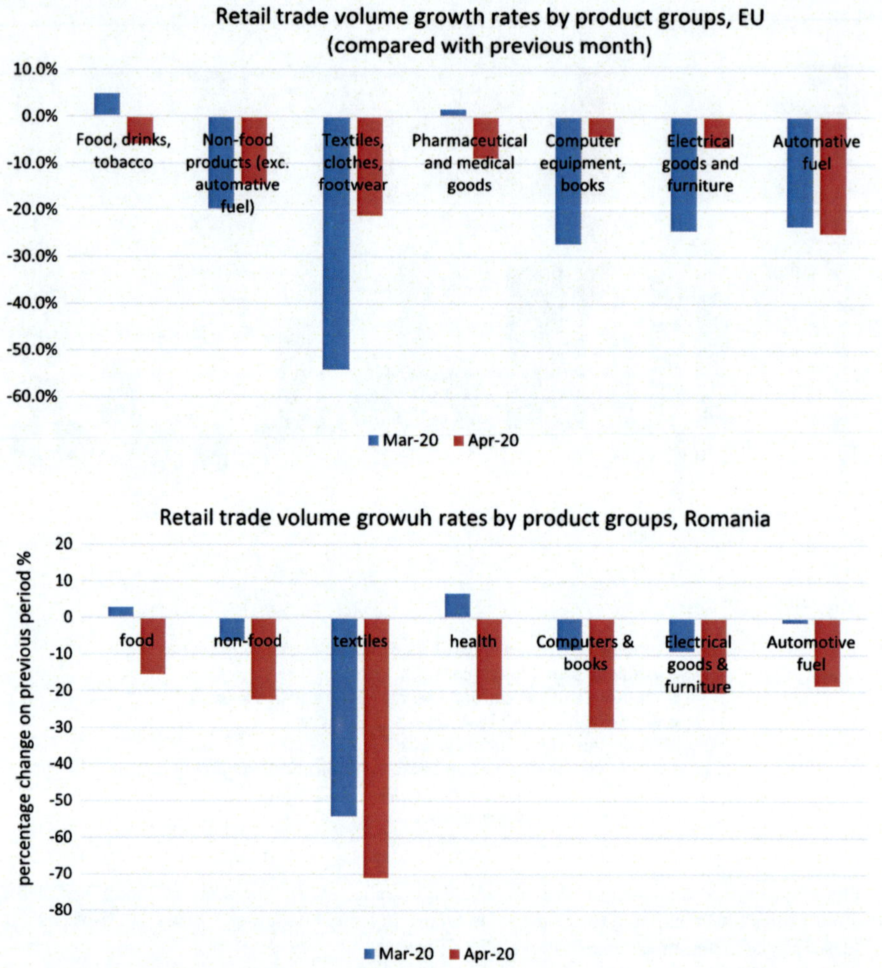

Fig. 17 Rate of increase of the volume of retail trade by product groups, at the level of the EU and Romania. *Source* STS, Eurostat

Table 1 Rate of increase of the volume of retail trade by product groups—rate of increase for April compared to February during (2010–2019) and in 2020

	Food products		Non-food products		Automotive fuel	
	Average	2020	Average	2020	Average	2020
EU-27	0.0	−1.3	0.4	−31.5	0.0	−42.6
Romania	0.4	−13.2	1.8	−27.4	2.5	−42.5

Source STS, Eurostat

Table 2 Rate of increase of the volume of retail trade by sales channel—rate of increase for April compared to February for (2010–2019) and in 2020

	Total retail trade		Supermarkets		Large stores		Internet	
	Average	2020	Average	2020	Average	2020	Average	2020
EU-27	0.1	−20.1	−0.1	0.8	0.4	−30.5	1.1	13.8
Romania	1.2	−24.9	0.3	-13.8	4.1	−23.7	2.9	17.6

Source STS, Eurostat

10.6% in supermarkets) and Croatia (−27.1% overall and −10.1% in supermarkets). In Romania, retail sales decreased by 24.9% overall and by 13.8% in supermarkets.

Sales in big stores, which were closed in large part after mid-March, dropped in all member states and very much in some of them: in Ireland (−77.7%), Belgium (−69.6%), Italy (−62.8%) and Spain (−59.2%). In Romania, this decrease tendency is also reflected, even if the percentage is relatively lower: 23.7%.

The volume of internet sales increased in all member states, with the highest increases registered in Hungary (61%), Lithuania (42.3%) and Spain (41.9%). In Romania, the volume of online sales also grew by 17.6%. However, it is important to note that online trade, statistically speaking, covers only enterprises the main activity of which is Internet sales.

With respect to labor market indicators, labor force occupation, the number of hours worked and the evolution of salaries, we can find that there is a decrease in labor force occupation at sector level of 4% in April 2020 as compared to the previous month, with very sharp drops in the sub-sector wholesale and retail trade and repairs of motor vehicles and motorcycles (−8.9%), followed by retail trade, except for motor vehicles and motorcycles, characterized by a decrease in labor force by 1.8% (Fig. 18).

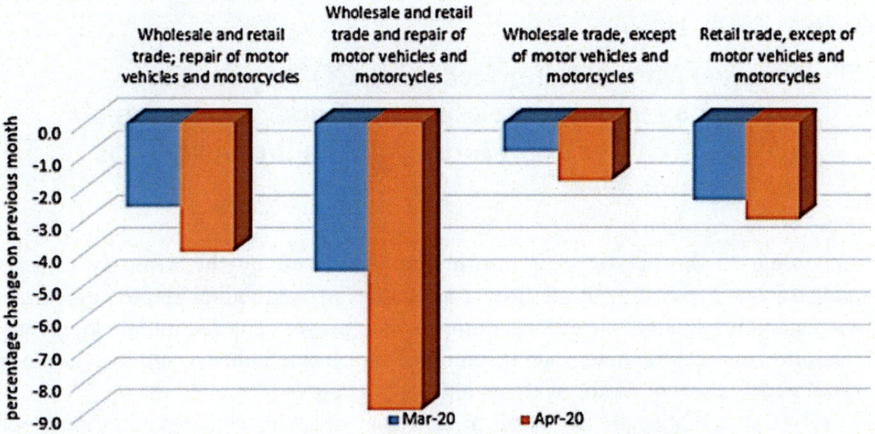

Fig. 18 Labor force occupation (number of employed persons) in the sector Wholesale and retail trade; repair of motor vehicles and motorcycles in 2020. *Source* STS, Eurostat

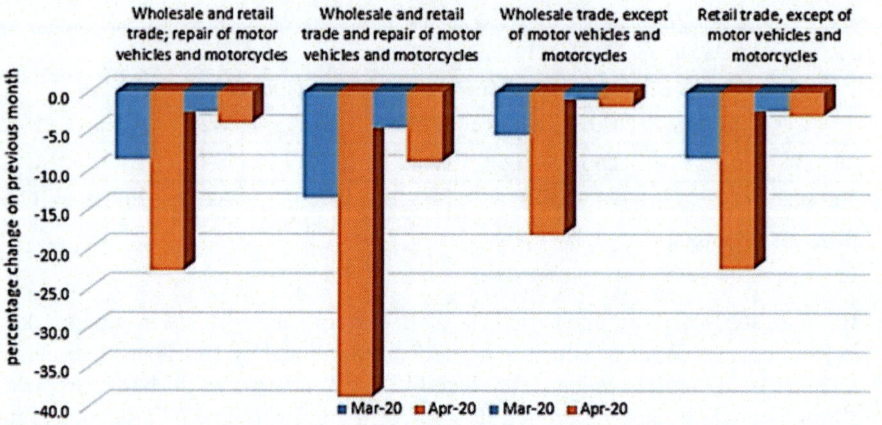

Fig. 19 Work volume (number of hours worked) in the Wholesale and retail trade, maintenance and repair of motor vehicles and motorcycles Sector in 2020. *Source* STS, Eurostat

Severe decreases were also registered with respect to the volume of hours worked, both at the level of the entire sector and by divisions. Thus, if in April 2020, the number of hours worked in the wholesale and retail sector; the repair of motor vehicles and motorcycles decreased by 22.7% from March 2020, and the biggest drop was registered in in April 2020 for the wholesale and retail trade and repairs of motor vehicles and motorcycles (−38.8%), followed by retail trade except for motor vehicles and motorcycles (−22.4%) (Fig. 19).

Gross salaries for the entire sector dropped in March compared to February 2020 by 1.7%, and this is considered to be the beginning of the pandemic. The sharpest drop was registered in division 45—Wholesale and retail trade and repair of motor vehicles and motorcycles (−7.6%) (Fig. 20).

7 Proposed Measures for Reducing COVID-19 Effects and Re-Launching Wholesale and Retail Trade, Repair of Motor Vehicles and Motorcycles on the Long-Term and Medium-Term Run

According to the most recent information published by the Ministry of Labor and Social Protection regarding the status of individual labor agreements suspended/terminated, the highest number of employees entered into furlough are in the following sectors: hotels and restaurants, processing industry and Wholesale and retail trade, repair of motor vehicles and motorcycles.

Given that Wholesale and retail trade, repair of motor vehicles and motorcycles was the sector that came in third in this ranking of sectors with most employees in furlough, we consider that the measures regarding the attenuation of the social impact

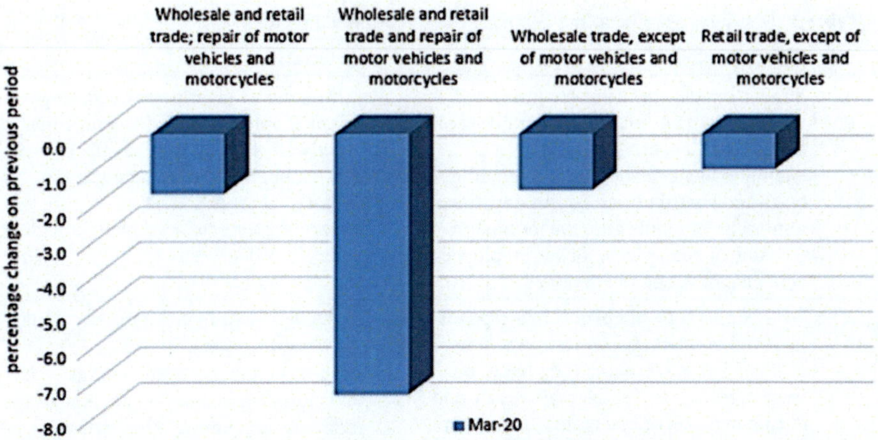

Fig. 20 Decrease in gross salaries for Wholesale and retail trade; repair of motor vehicles and motorcycles in March 2020 compared to February 2020. *Source* STS, Eurostat

of the effects of COVID-19 on the companies that reduced their working hours or placed their employees in unemployment should be a priority.

In addition to social measures, in order to attenuate the negative effects of the COVID-19 pandemic on Wholesale and retail trade, repair of motor vehicles and motorcycles, additional economic measures must be implemented. All these categories of measures are presented below (Table 3).

8 Conclusions

The main objective of this chapter is to analyze the potential impact of COVID-19 on the wholesale and retail trade sector—repair of motor vehicles and motorcycles and outlining the main measures proposed for diminishing the effects of COVID-19 and re-launching the sector.

The analysis of the dynamics of the economic–financial indicators highlighted the fact that the sector Wholesale and retail trade—repair of motor vehicles and motorcycles (section G of the National Classification of Economic Activities) represents a fundamental component of the economic mechanism, and understanding its economic and social impact is important both through the angle of substantiating the strategies of the companies that compete in the sector and that of the public policies that impact this sector and the economic–social environment.

Of particular relevance is the fact that the recovery time after the previous crisis of 2008 was 6 years (at the level of 2014) for the wholesale and retail sector as a whole. Thus, we expect in this case the recovery time after the pandemic caused by the SARS-CoV-2 virus to be also approximately 6 years. In the prior crisis, the

Table 3 Measures specific to the Wholesale and retail trade sector

No	Proposed action	Expected effect
1	Supporting the companies that reduced working hours or placed their employees in furlough, by covering in full the unemployment-related funds, including taxes and contributions, for **an additional** minimum 3 months after the termination of the state of emergency, for the employees who cannot yet be re-employed	– Preventing an increase in unemployment – Keeping employees in the companies directly affected by the COVID-19 virus (e.g., companies that function in commercial centers) – Supporting companies directly affected by the COVID-19 virus
2	Accessing a state aid plan for enterprises involved in retail business or providing services in rented spaces (i.e., based on lease agreements) for the recovery of rent during the state of emergency, a measure that will also indirectly benefit economic agents that carry out activities in commercial spaces	– Reducing bankruptcies by maintaining commercial spaces – Supporting the real estate market – Preventing an increase in unemployment – Indirectly supporting other industries with which sector G interacts
3	Supporting **investments in e-commerce** by granting certain ***subsidized loans***	– Developing online commerce – Growing jobs in the IT sector – Professional reconversion (e.g., many workers will migrate toward the IT, web design sectors)
4	Developing **long-term relationships between the local traders and producers**, especially in the food processing industry, as well as clothing, footwear and other necessary household items, by creating an **online platform,** which will bring together producers and traders Implementing a platform that would provide **a list of local producers of goods** or **producers from other regions in the country,** by product category	– Facilitating the conclusion of online contracts between providers and traders – Stimulating domestic consumption – Increasing domestic production as a result of stimulating the consumption of local products – Reducing imports – Promoting domestic products – Setting up cooperatives in rural areas – Encouraging entrepreneurships – Increasing employment – Avoiding storage problems
5	Granting ***lines of credit*** for companies that engage in **export activities**, which were economically sound before the effects of COVID-19 occurred	– Increasing exports – Increasing employment
6	Promoting local producers through **marketing and PR policies** (such as: using certain nudges that show the impact of the increase of local/traditional products on the employment market, tourism, etc.)	– Increasing consumption of local products – Reducing imports – Increasing employment in these activity sectors; creating a national brand

most relevant economic indicators used to calculate the recovery time were: turnover, gross result and gross value added.

From the perspective of the impact of COVID-19 on trade during the state of emergency, it differed depending on the type of goods and on the method of trading them. The trading of food products grew, whereas non-food commerce registered massive decline due to the closing of all major commercial centers.

The impact of COVID-19 is also reflected in the number of individual labor agreements that were suspended or annulled, with many people entering into furlough or losing their jobs.

The proposed plan for measures outlined in this chapter emphasizes the importance of measures aimed at attenuating the social impact of the effects of the COVID-19 pandemic—recognizing COVID-19 as grounds for reducing working hours and/or for instating furlough, as well as of measured intended to reignite activity.

References

Abrihan, R.: The shopping basket of Romanians, growing. But small businesses are at a disadvantage - study. STARTUPCAFE. https://www.startupcafe.ro/afaceri/cumparaturi-romani-afaceri-profit.htm (2020). Accessed 28 April 2020

Bolisani, E., Scarso, E., Ipsen, C., Kirchner, K., Hansen, J.P.: Working from home during COVID-19 pandemic: lessons learned and issues. Manag. Market. Challenges Knowl Soc. **15**(Special Issue), 458–476. https://doi.org/10.2478/mmcks-2020-0027 (2020)

Chamber of Commerce and Industry of Romania: Measures taken by the European Union to support the business community in the context of the spread of the COVID-19 pandemic. https://ccir.ro/2020/03/31/masurile-adoptate-de-uniunea-europeana-pentru-sprijinirea-comunitatii-de-afaceri-contextul-raspandirii-pandemiei-de-covid-19/) (2020). Accessed 1 Jan 2020

DECISION no. 394 of 18 May 2020 on the declaration of the state of alert and the measures applied during it to prevent and combat the effects of the COVID-19 pandemic (2020)

DECISION no. 476 of 16 June 2020 on the extension of the alert status on the Romanian territory and the measures applied during it to prevent and combat the effects of the COVID-19 pandemic (2020)

Decree no. 195 of 16 March 2020 on the establishment of the state of emergency on the territory of Romania, published in the Official Gazette number 212 of 16 March 2020 (2020)

Decree no. 240 of 14 April 2020 on the extension of the state of emergency on the territory of Romania, published in the Official Gazette number 311 of 14 April 2020 (2020)

ECONOMICA.net: How to see the COVID-19 crisis in your pocket. https://www.economica.net/s-a-scumpit-mancarea_184035.html (2020). Accessed 7 May 2020

Emergency Ordinance no. 29 of 18 March 2020 on some economic and fiscal-budgetary measures, published in the Official Gazette number 230 of 21 March 2020 (2020)

Emergency Ordinance no. 33 of 26 March 2020 regarding some fiscal measures and the modification of some normative acts, published in the Official Gazette number 260 of March 2020 (2020)

Emergency Ordinance no. 48 of April 9, 2020 on some financial-fiscal measures, published in the Official Gazette with number 319 of April 16, 2020 (2020)

Emergency Ordinance no. 43 of 6 April 2020 for the approval of some support measures settled from European funds, as a result of the spread of COVID-19 coronavirus, during the state of emergency, published in the Official Gazette number 292 of 7 April 2020 (2020)

EUROSTAT: Retail trade down compared to last years. https://ec.europa.eu/eurostat/web/products-eurostat-news/-/DDN-20200507-2?inheritRedirect=true&redirect=%2Feurostat%2Fweb%2Fcovid-19%2Foverview (2020). Accessed 10 May 2020

GpeC: The current situation in Romanian eCommerce in the context of COVID-19. Iulian Stanciu, CEO of eMAG, in open dialogue with GPeC. https://www.gpec.ro/blog/situatia-actuala-din-ecommerce-ul-romanesc-in-contextul-covid-19-iulian-stanciu (2020). Accessed 7 May 2020

Lalou, P., Ponis, S.T., Efthymiou, O.K.: Demand forecasting of retail distribution networks using data analytics and statistical programming, vol. 15, no. 2, pp. 186–202. https://doi.org/10.2478/mmcks-2020-0012 (2020)

Law 227/2015 on the Fiscal Code, published in the Official Gazette with number 688 of September 10, 2015 (2015)

Law no. 76 of January 16, 2002 on the unemployment insurance system and employment stimulation, published in the Official Gazette number 103 of February 6, 2002 (2002)

Ministry of Labor and Social Protection: The situation of the suspended / terminated individual employment contracts, on May 8, 2020. http://mmuncii.ro/j33/index.php/ro/comunicare/comunicate-de-presa/5926-situatia-contractelor-individuale-de-munca-suspendate-incetate,-la-data-de-08-mai-2020 (2020). Accessed 7 May 2020

MKOR: Study of the Impact of the CoronaVirus Epidemic on the Life of Romanians 2020. https://mkor.ro/studii/studiu-coronavirus-romania-2020/ (2020). Accessed 1 May 2020

Morard, B., Balu, F.O., Crețu, R.F.: Managing and predicting turning points in commodity trading market, Proceedings of Annual Tokyo Business Research Conference 15–16 December 2014, Waseda University, Tokyo, Japan, ISBN:978–1–922069–67–2. http://www.wbiworldconpro.com/uploads/japan-conference-2014/finance/1418034364_339-Florentina.pdf (2014)

National Institute of Statistics: Enterprise statistics - TEMPO ONLINE. http://statistici.insse.ro:8077/tempo-online/#/pages/tables/insse-table (2020). Accessed 27 April 2020

Online Retail Conference - Arena Sessions: Non-food retail, where to? Impact of COVID-19 on industry, resumption challenges and possible solutions (2020)

Retail-FMCG: Proximity formats bring the greatest growth. https://www.retail-fmcg.ro/servicii/studii-de-piata-servicii/vanzari-bunuri-de-larg-consum-March-2020.html (2020). Accessed 28 April 2020

Retail-FMCG: EY study: The Romanian consumer becomes attentive to quality, prefers local products and is ready to migrate to online shopping. https://www.retail-fmcg.ro/servicii/studii-de-piata-servicii/studiu-ey-consumator-cumparaturi-online.html (2020). Accessed 11 Aug 2020

The Financial Newspaper: *How did the sales in the food trade evolve in Q1.* https://www.zf.ro/companii/cum-au-evoluat-vanzarile-in-comertul-alimentar-in-t1-magazinele-mici-19093633, (2020). Accessed 28 April 2020

Vrânceanu, D.M., Țuclea, C.E., Țigu, G.: Price search behaviour in digital markets–a perspective from Romania. Manag. Market. Chall. Knowl. Soc. **15**(2), 219–235. https://doi.org/10.2478/mmcks-2020-0014 (2020)

Effects of the Covid-19 Pandemic on the Water Distribution, Sanitation, Waste Management, Decontamination Activities Sector

Florescu Margareta Stela, Cretu Raluca Floretina, and Trica Carmen Lenuta

1 Introduction

Sector E–water distribution, sanitation, waste management, decontamination activities has a great potential for development, due to the wide range of activities performed, from waste collection to treatment and disposal, from recovery of recyclable materials to reintroduction into the production circuit, in the context of the development of a sustainable and circular bio-economy in Romania.

The main objective in the field of environmental protection, assumed by the Treaty of Accession to the European Union, is represented by the improvement of living standards of the population and at the same time of environmental standards, for the fulfilment of which it is necessary to continue investments in environmental infrastructure (drinking water supply, waste management), as well as in the decontamination of historically polluted sites, air quality improvement and biodiversity protection/conservation in the context of the implementation of the Natura 2000 Network. In the field of environmental infrastructure and environmental protection—through the EU—has assumed the fulfilment of some obligations regarding the implementation of the European Environment acquits. Combined with these commitments, the improvement of the living standards of the population and at the same time of the environmental standards continues to represent the main objective in the field of environmental protection. Thus, the aim is to reduce the difference between the environmental infrastructure that exists between Romania and the European Union, in terms of both quantity and quality. In the current period, marked by the pandemic, in

F. M. Stela (✉) · C. R. Floretina · T. C. Lenuta
Bucharest University of Economic Studies, Bucharest, Romania
e-mail: margareta.florescu@ari.ase.ro

C. R. Floretina
e-mail: raluca.cretu@cig.ase.ro

T. C. Lenuta
e-mail: carmen.trica@eam.ase.ro

A. M. Dima et al. (eds.), *Economic Recovery After COVID-19*, Springer Proceedings in Business and Economics, https://doi.org/10.1007/978-3-030-86641-9_14

parallel with the unprecedented actions required for the health system (Crețu 2017), it is necessary to prepare the economy for a crisis, also unprecedented. The elaboration of a set of measures for this economic sector was carried out taking into account the extraordinarily abrupt dynamics from day to day of the data on the spread of infections, doubled by the actions of the authorities for home isolation and implicitly the severe restriction of economic activities (Albu et al. 2020), which makes the set of measures proposed at the end of this paper to give resilience to this economic sector.

The COVID-19 pandemic had a relatively small impact on the economic activities of sector E–water distribution, sanitation, waste management, decontamination activities, according to data provided by the Romanian Employers' Association—Study on labour market dynamics in 2015–2018 at the level of economic sectors, sector E–water distribution, sanitation, waste management, decontamination activities had in 2015, a number of 98,262 individual employment contracts (CIM), with a share of 2.01% in total employment contracts, while in 2018 the number of CIMs will increase to 100,447, respectively a share of 1.87% in total, the absolute dynamics in the period 2015–2018 being 2,185 CIMs, which represents a share of 2.22%.

In addition, the information provided by the competent authorities in the midst of the pandemic, respectively March–December 2020, compared to the same period of 2019, helps us to conclude that the number of company dissolutions, deletions, suspensions of companies in the sector. It is analysed, of the registrations, it was lower in 2020 compared to 2019.

The analysed sector has a great potential for development, due to the wide range of activities that can be highlighted by the evolution of relevant economic and financial indicators, from 2008–2018, corroborated with data provided by competent authorities in the first year of the Covid-19 pandemic, is a support for the development of short-medium and long-term measures. The bio-economy can recycle plastic, turn waste into furniture or turn industrial by-products into organic fertilizers, as the European Union Commission has been advocating since October 2018.

The effects of Covid-19, of a medical and economic nature, as well as the shocks produced by the pandemic in the economy determined a series of constraints at the level of the economy generated by the need to protect employees, but also by opportunities for the labour market (Crețu 2013). In Romania, the data provided by the ministries indicate costs ranging between 8103.9 million lei allowances following the suspension of the activity (GEO no. 30/2020) and 6,042.4 million lei transfers for balancing the social insurance budget and 16 billion lei IMMINVEST ROMANIA Programme support for small and medium enterprises for the relaunch of the activity, to which are added other costs (200 million lei aid scheme for SMEs affected by Covid-19, repatriation costs, quarantine costs, parental costs, allowances, etc.).

The Covid-19 pandemic has caused all employees worldwide to suddenly experience significant changes, both in the family and in their professional activity, the most affected being low-wage workers without access to social protection.

At present, our company faces major problems in terms of water distribution, sanitation, waste management and decontamination activities. Improper management of these issues contributes to climate change and water, air and soil pollution, directly and indirectly affecting the population and the environment. Waste activities, such as dumping, incineration or illegal imports of waste, have a negative impact on the environment, and the extent of this impact is difficult to assess. Due to the lack of a coherent policy at national and local levels, regarding water distribution, sanitation, waste management, decontamination activities, the quality of the environment has constantly deteriorated.

The paper includes the following parts: introduction (description of the water distribution, sanitation, waste management, decontamination activities and European and national environmental policy sector); literature review; research methodology; results and discussions (the correlation of the analysed sector with the other sectors and the national economy—the analysis of the result of the Leontief model; the evolution of sector E–water distribution, sanitation, waste management, decontamination activities during the Covid-19 pandemic, results of the online questionnaire from 28 May to 2 June 2020 and the evolution of sector E from 1 January to 30 June 2020; circular economy and introduction the guarantee system for packaging, the European environmental pact—green deal); conclusions (economic and social measures in the context of the crisis generated by Covid-19).

During this paper, we will analyse both the correlation of the sector with other sectors of the national economy through Leontief's input–output model, which describes how an output from a particular sector can become input to a particular sector and the direct and indirect effects registered.

The results of the online questionnaire launched between 28 May and 2 June 2020 show the desire of the population to introduce an integrated waste management system, by involving public authorities in limiting the spread of coronavirus, by applying ecological, economic and social measures, thus helping to reduce waste spread of any nature and water pollution through their illegal storage in the major and minor riverbeds of river basins. Only by introducing a national guarantee system and as soon as possible can the "green business", the waste recycling system, packaging in the context of the circular economy be encouraged.

2 Literature Review

Water management in Romania, according to the Nations Strategy for Sustainable Development, is done in a decentralized system. In Romania, there are 42 regional operators and one in Bucharest. According to the National Institute of Statistics, 76.1% of water is used for domestic consumption. In the last 10 years, household water consumption in Romania decreased by 28.5%, simultaneously with the decrease of the share of drinking water consumed for other users of approx. 33% as a result of the reduction and restructuring of industrial and agricultural activity, the metering of household consumption and last but not least the increase of the citizen's education regarding the elimination of waste. The value of water on a global scale could be perceived by analysing all water on Earth, from the perspective of how basic concepts about the place of water in global existence have changed, how they have been in equilibrium or tension in different periods but and how they are viewed, on a small or large scale (Burlacu et al. 2020).

Integrated waste management is organically part of the vision of sustainable development and is the embodiment of the concept of circular economy, based on recycling and conservation, according to the Sustainable Development Strategy 2030. Products processed by man and become unusable are treated as raw material for the generation of other products or services (Busu et al. 2019). According to the National Waste Management Plan, the recycling rate (including compost) reported by Eurostat was 13% in 2016, and the landfill rate was 69%. The analysed sector (Anghel et al. 2014) includes activities related to the management of water, waste and contaminated sites, management activities (including collection, treatment and disposal) of different types of waste, such as industrial or municipal waste, solid or not, as well as land decontamination activities. The results of waste treatment processes can be disposed of or become raw materials for other production processes.

The analysis of the sector based on relevant economic and financial indicators, which highlight the effects for 10 years, respectively the period 2008–2018, is the support for the development of short, medium- and long-term measures in each division: **36 Water capture**, treatment and distribution—during the analysed period, the number of companies increased by 75.67%, while the number of employees increased by 7.13%. **37 Water collection and treatment**—if the number of companies increased by 25.9%, and the number of employees by 72.80% in the analysed period, the indicator for quantifying economic performance (Anica-Popa et al., 2017), respectively turnover, increased by 51.83%, while gross value added at factor cost increased by 104%; **38 Collection, treatment and disposal of waste, recovery activity of recyclable materials**—an in-depth analysis of labour productivity shows an increase in labour efficiency in the analysed period by 6.54% per total division, the number of companies registered the largest increase at the level of the waste treatment and disposal group by 112.5% (Table 1).

The 39 Decontamination activities and services—include the provision of remediation services, i.e. cleaning of contaminated buildings and sites, soil, surface or groundwater.

All the results, scientifically based on the data provided by the competent authorities in the field, oblige us in a world affected by the Covid-19 pandemic to focus our efforts to provide people with a society in which water distribution, sanitation, waste management, decontamination to be achieved sustainably with immediate economic and social effects. The bio-economy can recycle plastic, turn waste into furniture or turn industrial by-products into organic fertilizers, as the European Union Commission has been advocating since October 2018.

European environmental policy was adopted at the Paris European Council in 1972. The documents underlying the European Union's environmental policy were the Environment Action Programs (MAPs). Thus, community action in the field of the environment is based on four successive programs of action on the environment, based on environmental issues, with both a vertical and a sectoral approach.

Among the strategic documents at European level, with an impact on waste management policies, we must mention: Directive no. Regulation (EC) No 850/2018

Table 1 Dynamics of the number of companies in the industry, division 38, period 2008–2018

CAEN code	Total industry	2008	2009	2010	2011	2012	2013	2014	2015	2016	2017	2018
	No. companies CA>0	**1,696**	**1,699**	**1,829**	**2,030**	**2,255**	**2,395**	**2,504**	**2,395**	**2,093**	**2,162**	**2,155**
381	Waste collection	464	486	569	702	814	926	975	964	809	844	826
382	Waste treatment and disposal	48	56	81	98	95	106	117	125	101	106	102
383	Materials recovery	1,184	1,157	1,179	1,230	1,346	1,363	1,412	1,306	1,183	1,212	1,227
	Evolution no. companies		*3*	*130*	*201*	*225*	*140*	*109*	*-109*	*-302*	*69*	*-7*
	Evolution no. companies %		*0.2*	*7.7*	*11.0*	*11.1*	*6.2*	*4.6*	*-4.4*	*-12.6*	*3.3*	*-0.3*

Source www.insse.ro, accessed on May 15, 2020, author's processing amending Directive 1999/31/EC on the landfill of waste (Text with EEA relevance)—European Parliament and Council of the European Union; Directive no. 852/2018 amending Directive 94/62/EC on packaging and packaging waste (Text with EEA relevance)—European Parliament and Council of the European Union; European Union Sustainable Development Strategy; thematic strategy on the sustainable use of natural resources.

Given that waste management is one of the important issues facing Romania, the legislative framework is an essential condition for implementing an integrated system in line with EU requirements. Waste management involves activities of collection, transport, treatment, recovery and disposal of waste, each of these activities being regulated by a series of regulations.

National waste management policy (Guerrieri et al. 2020) must be in line with the objectives of European waste prevention policy and aim at reducing resource consumption and the practical application of the waste hierarchy.

Wastewater (Rodriguez et al. 2020) can be treated and returned to the economic circuit at various qualities for different sectors, including agriculture and industry. Wastewater treatment for reuse is one of the most effective and efficient solutions to the problem of global water scarcity. In addition, by-products from wastewater treatment can become valuable for agriculture and green energy production. Therefore, improving the wastewater management process offers a triple value to society by adopting the principles of the circular economy: in addition to environmental protection and health benefits, it contributes to reducing decontamination costs.

The rapid changes of recent times in the management of urban water, waste and climate change - amplified by urbanization and economic development, are growing day by day in all cities of our planet (Rahmasary et al. 2019). The population of cities, but especially public and private institutions that have responsibilities in the field of administration, must be aware of the threats and opportunities to improve their ability to address these rapid changes. Together they need to identify the priorities, barriers and facilitators of these capabilities. The new "City Blueprint®" concept performs a basic, integrated assessment of the urban water cycle. Thus, cities can be assessed in terms of their governance capacity for challenges, with a focus on floods, solid waste collection and treatment, and access to improved drinking water and sanitation (for cities with large slum populations). These people are also disproportionately affected by the impact of climate hazards. The high variation in water management performance between different cities on the same continent shows a high potential for learning from city to city through the exchange of good practices in the field of clean, clean technologies and water management. Combining interventions between different sectors, by analysing the benefits that can be obtained (agriculture, transport and energy) will increase work efficiency, improve resilience and reduce cost. Cities need to increase their capacity to implement community involvement policies. Consequently, the process of transforming the city must be concrete, efficient and inclusive.

More and more cities in the global south are facing high climate vulnerabilities compared to them in the global north (Aartsen et al. 2018). Moreover, the transposition of relevant scientific ideas into city administration policy and practice is the major problem of misunderstandings. Feasible interactive approaches are needed to facilitate the collaboration between advanced science in the field of green technologies and the policy implemented by the institutions that ensure the administration of cities. The authors of the article assessed the extent to which the city plan approach can facilitate such a significant science - policy interaction in Ahmedabad, India. An overall assessment of trends, pressures and integrated water resources management in Ahmedabad was conducted. The challenges are related to water pollution, lack of water (lowering of groundwater levels), the risk of heat and excessive urbanization, but also to the administration and governance capacities of the city. The result of the study is that learning, stakeholder involvement and implementation capacity are most in need of improvement.

3 Research Methodology

It was relevant for the research team to identify a target group willing to collaborate and provide relevant answers, rather than gathering quantitative information. This information was treated as a qualitative research, from the results of which it is possible to move to a quantitative research, with a nationally representative sample. The information was collected in the form of an EXCEL database, and the results of the research will be presented below. The research was conducted in the form of a questionnaire with 20 questions, three of which were demographic, and the questionnaire was completed online, between 28 May and 2 June 2020. Answers were collected from 288 participants. A total answers is the sum of the answers selected by the participants to a certain question. The percentage for each option is calculated by dividing the sum of the same options by the total answers. The results of the questionnaire are presented in Annex.

The authors tried to identify, following this survey, economic and social measures for the analysed sector, in the context of the crisis generated by Covid-19 and the creation of premises for quantifying the impact that these measures will have for the most exposed target group, namely the population. The motivation for choosing this target group was supported by the fact that the population is the social group most interested in services in the water distribution sector, sanitation, waste management and decontamination activities. The national guarantee system can encourage the development of green business and the waste recycling system in the context of the circular economy.

Tested hypotheses:

Hypothesis 1: Does the population want to introduce an integrated waste management system?

Hypothesis 2: Does the population understand the role of public authorities (National Agency for Environmental Protection) in implementing the integrated waste management system?

Table 2 Leontief matrix

Production/Demand	Sector 1	Sector 2
Sector 1	a	b
Sector 2	c	d

Hypothesis 3: Does the population want to improve the ecological measures included in a river basin management plan during the Covid-19 pandemic?

Hypothesis 4: Does the population want to be informed and consulted about the additional measures taken during the Covid-19 pandemic in the water distribution, sanitation, waste management, decontamination activities?

Extrapolating, not only the population is affected by this deadly virus but the entire economy of a country. This can be explained by using Leontief's input–output model.

The concept of productive matrix was developed by economist Wassily Leontief in 1973, when he won the Nobel Prize for economics. Leontief modelled and analysed the relationships between different sectors of an economy. The interdependencies between the latter can be examined by the input–output model with empirical data over a certain period of time.

The Leontief model consists of a matrix equation to determine the relationships between the different sectors of a specific region. This assumes that the economy is made up of various production and service sectors, among which there is a domestic demand to be met, as well as an external demand that must also be met (Table 2).

The table shows the relationship between sector 1 and sector 2. The value "a" expresses the fact that sector 1 requires so much from its own production. The value "b" expresses that sector 2 needs so much of the production of sector 1. The value "c" expresses the fact that sector 1 needs so much of the production of sector 2. And the value "d" expresses the fact that sector 2 requires so much production own.

The following matrices are defined:

$$\mathrm{A} = \begin{pmatrix} a\ b \\ c\ d \end{pmatrix};\ \mathrm{D} = \begin{pmatrix} \textit{external demand sector}\ 1 \\ \textit{external demand sector}\ 2 \end{pmatrix};\ \mathrm{X} = \begin{pmatrix} \textit{production sector}\ 1 \\ \textit{production sector}\ 2 \end{pmatrix}$$

- Matrix A represents the initial values of the table placed in the matrix.
- Matrix D is the vector of external demand
- The matrix X is the production vector, for which we have to calculate the value of its elements.

Matrix equation:

$$X = AX + D$$

And the production vector is isolated to be able to solve the system:

$$IX - AX = D; (IA)X = D; X = (I - A)-1D$$

To show the role played by the four divisions of activity of the sector water distribution, sanitation, waste management, decontamination activities in the economy, we will analyse:

- Matrix of technical coefficients;
- Multipliers.

Sector dependence water distribution, sanitation, waste management, decontamination activities from inputs provided by other sectors is highlighted by technical coefficients, which show the speed with which inputs are transformed into results.

Multiplier analysis

Based on the input–output matrix, we can calculate two distinct results:

- Backward linkages are used to indicate the interconnection of the analysed sector with other sectors of the economy that are used as inputs by that sector and focus mainly on demand;
- Forward linkages show us the impact of increasing the total production in the analysed sector on the other sectors of the economy that use the products in that sector as inputs in their production process. These multipliers focus on supply.

4 Results and Discussions

The respondents of this questionnaire are part of the population category 96.2%, and the operators in sanitation and water distribution services 3.8%, are from urban areas 67% and rural 31%, have high school studies 42.7%, university studies 38, 9%, master studies 18.4%, aged between 18–35 years 87.2% and over 35 years 12.8%.

Although they are young people, they believe that the effectiveness of the pandemic waste management system is good and very good 66.3% and not very good 33.7%, this sector being responsible for limiting the spread of coronavirus by collecting waste from hospitals, centres quarantine, etc.

Seventy-six percent of respondents consider the current price/quality ratio of waste collection services as medium, 17.7% as high and only 6.3% consider it low, which justifies the affirmative answer in the proportion of 77.4%, for the differentiation of tariffs for the selective collection of waste, which will increase the degree of recycling by introducing the guarantee system, a system implemented since the 2000s in many countries, with remarkable results in the circular economy. Fifty-one percent of respondents do not know how the costs in this sector were estimated, 25% do not agree with the estimate and only 24% agree with them.

The current waste management system ensures the protection of the environment and the health of the population, according to the respondents in average and low proportion of 93.4%, and 6.6% consider it efficient, which justifies the answer “yes” in 91.3% for the implementation of an integrated waste management system and 72.9% of respondents believe that sanitation services in the county will be efficient if this system is implemented as soon as possible. For the success of the implementation of this integrated system, a population information campaign is "needed", according to 85.4% of respondents, and for this campaign 74% must be involved, the Environmental Protection Agency, 14.6% environment and school 11.5%, because the pandemic affects both directly and indirectly, 65.6% and cumulatively, 34.4% sector water distribution, sanitation, waste management, decontamination activities. According to the respondents, although they do not know the content of a river basin management plan, 60.8%, but are interested in finding out, 33.3% are convinced 61.5% that ecological measures are the most effective for keeping river basins clean, 21.9% economic measures and 16.7% social measures.

The population wants to have access to information available about this sector during the pandemic, and to be available especially on websites, 69.1%, e-mail, 19.4% and brochures/leaflets, 11.5%.

The population (78.8%) consider that they do not have enough information about this serious situation, which they have not faced so far and request as much information about this virus. They want to know how dangerous this virus is, what effects it has on health over time and how contamination with this killer virus can be avoided.

Most respondents (87.5%) expressed their desire to be informed and consulted on the additional measures taken during the pandemic in the sector of water distribution, sanitation, waste management, decontamination activities. Only 12.5% do not want or do not know if they want to know more information about this killer virus. Therefore, over 80% of respondents understand the size of this pandemic and want to be informed and consulted about the measures that will be taken, in the short, medium and long terms.

The four hypotheses of this questionnaire are confirmed, in the sense that the population wants to introduce an integrated waste management system, by involving public authorities in limiting the spread of coronavirus, by applying ecological, economic and social measures, thus helping to reduce the spread of waste of any kind and water pollution through illegal storage in the major and minor riverbeds of river basins. At the same time, it wishes to be informed and consulted about the additional measures taken during the Covid-19 pandemic, in the sector of water distribution, sanitation, waste management, decontamination activities.

Only by introducing a system of guarantee at national level and as soon as possible can be encouraged "green business", the system of recycling waste, packaging in the context of the circular economy.

Leontief's input–output model describes how an output from a particular sector can become input to a particular sector. The premise for input–output models is the balance between limited resources (supply) and unlimited consumption (demand), based on which a matrix of inputs and outputs between the sectors of the economy is defined.

To show the role played by the four divisions of activity of the sector water distribution, sanitation, waste management, decontamination activities in the economy, we will analyse:

- Matrix of technical coefficients;
- Multipliers.

In the matrix of technical coefficients, the four divisions were grouped into two, according to the NACE Rev. 2 classification. 2, as follows: E36-Water capture, treatment and distribution; E37–E39 Wastewater collection and treatment, Waste collection, treatment and disposal; Recyclable materials recovery activities; Decontamination activities and services. Sector dependence water distribution, sanitation, waste management, decontamination activities from inputs provided by other sectors is highlighted by technical coefficients, which show the speed with which inputs are transformed into results. In the graph below, we present the matrix of these coefficients for division 36-Water capture, treatment and distribution. From the analysis of these coefficients, it can be observed that the highest values of inputs for this division come from the following branches: manufacture of coke oven products and products obtained from crude oil processing (0.111 lei); fishing and aquaculture (0.027 lei); agriculture, hunting and ancillary services (0.023 lei); food industry, beverage manufacturing, tobacco products manufacturing (0.018 lei); and so on The value of 0.111 lei shows us that, in order to achieve an output of 1 lei, the sector with CANE code 36 needs 0.111 lei from the sector for the manufacture of coke oven products and products obtained from crude oil processing. Matrix of technical coefficients for sectors E37–E39 Wastewater collection and treatment; waste collection, treatment and disposal; recyclable materials recovery activities; decontamination activities and services, shows us that the main inputs in this sector come from the following sectors: food industry, beverage manufacturing, tobacco products manufacturing (0.067 lei); storage and auxiliary activities for transports (0.059 lei); production and supply of electricity and heat, gas, hot water and air conditioning (0.049 lei); manufacture of basic pharmaceutical products and pharmaceutical preparations (0.048 lei); fishing and aquaculture (0.043 lei); manufacture of coke oven products and products obtained from crude oil processing (0.034 lei); agriculture, hunting and ancillary services (0.025 lei); wood processing, manufacture of wood and cork products, except furniture; manufacture of articles of straw and other woven vegetable materials (0.025 lei); furniture manufacturing, other industrial activities (0.021 lei); extractive industry (0.020 lei), etc. From the analysis of the data provided by the Leontief matrix, we found that the division E36-Water capture, treatment and distribution contributes as input, very little significant for each sector of the economy. Divisions E37–E39 Wastewater collection and treatment, Waste collection, treatment and disposal; recyclable materials recovery activities; Decontamination activities and services contribute as input in the following sectors of activity: constructions (0.0324 lei); activities related to human health (0.0155 lei); fishing and aquaculture (0.0155 lei); education (0.0113 lei); postal and courier activities (0.0084 lei); advertising and market research activities (0.0081 lei); wastewater collection and treatment, waste collection, treatment and disposal; recyclable materials recovery activities, decontamination activities and services (0.0078 lei); activities of tourist agencies and tour operators, other reservation services and tourist assistance (0.0077 lei); storage and auxiliary activities for transports (0.0071 lei); other professional, scientific and technical activities, veterinary activities (0.0063 lei), etc.

Multiplier analysis

Based on the input–output matrix, we can calculate two distinct results:

- **Backward linkages** are used to indicate the interconnection of the analysed sector with other sectors of the economy that are used as inputs by that sector and focus mainly on demand;
- **Forward linkages** show us the impact of increasing the total production in the analysed sector on the other sectors of the economy that use the products in that sector as inputs in their production process. These multipliers focus on supply.

a. **Backward impact multipliers analysis** involves the analysis of:

1. **The type I output multiplier, which shows us** the contribution of the "E" sector to the total output at the level of the entire economy, as a result of the increase of the final demand for the final goods and services offered by the analysed sector by 1 lei.

Sector 36 contributes to the total output by 1.55 lei to an increase of 1 lei of the demand for goods and services offered by this sector, and sectors E37-E39 by 1.950 lei (Table 3).

2. **Type II output multiplier**-captures the direct, indirect and induced effects of 1 lei increase in final demand from a certain branch on total output. From the table above, it can be seen that, **for the activity branch 36**, the type II multiplier is 2.512 lei, of which the value of 1.550 lei **is due to the direct and indirect effects of production** (type I output multiplier) and **0.963 lei to the induced effects** (cash flows in and out of households and the effect of these flows on other industries).

Table 3 Output multipliers

CAEN CODE	Branch	Type I output multiplier (direct and indirect effects)	Type II output multiplier	Induced effects
E36	Water capture, treatment and distribution	1.550	2.512	0.963
E37–E39	Wastewater collection and treatment, Waste collection, treatment and disposal; recyclable materials recovery activities; Decontamination activities and services	1.950	2.590	0.640

Source calculations taken from sector G

Table 4 Income multiplier for branches of activity E36, E37–39

CAEN CODE	EFFECTS			Type II multiplier
	Direct	Indirect	Induced	
E36	0.417	0.084	0.114	0.616
E37–39	0.164	0.169	0.076	0.410

Source calculations taken from sector G

The output multiplier can, in turn, be calculated in relation to:

- Income;
- Gross value added (GVA).

The income–output multiplier for the branch of activity with CAEN code 36 is 0.616 lei. This means that an increase of 1 lei in the demand for goods in this sector generated on average 0.616 lei in household income. Of this value: 0.501 lei represents the increase of workers' incomes both from the water capture, treatment and distribution industry (direct effect with 0.417 lei), and from the industries with which this sector of activity intertwines (indirect effect with 0.084 lei), and 0.114 lei represents an induced effect.

Analysing comparatively the two sectors E36 and E37-39 it can be seen that the highest effect in the economy (0.616 lei) at a change of one leu of the demand for goods in this sector of activity has the E36 sector. However, the indirect effect is smaller than that of the other activity sector (0.084 lei) (Table 4).

Gross value added multiplier (GVA)

The type I multiplier of GVA shows us the effect of the additional increase by 1 lei of the final consumption for goods (output) made in industry E, on the gross value added in the economy, as a result of direct and indirect effects from the production process. The type II multiplier also takes into account the **effect induced on GVA** (Table 5).

From the table above we can see that the activity sector with CANE code 36: Water capture, treatment and distribution registers a value of 1.27 lei at an increase of 1 lei in the demand for goods and services for this industry. Of this total: the value of 0.68 lei is generated directly by this industry, the value of 0.22 lei is generated indirectly by the industries with which the water capture, treatment and distribution industry (CAEN code 36) interacts, and the rest, the value of 0.38 lei represents

Table 5 GVA multipliers for branches of activity: E36, E37-39

CAEN CODE	Direct effects	Indirect effects	Induced effects	Type II multiplier
E36	0.68	0.22	0.38	1.27
E37-39	0.29	0.41	0.25	0.95

Source calculations taken from sector G

an induced effect of all sectors of the economy, which can stimulate the additional increase of consumption expenditures in this sector of activity.

b. **Impact multiplier analysis**—Forward shows us the impact of increasing total production in sector E on other sectors of the economy that use products in sector E as inputs in their production process. These multipliers focus on supply.

1. The output multiplier shows us that an increase in supply by 1 lei in the E36 sector generates an output at the level of the entire economy of 1.14 lei. Of this amount, 1.01 lei represents the type I multiplier (direct and indirect effects), and.

2. The income multiplier shows us that, with an increase in supply by 1 lei in sector 36, the total income from the economy will increase by about 1 lei, of which: 0.41 lei represents the increase in income in sector 36, 0.003 lei shows us the value with which the incomes of the sectors that use as input the goods from sector 36 change (indirect effect), and 0.03 lei induced effect for the other sectors of the economy.

3. The GVA multiplier shows us how the supply growth by 1 leu impacts, the GVA from the level of the entire economy. The activity sector E36 registered the value of 0.74 lei. Of this amount 0.67 lei represents the value generated directly in this industry, 0.006 lei represents the value obtained in the sectors with which the branch of activity 36 interacts, and the difference represents the induced effect (0.063 lei) (Table 6).

From the data provided by the National Office of the Trade Register on June 30, 2020 on company dissolutions, it results that, since the beginning of 2020, 12,046 companies in the water distribution, sanitation, waste management, decontamination activities compared to 16,626 in the same period have been dissolved from 2019, so a decrease of 27.55% in 2020. Of the 12,046 companies dissolved at the beginning of 2020, 2,371 companies were dissolved in June 2020.

The situation of deregistration in sector E, on 30 June 2020 compared to the similar period of 2019 is shown in the following table. Of the 23,007 companies deregistered at the beginning of 2020, 4,904 companies were deregistered only in June, compared to 67,807 in the similar period of 2019, so 66.07% fewer companies deregistered in 2020.

Regarding the suspensions of activities of companies operating in sector E, it can be seen that, of the 5,136 suspensions at the beginning of 2020, 1,026 companies were suspended only in June, compared to 7,601 companies suspended in the similar period of 2019, so by 32.43% less suspensions of companies' activities in 2020 compared to 2019 (Table 7).

Regarding the situation of company registrations in sector E, from the beginning of 2020 to 30 June 2020, 144 companies were registered, compared to 239 companies registered in the similar period of 2019, so 39.75% less in 2020. Of the 144 companies registered in sector E, 37 companies were registered only in June 2020. As a share in the total number of registrations, there is a slight decrease from 0.30–0.29% in 2019 compared to 2020.

Circular Economy and Introduction of the Packaging Guarantee System Achieving a circular economy brings to the fore the need to implement a sustainable

Table 6 Impact multipliers—Forward for sectors E36, E37–39

	Type I	Type II		Decomposition of type I and type II income–output multipliers				Decomposition of type I and type II VAB-output multipliers			
	Output multiplier	Output multiplier	Induced effects	Direct Effects	Indirect Effects	Induced Effects	Type II Multipliers	Direct Effects	Indirect Effects	Induced Effects	Type II Multipliers
Water capture, treatment and distribution	1.013	1.144	0.131	0.418	0.003	0.033	0.453	0.676	0.006	0.063	0.745
Wastewater collection and treatment, waste collection, treatment and disposal; recyclable materials recovery activities; Decontamination activities and services	1.359	1.490	0.131	0.164	0.070	0.032	0.267	0.292	0.161	0.062	0.515

Source calculations taken from sector G

Table 7 Situation of suspensions of the activities of companies in sector E-Year 2020 compared to 2019

CAEN version	Activity name	No. suspensions in the period 01.01.2020–30.06.2020	No. suspensions in the period 01.01.2019–30.06.2019	Dynamics	No. suspensions between 01.06.2020–30.06.2020
1998		2	9	−77.78%	
	Water distribution; sanitation, waste management, decontamination activities	1	1	0.00%	
2003		12	44	−72.73%	2
	Water distribution; sanitation, waste management, decontamination activities	13	31	−58.06%	3
2008		5,122	7,548	−32.14%	1,023
Total		5,136	7,601	– 32.43%	1,026

Source https://www.onrc.ro/index.php/ro/statistici?id=249

approach to all economic activities. The transition to a circular economy promotes sustainable production and consumption patterns that can be implemented in a society in constant search of new sources for self-sustaining economic growth. The process of transforming the classical-linear model into a circular one involves reconsidering unsustainable aspects in order to identify future development opportunities. The process of transforming the classical-linear model into a circular one involves reconsidering unsustainable aspects in order to identify future development opportunities.

At EU level, an ambitious action plan on the circular economy has been adopted since 2015, with the aim of stimulating the transition to a competitive, competitive economy so as to accelerate sustainable economic growth and job creation. This approach is known as the "Circular Economy Package (II)" including a series of legislative proposals and a detailed plan of necessary measures adopted by the end of 2019.

Regarding the integrated waste management, the objective considered in the National Strategy for Sustainable Development of Romania Horizons 2013 - 2020 - 2030 refers to the transition "from waste storage to selective collection and recovery in a higher proportion of recyclable waste, including by transforming organic waste into compost, and the exclusive use, for the urban environment, of ecological landfills".

Advantages of Using the Guarantee System The success factors and advantages of the guarantee system are multiple and can be addressed depending on the forms of implementation of this system at the level of each state.

Ecological perspective: For single-use packaging, they are used in a single bottling cycle; after use they are recycled. Recycling produces much lower greenhouse gases compared to the production of new packaging; in the transport process, disposable packaging intended for recycling and resumption of the production process does not consume large volumes and resources, as they are compacted and/or broken for this activity; a great advantage is the substantial decrease of the phenomenon of abandonment of packaging waste (littering) in the states where the landfill system was introduced, a phenomenon that seriously affects Romania. There are studies that show the direct link between reducing environmental pollution with packaging and introducing the guarantee system; increasing aggregate waste recycling and recovery rates at national level by improving packaging recycling and recovery rates.

Economic outlook—System costs: in the guarantee system, costs are generally borne by beverage manufacturers; revenues slightly exceed costs, according to Swedish operator Returpack; costs in the system do not affect retailers; costs increase for producers, as they bear the investment in collection systems, as well as the costs of handling returned packaging, etc.

The limits of the guarantee system are: the initial increase in the shelf price of the product whose packaging is covered by the guarantee system; increasing the costs of producers and traders of products whose packaging is covered by the guarantee system; the guarantee system does not cover all types of packaging on the market; however, due to the improvement of collection systems, new types of packaging can be added after the implementation of the storage system; change in consumer behaviour, influenced by the initial increase in shelf prices for products whose packaging is covered by the guarantee system. There are therefore many limitations, but they must be taken into account in order to maximize the economic, social and environmental benefits.

The European Green Pact aims to improve people's well-being. Taking the necessary steps to make Europe climate neutral and to protect our natural habitat will be good for people, the planet and the economy. No one will be left behind: 93% of Europeans consider climate change to be a serious problem, 93% of Europeans have taken at least action to combat climate change, and 79% of Europeans agree that taking action in the field of climate change Climate change will lead to innovation.

The European Commission (EC) presented in December 2019 the European Green Pact, the most ambitious package of measures that should enable European citizens and businesses to benefit from the transition to a green and sustainable economy.

The European Green Pact presents a new growth strategy aimed at transforming the EU into a fair and prosperous society, with a modern, competitive and resource-efficient economy, without net greenhouse gas emissions by 2050 and in which eco-nomic growth is decoupled from the use of resources.

The pact's ambitious environmental goals will not be achieved through Europe's isolated efforts. The determinants of climate change and the decline of biodiversity are the same worldwide and are not limited to national borders. The EU can leverage its influence, expertise and financial resources to co-opt its neighbours and partners on this sustainable path. The EU will continue to be at the forefront of international efforts in this regard and wants to forge alliances with countries that share the same vision, while recognizing the need to maintain security of supply and competitiveness, even when other countries do not want to take a stand.

Elaboration of a Deeply Transformative Set of Policies In order to implement the European Green Pact, a rethinking of clean energy supply policies in all economic and industrial sectors, along the production and consumption chain, is needed for large-scale infrastructure projects in the sector transport, food and agriculture, construction, taxation and social benefits. To achieve these goals, it is essential to place greater value on the protection and restoration of natural ecosys-tems, the sustainable use of resources and the improvement of human health. It is in these areas that a profound change is imperative, which can be extremely beneficial to the EU's economy, society and natural environment. The EU should also promote and invest in the necessary digital transformation and related tools, as these are key drivers of change. The following directions are being considered: increasing the EU's level of climate ambition for 2030 and 2050; providing clean, safe and affordable energy; mobilizing the industrial sector for a clean and circular economy; building and renovating buildings in an energy and resource efficient way; accelerating the transition to sustainable and smart mobility; "From farm to consumer": designing a fair, healthy and environmentally friendly food system; conservation and restoration of ecosystems and biodiversity; an ambitious goal of reducing pollution to zero for an environment free of toxic substances.

5 Conclusions

Sector analysed water distribution, sanitation, waste management, decontamination activities has a great potential for development, due to the wide range of activities, from waste collection to treatment and disposal, from recovery of recyclable materials to reintroduction into the production circuit, in the context of the development of a sustainable and circular bio-economy in Romania.

The main objective in the field of environmental protection, assumed by the Treaty of Accession to the European Union, is represented by the improvement of living standards of the population and at the same time of environmental standards, for the fulfilments of which it is necessary to continue investments in environmental infrastructure drinking water supply, waste management), as well as in the decontamination of historically polluted sites, air quality improvement and biodiversity protection/conservation in the context of the implementation of the Nature 2000 Network. In the field of environmental infrastructure and environmental protection, through the EU-has assumed the fulfilment of some obligations regarding the implementation of the European Environment acquit. Combined with these commitments, the improvement of the living standards of the population and at the same time of the environmental standards continues to represent the main objective in the field of environmental protection. Thus, the aim is to reduce the difference between the environmental infrastructure that exists between Romania and the European Union, in terms of both quantity and quality.

Given this fundamental objective, in order to create the premises for full compliance with Romania's obligations under its status as an EU member state, it is necessary to continue investing in environmental infrastructure (collection and treatment of wastewater, drinking water supply, waste management), as well as in the decontamination of historically polluted sites, the improvement of air quality and the protection/conservation of biodiversity in the context of the implementation of the Natura 2000 Network.

In the current period, marked by the pandemic, in parallel with the unprecedented actions required for the health system, it is necessary to prepare the economy for a crisis, also unprecedented. The elaboration of a set of measures for this economic sector was carried out taking into account the extraordinarily abrupt dynamics from day to day of the data on the spread of infections, doubled by the actions of the authorities for home isolation and implicitly the severe restriction of economic activities, which makes the proposed set of measures frequently changed.

The Covid-19 pandemic had a relatively small impact on the economic activities of the analysed field: according to the data provided by the Romanian Employers' Association - Study on labour market dynamics in 2015–2018 at the level of economic sectors, sector E-water distribution, sanitation, waste management, decontamination activities had in 2015, a number of 98,262 individual employment contracts (CIM), with a share of 2.01% in total employment contracts, while in 2018 the number of CIM to increase at 100,447, respectively a share of 1.87% in total, the absolute dynamics in the period 2015–2018 being 2,185 CIM, which represents a share of

2.22%. The information provided by the competent authorities during the pandemic, respectively January–June 2020, compared to the same period of 2019, helps us to conclude that the number of company dissolutions, eliminations, suspensions of companies in the sector is analysed, registrations, was lower in 2020 compared to 2019.

The four hypotheses of the questionnaire launched online between May 28 and June 2 are confirmed, in the sense that the population wants to introduce an integrated waste management system, by involving public authorities in limiting the spread of coronavirus, by applying ecological, economic and social measures, contributing thus reducing the spread of waste of any kind and water pollution through illegal storage in major and minor riverbeds of river basins. At the same time, it wishes to be informed and consulted about the additional measures taken during the Covid-19 pandemic, in the sector of water distribution, sanitation, waste management, decontamination activities.

Only by introducing a national guarantee system and as soon as possible can the "green business", the waste recycling system, packaging in the context of the circular economy be encouraged.

All the scientifically based results, based on data provided by the competent authorities in the field, oblige us, in a world affected by the coronavirus pandemic, to focus our efforts to provide people with a society in which water capture, treatment and distribution, collection and make wastewater treatment and waste collection, treatment and disposal sustainable. The bio-economy can recycle plastic, turn waste into furniture or turn industrial by-products into organic fertilizers, as the European Union Commission has been advocating since October 2018.

The analysed sector has a great potential for development, due to the wide range of activities, from waste collection to treatment and disposal, from recovery of recyclable materials to reintroduction into the production circuit, in the context of developing a sustainable and circular bio-economy in Romania;

- The effects of Covid-19, of a medical and economic nature, as well as the shocks produced by the pandemic in the economy determined a series of constraints at the level of the economy generated by the need to protect employees, but also by opportunities for the labour market. In Romania, the data provided by the ministries indicate costs ranging between 8,103.9 million lei allowances following the suspension of the activity (GEO no. 30/2020) and 6,042.4 million lei transfers for balancing the social insurance budget and 16 billion lei IMMINVEST ROMANIA Programme support for In addition, the analysis of the sector based on relevant economic and financial indicators, which highlight the effects for 10 years, respectively 2008–2018, in conjunction with the data provided by the competent authorities in the first 6 months of 2020, so in full of the Covid-19 pandemic, is a support for the development of short-, medium- and long-term measures;
- All these scientifically based results, based on data provided by the competent authorities in the field, oblige us in a world affected by the coronavirus pandemic

to focus our efforts to provide people with a society in which waste management is sustainable.
- The bio-economy can recycle plastic, turn waste into furniture or turn industrial by-products into organic fertilizers, as the European Union Commission has been advocating since October 2018.

Small and medium enterprises for the prelaunch of the activity, to which are added other costs (200 million lei aid scheme for SMEs affected by Covid-19, repatriation costs, quarantine costs, parental costs, allowances, etc.).

The Covid-19 pandemic has caused all employees worldwide to suddenly experience significant changes, both in the family and in their professional activity, the most affected being low-wage workers without access to social protection.

Economic and Social Measures in the Context of the Crisis Generated by Covid-19 The outbreak of the Covid-19 pandemic changed the economic outlook for the coming years in the Union. The short-term impact in each Member State will depend on the duration and severity of the containment measures, the production structure and the economic policy measures taken to mitigate the immediate impact of the crisis. The medium- and long-term effects will depend on the intensity of the economic activity shock caused by the Covid-19 pandemic in all sectors of the economy, the economic resilience of the economies and the ability to take appropriate action. In the absence of decisive policy action, the risk of distorting a level playing field in the single market may lead to increasing economic disparities in the Union and to increasing Europe's long-term growth challenges.

Given the phasing out of containment measures, a sustainable recovery requires strategic policy orientation to mitigate the economic and social impact of the crisis, by encouraging economic convergence and resilience, thus contributing to long-term sustainable growth. This includes facilitating the double transition to a greener and more digital society, while ensuring the Union's strategic autonomy. Previous experience has shown that investment is often drastically reduced during crises. However, it is essential to support investments in this special situation. In addition, it is necessary to address the major economic and social challenges associated with this crisis in order to prevent a lasting loss of production capacity and employment (the hysteresis effect), thus protecting economic and social resilience. In addition, a sustainable and resilient recovery requires a framework conducive to the right kind of investment and reform. It is also crucial that Member States' recovery strategies adequately integrate the challenges of the green and digital transition and support investment and reform in these two key areas.

The analysed sector has a great potential for development, due to the wide range of activities, from waste collection to treatment and disposal, from recovery of recyclable materials to reintroduction into the production circuit, in the context of developing a sustainable and circular bio-economy in Romania. In addition, the analysis of the sector on the basis of relevant economic and financial indicators, which highlight the effects for 10 years, respectively 2008–2018, is a support for the development of short-, medium- and long-term measures.

All these scientifically based results, based on data provided by the competent authorities in the field, oblige us in a world affected by the coronavirus pandemic to focus our efforts to provide people with a society in which waste management is sustainable. The bio-economy can recycle plastic, turn waste into furniture or turn industrial by-products into organic fertilizers, as the European Union Commission has been advocating since October 2018.

Proposed measures in the sector of water distribution, sanitation, waste management, decontamination activities: Intensification of information campaigns, education and awareness of the population on how to collect waste separately; public awareness in the field of waste management depends on education strategies and programs defined at local, regional and/or national levels; Strict prohibition regarding the storage of bulk (spilled) waste in the trash/and the disposal of protective equipment masks, gloves, etc. without being hermetically sealed in bags in the rubbish bin or in the container where the waste is temporarily stored in the household to prevent accidental contamination of the contents of the rubbish bin; Identification of measures for monitoring contaminated waste in the context of the Covid-19 pandemic; Creating the national database on waste resulting from medical activities, by including centralized data from all entities subordinated to the ministry according to legal provisions; Intensification of the control activity in the sanitary units regarding the management of waste and/or contaminated results from medical activities; Realization of a management/collection plan for transport and disposal of waste by using the method of thermal decontamination at low temperatures and final disposal in appropriate conditions centralized at regional/national level; Public announcements, information of the target group, public debates, press releases and press conference on waste management and collection in the Covid-19 pandemic; Introduction in the school curriculum for the pre-university/university education of topics regarding the way of separate waste collection and the management of its contamination in the conditions of a pandemic; Promoting research programs that have as environment the quality of life.

Attracting European funds to finance projects on water distribution, sanitation, waste management, decontamination activities at local level; Introduction of coercive tools at local level to avoid water contamination by illegal waste storage; Separate collection of household and similar residual waste, of recyclable household and similar waste; household and similar bio-waste, bulky waste; hazardous household waste; The application of the instrument "pays for how much and how you throw" (contraventions that are sanctioned with a fine according to the provisions of art. 61 of Law 211/2011); Increasing the degree of readiness for reuse and recycling of waste; Bi-waste treatment; Adoption of new biological technologies: bio stabilization and bio scare; Storage of waste only in compliant landfills—permanently; Creating a database of quantities of bio-waste resulting from food preparation (HoReCa) and expired foods from the commercial chain; Clarification of the legislative provisions regarding the reporting obligations; Introduction of the guarantee-return system for reusable primary packaging; Regulation of extended producer responsibility in accordance with the latest legislative changes at European level (Directive 852/2018); Elaboration of guides of good practices for the local public authorities, which will aim at the following aspects: prevention of waste generation; data management and data entry; Realization of partnerships with NGOs, interested factors for carrying out awareness campaigns; Implementation of river basin management plans, in accordance with the provisions of the Water Framework Directive of the European Union; Elaboration of the Master Plans for the Arrangement of the Hydrographic Basins for the water uses; Actions to raise public awareness of the potential for pollution of human activities on water resources; Extension and rehabilitation of supply and distribution networks;

Monitoring the quality of drinking water through programs approved by the Public Health Directorate; Permanent monitoring through monitoring, control and data acquisition systems (Supervisory Control And Data Acquisition—SCADA) of water quality at the exit of the treatment plant and network operation parameters; self-monitoring, on water treatment stages, as well as for storage and distribution tanks to the consumer; Ensuring an efficient maintenance system; Ensuring the control of water losses; Program—type of hygienic training for the employees of the water treatment stations, the aqueduct installations, (who have the direct attribution to the water treatment and disinfection) and the persons, who serve the aqueduct networks;

Program—type of hygienic training for employees of wastewater treatment plants, sanitation facilities, garbage collectors and those involved in the disposal of household waste and industrial waste; the toilets of public toilets; Measures of administrative coercion applied to natural and legal persons for sanitary-epidemiological violations admitted to the activity.

The limits of this research refer to the fact that, in Romania, waste is not collected sorted by population, although the European Union launched this policy a long time ago. During the pandemic, the economic operators responsible for collecting the waste did not act efficiently and effectively, and the medical and hospital waste was not properly managed. The amount of waste stored anywhere has deteriorated and the quality of the water. The research does not show the areas contaminated with nitrites and nitrates in Romania or other dangerous substances, although many waters have a poor quality, especially those from shallow boreholes.

In the current context of prolonging the pandemic for an indefinite period, the authors of this article will continue research in the following directions:

- Assessing the impact of the dynamics of the Covid-19 epidemic on the water distribution, sanitation, waste management and decontamination activities sector;
- Measures to reduce the negative effects on the labour market in the analysed sector;
- Assessing the impact of telework—a modern form of economic resilience—in the sector of water distribution, sanitation, waste management and decontamination activities.

Annex

1. What category of stakeholders do you belong to?		
(a) sanitation service operators	4	1.4%
(b) operators of drinking water distribution services	7	2.4%
(c) population	277	96.2%
	288	100.0%
2. What do you think about the effectiveness of the waste management system during the Covid-19 pandemic?		
(a) not very good	97	33.7%
(b) good	180	62.5%
(c) very good	11	3.8%
	288	100.0%
3. What do you think of the current price/quality ratio of waste collection services?		
(a) large	51	17.7%
(b) medium	219	76.0%
(c) small	18	6.3%
	288	100.0%
4. Could the differentiation of tariffs for selective waste collection lead to an increase in recycling during the Covid-19 pandemic?		
(a) yes, in an insignificant percentage	98	34.0%
(b) no	65	22.6%
(c) yes, in a significant percentage	125	43.4%
	288	100.0%
5. What do you think is the degree to which the current waste management system ensures the protection of the environment and the health of the population?		
(a) low	129	44.8%
(b) medium	140	48.6%
(c) high	19	6.6%
	288	100.0%
6. Do you consider that the implementation of an integrated waste management system (selective collection, sorting, composting and controlled storage) will contribute to improving the quality of the environment?		
(a) yes	263	91.3%
(b) no	10	3.5%
(c) I don't know/I didn't think	15	5.2%
	288	100.0%

(continued)

(continued)

7. Do you consider that the sanitation services in the county will be efficient with the implementation of the new system?		
(a) yes	210	72.9%
(b) no	18	6.3%
(c) I don't know/I didn't think	60	20.8%
	288	100.0%
8. Do you consider that a sustained information campaign among the population is useful for the successful implementation of the integrated waste management system, especially during the Covid-19 pandemic?		
(a) yes	246	85.4%
(b) no	18	6.3%
(c) I don't know/I didn't think	24	8.3%
	288	100.0%
9. If your answer is yes, which institutions do you think should be involved?		
(a) Environmental Protection Agency	213	74.0
(b) The school	33	11.5
(c) Environmental Guard	42	14.6
	288	100
10. How does the Covid-19 pandemic affect the water distribution, sanitation, waste management, decontamination activities sector?		
(a) directly by increasing the amount of waste and the high degree of contamination	127	44.1
(b) indirectly, by increasing the tariffs for sanitation services	62	21.5
(c) cumulatively	99	34.4
	288	100
11. Do you know the content of a River Basin Management Plan?		
(a) yes	17	5.9%
(b) no	75	60.8%
(c) I will be interested	96	33.3%
	288	100.0%
12. What specific measures under a basin management plan do you consider to be a priority during the Covid-19 pandemic?		
(a) ecological measures	177	61.5%
(b) social measures	48	16.7%
(c) economic measures	63	21.9%
	288	100.0%

(continued)

(continued)

13. Do you agree with the estimated costs of the water distribution, sanitation, waste management, decontamination activities during the Covid-19 pandemic?		
(a) yes	69	24.0%
(b) no	72	25.0%
(c) I don't know	147	51.0%
	288	100,0%
14. Can you identify other sources of funding for the implementation of additional measures imposed during the Covid-19 pandemic period in the water distribution, sanitation, waste management, decontamination activities?		
(a) yes	88	30.6%
(b) no	102	35.4%
(c) in an insignificant percentage	98	34.0%
	288	100.0%
15. Do you think it is important to be informed and consulted about the additional measures taken during the pandemic in the water distribution, sanitation, waste management, decontamination activities?		
(a) yes	252	87.5%
(b) no	12	4.2%
(c) I don't know	24	8.3%
	288	100.0%
16. Do you consider that there is available and sufficient information for the population during the pandemic related to the analysed sector?		
(a) yes	61	21.2%
(b) no	106	36.8%
(c) too little, insignificant	121	42.0%
	288	100.0%
17. What information methods do you prefer and find most effective for your active involvement in environmental issues during the Covid-19 pandemic?		
(a) Website	199	69.1%
(b) brochures/leaflets	33	11.5%
(c) e-mail	56	19.4%
	288	100.0%
18. What is the respondent's highest level of education?		
(a) high school studies	123	42.7%
(b) university studies	112	38.9%
(c) master studies	53	18.4%
	288	100.0%
19. What is your age?		
18–35 years old	251	87.2%
36–50 years	29	10.1%

(continued)

(continued)

51–65 years old	7	2.4%
over 65 years	1	0.3%
	288	100.0%
20. What is your environment of residence?		
(a) rural	90	31.3%
(b) urban	194	67.4%
(c) I prefer not to answer	4	1.4%
	288	100.0%

References

Aartsen, M., Koop, S., Hegger, D., Goswami, B., Oost, J, Leeuwen, K. V.: Connecting water science and policy in India: lessons from a systematic water governance assessment in the city of Ahmedabad. Reg. Nal Environ. Chang. **18**, 2445–2457 (2018). https://doi.org/10.1007/s10113-018-1363-1.

Albu, L. L.: Academician: macroeconomic impact assessments of Covid-19, Romanian Academy, department of economic, legal and sociological sciences, institute of economic forecasting (2020)

Banacu, C.S., Busu, M., Ignat, R., Trica, C.L.: Entrepreneurial innovation impact on recycling municipal waste. a panel data analysis at the EU level. Sustain. **11**(18), 5125 (2019). https://doi.org/10.3390/su11185125.

Best Environmental Management Practice in the tourism sector: Waste sorting and sending for recycling, https://ec.europa.eu/environment/emas/takeagreenstep/pdf/BEMP-6.2-FINAL.pdf (2017).

Burlacu, S., Vasilache, P.C., Velicu, E.R., Curea, S.C., Margina, O.: Management of water resources at global level. In Proceedings of the International Conference on Economics and Social Sciences, pp. 998–1009. Sciendo. (2020)

Crețu, R.F.: Drug Industry Medical and Waste, Supplement of "Quality-access to success" Journal Vol. 18, S2, The journal is published by the Romanian Society for Quality Assurance, CNCSIS recognized, category B+ and it is included in SCOPUS, EBSCO, PROQUEST, CABELL'S, pp. 160–165, din 490 p., anul 2017, ISSN 1582–2559, http://www.srac.ro/calitatea/arhiva/supliment/2017/Q-asContents_Vol.18_S2_March-2017.pdf (2017).

Crețu, R.F., Cretu, R.C.: Company value and structure of the corporate governance under the circumstances of diversification and economic instability, International Conferance sustainable development in conditions of economic instability Satu Mare Academy Comercial, 21–22 june 2013, CIBERNETICA MC Bucharest 2013, ISBN 978-606-8288-19-2 (2013).

Communication from the Commission to the European Parliament, the Council, the European Economic and Social Committee and the Committee of the Regions, European Green Pact, Brussels, 11.12.2019, COM (2019), 640 final (2019).

Directive (EU) 2018/851 of the European Parliament and of the Council of 30 May 2018 amending Directive 2008/98 / EC on waste (2018).

Directive 2008/98 / EC of the European Parliament and of the Council of Directive (EU) 2018/851 of 19 November 2008 on waste and repealing certain Directives.

Government Emergency Ordinance no. 196/2005 on the Environmental Fund.

Government Emergency Ordinance no. 74/2018 of July 17, 2018 for the amendment and completion of Law no. 211/2011 on the waste regime.

Guerrieri, V.G., Lorenzoni, L.S., Werning, I.: Macroeconomic Implications of COVID-19: Can Negative Supply Shocks Cause Demand Shortages?, NBER Working Paper 29618 (2020).

Institutions responsible for collecting data on the quantities of waste generated and managed—Bucharest Environmental Protection Agency, respectively Ilfov Environmental Protection Agency.

Local institutions responsible for ensuring sanitation in Bucharest—Bucharest City Hall and the mayoralties of the 6 sectors.

Minju, K.: Leontief Input–Output Model (Application of Linear Algebra to Economics) Archived 2014-12-15 at the Wayback Machine (2014).

National Waste Management Strategy and National Waste Management Plan.

Rahmasary, A.N., Robert, S., Chang, I.-S., Jing, W., Park, J., Bluemling, B., Koop, S., Leeuwen van, K.: Overcoming the Challenges of Water, Waste and Climate Change in Asian Cities, Environmental Management, volume 63, pp. 520–535, https://link.springer.com/article/https://doi.org/10.1007/s00267-019-01137-y.10 (2019).

Robu, V., Anghel, I., Serban, E.C.: Economic-financial analysis of the company. Economic Publishing House, Bucharest (2014)

Robu, V., Anica-Popa, A., Curea, S.C.: Economic-financial analysis of the company. vol. I. ASE Publishing House, Bucharest (2017)

Rodriguez, D.J., Serrano, H.A., Delgado, A., Nolasco, D., Saltiel, G.: Wastewater? From Waste to Resource, World Bank Water Global Practice, https://www.worldbank.org/en/topic/water/publication/wastewater-initiative (2020).

Report from the Commission to the European Parliament, the Council, the European Economic and Social Committee and the Committee of the Regions on the implementation of the Circular Economy Action Plan, Brussels, 26.1.2017 COM (2017), 33 final.

Romania's National Strategy for Sustainable Development 2030.

Study on the evaluation of the guarantee system, component of the waste management system in Romania, coordinator Cristian Teodor et al., Bucharest, Ministry of Environment.

www.inss.ro, accessed on May 15, 2020, Data from the National Institute of Statistics 2008–2018.

www.mfinante.ro, Data from the Ministry of Public Finance.

www.eurostat.ro, Eurostat data.

www.piarom.ro, Data from the Patronage of Local Investors in Romania.

www.onrc.ro, Data of the National Office of the Trade Register.

The Impact of the Early Stages of COVID Pandemic Lockdown on Romania's Consumers' Behavior

Mosora Mihaela Hrisanta, Orzan Mihai Cristian, Vălimărean Ileana, and Caescu Stefan Claudiu

1 Introduction

The COVID-19 (Coronavirus) pandemic is a somatic marker that will change our behavior forever. In this moment, we are witnessing many changes in the economy: unemployment is rising, people are running out of jobs, some businesses are closing, and other businesses are growing. Any economic crisis ultimately leads to the emergence of new competitive business and improved success models.

Digitization will certainly receive a strong impetus and digital solutions will find their way into professional and private life much faster than before (Dunleavy and Margetts 2010). We are witnessing a development of telework that we will certainly not give up because we save time, and efficiency is not given by physical proximity.

2 Literature Review

Strict quarantine measures have changed consumer behavior in terms of consumption of goods, services, etc. and affected the economies of all countries in the world (Baicu et al. 2020; Stanciu et al. 2020; Seema et al. 2020). These measures have produced

M. M. Hrisanta (✉) · O. M. Cristian · V. Ileana · C. S. Claudiu
Bucharest University of Economic Studies, Bucarest, Romania
e-mail: mihaela.mosora@economie.ase.ro

O. M. Cristian
e-mail: mihai.orzan@ase.ro

V. Ileana
e-mail: ileana.mircioi@ase.ro

C. S. Claudiu
e-mail: stefan.caescu@mk.ase.ro

A. M. Dima et al. (eds.), *Economic Recovery After COVID-19*, Springer Proceedings in Business and Economics, https://doi.org/10.1007/978-3-030-86641-9_15

radical changes in the lifestyle of people and the business environment (Ho et al. 2020).

Approaches that can explain consumer behavior can be grouped into three categories (Donthu & Gustafsson 2020): sociological (consumer attitudes are influenced by various social occasions and social leaders), psychic (behavior is influenced by how individuals react to different factors, such as: an economic crisis, a war, a pandemic), and economic (behavior is related to the choices of individuals and their financial situation).

Flatters and Willmott (2009) identified several consumer trends during a crisis, namely: simplification of demand, people buy simpler offering with great value, people are more attentive to what and how much they consume and try to be more rational considers that this behavior tends to persist even after the crisis.

In a normal situation, an individual's choice regarding the consumption of goods is based on the intrinsic and extrinsic characteristics of the respective products (Asioli et al. 2017; Richardson et al. 1994). On the other hand, during the lockdown period, the emphasis was mainly on the supply of food and products of strict necessity (OECD 2020a).

Abe (2020) observed that during the lockdown period, people had the following behavior: they spent less of their income on things perceived as non-essential (clothing, footwear, makeup, and jewelry), increased demand for edible products, while demand for non-edible products was moderate (homecare, cosmetics, and personal care products).

Sangetta M. et al. (2021) based on a structural equation modeling (SEM) showed that: benefits, perceived social norms, and social influence significantly influence the tendency of people to respect the actions taken by the government to limit the spread of the virus. SARS-COV-2. The measures taken by the authorities during the lockdown period had a high impact on the following sectors of activity: tourism, retail, transport, and agriculture.

Today, both nationally and globally, we face threats, uncertainty, and anxiety. All of these things have a major impact on people's behavior and the way they act and make decisions (Campbell et al. 2020).

There is a large body of literature that tries to explain the decision-making process, both in business-to-business and business-to-consumer contexts (Peña-Lévano et al. 2020; Sheth 2020; Donthu & Gustafsson 2020). However, the general lockdown faced by the world economy during most of 2020 has been unprecedented and, corroborated with a barrage of fake news and increased difficulty of assessing the reliability and trustworthiness of modern media outlets, it lead to shifts in consumer behavior that would take scientists serious efforts to understand (Orzan et al. 2020). Our paper tries to pinpoint a moment in time (the first two months of lockdown) and how it affected the consumer behavior for general products.

3 Research Methodology

The Bucharest University of Economic Studies initiated a market research study on the Romanian consumers, aimed at identifying the main effects of the crisis caused by the COVID-19 pandemic on Romania's economy and in particular on the population's consumer behavior. The study was conducted during the May 4–8, 2020 period, on a nationally representative panel of 1015 consumers. The survey instrument was pretested on a sample of 62 respondents. The collected data were analyzed using the IBM SPSS Statistics Package v. 22 and Warp PLS 6.0 (Orzan et al. 2013). The items corresponding to each construct have a Cronbach's Alpha value over 0.7, the items being accurate and describing well the latent construct. Average variance extracted (AVE) values are above 0.5 showing constructs' good convergent validity and the square roots of AVE, with good discriminant validity (Pentescu et al. 2014).

4 Economic Effects of the COVID Pandemic

The study shows that the majority (50,7%) of respondents believe that the Coronavirus (COVID-19) outbreak will have a significant impact on the Romanian economy (Fig. 1), and almost 65% of the respondents believe that their family financial situation is more difficult now than before the beginning of this pandemic (Fig. 2). However, even more important is the fact that almost half of Romanians (46.3%) believe that in the near future, the financial situation will become even more difficult, and they will have to resort to their savings (33.4%), loans from friends (14.5%), or from banks (5.6%) in order to successfully overcome this period (Fig. 3).

Approximately, 75% of Romanians believe that the prices they paid during the state of emergency period for daily consumer products were higher than the prices paid before the state of emergency was declared, and they anticipated an increase in prices in the immediately following period (Fig. 4).

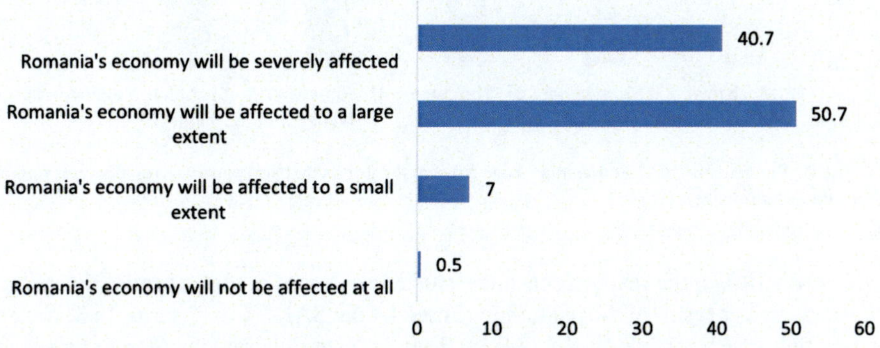

Fig. 1 Will the COVID-19 outbreak affect Romania's economy overall?

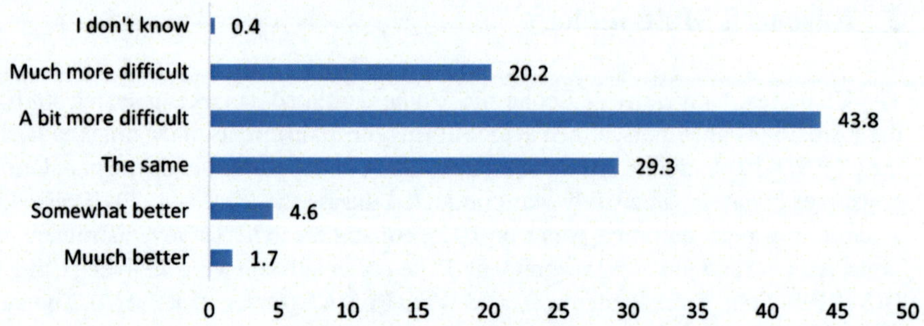

Fig. 2 Please estimate your family's financial situation now as opposed to three months ago (%)?

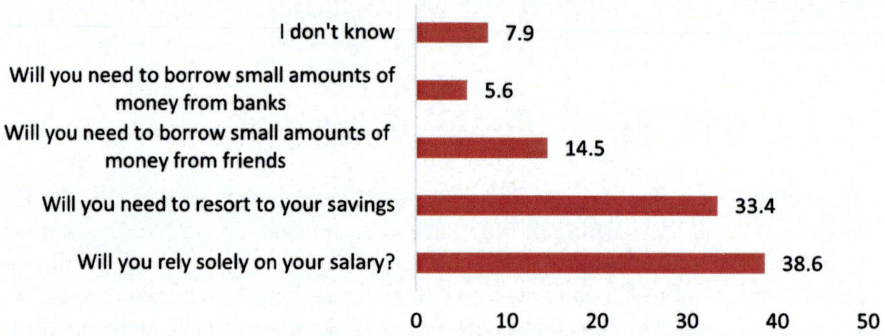

Fig. 3 How would you cover your anticipated expenses over the next three months?

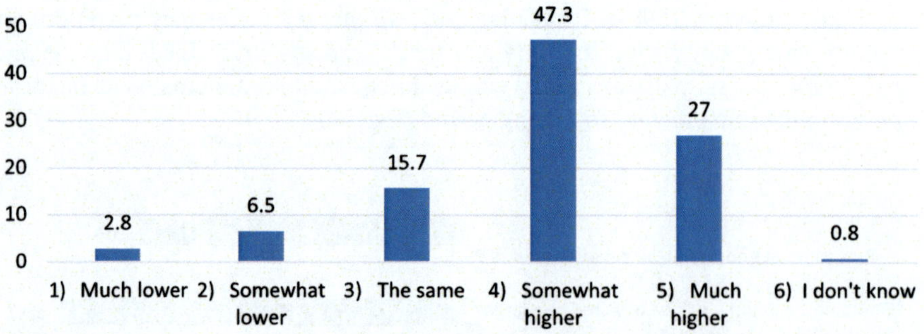

Fig. 4 Please estimate the current average price of the goods that you purchase regularly, as opposed to three months ago (%)?

Over 70% of the respondents anticipated an increase in the unemployment rate in Romania as a result of the pandemic caused by the SARS-Cov-2 virus. In March, the unemployment rate reached 4.6%, up from 3.9% in the previous month; however, a large part of the respondents (41.4%) believe that they will keep the same jobs in the future.

The vast majority of the respondents believed that the state of emergency will lead to a rise in the rate of unemployment (61.3%), combined with a decrease in the population income (58.2%), inflation (59.5%), and the bankruptcy of a significant number of local companies (60.2%), as reflected in Fig. 5.

The respondents' perception regarding the evolution of unemployment in the period following the "state of emergency" depends only in small part on the job sector in which the interviewee is active (9.4%). We can thus conclude that the general perception on this phenomenon is the same regardless of industry, namely: **the unemployment rate in the economy will increase due to the crisis caused by the SARS -COV-2 virus** (Table 1).

From the table above, we could conclude that the correlation coefficients between employment area and expectations regarding short-term job stability are statistically significant (p < 0,01).

We can also infer that there is a significant correlation between the respondents' employment fields and their fear for the future. In areas such as commerce, tourism, and hospitality, job security perspectives seem much lower, as opposed to ICT, energy, and education, where employees have a much lesser degree of concern for their workplace (p < 0,01).

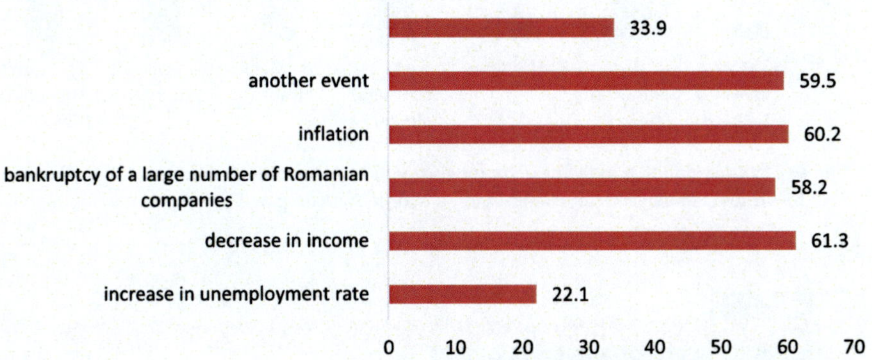

Fig. 5 Main events we will face in Romania in the first three months after the end of the state of emergency (%)

Table 1 Correlations between employment area and short-term job stability expectations

	Perceptions regarding short-term job stability
In what field do you work?	
Correlation Coefficient	0.094**
Sig. (2-tailed)	0.003
N	1015

** Correlation is significant at the 0.01 level (2-tailed)

With respect to consumer intentions, approximately, **30%** of respondents declare that they do not intend **to purchase durable goods,** whereas 35% of the survey subjects intend to reduce these expenses (Fig. 6). Almost identical percentages were obtained in the case of **purchases of tourism services: 37.1% of the persons surveyed will not buy any kind of service,** and those who will, will prefer less crowded vacation spots (Fig. 7).

With respect to **purchasing a car** for themselves or their family in the next **12** months, only 14.4% of the respondents considered this possibility and only **2% of them are actually determined to make such investment** (Fig. 8).

With respect to **real estate investments,** the percentage of people who want to buy new houses or homes is also very small: 2.7% are sure they intend to do this, and 9.3% are contemplating this possibility (Fig. 9).

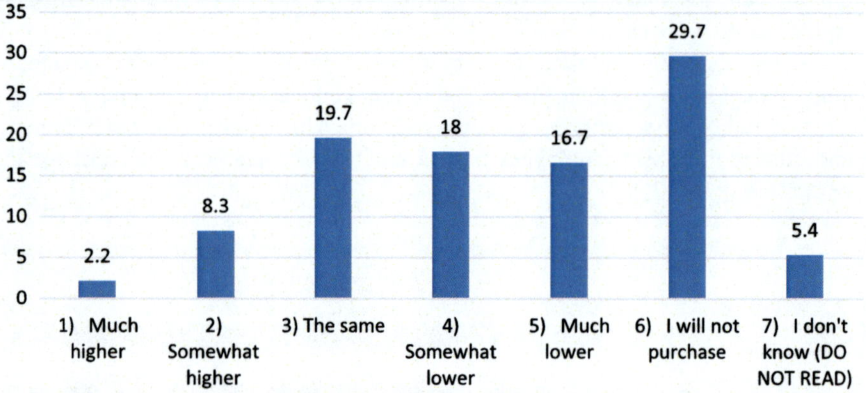

Fig. 6 Do you think that in the next six months, you will invest in the purchase of durable goods (ex.: household appliances, furnishings, etc.) a budget that compared to the previous six months

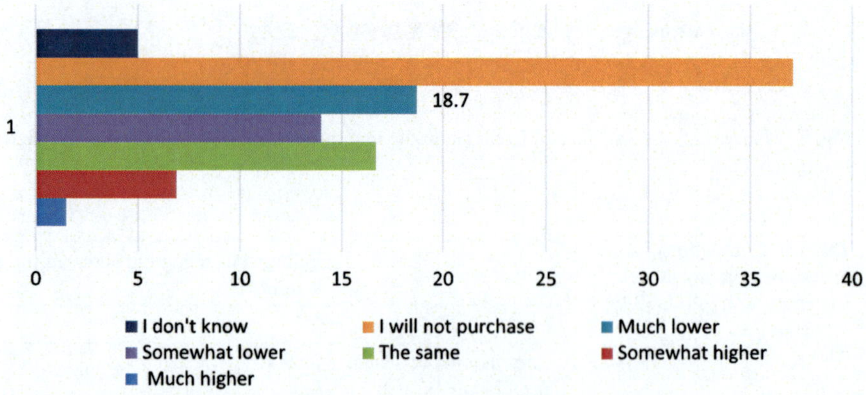

Fig. 7 Do you think that, in the next six months, you will allocate for the purchase of tourism products a budget that, compared to the previous six months, will be (%)?

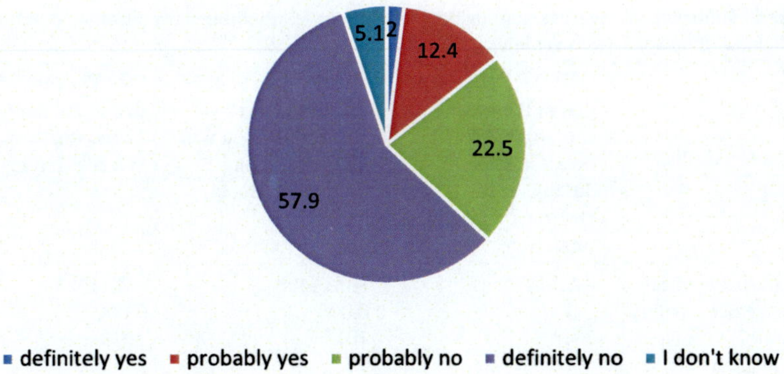

Fig. 8 Do you believe that in the next 12 months, you will invest in buying a car?

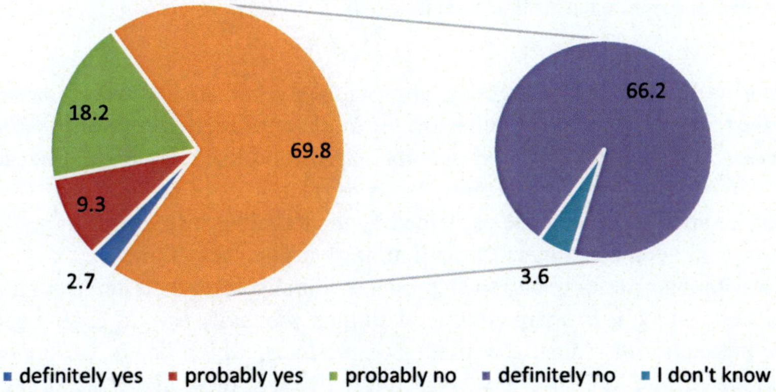

Fig. 9 Do you believe that in the next 12 months, you will invest in buying a house or a new home for you or for another family member (%)?

The preferences of respondents with respect to purchasing the aforementioned goods/services are not strongly correlated to their income. The table below reflects that the income of the survey respondents may negatively and to a small extent explain their tendency to buy: durable goods (−11.4%), package vacations (−16.4%), and a car in the next six months (−11.3%). The negative sign shows us that, given an increase in income, there will not be a corresponding increase in the demand for these goods/services. This behavior shows us that the respondents' choices depend mostly on other factors, such as job uncertainty, the evolution of the economy, etc. (Table 2).

From the table above, we could conclude that the correlation coefficients between Q35 and Q10, Q11 and Q12 are statistically significant ($p < 0{,}01$), people with higher income being a lot more likely to acquire durable good, personal vehicles, or in recreational travel in the near future.

Table 2 Influence of average net income on purchase intentions for durable goods, touristic products, and personal auto vehicles

	Q10 Do you believe that in the next six months, you will invest in buying durable goods (ex.: electrical appliances, furnishings, etc.)	Q11 Do you believe that in the next six months, you will invest in buying tourism products	Q12 Do you believe that in the next 12 months, you will invest in buying a car?
Q35 What is your average net monthly income? Correlation Coefficient Sig. (2-tailed) N	−0.114** 0.000 1015	−0.164** 0.000 1015	−0.113** 0.000 1015

Correlation is significant at the 0.01 level (2-tailed)

During the state of emergency, approximately half of Romanians believe they changed their food spending behavior: for **food supplies, they prefer mostly supermarkets, as** hypermarkets, corner stores, agro-food markets, and online stores are still ranked very low on the Romanian consumers' list of preferences. The preference for supermarkets can be explained by the traveling restrictions imposed by the government upon consumers through military ordinances (Table 3).

Respondents prefer to buy fresh products from hypermarkets and from individual producers, which is in sharp contract with their proclivity toward buying ecological (bio) products and industrially processed products, which lies at the opposite end of the spectrum (Table 4). In the near future, we will most likely see an increase in the consumers' predilection for traditional goods. Over **80% of respondents prefer buying locally produced agricultural goods**, an aspect that could also be taken into account in the public strategies for encouraging consumption (Fig. 10). The only inconvenience in this case is related to price, which will be higher than the one in the supermarket/hypermarket (Table 4).

Table 3 Main source of food supplies during the social distancing period

Supply source	Preferences
Supermarket	1
Hypermarket	2
Corner stores-proximity	3
Agro-food markets	4
Online (individuals and small producers)	5
Online (supermarket/hypermarket)	6
Online (restaurant/fast-food)	7

Table 4 Consumption preferences for food products during the social distancing period

Food product categories	Preferences
Fresh from the supermarket/hypermarket	1
Fresh from local producers	2
Traditionally prepared and semi-prepared	3
Ecological (bio products)	4
Industrially processed and semi-processed	5

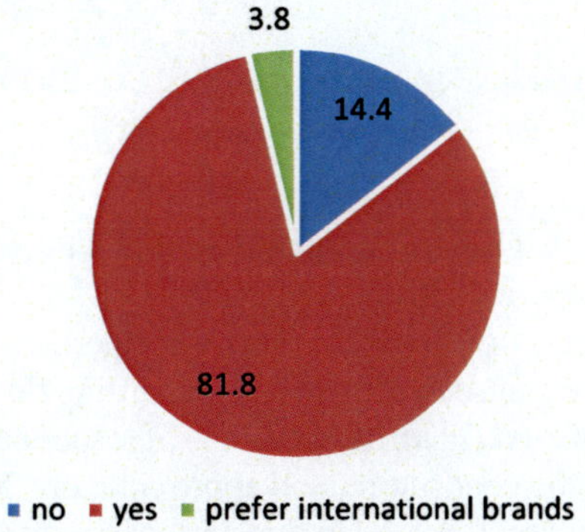

Fig. 10 Do you explicitly intend in the near future to buy products through local/national producers and distributors (%)?

Respondents are divided on the issue of **food consumption** during this period: 48.7% believe they consumed more food, and 51.3% that they did not increase their food consumption (Fig. 11). Other market studies show that, during the week of March 9–March 15, the consumption of food and hygiene products grew significantly,

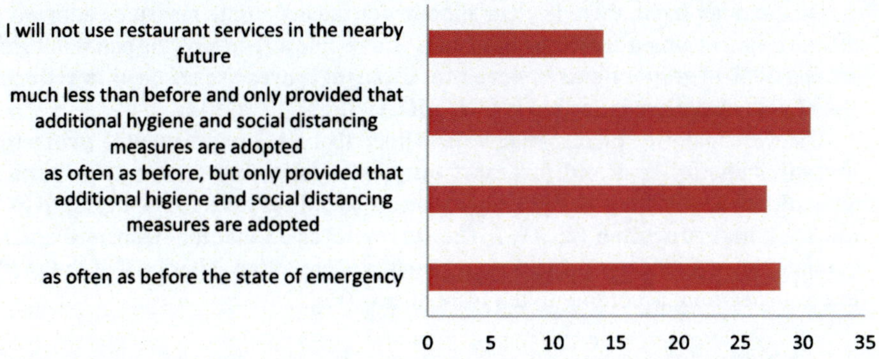

Fig. 11 To what extent will you resort to the services of a restaurant (of any kind) in the near future (%)?

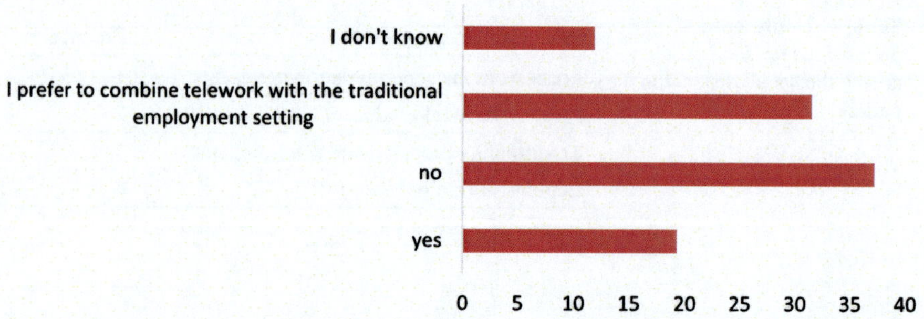

Fig. 12 After the state of emergency declared due to the COVID-19 outbreak ends, will you prefer to telework for your job (%)?

as this is considered to have been the "panic week." A decrease in consumption could be observed after this period (Retail-FMCG 2020).

Tourism industry and non-food commerce are perhaps the sectors most affected by this pandemic. In response to the question regarding ***the possibility of resorting to the services of a restaurant (of any kind):*** 14% of respondents will no longer dine out in public locations in the near future, and approximately, 57% of respondents intend to patronize restaurants only provided that certain heightened hygiene measures are implemented that would ensure consumer protection (Fig. 11).

As a result of the large-scale instatement of the **telework regime** at society level in Romania, more and more people started engaging in remote professional activities. However, only 19.3% of respondents indicate that they are interested in conducting their professional activity in the telework regime, and **31.5% of respondents are interested in a hybrid scenario where telework would supplement the current activities that would be carried out in the regular workspace.** We will therefore witness in the future a change in the way in which activities are carried out, both at company and state institution levels (Fig. 12).

On the other hand, there is clear support for the economic measures adopted by the government aimed at aiding companies and people affected by the pandemic, **and almost 60% of respondents believe that these measures are efficient in reducing the effects of the crisis caused by COVID-19** (Figs. 13 and 14).

The vast majority of respondents consider that the **governmental protection measures should first and foremost target the following sectors: agriculture, silviculture and fishing (75.1%), health and social services (51.4%), HORECA (33.8%), and education (25.7%).** The survey revealed that the financial-banking, administrative services, and real estate sectors were at the other end of the public interest spectrum, according to the respondents (Fig. 15).

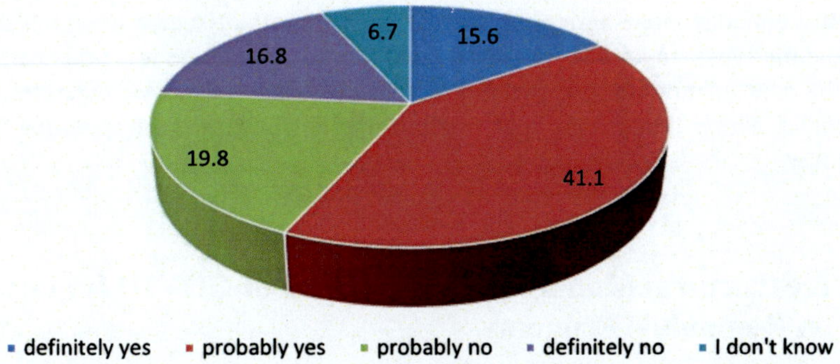

Fig. 13 Efficiency of public policy changes aimed at improving macroeconomic health

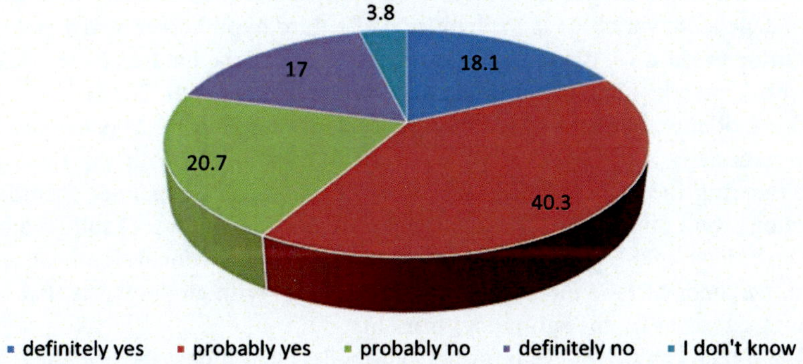

Fig. 14 Efficiency of public policy changes aimed at improving citizens' personal economic standing during the COVID crisis

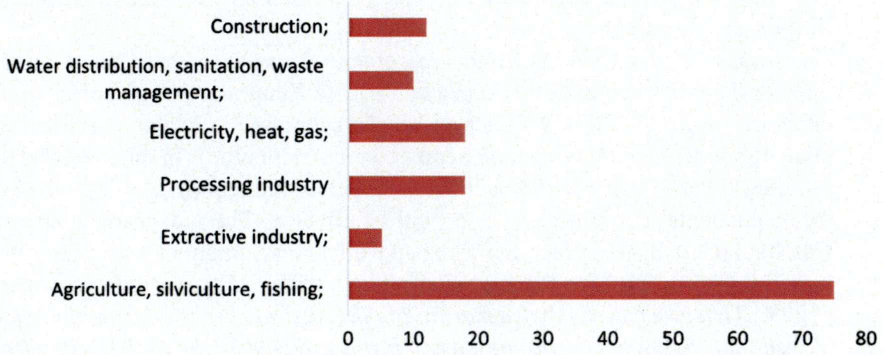

Fig. 15 Preferences regarding governmental support priorities

Respondents chose agriculture as the most important sector in which the state should intervene, regardless of their field of work. This choice was practically based on the near-unanimous perception (75.1%) of the interviewees, regardless of the sector in which they work, **that agriculture is of utmost importance for our country**.

5 A Structural Model of the Perception of COVID Impact on Romania's Economy

The SEM Path Analysis is a mediation model that seeks to identify and explain the mechanism that underlies an observed relationship between an independent variable and a dependent variable via the inclusion of a third hypothetical variable, known as **mediator variable. This variable is used** to identify the nature of the relationship between dependent and independent variables (Purcarea et al. 2013).

Our model was created based on a study conducted during May 4–May 8, 2020 on a nationally representative panel of 1015 consumers, with the final purpose of measuring the effect of COVID on the respondents' consumer spending. The questions were divided by type into seven variables, as follows (Tables 5 and 6).

On the basis of the variables presented above and the statistical significance assessment, we theorized the model presented in Fig. 16, with an emphasis that we want to further discuss on the sub-model from Fig. 17.

The model can be split into further sub-models that reflect the role played by the mediator variables.

The model above allows us to conclude that:

- The COVID Effect negatively affects **respondents' consumer expenses (Expenses, $\beta = 0.16$)**.
- **The impact of the COVID Effect on consumer expenses** may be attenuated through the intervention of the mediator variable **Economy** (which refers to the influence of the COVID-19 Effect on certain economic indicators, such as: the price of goods, unemployment, general economic situation). In other words, the less the COVID-19 Effect will be reflected in prices, unemployment, etc., the less the respondents' consumer expenses will be affected. The independent variable **CoEffect** (COVID-19 Effect) has a negative effect on Romania's economic situation (β-0.44) and explains the evolution of this variable (Economy) in proportion of 20%. Thus, we can say that, ***according to the answers received from the interviewees, our country's economic situation was affected by the COVID-19 Effect during the pandemic in proportion of 20%.*** The mediator variable Economy, in its turn, has a negative impact on consumer expenses ($\beta = 0.3$). An increase in unemployment will lead to a decrease in revenues and implicitly to a decrease in consumer spending, especially for durable goods, homes, package vacations.

Table 5 Types of questions

1. COVID-19 Effect - **independent variable**	Q1 **Has your professional activity been affected by the Coronavirus** (Covid-19) outbreak? 1-Not at all …0.4- Complete shutdown of the activity
2. Economy (The impact of Covid on the Romanian economy)- **dependent variable**	Q2 In your opinion, will the Coronavirus (Covid-19) outbreak affect **Romania's overall economy**? (1- Not at all…4-Severely) Q6 Please estimate **the average price levels of the goods that you buy frequently** now, as opposed to 3 months ago Do you believe that the average prices you pay now are: (1-Low…5-High) Q7 Thinking forward to the next 3 months, how do you think that **the prices for the goods** that you buy frequently **will change**? (1-Low…5-High) Q9 Do you think that 3 months from now **the unemployment level in Romania**: (1-Low…5-High)
3. Measures (economic and administrative measures adopted by the Government)- **dependent variable**	Q14 Over the past months, the Government adopted a series of **measures intended to limit the effect of the Coronavirus** (Covid-19) **outbreak on Romania's economy (supporting furloughs, IMM Invest, etc.)** Do you believe these measures are efficient (1-Definitely Yes…4-Definitely No) Q15 Over the past months, the Government adopted a series of **measures intended to limit the effect of the Coronavirus** (Covid-19) **outbreak, which directly affects Romanian citizens** (measures such as deferrals of bank loan installments, price-capping, etc.) (1-Definitely Yes.4-Definitely No) Q16 In your opinion, to what extent did **the public institutions succeed in implementing the measures taken to support the business environment** (such as granting furloughs or compensating medical leave)? (1.Very high extent. 5-Very low extent) Q17 How do you rate **the functioning of the electronic services used in the relationship with the public administration during the state of emergency**? (1-Unsatisfactory…4-Very good) – reversed scale

(continued)

Table 5 (continued)

4. FiHealth (Financial situation) - **dependent variable**	Q3 Please assess **your family's financial situation now as opposed to 3 months ago** Do you believe it is: (1-Much better…5-Much worse) Q4 **Do you believe that in the following 3 months your family's financial situation will be:** (1-Much better…5-Much more difficult)
5. EcEvents (Economic events): 1-Least likely … 5-Most likely) - **dependent variable**	Q19.1 **Food crisis**:Q19 On a scale of 1 to 5, how likely do you think it is that the following events will occur in Romania in the next 3 months due to the Coronavirus pandemic? Q19.2 **Raise in the unemployment rate:** Q19 On a scale of 1 to 5, how likely do you think it is that the following events will occur in Romania in the next 3 months due to the Coronavirus pandemic? Q19.3 **Decrease in income:** Q19 On a scale of 1 to 5, how likely do you think it is that the following events will occur in Romania in the next 3 months due to the Coronavirus pandemic? Q19.4 **Bankruptcy of a significant number of Romanian companies:** Q19 On a scale of 1 to 5, how likely do you think it is that the following events will occur in Romania in the next 3 months due to the Coronavirus pandemic? Q19.5 **Significant inflation:** Q19 On a scale of 1 to 5, how likely do you think it is that the following events will occur in Romania in the next 3 months due to the Coronavirus pandemic?
6. Expenses (Expenses: 1-Significantly higher … 5-Significantly lower) - **dependent variable**	Q10 Do you think that in the next 6 months **you will invest in the purchase of durable goods** (ex: household appliances, furnishings, etc.) a budget that, compared to the previous 6 months, will be: Q11 Do you think that in the next 6 months **you will invest in the purchase of tourism products** un buget care, in comparatie cu precedentele 6 luni, va fi: Q12 Do you think that in the next 12 months **you will invest in the purchase of a car**? Q13 Do you think that in the next 12 months **you will invest in buying a new house or home for you or for another family member?**
7. Job Change (Change in job:1-Definitiely Yes … 4-Definitely No) - **dependent variable**	Q8 Do you believe that **3 months from now you will have the same job?**

Table 6 Model fit and quality indices

Indices	Criterion
Average path coefficient (APC) = 0.242,	P < 0.001
Average R-squared (ARS) = 0.585,	P < 0.001
Average adjusted R-squared (AARS) = 0.580,	P < 0.001
Average block VIF (AVIF) = 1.836,	acceptable if < = 5, ideally < = 3.3
Average full collinearity VIF (AFVIF) = 2.051,	acceptable if < = 5, ideally < = 3.3
Tenenhaus GoF (GoF) = 0.570,	small > = 0.1, medium > = 0.25, large > = 0.36
Sympson's paradox ratio (SPR) = 1.000,	acceptable if > = 0.7, ideally = 1
R-squared contribution ratio (RSCR) = 1.000,	acceptable if > = 0.9, ideally = 1
Statistical suppression ratio (SSR) = 1.000,	acceptable if > = 0.7
Nonlinear bivariate causality direction ratio (NLBCDR) = 1.000,	acceptable if > = 0.7

* Computed with WarpPLS 5.0

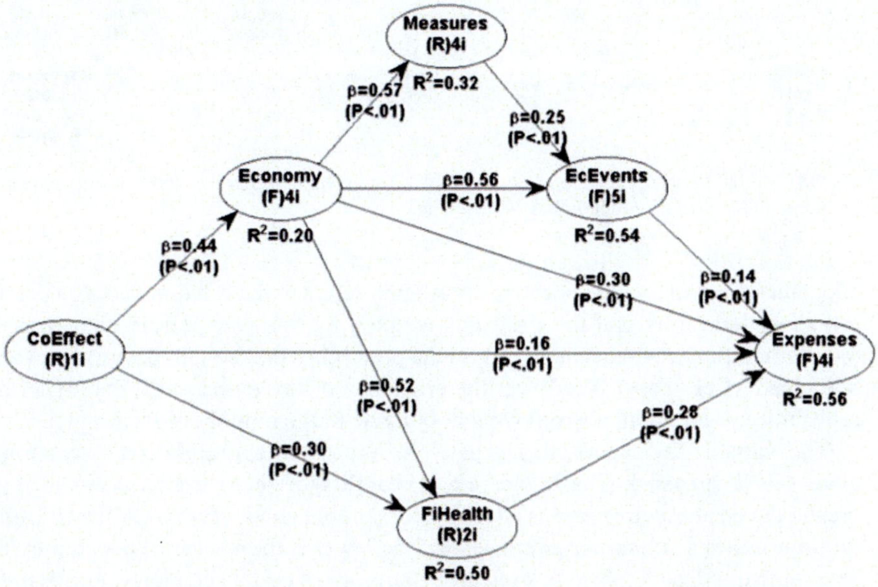

Fig. 16 Model of the perceptions of the COVID pandemic impact on consumers' behavior

Based on Fig. 18, we can say that the impact of the COVID Effect on consumer expenses may be attenuated even further through three mediator variables: **Economy, Measures and EcEvents.** Romania's economic situation negatively influences the measures adopted by the government and explains in proportion of 32% the need to

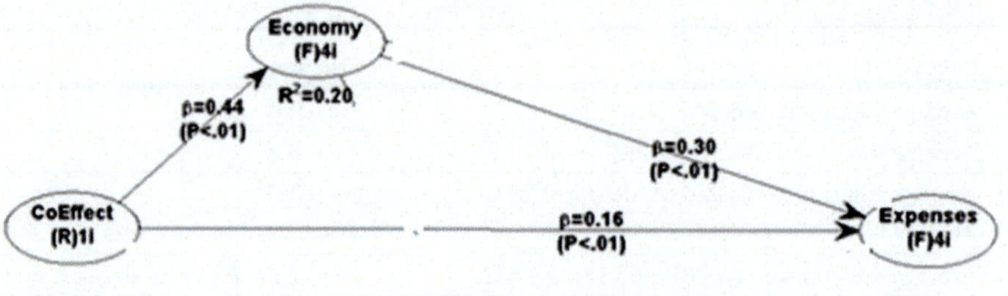

Fig. 17 Model of the perceptions of the COVID pandemic impact on consumers' expenses

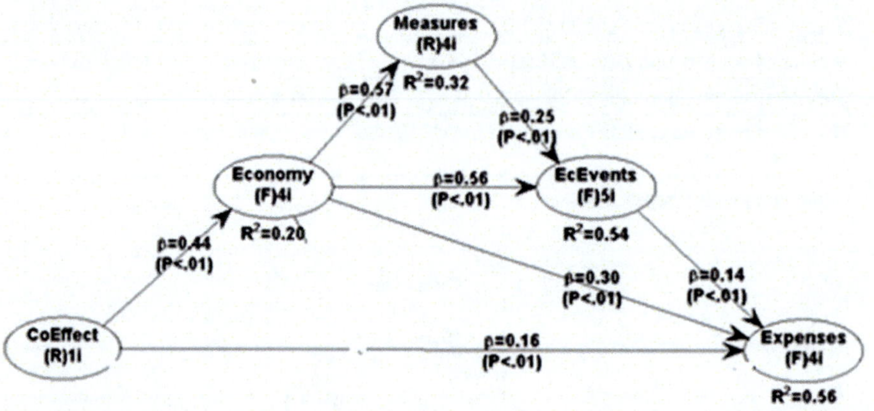

Fig. 18 Model of the perceptions of the COVID pandemic impact on consumers' expenses including the impact of Public Policy adjustments

adopt these measures. The negative correlation refers to the relation between certain economic indicators and the measures adopted by the state. These **measures**, in their turn, influence—also negatively—the possibility that certain **economic events will occur (EcEvents)**. The lower the efficiency of these measures, the higher the probability of inflation, unemployment, of a rise in the number of bankruptcies.

The variable **EcEvents** also negatively impacts **the population's consumer expenses (Expenses).** The higher the probability of these events occurring, the greater the decrease in expenses allocated for durable goods. **The COVID-19 Effect on population's consumer expenses** will be lower if the measures adopted by the government will be likely to foresee the occurrence of certain economic events unfavorable for the consumers and will efficiently address the problems faced by the economy during this period, as well as in the near future.

Figure 18 also shows that the economic situation directly influences the probability of certain economic events happening; however, this relationship can be mediated through the variable **Measures.** The two variables **Measures** and **Economy** explain in a proportion of 54% the variable **EcEvents** (R^2-54%). In other words, **the occurrence of a food crisis or a rise in inflation may be explained in the proportion**

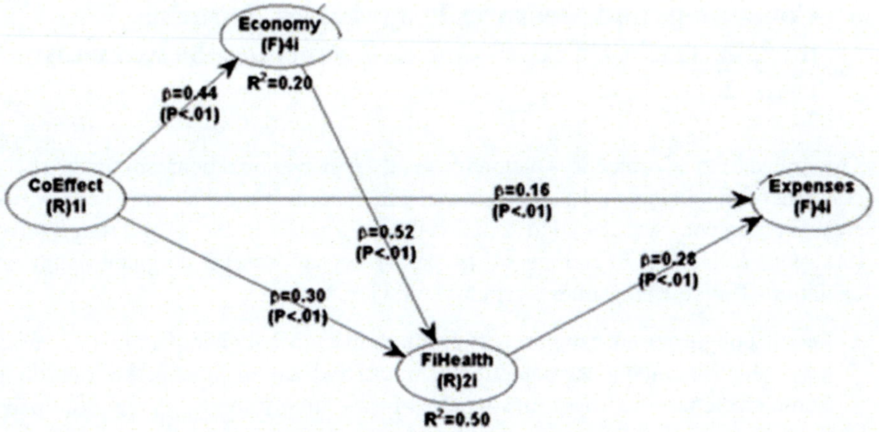

Fig. 19 Model of the perceptions of the COVID pandemic impact on consumers' expenses including the impact of individual financial health

of 54% by the two variables: the measures adopted by the government and the economic situation.

The impact of the **COVID-19 Effect** on **consumer expenses** may also be analyzed through the mediator variable **FiHealth**. We can observe from Fig. 19 that the COVID-19 Effect negatively influences respondents' financial situation, which, in turn, influences negatively consumer expenses.

The COVID-19 Effect on the variable FiHealth may be mediated by the variable **Economy**, which negatively impacts respondents' financial situation. An increase in unemployment or in prices will directly and negatively impact the population's financial situation. The same diagram above reflects that the evolution of the variable FiHealth may be explained in proportion of 50% by the COVID-19 Effect and by the economic situation in our country.

As a result, we can conclude that **the evolution of respondents' consumer expenses depends in proportion of 56% on 4 variables that are in turn mediated by other variables:**

- COVID-19 Effect—negative impact;
- The probability that certain economic events will occur (food crisis, decrease in income)—negative impact.
- Our country's economic situation is in its turn influenced in proportion of 20% by the COVID-19 Effect (evolution of prices, unemployment, number of bankruptcies)—negative impact.
- Respondents' financial situation currently and in the near future—negative impact.

6 Conclusions and Measures Proposed for Reducing the Effects of COVID-19 and Re-Launching the Economy in the Short Run

The spread of the Coronavirus pandemic resulted in irrational behavior on the part of consumers globally as well as in Romania, which became more accentuated once the state of emergency was declared at national level, on March 16, 2020. From a behavioral perspective, the beginning of the pandemic saw several poignant behavioral deviations from the consumers' regular behavior, such as:

- People bought certain categories of products in a much higher quantity than necessary, which resulted in the depletion of stocks and caused panic in the community. Some of the product categories where we saw supply shortages are toilet paper, flour, corn, yeast, hygiene products, and water.
- It took a while for people to get used to washing their hands more frequently, to social distancing, filling out a declaration every time they leave home, teleworking, and wearing protective masks.
- The value that people place on losing something is higher than the desire to obtain something of the same value. This bias had a strong impact on people during the Coronavirus pandemic, because people lost the full extent of their right to liberty which they had before the state of emergency was instated.
- People tend to read all sorts of news without checking their accuracy, which promoted the spread of false news.

The marketing research conducted by the University of Economic Studies at consumer level in Romania reflects the following conclusions: the Coronavirus (COVID-19) outbreak will significantly impact Romania's economy; over 70% of respondents believe that we will see an imminent increase in the unemployment rate in Romania; Romanians' expectations with respect to economic evolution are generally negative, with the vast majority of respondents believing that we will face an increase in unemployment rate, combined with a decrease in the population income, inflation, and the bankruptcy of a significant number of domestic companies; tourism, the consumer goods market, the automotive market and the real estate market will be among the most affected markets in the economy as a result of the SARS-COV-2 virus outbreak; governmental protection measures should target the following sectors with utmost priority: agriculture, silviculture and fishing, health and social services, HORECA and education, with the financial-banking, administrative services, and real estate sectors being at the other end of the public interest spectrum.

Pursuant to the analysis of the SEM model, we can confidently say that the highest impact on the respondents' consumer spending (the key variable in this model) is exercised by the Economy variable (which reflects the economic situation in our country), followed by the measures adopted by the government, the probability of certain events happening and, finally, the respondents' financial situation.

The analysis identified the following **measures** that would attenuate the effects of the pandemic:

1. **Monitoring the evolution of the prices of the main food and non-food goods:**
2. **Lowering unemployment rate**, as well as measures to prevent an increase in this indicator, especially in the most affected sectors: tourism, non-food trade, horeca, etc. Initiative proposals:
   - Vacation vouchers;
   - Vouchers for the purchase of cars manufactured in the EU;
   - Vouchers for the purchase of cars manufactured in the EU;
   - Supporting infrastructure investments from European funds (national roads, highways, etc.);
   - Supporting the purchase of durable goods;
   - Developing traditional trade by creating cooperatives/associations financed by European funds targeting in particular the local store chains, groceries, etc.;
3. **Developing and promoting ecotourism financed by European funds**—in the future, tourists will prefer small and less crowded accommodations, nature walks, local products, etc.;
4. **Identifying measures for monitoring tourist traffic** in the context of the COVID-19 pandemic so as to respect social distancing (the use of crowd alerts);
5. **Encouraging online shopping** by creating platforms for small-scale producers/craftsmen and reducing VAT to distribution services;
6. **Continuing to promote handwashing** by combining awareness campaigns with behavioral attitudes and social norms. For example:
   - Placing the hand sanitizer in a visible place;
   - Using colored signs to attract attention;
   - Asking direct questions "did you use soap when you washed?"
7. Adopting certain public policies intended to encourage and facilitate teleworking (exclusively or in combination with physical work in the office).

As an avenue for future research we could analyze the effects of perceived behavioral control Ajzen (1991) and attitude toward risk (Mandrik and Bao 2005) as mediating variables. Also, the effect of multiple family members being affected by the economic crisis associated with the pandemic should be analyzed, because in these cases consumers can experience multiple, possibly conflicting, issues (Featherman and Pavlou 2003). Our research limitations arise mainly from our sampling of Romanian households. Better data could be obtained by expanding our research to other markets and different cultures. Furthermore, different research techniques, such as focus groups, in-depth interviews, and social experiments, would probably yield better insights into the causes of the observed behaviors, and this could also be explored into a future study.

References

Abe, S.: Market trends and D2C opportunities in the COVID-19 landscape. the AdRoll blog. adroll.com/blog/marketing/market-trends-and-d2c-opportunities-in-thecovid-19-landscape (2020)

Ajzen, I.: The theory of planned behavior. Organ. Behav. Hum. Decis. Process. **50**(2), 179–211 (1991)

Asioli, D., Varela, P., Hersleth, M., Almli, V.L., Olsen, N.V., Naes, T.: A discussion of recent methodologies for combining sensory and extrinsic product properties in consumer studies. Food Qual. Prefer. **56**, 266–273 (2017)

Baicu et al.: The impact of COVID-19 on consumer behavior in retail banking. evidence from Romania. Mamagement Mark. **15**(s1), 534–556 (2020), https://doi.org/10.2478/mmcks-2020-0031

Campbell, M.C., Inman, J.J., Kirmani, A., Price, L.L.. : In times of trouble: a framework for understanding consumers' responses to threats. J. Consum. Res. **47**(3), 311–326 (2020). https://doi.org/10.1093/jcr/ucaa036

Donthu, N., Gustafsson, A.: Effects of COVID-19 on business and research. J. Bus. Res. **117**, 284–289 (2020). https://doi.org/10.1016/j.jbusres.2020.06.008

Dunleavy, P., Margetts, H.Z.: The second wave of digital era governance, in APSA 2010 annual meeting paper, available online at SSRN: https://ssrn.com/abstract=1643850 (2010).

Featherman, M.S., Pavlou, P.A.: Predicting e-services adoption: a perceived risk facets perspective. Int. J. Hum Comput Stud. **59**(4), 451–474 (2003)

Flatters, P., Willmott, M.: Understanding the postrecession consumer. Harv. Bus. Rev. **87**(7/8), 64–72 (2009)

Ho, J., Hui, D., Kim, A., Zhang, Y.: Cautiously optimistic: Chinese consumer behavior post-COVID-19, McKinsey & Company, (online), available at https://www.mckinsey.com/industries/consumer-packaged-goods/our-insights/cautiously-optimistic-chinese-consumer-behavior-post-covid-19 (2020)

Mandrik, C.A., Bao, Y.: Exploring the concept and measurement of general risk aversion. Adv. Consum. Res. **32**, 531–539 (2005)

Organization for economic co-operation and development OECD: COVID-19 and the food and agriculture sector: issues and policy responses, (online), http://www.oecd.org/coronavirus/en (2020a)

Orzan, G., Iconaru, C., Popescu, I.C., Orzan, M.C., Macovei, O.I.: PLS-based SEM analysis of apparel online buying behavior. Importance eWOM, Ind. Text.a **64**(6), 362–367 (2013)

Orzan, M., Zara, A., Florescu, M.S., Orzan, O.A.: Smart textiles perspective for the Romanian fashion industry. Ind. Text.a **71**(6), 572–575 (2020)

Peña-Lévano, L., Burney, S., Melo, G., Escalante, C.: COVID-19: effects on US labor, in supply chains and consumption imagery article. Choices **35**(3) (2020)

Pentescu, A., Orzan, M., Ştefănescu, C.D., Orzan, O.A.: Modelling patient satisfaction in healthcare. Econ. Comput. Econ. Cybern. Stud. Res. **48**(4), 153–166 (2014)

Purcărea, T.V., Orzan, G., Orzan, M., Stoica, I.: Romanian consumer behavior regarding traditional foods: contributing to the rebuilding of a healthier food culture. J. Food Prod. Mark. **19**(2), 119–137 (2013)

Retail-FMCG: Formatele de proximitate aduc cea mai mare creştere... https://www.retail-fmcg.ro/servicii/studii-de-piata-servicii/vanzari-bunuri-de-larg-consum-martie-2020.html, last Accessed 28 Apr (2020)

Richardson, P.S., Dick, A.S., Jain, A.K.: Extrinsic and intrinsic cue effects on perceptions of store brand quality. J. Mark. **58**(4), 28–36 (1994)

Sangeeta M. et al.: Assessing perceptions of COVID-19 self-protective measures: a structural equation modeling (SEM) approach, J. Health Res. **35**(4), ISSN: 2586–940X (2021)

Seema M. et al.: The new consumer behaviour paradigm amid COVID-19: permanent or transient? J. Health Manag. 1–11, DOI: https://doi.org/10.1177/0972063420940834 (2020)

Sheth, J.: Impact of Covid-19 on consumer behavior: will the old habits return or die? J. Bus. Res. **117**, 280–283 (2020). https://doi.org/10.1016/j.jbusres.2020.05.059

Stanciu S.: Consumer behavior in crisis situations. research on the effects of COVID-19 in Romania, Annals of Dunarea de Jos University of Galati I Economics and Applied Informatics, 1/2020, 5–13, DOI:https://doi.org/10.35219/eai1584040975 (2020)